Virtue, Nature,  Moral Agency in the *Xunzi*

Virtue, Nature, and
Moral Agency in the *Xunzi*

Edited, with Introduction, by

T. C. Kline III
and
Philip J. Ivanhoe

Hackett Publishing Company, Inc.
Indianapolis/Cambridge

Cover design by Deborah Wilkes

For further information, please address

Hackett Publishing Company, Inc.
P.O. Box 44937
Indianapolis, Indiana 46244-0937

www.hackettpublishing.com

Library of Congress Cataloging in Publication Data

Virtue, nature, and moral agnecy in the Xunzi / edited, with
introduction by T. C. Kline III and Philip J. Ivanhoe
    p.   cm.
Includes bibliographical references and indexes.
ISBN 0-87220-523-1 (alk. paper)
ISBN 0-87220-522-3 (pbk.)
    1. Hsèn-tzu, 340-245 B.C Hsèn-tzu. 2. Ethics—China. I.
Kline, T. C., 1966- II. Ivanhoe, P.J.
B128. H7 V57 2000
181'.112—dc21   99-052072

水行者表深，表不明則陷；治民者表道，表不明則亂。

荀子: 天論 17/82/22

When people cross the water at fords, they mark the deep places;
but if the markers are unclear, those who come after will drown.
Those who govern the people mark the Way, but if the markers
are not clear, then the people will fall into disorder.

Knoblock 17.11

For his pioneering work in the philosophical study of Xunzi's
thought—setting the markers in the river that so many have used to
cross—we dedicate this volume to John Knoblock (1938-1999).

Contents

Introduction   ix

Acknowledgments   xix

Note on Conventions and Abbreviations   xxi

1. State and Society in the *Xunzi*: A Philosophical Commentary   1
   Henry Rosemont, Jr.

2. Ethical Uses of the Past in Early Confucianism: The Case
   of Xunzi   39
   Antonio S. Cua

3. Virtues in Xunzi's Thought   69
   Jonathan W. Schofer

4. Xunzi: Morality as Psychological Constraint   89
   Joel J. Kupperman

5. Mengzi and Xunzi: Two Views of Human Agency   103
   Bryan W. Van Norden

6. Xunzi on Moral Motivation   135
   David B. Wong

7. Moral Agency and Motivation in the *Xunzi*   155
   T. C. Kline III

8. Xunzi and Zhuangzi   176
   David S. Nivison

9. Theories of Human Nature in *Mencius* and *Xunzi*   188
   D. C. Lau

10. Does Xunzi Have a Consistent Theory of Human Nature?   220
    Eric Hutton

11. Human Nature and Moral Understanding in the *Xunzi*   237
    Philip J. Ivanhoe

Contributors   251

Bibliography   253

Subject Index   259

Name Index   266

Introduction

Henry Rosemont, Jr., began his 1971 article on the political and social philosophy of Xunzi 荀子 with the following lament: "The study of early Chinese philosophy *qua* philosophy does not attract much attention in contemporary scholarly circles . . . the philosophical depths of the classical texts are rarely plumbed anymore."[1] He hoped that his study of Xunzi as political and social philosopher would take "a small step in catching up and reversing an untoward trend."[2] Due to the work of scholars such as Rosemont, the "untoward trend" has been reversed and the study of Chinese philosophy is beginning to catch up to the rest of the field. Happily, we need not lament that Chinese philosophy is of *no* interest to contemporary scholars. Yet, much work remains to be done.

This volume of essays, focused on Xunzi's ethical philosophy, continues the well-established trend of increased interest in and scholarship on early Chinese philosophy. Taken as a group, these essays support two related claims. First, contrary to what one might gather from orthodox Confucian criticisms of Xunzi's work, his writings are of great importance to the development of Confucianism and to the larger field of Chinese philosophy. There is even a case to be made for the claim that Xunzi's writings constitute the single most sophisticated philosophical explanation and defense of the Confucian point of view. Second, a careful consideration of these essays reveals Xunzi's writings to be of general philosophical interest and importance. Xunzi is not simply a significant Chinese philosopher, but an important *world* philosopher. His insights into various aspects of virtue, nature, and moral agency speak to our own concerns as well as to those of his second-century Chinese peers.

These claims about the significance of Xunzi's work gain further support if we consider Xunzi and his writings in light of their influence on later generations of Chinese thinkers. In contrast to our limited biographical knowledge of many of the philosophers in early China, we have historical sources that record a good deal of information about the development of Xunzi's political and philosophical career.[3] Xunzi, literally "Master Xun," was born in the state of Zhao 趙 around 310 B.C.E. during the Warring States period (403-221 B.C.E.).[4] We know little about his family or childhood, but through his writings, Xunzi reveals a thorough training in the arts of the aristocracy—hunting, archery, warfare, reading and writing, ritual activity, etc.—as well as an education in classical literature. Since only wealthy families could afford an education of this sort, we can safely surmise that he was born into a relatively affluent family. In addition, we know that Xunzi's public life began quite early. At the age of fifteen, he left his home in Zhao and traveled to the state of Qi 齊 in order to expand the range of his studies. In Qi he studied and later taught at the Ji Xia 稷下 Academy, an important center of intellectual life in early China that attracted scholars from many different states. While at the academy, he would be recognized as a leading thinker and teacher whose fame spread throughout and well beyond Qi. His distinguished place among the intellectuals of his time is attested to by his being appointed head libationer of the Ji Xia Academy—the honorary, highest-ranking participant in an official state ritual—an unprecedented three times. Xunzi's connection to the academy shows his active participation and leadership within the philosophical community at a time when philosophical discussion and the work of governing the state were thought to require and complement one another. This intellectual environment afforded him the opportunity first to study under the most distinguished philosophers of his day, to influence many of them through discussion and debate, and then to instruct a number of exceptionally talented students. Despite his recognition as a scholar and teacher, while in Qi, Xunzi did not hold any government position. Only after leaving Qi and moving to Chu 楚 was he granted a political office. Eventually dismissed from office, apparently for political reasons, Xunzi retired and lived to see the unification of China under the Qin 秦, a process that to a large extent was accomplished through the work of his student Li Si 李斯.

During his career, Xunzi wrote numerous essays on the pressing topics of the day. In his view, there were plenty of problems to be solved.[5] The power and moral authority of the Zhou dynasty were in serious decline, and the rulers of various states vied for political supremacy. Turmoil and intrigue, rather than harmony and benevolence, had become the predominant characteristics of those in positions of power. Neither the majority of the populace nor their rulers followed the ritual order of the early Zhou kings. Lacking the proper guides for moral cultivation, people were led to ruin by deceptive and misguided philosophies. Xunzi addressed these problems and described solutions that he believed would allow both individuals and the state to harmoniously follow the proper way of life, or Dao 道.

Like his Greek contemporary, Aristotle, Xunzi wrote on a wide variety of topics and organized them within the context of a larger, unified philosophical system. His sustained, philosophical arguments respond to the challenges of competing philosophical positions as well as explain and justify his own advocacy of Confucian ritual cultivation. As we have seen, Xunzi's views had a profound influence on his contemporaries, and this influence continued long after his death. For example, in the subsequent Han 漢 dynasty, the great historian Sima Qian 司馬遷 recognized Xunzi's importance and included him, alongside the other leading philosophical figures of the past, in the biographies of his monumental *Shiji* 史記 *"The Records of the Grand Historian."*

Many of Xunzi's most significant achievements can be seen in the development of the later Confucian tradition. He was the first philosopher to designate a textual canon, a canon that he believed was crucial to the process of moral cultivation. He included five works in the canon—*Li* 禮 *"Rites," Yue* 樂 *"Music," Shi* 詩 *"Odes," Shu* 書 *"History,"* and *Chunqiu* 春秋 *"Spring and Autumn Annals."* [6] Over the course of time the Confucian canon would change, yet the set of texts established by Xunzi would endure as its central core. More importantly, the notion of a canon and its contribution to moral cultivation would remain a mainstay of the tradition.[7] Along with the canon, Xunzi emphasized the fundamental role of the teacher in classical Confucian education. Although the importance of the teacher is implicit in the writings of Confucius and Mencius 孟子, Xunzi provided explicit justification for the role teachers must play in moral cultivation. Moreover, he more thoroughly described the role of teachers and their significance in the process of guiding others through moral cultivation. Both his emphasis on the importance of teachers and his explicit justification of their role in moral education remained characteristic features of the later tradition. In addition, Xunzi expanded the understanding of tradition and argued for the necessity of both hierarchy and a unified set of standards with which to guide cultivation. All of these ideas became integrated into and came to be defining features of the Chinese imperial orthodoxy. It should be noted that Xunzi was not the only philosopher in the early tradition to discuss these issues, but he offered some of the most sophisticated analyses of these topics and was the only thinker to bring them together in a systematic fashion. For these reasons he may be identified as the most influential proponent of these ideas in the early Confucian tradition.

As significant as these achievements are, Xunzi's most direct influence can be seen in the accomplishments of his students. It can be argued that it was through the influence of his students that many of the ideas described above became orthodox imperial beliefs and practices. Three of Xunzi's students are responsible for the transmission of extant classical texts. Fouqiu Bo 浮邱伯 conveyed the text of the *Guliang Commentary* 穀梁傳 to the *Spring and Autumn Annals* to Shen Pei 申培. Zhang Cang 張蒼 transmitted the *Zuo Zhuan* 左傳. Mao Heng 毛亨 learned the interpretations of the *Odes* from Xunzi and then taught them to his son Mao Chang 毛萇. Together the Maos wrote what became the orthodox commentary on the *Odes*. In each case, these students of Xunzi disseminated important classical texts, bringing them to the attention of Han scholars and transmitting them to later generations.

Xunzi's two most politically successful, as well as notorious, students were Li Si and Han Feizi 韓非子. As mentioned above, Li Si was an advisor to the Qin court and played an instrumental role in creating the policies that aided King Zheng of Qin 秦政王 in his campaign of conquest that culminated in the unification of China and the founding of the first imperial dynasty—the Qin dynasty. Although King Zheng never directly employed Han Feizi, his ideas also contributed to the king's success. Han Feizi believed that the means of effective governing lay in developing bureaucratic methods for the control of political power. Like Xunzi, he wrote numerous essays explaining the techniques of governing and providing philosophical justifications for them. But, unlike his teacher, Han Feizi focused not on the power of ritual, moral cultivation, or the virtue of the ruler, but exclusively on the techniques for exercising and maintaining political power. After reading Han Feizi's essays, King Zheng implemented many of his policies during his campaign of conquest and in the administration of the subsequent Qin dynasty. Thus, taken together, the political skill of Li Si and the writings of Han Feizi constitute a central component in the foundation of the Chinese imperial state.

In spite of the remarkable contribution these two students made in orchestrating the unification of China and the creation of the imperial bureaucracy, their success had a negative as well as positive impact on Xunzi's standing as a philosopher. For traditionally, the Qin dynasty was understood as a brutal and repressive regime. Since, from the Chinese point of view, teachers are responsible for the actions of their students, Xunzi was held accountable for the repressive measures used in the campaign that unified the empire and ensured the emperor's political power.

Despite the negative impact of being associated with these two students, Xunzi enjoyed growing philosophical influence and reputation throughout the Han dynasty. Yet, by the early ninth century C.E., his public standing began to wane. Han Yu 韓愈, a prominent scholar and literary figure of the late eighth and early ninth century C.E., in a short essay entitled *Duxun* 讀荀 "Reading Xunzi,"[8] judges Xunzi to be inferior to Mencius. According to Han Yu, Xunzi's writings are "mostly pure with minor defects," while Mencius' philosophy is "the purest of the pure."[9] By the eleventh century, for a variety of complex reasons, philosophical interest turned toward Mencius and away from Xunzi. Primarily because Xunzi was recognized as opposing the Mencian interpretation of Confucius' philosophy, the neo-Confucians of the Song 宋 dynasty excised Xunzi from the grand Confucian narrative. As a result, the writings of Mencius and not Xunzi were included in the orthodox Confucian canon. Xunzi's claim that "human nature is bad" 性惡 *xing'e* directly opposed Mencius' claim that "human nature is good" 性善 *xingshan* and came to be regarded as a mark of Xunzi's inferior philosophical insight. Nevertheless, much of the rest of Xunzi's philosophy endured in practice even if publicly unacknowledged. Given this Mencian turn in the Confucian tradition, from the Song dynasty onward, scholars spent little time or effort studying Xunzi's philosophy.[10]

In the nineteenth and early twentieth century, Western writers and translators studying Chinese philosophy followed the orthodox neo-Confucian narrative. As a result, Xunzi was once again the subject of relatively little scholarly attention. James Legge, one of the most productive and influential translators of the nineteenth century, translated only a single chapter of Xunzi's writings. As part of the introductory material to his translation of the *Mencius*, Legge presented the *Xing'e* 性惡 chapter along with various other short essays by early Chinese philosophers who had written on the topic of human nature.[11] In the late 1920s, Homer Dubs became the first person to publish a book-length study of Xunzi's philosophy—*Hsüntze: The Moulder of Ancient Confucianism*.[12] This monograph was followed one year later by Dubs' selected English translation of Xunzi's writings.[13] The publication of Burton Watson's partial translation in 1963 marked the next major event in Xunzi scholarship.[14] Yet not until the mid-eighties was the second book-length study of Xunzi's philosophy published, Antonio Cua's *Ethical Argumentation: A Study in Hsün Tzu's Moral Epistemology*.[15] In the last ten years scholarly interest in Xunzi's work has grown significantly. John Knoblock published, over a period of six years, his three-volume translation and study of the complete works of Xunzi.[16] The publication of this full translation meant that the entire text was now accessible to non-Chinese readers. While Knoblock was publishing his complete translation, Edward Machle wrote a translation and study of the *Tianlun* 天論 chapter.[17] And, most recently, Paul Goldin has written a book on Xunzi's philosophy.[18] Yet, even taken together, these works only begin to sketch the outlines of Xunzi's philosophical system. These observations concerning Xunzi and his influence argue for his importance to the field of Chinese philosophy. Yet, what can be added to support the additional claim that Xunzi is of philosophical interest to us—Western philosophers? To begin, Xunzi writes sustained philosophical arguments. His writings form a surprisingly consistent group of essays that, when taken together, form a complex and rich system of Confucian philosophy. The developed and systematic nature of his writings recommend him as a more accessible conversation partner for Western philosophers. In addition, Xunzi's broad knowledge of the early Chinese philosophical tradition outside of Confucianism makes his work exceptional. Although he devotes a great deal of time to criticizing rival philosophies, he adopts and adapts almost as much of their work as he condemns. For example, Xunzi criticizes Zhuangzi for being obsessed with Heaven and unable to understand either the importance of culture or the need for self-cultivation. Nonetheless, despite these criticisms, Xunzi adopts many aspects of Zhuangzi's conception of language and draws upon his understanding of moral psychology. In a similar manner, in the course of criticizing both Mencius, a fellow Confucian, and Mozi 墨子, founder of a powerful, competing school of philosophy, Xunzi not only sheds significant light on important aspects of their philosophies but also deepens and sharpens his own work in the process.

All these comments point toward Xunzi's involvement in an ongoing debate among early Chinese thinkers concerning the proper understanding of human nature, language, culture, and the need for or irrelevance of a ritual system of moral cultivation. He significantly adds to this debate by knitting together and defending a conception of human nature alongside a more complex theory of moral psychology and an understanding of moral cultivation and its connection to the mechanisms of tradition. While many of his views on this range of problems are distinctively Chinese—and uniquely Xunzian—the problems he confronts are recognizable and familiar to any philosophically-minded reader. These are our problems as well as his. We still grapple with questions concerning moral psychology and the proper role and form of education. We too worry about how to become better people, how to cultivate virtues in ourselves and inculcate them in others. We too try to explain the function of our social practices and describe their connection to tradition. Xunzi brings to these debates a rich conception of human nature, an element that is missing from many contemporary philosophical discussions of moral agency, and he is interested not only or even primarily in the synchronic aspects of moral psychology that are revealed in discrete moral actions, but also in the diachronic aspects of moral development—how we learn to understand, perceive, evaluate, and perform good actions.

Each of the essays in this volume aims to accurately and richly describe a particular aspect of Xunzi's philosophy and brings Xunzi into conversation with Western philosophical concerns about these same issues. For the authors represented here, understanding Xunzi's philosophy is an exercise in contemporary reflection, not antiquarian curiosity. Perhaps more than any other philosopher of the early period, he can speak to us across the distance of time and culture, and we can benefit from much of what he has to say. In philosophy as in life, good conversation partners allow us to better understand and appreciate ourselves and others, and Xunzi is an important and challenging participant in this ongoing endeavor.

Notes

1. See the present volume, p. 1.

2. Ibid.

3. For an extensive discussion of Xunzi's biography as well as his intellectual career, see the introductory chapters of John Knoblock, *Xunzi: A Translation and Study of the Complete Works*, vol. 1 (Stanford: Stanford Univ. Press, 1988).

4. As with most dates in early Chinese history, scholars disagree over the precise dates of Xunzi's birth and death. The range of different opinions is quite wide. For example, Qian Mu 錢穆 puts Xunzi's dates at 340-245 B.C.E., about thirty years earlier than Knoblock. Here we have followed Knoblock's dates. An interesting mix of theories about these dates can be found in the essays on Xunzi collected by Gu Jiegang 顧頡剛 in *Gushibian* 古史辨 (藍燈文化事業, 1987) 94-140.

5. Xunzi's extant writings consist of thirty-two chapters of varying length. These writings did not reach their present form as the extant text the *Xunzi* until Liu Xiang 劉向 compiled and edited them sometime shortly after 26 C.E. According to Liu's preface to the *Xunzi*, he began with 322 chapter manuscripts and eliminated duplicates, leaving only the present thirty-two. For a more detailed description of the text, its transmission, and authenticity see Knoblock, *Xunzi: A Translation and Study of the Complete Works*, vol. 1, 105-28.

6. Of these texts, the *Shi*, *Shu*, and *Chunqiu* are still extant in what appear to be versions relatively similar to those that Xunzi would have read. Neither the *Li* nor *Yue* still exist in the forms with which Xunzi would have been

familiar. The *Li* may or may not be related to the extant *Liji* 禮記 *"Records of the Rites."* Similarly, a chapter of the *Liji* is entitled *Yue*, but its connection to the text mentioned by Xunzi is unknown.

7. For an interesting comparative study of the role of canons in religious traditions, see John B. Henderson, *Scripture, Canon, and Commentary: A Comparison of Confucian and Western Exegesis* (Princeton: Princeton Univ. Press, 1991).

8. The Chinese is ambiguous as to whether or not Han Yu is referring to the text *Xunzi* or to the person Xunzi. A similar locution exists in English. We often say that we have been "reading Dante" when we mean that we have been reading what Dante wrote. Since in this case the text is named after the author, there is no way definitively to determine the reference. Hence, we have chosen to follow the English idiom and translate the title as "Reading Xunzi" rather than "Reading the *Xunzi.*"

9. Han Yu, *Duxun* 讀荀, *Hanchangli quanji* 韓昌黎全集 in *Sibubeiyao* 四部備要 (台灣: 中華書局, 1965) vol. 443:1, Juan 11, p. 15b. It is interesting to note that the first commentary on the Xunzi comes rather late in the philosophical tradition. At roughly the same time that Han Yu writes about reading Xunzi's works, Yang Liang 楊惊 authors the first commentary in 818 C.E.

10. As Paul Goldin has pointed out, those scholars who did write on Xunzi focused primarily on his arguments supporting the claim that "human nature is bad." See Paul Goldin, *Rituals of the Way: The Philosophy of Xunzi* (Chicago: Open Court, 1999) 100.

11. James Legge, "That the Nature Is Evil," in *The Chinese Classics: The Works of Mencius*, vol. 2 (Oxford: Clarendon Press, 1895) 79-88.

12. Homer Dubs, *Hsüntze: The Moulder of Ancient Confucianism* (London: Arthur Probsthain, 1927).

13. Homer Dubs, *The Works of Hsüntze* (London: Arthur Probsthain, 1928).

14. Burton Watson, *Hsün Tzu: Basic Writings* (New York: Columbia Univ. Press, 1963).

15. Antonio Cua, *Ethical Argumentation: A Study in Hsün Tzu's Moral Epistemology* (Honolulu: Univ. of Hawaii Press, 1985). Notably, Cua's study of Xunzi was the first book-length study authored by someone trained in philosophy. Cua is also the most prolific writer of essays on Xunzi's philosophy.

16. John Knoblock, *Xunzi: A Translation and Study of the Complete Works*, 3 vols. (Stanford: Stanford Univ. Press, 1988-94).

17. Edward Machle, *Nature and Heaven in the Xunzi: A Study of the Tian Lun* (Albany: SUNY Press, 1993).

18. Paul Goldin, *Rituals of the Way: The Philosophy of Xunzi* (Chicago: Open Court, 1999).

Acknowledgments

We would like to thank the contributors for their willingness to work with us in producing this volume. In addition, Deborah Wilkes and Meera Dash at Hackett Publishing provided the support and guidance necessary to turn the manuscript into a book. We would like to thank Roger T. Ames for allowing us to publish Eric Hutton's article, chapter ten in this volume, which was forthcoming in *Philosophy East and West* when we solicited it for the present work. Special thanks also go to Laura Hengehold and Amy Olberding, who spent a great deal of time helping to prepare the manuscript.

Several of the articles in this volume were previously published. Only with the generous permission of the various publishers were we able to gather them here together. These articles were originally published in the following locations:

Chapter one: Henry Rosemont, Jr., "State and Society in the *Hsün Tzu*: A Philosophical Commentary," *Monumenta Serica* 29 (1970-1) 38-78.

Chapter two: Antonio S. Cua, "Ethical Uses of the Past in Early Confucianism: The Case of Hsün Tzu," *PEW* 35:2 (1985) 133-56.

Chapter three: Jonathan W. Schofer, "Virtues in Xunzi's Thought: Issues in Comparative Analysis," *The Journal of Religious Ethics* 21 (1993) 117-36.

Chapter five: Bryan W. Van Norden, "Mengzi and Xunzi: Two Views of Human Agency," *IPQ* 32:2 (1992) 161-84.

Chapter six: David B. Wong, "Xunzi on Moral Motivation," in *Chinese Language, Thought, and Culture: Nivison and His Critics*, Philip J. Ivanhoe, ed. (Chicago: Open Court, 1996) 202-23.

Chapter eight: David S. Nivison, "Hsün Tzu and Chuang Tzu," *Chinese Texts and Philosophical Contexts: Essays Dedicated to Angus C. Graham*, H. Rosemont, ed. (Chicago: Open Court, 1991) 129-42.

Chapter nine: D. C. Lau, "Theories of Human Nature in *Mencius* and *Shyuntzyy*," *BOAS* 15 (1953) 541-65.

Chapter eleven: Philip J. Ivanhoe, "Human Nature and Moral Understanding in *Xunzi*," *IPQ* 34:2 (1994) 167-75.

— T. C. Kline III and Philip J. Ivanhoe

Note on Conventions and Abbreviations

There are three notes with regard to textual conventions. First, all romanizations of Chinese are in Pinyin except for proper names, of either people or published works, that are traditionally romanized in some other system. To keep the text consistent, romanizations in quoted sources have also been changed to Pinyin. In addition, in order to better distinguish proper names, the romanizations of proper names or titles precede the Chinese characters rather than follow them.

Second, translations found in the text are from readily available editions of the Chinese texts or from the contributors themselves. In places where contributors disagree with a translation and have altered it, these altered translations are identified as "adapted" in the citation. References to other translations of the passage can also often be found in the endnotes. References to translations are by page number, except in the case of John Knoblock's translation. For Knoblock's translation, references use his own system of chapter and section notation—chapter number followed by section number.

Third, whenever possible, citations of Chinese sources refer to the new series of concordances edited by D. C. Lau and Chen Fong Ching and published by The Chinese University of Hong Kong's Institute of Chinese Studies 香港中文大學中國文化研究所 and The Commercial Press 商務印書館 in Hong Kong. We have chosen to use these texts as standard rather than the Harvard-Yenching series. The advantages are that the new series is in print and can be purchased. Furthermore, the printing itself is more readable than the earlier typeset of the Harvard-Yenching series. All references to the *Xunzi* are to the concordance in this series: 荀子逐字索引 *A Concordance to the Xunzi.*

As for abbreviations, in the endnotes we have used the following standard abbreviations for certain journals:

BOAS	*Bulletin of the School of Oriental and African Studies*
IPQ	*International Philosophical Quarterly*
JAAR	*Journal of the American Academy of Religion*
JCP	*Journal of Chinese Philosophy*
PEW	*Philosophy East and West*
Phil Rev	*Philosophical Review*

One

State and Society in the *Xunzi*:
A Philosophical Commentary

Henry Rosemont, Jr.

Introduction

The study of early Chinese philosophy *qua* philosophy does not attract much attention in contemporary scholarly circles. Historical and literary studies of the Zhou have grown apace in recent decades,[1] philosophical work has lagged far behind. Thus while we have gained invaluable insights into the cultural milieu of the late Zhou period and its influence on the personages and institutions of later Chinese history it is nevertheless the case that the philosophical depths of the classical texts are rarely plumbed anymore. The present work is intended as a small step in catching up and reversing an untoward trend.

To justify this exhortation for a change of academic heart regarding Chinese philosophy the social and political views of the early Confucian Xunzi will be examined in an attempt to enlist support for the following positions: (1) there is a unity to his views that places him among the seminal contributors to the fields of social and political philosophy; (2) the philosophical problems to which Master Xunzi addressed himself are no less significant today than they were twenty-two hundred years ago. If the effort to rescue Xunzi from the philosophical obscurity into which he has fallen is at all successful it may concomitantly serve to encourage sympathy for a reassessment of his Zhou colleagues.

Any attempt to demonstrate the philosophical sophistication of the early Chinese thinkers, however, must first meet a fundamental objection if the demonstration is not to be construed simply as a case of special pleading. On the one hand Chinese philosophical writings do not generally exhibit the hypothetico-deductive form common to Western texts, and on the other hand the Zhou texts are perceived to be culture-specific. Hence the objection: whatever intellectual substance is found in those texts is a function of their being unique to China; they are otherwise little more than a congeries of arguments *non sequitur.*

In order to meet this objection it is necessary to see that the two problems facing the reader of the Chinese texts are not philosophically unrelated; indeed it is by attending carefully to their interconnections that they can often be eliminated as problems. That is to say, supplementing Xunzi's arguments with specific materials from the Chinese situation does not necessarily demonstrate his cultural-specificity or his philosophical *naiveté*; the supplementation can also be viewed as providing premises for general arguments that are otherwise enthymemic in character. To be sure, Xunzi does not argue all of his views; some are merely stated. This fact does not make these views any less true or any less worthy of examination when placed in context with his other views and the realities of the Chinese situation.

At the same time, attentiveness to the Chinese environment in which Xunzi wrote can also serve as a check on the temptation to read current concerns and perspectives into the thoughts of someone half a world and twenty-two centuries distant. (Some of those concerns and perspectives, however, cannot but intrude; scholars too are integral parts of a set of historical circumstances.)

These points may be illustrated by outlining the major thesis of this paper and the philosophical perspective from which it was written. In Western thought the fundamental political question has traditionally been formulated: given that men are basically free in a "state of nature" what constraints can justifiably be placed on their freedom by the state? When viewed from this standpoint the philosophy of Xunzi seems to be occasionally platitudinous, usually authoritarian, and almost always beside the basic question. But there is another standpoint, exemplified in Xunzi's dictum "desires are many, things are few."[2] This insight reflects an appreciation of the harsh meteorological, topographic and soil environments of China, environments that make the legend of a Johnny Appleseed seem no less incredible than the awesome dragons that fly into and out of Chinese folk tales. By thus altering our vantage point we will be reminded—as Xunzi did not need to be—that without large-scale cooperative public works the recalcitrant East Asian earth will not surrender a bounty sufficient to nurture the population, and consequently we might put the fundamental question differently: given that men must be basically constrained in order to survive, how much freedom and humanism can the state justifiably allow?

What is noteworthy here is that the fundamental question does not become any less philosophical for being turned around. If it is maintained that Xunzi assumes a legitimacy for political institutions which his Western counterparts question, he can obviously reply that his Western counterparts have assumed a minimal level of economic well-being which he cannot even question, but must flatly reject. By thus interpolating Chinese materials (premises) into Xunzi's writings we can attempt to make a case for his philosophical acumen. And clearly his work, seen in this light, is not out of date; more than two-thirds of the human race have not yet reached the minimal level of economic affluence most Western philosophers since Plato have unfortunately taken for granted. From this perspective it is also clear that the present work differs somewhat from other philosophical critiques of the Zhou thinkers for no effort is made herein to salute Xunzi's sophistication on the grounds that his writings are here and there analogous to the views of this, that or the other Western philosopher. This is not a comparative study; rather will Xunzi be considered as a philosopher in his own right, and we shall focus on his concerned efforts to humanize a collectivistic state and ethical system he felt compelled by his environmental constraints to advocate. Simultaneously we will focus on the avowedly atheistic nature of his philosophical position which forced him to show how and why human life could be significant without recourse to supernatural support.

The unity of Xunzi's views and their current import will be argued first of all by proffering an integrated model of his ideal state drawn from his writings. Secondly, the model will be placed in a current philosophical context by showing how well Xunzi's writings fit together (and hold up) when criticized by proponents of Western democratic institutions. Specifically, Karl Popper's *The Open Society and Its Enemies*[3] will be taken as exemplary of philosophical critiques of sociopolitical institutions.[4] After showing that Xunzi's model meets Popper's major specifications of a "closed society" it will be maintained that a number of Popper's criticisms are irrelevant to Xunzi's model, other criticisms are effectively met by it, and still other of those criticisms are based on assumptions that the Chinese model seriously calls into question. In sum, it will be argued that perhaps Popper's two main opponents—Plato and Marx—were philosophical pushovers for him when compared to Xunzi, and that the ancient Confucian's advocacy of his system shows clearly that he faced squarely and attempted to answer a number of significant philosophical questions that have all too often been begged.

A final introductory remark. In order to develop the view that Xunzi's philosophy can be interpreted as a unified system it is necessary for this paper to have a larger scope than is common in contemporary philosophical writings. The more controversial interpretations suggested herein are defended in the footnotes, and for the rest it can be said that the present work does not pretend to be definitive—it is doubtful whether any such work is possible in philosophy—but on the contrary, should merely be seen as a first approximation to a systematic interpretation of one of the more sophisticated political philosophies ever formulated.

Xunzi's Ideal State: The Model

1. Geography and Population

Unlike the city-sized republic of Plato, Xunzi's state encompasses a massive area and diverse population. It takes in at least the whole of China and will include non-Chinese groups living beyond the borders.[5] These groups will stand in a satellite relation to the larger body, and their members, singly or collectively, may elect to become an integral part of the state at any time.[6] It has generally gone unremarked that Xunzi's theory of the perfectibility of man through education generates the notion of racial tolerance as a concomitant: if all men are capable of becoming a Yao or a Shun it makes no sense, of course, to distinguish them *a priori* on the basis of their race or skin color.[7] Perhaps this view is naïve, but it points up some dissimilarities between his philosophical concerns and those of his Western peers. By believing that men are born equal in all ethically relevant respects Xunzi has not provided us with sophisticated Aristotelian arguments justifying the institution of slavery, nor has he provided us with a Platonic conceptual framework in which selective breeding is ethically desirable.[8] In short, Xunzi's state is non-exclusionary, and hence is in principle a world state; the prerequisite for full participation is subscription to the official (Confucian) ideology, an issue to be examined in detail below.

2. The Economy

The economic foundation of the state is agriculture, a foundation that continues to support China to this day. Xunzi sketches his economic views in the following passage:

> These are the king's laws. They fix the various rates of taxation, regulate all affairs, exploit the ten thousand things, and thereby provide nourishment for all people. The tax on the fields shall be one tenth. At barriers and in markets, the officials shall examine the goods but levy no tax. The mountains,

forests, lakes, and fish weirs shall at certain seasons be closed and at others opened for use, but no taxes shall be levied on their resources. Lands shall be inspected and the amount of tax graded according to their productivity. The distance over which articles of tribute must be transported shall be taken into consideration and the amount of tribute fixed accordingly. Goods and grain shall be allowed to circulate freely, so that there is no hindrance or stagnation in distribution; they shall be transported from one place to another as the need may arise, so that the entire region within the four seas becomes like one family.[9]

He then goes on to extol the virtues of commerce, concluding with:

Thus, wherever the sky stretches and the earth extends, there is nothing beautiful left unfound, nothing useful left unused. Such goods serve above to adorn worthy and good men, and below to nourish the common people and bring them security and happiness.[10]

Several points in the above quotations require attention. First, Xunzi justifies his proposals by arguing that they will bring security and a measure of well-being to every member of the state. At the most fundamental level the welfare of the people is always the basis on which he defends his views.[11] He insists upon at least a minimal share in the state's resources for everyone irrespective of their social station. Some will receive a greater share than others, depending on the importance of the functions they perform in the society;[12] but no one shall be in dire poverty while others are in wealth. Xunzi believed that the state existed because man was a social animal who could not survive without societal institutions because cooperative economic efforts in the form of public works projects were necessary to guarantee that flood or drought would not wreak havoc with the crops each year.[13] In this way each man's work makes a contribution to the state and thereby to everyone else, and hence on Xunzi's grounds every citizen of the state is entitled to and must receive benefits from his membership therein.

Second, it is worth noting here the historical point made by Dubs,[14] that Xunzi (and the early Confucians in general) encouraged trade. The curtailment of mercantile activities that accompanied the rise of the empire after his time was not suggested by him, nor, on the basis of his writings, is there any reason to believe that he would have endorsed the restrictive policies that were later to become standard.[15]

Third, and of ethical as well as historical significance, is the fact that Xunzi's economic statements are as much descriptive of the actual conditions that obtained during the Warring States period as they are prescriptive of his ideal.[16] He was concerned to curb excesses, but no utopian human engineering or large-scale overhaul of extant economic institutions was necessary in order to implement his prescriptions. Xunzi's moderate program, again unlike Plato's, could have been effected without seriously disrupting the lives or activities of his countrymen living at that time. Xunzi, in other words, did not need a violent revolution in order to achieve his economic goals.[17]

To summarize: Xunzi would have retained the substance of the economic conditions that were operative during his lifetime (conditions which were obviously not restricted to that place or period). He wanted to promote all forms of agricultural activities, organize public works, encourage commerce, prevent monopoly or the excessive exploitation of natural resources—which belonged to everyone[18]—and to eliminate oppressive taxation policies.

3. Political Institutions

Xunzi's state will be headed by a hereditary monarch whose authority and decisions are unquestioned as long as the state is peaceful and prosperous. A lack of formal institutional checks on his authority is balanced by a set of social precedents and customs (the *li*) that circumscribe the options open to the ruler in decision-making situations.[19] He is further constrained by the policy suggestions and advice of the officials he appoints to manage the state; officials who do not, however, owe their primary allegiance to him, but rather to the state ideology which it is their primary duty to preserve.[20]

The ruler is also the cultural symbol of the state, with many ceremonial functions to perform; he is seen as the intermediary between heaven and earth, and as the "father and mother of the people."[21] His descendants will succeed him to the throne as long as the state continues to be well ordered. Significant loss of natural or social harmony is *prima facie* evidence of monarchical incompetence, furnishing a theoretical justification for ousting the ruling family and replacing it with another that will restore peace, prosperity and harmony to the state.[22]

Below the imperial line there may or may not be a feudal-like nobility. Xunzi discusses hereditary aristocrats in a number of his essays, but his occasional attentiveness to this class may have been no more than a reflection of the feudal-like times in which he lived.

Although he nowhere explicitly seems to advocate their abolition as a class the relevant point philosophically is that once the rule of a sage-king is realized the nobility do not seem to perform any necessary political, social or economic functions.[23] Hence it may be that Xunzi regarded the class as ultimately eliminable.

Following this aristocratic class, which will be limited in size if it exists at all, will be the civil servants, the scholars and officials. It is the members of this class who wield the real political power and influence in Xunzi's state. Inclusion in the class is not determined by wealth or birth, but is open to everyone who demonstrates a knowledge of and adherence to the state ideology. Literacy is the key by which each individual must seek admission. It follows that there will be both upward and downward mobility in Xunzi's model. He says:

> Yet although a man is the descendant of a king, duke, prefect or officer, if he does not observe the rules of proper conduct 禮 *li* and justice 義 *yi*, he must be relegated to the common ranks; although he is the descendant of a commoner, if he has acquired learning, developed a good character, and is able to observe the rules of proper conduct (*li*) and justice (*yi*), then elevate him to be minister, prime minister, officer or prefect.[24]

The officials are not only responsible for managing day-to-day bureaucratic affairs of the state, they are to be the determiners of policy as well, guided in their deliberations by custom and precedent. They will occupy all governmental offices from country clerk to prime minister. The members of this class not holding an official appointment will teach, adjudicate local disputes, and in general be the civic leaders in their communities.[25]

The above classes comprise the ruling group; all other members of the state, the common people, are the ruled. They make up the vast majority of the population, and include (in proper order) the farmers, artisans, merchants, soldiers, entertainers, and so on. There will be hierarchical divisions within this class, based on wealth or economic function. The members of this class give their primary political and social loyalty to their family and clan, and thereafter to their village, all of which serve largely as self-governing units. Authority-relationships at this level are determined according to age (in the family and clan), and by status (in the village).[26]

The political responsibilities of the state are manifold. First, there are numerous ceremonial functions to perform, both on the part of the ruler and on the parts of his officials. We have seen that the government must also promote agriculture, regulate commerce and collect revenues.[27] In addition, it must build and maintain state temples, highways, dikes, canals and other public works necessary for economic productivity, it must preserve natural resources, and provide for the common defense of the people.[28] Furthermore, the government of Xunzi's state is obliged to provide a wide range of social welfare services to its citizens. His insistence on these governmental responsibilities has been less emphasized by commentators than his authoritarianism, but Xunzi himself is quite explicit in the matter:

> In the case of those who belong to the five incapacitated groups [i.e., the handicapped], the government should gather them together, look after them, and give them whatever work they are able to do. Employ them, provide them with food and clothing, and take care to see that none are left out.[29]

And in another passage he urges the sage-king to

> . . . promote those who are kind and respectful, encourage filial piety and brotherly affection, look after orphans and widows and assist the poor, and then the common people will feel safe and at ease with the government.[30]

These passages (and the examples could be multiplied) underline the contention that Xunzi's ultimate aim was to provide security and a measure of economic well-being for his fellow men, all of whom, he felt, held their humanity in common. The point here is obviously a moral one, for Xunzi is insisting that at least a minimal allotment of wealth be given to a group of people who cannot pose any kind of political threat whatsoever.

4. Social Structure

The social structure of Xunzi's state reflects the political structure in most respects, with the political ordering reflected in the social hierarchy. The ruling classes enjoy privileges and prerogatives not available to the ruled, an inequality Xunzi defends by arguing that increased rewards—up to a point—should attend increased responsibilities.[31] Not all of these privileges involved wealth, for they were also closely interwoven with the cultural tradition; and as we will see below, one of the greatest privileges of all was being a standard-bearer of that tradition.[32] Xunzi held that all social distinctions of the sort he prescribes are necessary for the smooth functioning of any society, without which economic cooperation was impossible:

> In society, men can be in accord with the order of the seasons, properly allocate all goods and resources, and thereby uniformly bring profit to the whole world. This is possible because of social distinctions and a sense of righteousness.[33]

What we have then, is a clearly demarcated class structure, with membership in each class a function of the individual's ability and education. Minimal affluence was necessary in order to receive a formal education, and Xunzi may be faulted for failing to appreciate the extent to which the scholar-official class held an unfair advantage in perpetuating their descendants in the class, as the later history of China was to show;[34] but this sociological oversight, although not insignificant, does not vitiate his overall philosophical position of insisting upon proven ability rather than wealth or birth as the crucial determinant in securing leadership for the state.[35] Xunzi held that an hierarchical society was absolutely essential for equally essential collective economic efforts. At the same time an hierarchical society is unjust by definition. Hence the problem in his terms: no hierarchical society, no collective efforts; no collective efforts, no society whatsoever; no society, no justice whatsoever. Therefore the principal philosophical task was to minimize the injustice suffered and maximize the justice enjoyed—by all.

5. *The* Li *and Education*

The central notion in Xunzi's social philosophy is 禮 *li*—the rules of proper conduct, manners, etiquette, mores and morals. These ritualized norms are to govern the behavior of every member of the state from monarch to humble peasant. The *li* make up the "Way" of Confucianism as interpreted by Xunzi and they combine ethics, aesthetics and social manners in one encompassing set of social prescriptions. Different subsets of these norms will apply to different individuals, depending on their social and political position.[36] The *li* are not confined to the rituals of ancestral sacrifice, weddings, funerals and state protocol; on the contrary, for Xunzi they are all-pervasive and minutely detailed, dictating conduct in almost every facet of a person's life:

> That which enables a person to act appropriately to the occasion, that which enables him to be successful when in office, and to bear poverty when out of office, is the rules of proper conduct (*li*) and faithfulness. Whenever a person deals with flesh and blood,

purposes and plans, when it is according to the rules of proper conduct (*li*), then his government will be successful. If he does not act according to the rules of proper conduct (*li*), he is either wrong and confused, or careless and negligent. Food and drink, clothing, dwelling places, and movements, if in accordance with the rules of proper conduct (*li*), will accord to the situation; if not in accordance with the rules of proper conduct (*li*), they will meet with ruin and calamity. A person's appearance, his bearing, his advancing and retiring when he hastens or walks slowly, if according to the rules of proper conduct (*li*), is beautiful; if not according to the rules of proper conduct (*li*), then he will be haughty, intractable, depraved, banal, and rude. Hence a man who has no sense of what is proper (*li*) is without a means of livelihood; a matter which is not proper (*li*) will not be brought to accomplishment; a government without *li* will not be peaceful.[37]

The generalized forms in which the *li* are embodied are the "five relationships": ruler to subject, father to son, husband to wife, elder to younger brother, and friend to friend.[38] In each case the first member of the pair occupies a superordinate position, with his dual in a subordinate role. All other interpersonal relations are variations on these five basic themes. If one is tempted to recoil in egalitarian horror from the institutionalization of superior-inferior relationships he should keep in mind that no one spends all of his time in either position. Every middle male sibling will be both an elder and a younger brother; the son one day becomes a father; young friends turn into old friends; junior officials are promoted; indeed, in the extreme case, the subject becomes the ruler. Remember that Xunzi believes injustice cannot be eliminated. If displayed in interpersonal and familial relationships it becomes at least humanized, and in that way perhaps a little more tolerable—especially when one considers the Platonic alternative.

Xunzi's *li* were not, of course, to be cut out of whole cloth, nor were they to be grounded in any "grand lie," supernatural or otherwise; they were the ancient religious and other rituals and customs that already served as the cultural cement of the Chinese peoples.[39] These rituals were in danger of being lost because they were derived from an earlier set of supernatural and superstitious beliefs which had been almost universally abandoned by the educated in Xunzi's time. With considerable insight he saw that the *li* were an important link with the rich cultural past, and relatedly, that they provided a particular kind of human satisfaction which purely material comforts would be hard put to duplicate or replace.[40] In this respect he is similar to Santayana, who rejected totally the dogmas of religious institutions but rejoiced in the poetry, music and rituals of their ceremonies.[41] It is a good index of Xunzi's philosophical abilities and human sensitivities that he attempted to preserve the ethical and aesthetic functions of these cultural norms in an era when their religious *raison d'être* had vanished.

He preserved them by incorporating their study and practice into the "curriculum" of his educational system. All children receive extensive instruction in the *li*[42] and the advantaged will later continue to study the higher rites as a part of the formal education they receive under the direct supervision of a teacher:

> The rules of proper conduct (*li*) is that whereby a person's character is corrected; a teacher is that whereby the rules of proper conduct (*li*) are corrected. Without rules for proper conduct (*li*) how can I correct myself? Without a teacher how can I know what particular action is according to the rules of proper conduct? [43]

Xunzi insists that no one study in isolation because of the personal involvement one must have with the governing norms, which the student is to internalize as his tutor has done. He goes so far as to rank his scholars according to the extent of their personal commitment to the *li*.[44] By merely reading the ritual prescriptions someone might learn to go through the motions of their performance, but in all probability he could not perform them with grace or dignity, would lose the pleasure of appreciating the beauty of a proper performance, and also lose the pleasure of knowing that he has performed them well. The student must have a model then, a teacher who has integrated his own attitudes and behavior on the basis of the *li*.

Another reason for the centrality of the study of *li* in Xunzi's educational system is that they can channel men's desires toward worthwhile and attainable goals:

> The early kings . . . established the *li* . . . so that desires would not exceed material things, and material things would be sufficient to satisfy desires; desires and things would thus be in consonance. It was in this way that the *li* arose.[45]

The *li* thus serve a dual function in directing men's desires: (1) by establishing goals for each social level, it is insured that not everyone will desire the same things at the same time, increasing the probability that everyone will realize a certain percentage of his goals;[46] (2) by shifting attention away from material goods Xunzi increases the probability—especially among the literati—that goals will be reached and desires satisfied.[47] That is to say, if every budding official desires five thousand *mou* of land many of them will be frustrated in their desire and many more farmers would suffer great hardship; on the other hand, every budding official can achieve his goal if he desires to win fame as a moral exemplar, or write poetry, hear good music, or contemplate the beauty of a ritual state sacrifice.

The *li* then, are the basic "stuff" out of which Xunzi builds his ideal state. They are the social mores of the society, but they are much more than that. They are also the moral values, artistic standards and cultural norms. Their use affects economic actions, political decisions, indeed all interpersonal relationships; it is for this reason that everyone must learn the *li* appropriate to his station. Without them he could not be a functioning member of the society.

The balance of the educational curriculum for the advantaged will include study in the classics, history, philosophy, literature, art and music. Here, as elsewhere, the *li* dictate the correct forms in the several disciplines. Like Plato, Xunzi will proscribe not only unorthodox philosophy,[48] but licentious art, poetry and music as well.[49] Heretical artistic endeavors would serve to agitate the members of society rather than provide them with satisfaction, and such endeavors would thus tend to promote disorder, a consequence to be avoided even at the expense of censorship. In his essay *Yuelun* 樂論 Xunzi argues:

> Music enters deeply into men and transforms them rapidly. Therefore, the former kings were careful to give it the proper form. When music is moderate and tranquil, the people become harmonious and shun excess. When music is stern and majestic, the people become well-behaved and shun disorder. . . .

> But if music is seductive and depraved, then the people will become abandoned and mean-mannered. Those who are abandoned will fall into disorder. . . . In such a case, the common people will find no safety in their dwellings and no delight in their communities. . . . For this reason the former kings honored the proper rites and music and despised evil music. As I have said before, it is the duty of the chief director of music to enforce the ordinances and commands, to examine songs and writings, and to abolish licentious music, . . . so that

strange and barbaric music is not allowed to confuse the elegant classical modes.[50]

Along the same lines, Xunzi also held that it is only by following the proper norms that true artistic creativity could be appreciated; in concert with many other East Asian philosophers Xunzi believed that one's aesthetic sensibilities were enhanced rather than diminished by a rigid adherence to explicitly prescribed artistic norms.[51] Thus we have another reason for Xunzi's emphasis on the teacher. Formalization easily leads to fossilization without human involvement in the forms.[52]

Natural science as such occupies no place in Xunzi's educational philosophy. In one of his most celebrated essays, *Tianlun* 天論, Xunzi mounts a devastating attack on superstitious and supernatural beliefs, at the same time creating an intellectual atmosphere that was inimical to the conduct of pure scientific inquiry. He pointed out that it occasionally rained too little, and at other times too much; in either case, he argued, man could do nothing to remedy the situation by praying for rain or its abatement.[53] The thrust of his essay was to call attention to the human affairs which were within the powers of men to modify: namely, to organize the society in such a way that cooperative efforts could lessen and perhaps eliminate the horrors of flood or drought.[54] As a consequence, the scholar should not bother himself about the theoretical whys and wherefores of rain or other natural phenomena, rather he should concern himself with working to insure that no untoward natural phenomena would affect adversely the members of his state. This anti-superstitious and nonscientific stance of Xunzi's has several important consequences in relation to defending his overall philosophical position, as will be seen below.

We have, then, an hypothetical model of Xunzi's ideal state. The crucial group in his society is the scholar-official class, and their primary functions are to utilize and preserve the *li*, and by so doing enrich and enhance the lives of the members of the society. In their role as officials they employ the *li* to insure that there is a place for everyone; and in their role as scholars they employ the *li* to insure that everyone is in a place.

Having briefly described the model, we turn now to its characterization: what kind of state is it?

Xunzi's Ideal State: A "Closed Society"

In his influential *The Open Society and Its Enemies* Karl Popper levels a major philosophical attack on utopian states, focusing on the work of Plato and Marx. For present purposes Popper's book can be broken down into two broad themes: (1) his specific interpretations and criticisms of Plato's city-state and the communist ideal of Marx; (2) his general attack on totalitarianism, coupled with a defense of democratic institutions. Herein we shall only be concerned with the second theme. A number of controversies have arisen from Popper's analyses of those philosophers,[55] but his critiques of totalitarianism and democracy have been widely acknowledged to have made a substantive contribution to the field. We shall therefore not enter into the disputes involving his characterizations of Plato or Marx; rather we will restrict our attention to those parts of the work that are relevant to an analysis of Xunzi's model: (1) Popper's general categorizations of open and closed societies; (2) his detailed defense of the former; and (3) his equally detailed condemnation of the latter.

It might be objected here that no elements of Popper's analysis are relevant to Xunzi's model, simply because he did not take Xunzi—or any other Asian philosopher—into account while engaged in his analyses. In one sense this is a valid objection because it seems unfair to criticize Popper (as shall be done) for not responding to philosophical views he has not encountered. But in a more important way the objection is without force. Popper admittedly takes into direct account only those philosophical systems of the Western cultural tradition. But except when he is addressing himself to a specific passage from Plato, Hegel or Marx he intends his criticisms to be absolutely general, and his own views to be universal, applicable to all peoples.[56] Hence if he is prescribing for everyone, *a fortiori* he is prescribing for the Chinese, and it is therefore wholly legitimate to raise a Chinese challenge to both the form and the content of those prescriptions.

Popper characterizes an *open society* [57] as being superstition-free (or almost so), fundamentally democratic, individualistic and rational. A *closed society* [58] is just the opposite: superstition-ridden, dictatorial, collectivistic and irrational. That all of these terms are heavily value-laden Popper freely admits; hence more detailed definitions are necessary.

First, a society is *democratic* [59] if it contains political institutions by means of which the ruled may dismiss their rulers by peaceful means. A *dictatorship* or *tyranny* [60] has no such institutions, and hence the rulers of such a state can only be replaced by a resort to violence.

A society is *collectivistic* [61] if it requires the subservience of the individual's interest and desires to those of the whole group of which he is a part; an *individualistic* [62] society is noncollectivistic.

Rationalism is an especially important term in Popper's analyses. It is not used in distinction to "empiricism," but includes the latter term.[63] It is basically an attitude that seeks to solve problems by appealing to logical thought processes and experience rather than by appealing to the passions and emotions. He says of rationalism that it

> . . . is an attitude of readiness to listen to critical arguments and to learn from experience. It is fundamentally an attitude of admitting that "I may be wrong and you may be right, and by an effort, we may get nearer to the truth." It is an attitude which does not lightly give up hope that by such means as argument and careful observation, people may reach some kind of agreement on many problems of importance. . . .

> The fact that the rationalist attitude considers the argument rather than the person arguing is of far-reaching importance. It leads to the view that we must recognize everybody with whom we communicate as a potential source of argument and of reasonable information; it thus establishes what may be described as the "rational unity of mankind."[64]

Popper admits that the rationalist attitude he advocates cannot be conclusively argued on rationalist grounds; it involves an article of *irrational*[65] faith in reason. But only this much does he concede to irrationalism. If unchecked, he argues, irrationalism conduces to authoritarianism, emphasizes mystical and other forms of generally non-communicable intuitions, and is based on the assumption that man is determined in his actions much more by his emotions than by his reason.[66] He further maintains that it is irrationalism that leads to a closed society, with all of its untoward consequences for human freedom and responsibility.[67]

In analyzing Plato's republic—a closed society on his terms—Popper shows that it has (at least) the following totalitarian features:[68] (1) There is a strict division of the classes. (2) The fate of the state is identified with the fate of the ruling class. (3) The ruling class has a monopoly on military training and material, and on education. (4) There is a strict censorship of all intellectual and artistic activities. (5) The state is self-sufficient.

If we now overlay this pattern on the model of Xunzi's state, the fit is almost perfect. His ideal is not superstition-ridden, nor, as it will be argued below, does it meet Popper's specifications for being irrational; it does, however, have all five of the characteristics he ascribes to the Republic:

(1) In the first place, the classes are strictly divided in Xunzi's state. No one is denied admission to the scholar-official class by virtue of humble birth or lack of wealth, but at any particular time a gulf separates the rulers from the ruled.

(2) Xunzi can easily be interpreted as identifying the fate of the state with the fate of the ruling class. A primary function of the scholar-official class is to preserve and transmit the *li*. And as we have seen, the *li* define the culture which binds together all of the members of the society in an harmonious whole, a necessary condition for economic productivity. Hence on Xunzi's grounds the breakdown of the scholar-official class would almost surely result in the loss of the *li*, which in turn would result in the breakdown of the entire society. (A movement he believed to be occurring in his own time.)

(3) Although military considerations are not a basic interest for the scholar-official class, it is the case that in their governmental roles they enjoy a monopoly on military might. Moreover, this class clearly monopolizes education, which is the prerequisite for admission to it.

(4) Xunzi openly advocates censorship of unorthodox doctrines not only in politics and philosophy but in the literary and artistic fields as well. Tolerance of diverse opinions would only produce a divisive effect on the members of the society and hence must be proscribed if social harmony—a necessary condition for economic cooperation—is to be maintained.

(5) And of course Xunzi's state is economically self-sufficient. This last point is not particularly important with respect to Xunzi's state (as opposed to the city-state of Plato) because there is nothing in principle to prevent Xunzi's state from encompassing the whole world, which would obviously have to be economically self-sufficient.

By meeting these five conditions Xunzi's state is totalitarian in Popper's terms. Because no formal institutions exist for the peaceful replacement of the ruler(s) Xunzi's model also fits Popper's description of a dictatorship or tyranny; it is certainly not a democracy. Further, we have also seen that Xunzi justifies restrictions on individual actions and goals on the grounds of thereby securing a minimal economic and social well-being for all; hence his state is collectivistic.

In short, Popper would hold that Xunzi's state is a closed society; it is very nearly the antithesis of the democratic model he advocates as a universal doctrine.

Having specified the target, we turn now to an examination of some attacks that might be launched against it.

Xunzi's Ideal State: Rational and Moral?

In his critiques of open and closed societies Popper does not claim that his arguments are, or can be made conclusive, for he freely admits that most of them depend on premises which express value judgments.[69] Rather he attempts to show that the premises on which the advocacy of open societies rests are *more reasonable* than the premises employed to champion their closed counterparts.[70] It is by virtue of their reasonableness that Popper hopes to gain supporters for the former and concomitant adversaries of the latter. Reasonableness, however, is obviously a matter of degree and consequently the nature of the values Popper invokes must be of crucial importance in any decision to become advocates or adversaries of his views.

From Popper's characterizations of open and closed societies it is clear that he endorses the individualistic values, an integral part of the open society. Thus there is a strong temptation to reject Xunzi's position out of hand. Most of the values reflected in the Chinese model are collective values, and many of them are incompatible with the individualistic values a great many people would want to support. In order to gain Xunzi a hearing it must therefore be shown that some degree of moral reasonableness may be claimed for his system at the outset.

There may appear to be a fundamental tension between the value systems of Xunzi and Popper but the tension does not merely exist *between* them or anyone else; on the contrary, the fundamental tension exists *within* almost every person, plain man or philosopher-king. In the Western tradition there are not one set of ethical values but two. On the one hand we have those individualistic principles Popper champions, which may be called the "Athenian" principles. Economically these principles are reflected in the capitalist system, wherein each individual may in theory compete for profit in an open marketplace. Politically they are reflected in such things as the American Constitution, wherein each individual is guaranteed personal liberty and the pursuit of his own happiness. The Athenian principles are dominant in America and Europe today, and are abundantly embodied in our proverbs: "May the best man win"; "God helps them that help themselves"; "Every man's home is his castle," etc.

But the European and American peoples also subscribe to a set of "Spartan" ethical principles which de-emphasize the importance of the individual in favor of the well-being of a group.   The unparalleled prosperity of the industrialized societies causes most people to lose sight of these latter principles in the economic and political spheres except as they are reflected in agricultural and other cooperatives, credit unions, and similar institutions.   Yet those principles remain with us, for however certain we are that the best man should win we are equally certain that "it isn't whether you win or lose, but how you play the game that counts." To be sure, God helps them that help themselves, but the Good Book also insists that everyone "Love thy neighbor as thyself."   And while we are confident that every man's home is his castle, we agree with John Donne that "no man is an island."

The relevance of this point to a consideration of Xunzi's state is that it shows how and why a moral evaluation of his position should not divorce it from the environment in and for which it was written.   Recall again his dictum: "Desires are many, things are few."   A businessman may be permitted to invoke the "best man wins" principle when prevailing over his competition on Wall Street but he cannot use it to justify taking for himself a disproportionate share of the life supplies possessed by a shipwrecked party.   Athenian principles accompany economic abundance, when there is more than enough for all; they do not provide suitable warrants for self-aggrandizing behavior on the part of the mentally and/or physically advantaged when such behavior results in severe hardship for others.   In these latter cases, when things are few, the Spartan principles come to the fore.[71]

An analogy between China and a shipwrecked party cannot be pressed, but the Middle Kingdom (past or present) certainly bears scant resemblance to Wall Street.   And if this much be admitted we have at least a *prima facie* case for the moral reasonableness (although not conclusiveness) of Xunzi's advocacy of the collective values.

Prima facie cases do not always hold up, however, so Popper must be allowed to prosecute his own case in greater detail.

A basic theoretical objection that Popper raises against closed-society arguments is that they all appeal to *historicism*—"the doctrine that history is controlled by specific historical or evolutionary laws whose discovery would enable us to prophesy the future."[72]   This doctrine has been advanced by Christian theologians, Hegelian and other metaphysicians, and by social science theorists.   Popper rejects it in all forms regardless of ideological color, creed, or country of origin.[73]   He argues that the future of man, unlike that of the natural world, is essentially unpredictable,[74] and that the historicist doctrine obscures the highly significant fact that men can affect the course of events;[75] that it is within the power of men to change their surroundings, and to work toward an ideal even while realizing that it is not fully attainable.[76] He further argues that it is man's task to assume responsibility for events, rather than attempt to evade that responsibility on the grounds that the forces of history (God, evolution, etc.) have determined the future beyond the ability of any individual or group to alter.[77]

With everything Popper says about man's responsibility for events Xunzi would be in agreement. The ancient Confucian was explicit in pointing out that societies (and the *li*) are manmade,[78] and that history is no more than the prior efforts of men to come to terms with their environments:

> Heaven's ways are constant. It does not prevail because of a sage like Yao; it does not cease to prevail because of a tyrant like Jie. Respond to it with good government, and good fortune will result; respond to it with disorder, and misfortune will result. If you encourage agriculture and are frugal in expenditures, then Heaven cannot make you poor. . . . But if you neglect agriculture and spend lavishly, then Heaven cannot make you rich. If you are careless in your provisions and slow to act, then Heaven cannot make you whole. . . . Your people will starve even when there are no floods or droughts. . . . The seasons will visit you as they do in a well-ordered age, but you will suffer misfortunes that a well-ordered age does not know. Yet you must not curse Heaven, for it is merely the natural result of your own actions.[79]

Xunzi would certainly concur with Popper that man was in large measure responsible for his fate. But he would go beyond Popper in denying the whole historicist notion of "progress" in history. For him, history is neither evolving or devolving; on his account it remains pretty much the same.[80] He would argue that there are always severe constraints placed on men's actions, so that human history is relatively unchanging from generation to generation and from century to century. He would not deny that there are better and poorer times, depending on each generation's ability to order their societal lives, but the limits remain constant. It is important to note this view of Xunzi's, for when coupled with his thoroughgoing skepticism in religious matters he can be seen to be working in a situation that is "existential" to an extreme: no afterlife, and no possibility of a yet-to-be-realized paradise on earth. For him, the past and the future are alike in that they both resemble almost precisely the here and now. There is no supernatural *raison d'être* for human existence and no historical laws suggesting progress. Only the manmade cultural tradition (the *li*) can serve as a link with the past and to the future—and perhaps give them significance—by each succeeding generation's maintenance of that tradition in the present.

One is inclined to respond to Xunzi's skepticism about historical progress by arguing that the development of science and technology in the two millennia since his time have rendered his view wholly untenable. Advancements in agricultural productivity, for example, have raised the level of food production beyond the wildest dreams of anyone living in Xunzi's time. Or again, medical science has eliminated many diseases that earlier plagued mankind and the current state of the art has reached the threshold of the conquest of death.

But the truth of these examples does not necessarily obviate Xunzi's historical perspective. His shade could reply to them, it seems, that the constraints have remained fairly constant: increased crop yields have been accompanied by a corresponding increase in population, with little or no diminution of the percentage of human beings who go to bed hungry every night. Similarly, man's ability to arrest death has been more than matched by his ability to spread it; if the next generation survives at all, it might well survive indefinitely, but it is by no means clear yet which of the two possibilities stands the better chance of being realized. Were Xunzi a poker player his comment on the "march" of history might be that the game was the same—but the ante had been raised.

Resolving the question of progress in history is beyond the scope of this paper; we can only note that the study of history does not warrant unbridled optimism about man's ability to order and control the technology that has allowed him to order and control his natural environment. More important here is the fact that Xunzi's austere metaphysics is not necessarily anachronistic, it is not historicist, nor, unfortunately, is it unreasonable.

Turning now to some practical objections to closed societies raised by Popper, he argues that such societies will face crucial problems in the area of leadership: (1) How can the ruler justify taking for himself a disproportionate share of the state's productivity for his own purposes?[81] (2) Authoritarianism discourages criticism; hence the ruler will not easily learn of problems that arise concerning the actions he has taken.[82] (3) The ruler will have to ignore many legitimate complaints and suppress reasonable as well as unreasonable criticism.[83] (4) Even granting the benevolence of the ruler, how can he provide for an equally competent and benevolent successor?[84] We will take up each of these problems in turn.

(1) Xunzi will indeed provide the ruler of the state with all of the luxuries the state offers, but the amount of money spent on the imperial family should not be overestimated. In an earlier quotation it was seen that Xunzi will restrict the imposition of taxes on the people to one-tenth of the crop yield, with some supplemental revenues accruing to the state treasury in the form of tribute-taxes from groups living beyond the state's borders.[85] The sum thus collected will certainly not be insignificant but it must be pointed out that Xunzi's government will also have major expenditures: state shrines, temples, and other buildings must be built and maintained, a large civil-service payroll will have to be regularly met, monies must be spent on highways, dikes, canals and other public works, and welfare services must be provided for the poor, aged and infirm. Without figures it is impossible to calculate accurately, but the evidence suggests that governmental income and expenditures will very nearly equal each other in Xunzi's state.[86] If so, the surplus thus expended on the imperial family will be only a small percentage of the total budget, and on Xunzi's grounds, will be well spent.

Moreover, the ruler is the cultural symbol of the state, the highest visible exemplification of the *li*.[87] His role is therefore extremely important, for the *li* are the moral base of the state and it is imperative for the monarch to be looked upon as a moral paradigm. Hence Xunzi also had pragmatic reasons for wanting the imperial family to be well cared for. Knowing full well that sage-kings were few and far between Master Xun would give a flesh-and-blood ruler a full store of creature comforts and diversions and in that way sharply reduce any temptation on his part to ever act immorally.[88] If all that the ruler could desire can be assured by being an exemplar of the *li*, why should he behave in such a way as to subvert it?

(2) Popper is probably correct in arguing that authoritarianism discourages criticism, but the difficulty can be overcome if a part of the function of the governors of the state is to provide just that criticism. The office of the censorate initiated during the Tang is a historical illustration of this point.[89] The institution was admittedly perverted by the Ming,[90] but Xunzi would attribute the perversion to the officials who held the post and not to a theoretical weakness of the system. Obsequiousness was not a quality of Xunzi's scholar:

> When proper standards prevail in the world, to dare to bring
> your own conduct into accord with them; when the Way of the
> former kings prevails, to dare to follow its dictates; to refuse to
> bow before the ruler of a disordered age; to refuse to follow the

customs of the people of a disordered age, to accept poverty and hardship if they are in the cause of benevolent action; to reject wealth and eminence if they are not consonant with benevolent action; if the world recognizes you, to share in the world's joys; if the world does not recognize you, to stand alone and without fear: this is superior valor.[91]

(3) Equally important for encouraging complaints in Xunzi's state is the fact that criticisms will not reflect on the ruler personally. It has generally been overlooked by commentators that Xunzi's monarch was to reign more than to rule; it is not mere happenstance that Han Fei, who acknowledged the superfluity of the ruler, was a student of Xunzi. Subtly but surely his teacher said the same thing:

If the ruler desires safety, he should govern equitably and love the members of the clans. If he desires glory, he should honor *li* and treat scholars with respect. If he desires to establish his merit and his name, he should promote the worthy and employ the competent. These are the three great obligations of the ruler.[92]

Or again:

With care he will select men of talent and promote them to office, where he will offer rewards to encourage them and threaten strict punishments in order to restrain them from evil. He will choose men who know to handle such things and employ them to attend to and manage all affairs. Then he may sit back at ease and goods will pile up, all will be well-ordered, and there will be enough of all things to go around.[93]

From these quotations it should be clear that Xunzi's ruler has one major political function to serve, namely, the appointment of the officials who will otherwise manage the state's affairs. Thus if there are any deviations from the Way they should be called to the ruler's attention immediately so that he can replace the erring official(s). If he does not do so social harmony may be lost, a sign that the ruler's tenure might be short-lived:

Therefore, if the affairs of government are in disorder, it is the fault of the prime minister. If the customs of the country are faulty, it is due to the error of the high officials. And if the world is not unified and the feudal lords are rebellious, then the heavenly king is not the right man for the job.[94]

With competent officials at work the ruler has few tasks to perform. It is fairly safe to assume that his additional responsibilities—i.e., loving those below him, respecting scholars, and so on—will not prove to be an unduly heavy burden of state. For the rest, the ruler carries out his ceremonial duties and then "may sit back at ease and goods will pile up."

(4) By answering the prior questions we have also replied to Popper's fourth criticism of the ruler's successor. If the primary function of the ruler is to appoint his officials, and he is even to be guided in this task by the present office-holders, an unending procession of philosopher-kings will not have to be guaranteed in order to insure the continued harmony and prosperity of the state. As long as the appointments are made and the ceremonial duties fulfilled the ruler may otherwise deport himself in accordance with his desires. It might well require a man of exceptional ability to establish the state, but once founded, Xunzi believed the officials would be able to manage affairs well even during the reigns of less than ordinary monarchs.[95]

Xunzi's state can thus meet all four of Popper's basic criticisms concerning leadership in a closed society. (Xunzi has not specifically answered the question of why there should be a leader at all—but Popper didn't ask it. It is difficult to say whether this omission is more illustrative of the Chinese or the Western philosophical traditions).[96] Perhaps he will have some personal misgivings about the nature of the defense, but it is difficult to see on what grounds Popper would find it unreasonable.

Another objection to closed societies is that they engender an undesirable form of education. Popper says:

> The very idea of selecting or educating future leaders is self-contradictory . . . the secret of intellectual excellence is the spirit of criticism; it is intellectual independence. And this leads to difficulties which must prove insurmountable for any kind of authoritarianism. The authoritarian will in general select those who obey, who believe, who respond to his influence. But in doing so, he is bound to select mediocrities. For he excludes those who revolt, who doubt, who dare to resist his influence.[97]

The principle expressed in this quotation is sufficiently ingrained in Western educational philosophy as to make Popper's statement of it appear almost trivial. Xunzi, however, would flatly deny that it was true.

In the first place, Xunzi's scholars will not, on Popper's grounds, be intellectually independent because of their commitment to an ideology, the "Way." But does it follow that they will thus be "mediocrities"? We have already seen that Xunzi wants no obsequious men in his scholar-official class, and he urges the point repeatedly:

> The private desires of a gentleman are suppressed in favor of his sense of public obligation.[98]

> The gentleman . . . follows the principles of the Way with courage.[99]

Popper would reply, of course, that in the actual workings of the state the timid would far outnumber the brave. But Xunzi's point is that his gentlemen are committed to a set of principles, not to a particular monarch, and those principles give significance to the lives of those who adopt them (as will be seen below). Thus the psychological price paid for contravening the principles is extremely high. Further, Xunzi believed that the monarch would not seek to subvert those principles in any manner because they also served to legitimize his own imperial position.[100]

Equally important to Xunzi's educational concerns is the fact that an attitude of independence and disinterested inquiry is not a prerequisite for managing the affairs of his state competently. The governing *li*, remember, are or can be made explicit. The official, therefore, asks himself: "Does this action conform to the relevant standard?" He must know how to measure performance by criteria[101] and how to suggest remedies when the behavior (policies, etc.) falls short of the ideal; but it simply is not the case that a spirit of inquiry and criticism—in the scientific sense—must be fostered in order to train officials qualified to perform these functions. The official must certainly be a rational man; but that is not to say he must be a scientist.

One can see why Popper will insist upon intellectual independence, for he correctly perceives that it is at the heart of all work in science. And the potential goodness of scientific work is an assumption Popper makes throughout his work, notwithstanding his admission of the possibility that scientific achievements can be used to serve evil ends.[102] Xunzi however, would not grant the assumption. Indeed, he explicitly discourages such speculation as would today be considered scientific.[103] He would argue that we can learn all that is important to know about the natural world from careful observations at what would now be considered a gross level:

When he [the scholar] turns his thoughts to Heaven, he seeks to understand only those phenomena which can be regularly expected. When he turns his thoughts to earth, he seeks to understand only those aspects that can be taken advantage of. When he turns his thoughts to the four seasons, he seeks to understand only the changes that will affect his undertakings.[104]

Thus pure science and scientific curiosity for its own sake do not play any role in Xunzi's system and he would almost certainly concur with Pope's view that the proper study of mankind was man: how to morally organize him economically and politically:

There is no age that has not experienced eclipses of the sun and moon, unseasonable rain or wind, or strange stars seen in groups. . . . These are rare events. We may marvel at them, but we should not fear them. When human ominous signs come, then we should be really afraid.

What is a human ominous sign? Using a poor plough and thereby injuring the grain; the losing of the effect of the fertilizer in hoeing and weeding; the losing of the allegiance of the people by a government bent on evil; when the fields are uncultivated and the harvest is bad; when the price of grain is high and the people are starving; when there are dead bodies on the roads—these are what I mean by human ominous signs.[105]

The argument might be continued by pointing out that the educated are no less members of the human race than anyone else; and because man is basically a social animal an attempt to learn about him in a dispassionate manner could only result in the lessening of the investigator's humanity while engaged in his study, which Xunzi would be especially anxious to avoid.

It must be remembered that he rejects both the notion of a God-created universe with an attendant afterlife for those who follow His dictates and the notion of historical progress toward an almost unlimited happiness-state. An avowed atheist, Xunzi's vision is confined to this world in the concrete present. Men have their short three score and ten to walk the earth; when they die, they are dead: "Birth is the beginning of man, death his end."[106] In devising his education then, Xunzi was not merely concerned to train intellectual and political leaders in such a way that they did not seek to oppress, exploit, or otherwise subjugate the less fortunate. He was equally concerned to provide a way for those leaders to answer the question: "If it will all end one day soon for each of us, if there is no plan to be realized, no goal toward which we are advancing, why should I devote myself to the well-being of my fellows? To what purpose?" Xunzi's educational model was an attempt to provide answers to these kinds of questions. His solution to the problem of the meaning *of* life was to so construct his system that each person could find meaning *in* life.[107]

The problem of the meaning of life is uncomfortably vague, and there is probably no single formulation of it that would satisfy everyone. But this much is clear, that the problem involves morality, and the present point is that Xunzi thought a seeking after the unknown made a moral solution to the problem impossible. The unknown for Xunzi was more supernatural in flavor than scientific, but in both cases there is a shift of attention away from the human condition. If men are compartmentalized in their functions and obliged to dissociate themselves from their fellows—as the scientific temper demands by insisting upon objectivity—there will of necessity be a separation of moral from other behavior. Such separation could easily have at least two untoward consequences: (1) it could promote disharmony in the state, because no purely objective reasons could be adduced to support the contention that the strong should not tyrannize the weak,[108] especially in an economic environment that is a far cry from the Garden of Eden; (2) it would be more difficult for a man to see his life as significant, for the more he looked upon his fellow human beings as objects while engaged in his scientific pursuits the more difficult it would be for him to derive satisfaction from aiding them in the achievement of their cosmically insignificant aspirations.[109]

In Xunzi's model, on the other hand, morality infuses all attitudes and behavior. His cosmos is indeed barren, and hence for him the significance and beauty of human life must ultimately reside in interpersonal relationships, especially as those relations are defined by a rich cultural heritage which has the pragmatic concomitance of stimulating cooperative endeavors in the economic sphere. One man cannot build the Great Wall, nor a dike to stem the floodwaters of the Huang He, "Yellow River;" but together men can build for military security and economic productivity. When the social and ethical relations which form the cement of these endeavors are also seen to have strong psychological effects (or religious; either term is applicable), the scope and cohesiveness of Xunzi's entire philosophy becomes all the more impressive.

In his educational system each person will receive an all-pervasive ethical instruction by means of which he will come to define himself strictly in terms of his relationships to others (the function of the *li*),[110] and to evaluate his behavior in the same terms: he will know what to expect of his fellows and what is expected of him. One's actions are then significant in proportion to the significance they have for others, and hence one's aspirations and goals are human goals, determined by and for a consideration of other human beings.[111] Moreover, it bears repeating that: (1) the behavior-governing norms are *ritualized*, serving to bind the individual to his contemporaries, to those who have preceded him in time, and thereby to those who will follow him as well—a small but not inconsequential form of immortality; and (2) the proper performance of those rituals can provide the individual with an aesthetic satisfaction to complement his ethical, economic, and other accomplishments.

It can be seen then, that the strength of Xunzi's system lies in his insistence on the integration of economic, political, social, ethical and aesthetic behavior by means of the unifying *li*:

> The rules of proper conduct (*li*) are the utmost of human morality (*dao*). Moreover those who do not follow the rules of proper conduct (*li*) and are not satisfied with it, are people without a direction in life; they who follow the rules of proper conduct (*li*) and are satisfied with it are gentlemen who have a direction to their life.[112]

The *li*, of course, do not have the significance today that they had in Xunzi's time but it does not follow on that account alone that his philosophy is obsolete. On the contrary, problems of economic scarcity and psychological emptiness are no less acute today than they were when he faced them, and his solution—an integrated life made significant by defining it in terms of other human lives—is still worthy of careful consideration.

Being firmly entrenched in the scientific tradition Popper would probably believe that the integration of roles proposed by Xunzi would eventually lead to emotionalism and irrationality in many areas where it had no place, leading to an unjust arbitrariness or to a major loss of societal efficiency, either of which would more than offset the psychological gains claimed by Xunzi for his system. But the ancient Confucian would disagree:

> Fair-mindedness is the balance in which to weigh proposals; upright harmoniousness is the line by which to measure them. Where laws exist, to carry them out; where they do not exist, to act in the spirit of precedent and analogy—this is the best way

to hear proposals. To show favoritism and partisan feeling and be without any constant principles—this is the worst you can do.[113]

And similarly:

> With a benevolent mind he explains his ideas to others, with the mind of learning he listens to their words, and with a fair mind he makes his judgments.[114]

In short, Xunzi is saying that an integrated life is at the same time a rational life—the absence of the scientific temper notwithstanding. To Popper's call for a spirit of disinterested inquiry he would reply:

> If a person neglects what men can do and seeks for what Heaven does, he fails to understand the nature of things.[115]

Popper has a great many other objections to closed societies, but most of them do not apply to Xunzi's model because of the ethical pervasiveness of the *li*. Popper says, for example, that one pernicious quality of closed societies is that they dictate morality. Hence the individual member therein evades personal responsibility for his actions, making him amoral at best.[116] But when leveled against Xunzi the weakness of this charge becomes clear as soon as it is stated. Morality is the foundation of Xunzi's state, and each individual is morally responsible to himself and his fellows for the proper performance of *all* of his actions. These actions are integrated, making it impossible to distinguish moral behavior from any other human behavior. Moreover, while the *li* dictates the specific form of the behavior, it should be noted that the individual must *choose* to have the *li* govern his behavior. Admittedly the child learns many norms unreflectively, but the same cannot be said of the student. The young Confucian must make a basic moral choice, whether or not to assume responsibility for following the *li*; and the choice, once made, requires constancy and effort on his part thereafter:

> The superior man knows that his knowledge is not complete . . . ; so he recites the Classics sentence by sentence in order to make them part of himself, he seeks to search into them in order to understand them; he puts himself into the places of the writers in order to understand their viewpoint; he expels any wrong from his nature in order to grasp and mature his knowledge: he makes his eye unwilling to see what is not right; he makes his ears unwilling to hear what is not right; he makes his mouth unwilling to speak what is not right; he makes his heart unwilling to

think what is not right. . . . His life will be according to this,
and his death will be according to it.[117]

Thus to follow the *li* is to be moral. By failing in any of his duties the
individual of Xunzi's state may be immoral, but having chosen the *li* he
can no longer be considered amoral.[118]
Another objection Popper raises against closed societies is that they
are collectively selfish:

> This is the collectivist, the tribal, the totalitarian theory of
> morality: "Good is what is in the interest of my group; or my
> tribe; or my state." It is easy to see what this morality implied
> for international relations: that the state itself can never be wrong
> in any of its actions, as long as it is strong; that the state has the
> right, not only to do violence to its citizens, should that lead to
> an increase of strength, but also to attack other states, provided
> it does so without weakening itself.[119]

To this argument Xunzi has two replies: (1) if the state does not follow
the Way (i.e., subscribe to the *li*), military pugnacity can only add to its
depravity; in his writings Xunzi cites numerous instances of states that
were both strong and wrong.[120] Indeed, he regularly suggests that the
soldiers of a truly virtuous state will probably never have to engage in
combat, but will win over the opposition by moral example.[121] Like
Socrates, Xunzi believed that men did wrong only because they were
ignorant of what was right:

> All men will abide by what they think is good and reject what
> they think is bad. It is inconceivable, therefore, that any man
> could understand that there is nothing in the world to compare
> to the Way, and yet not abide by it.[122]

This position may well be naïve to a fault but it is clearly not a "might
makes right" foreign policy. While Xunzi will allow his ruler to retaliate
if attacked, he expressly forbids him to wage war.[123] (2) It must also be
kept in mind that there is no obstacle in principle preventing Xunzi's
model from having universal application; admitting the improbability of
the *li* becoming universally accepted it is nevertheless the case that to
whatever extent Xunzi's model could become the world state it would be
vacuous to charge it with collective selfishness.

Finally, we consider what is perhaps the most basic of all objections
to Xunzi's state: unlike the open society, it will be static. By proscrib-
ing unorthodox views in philosophy and the arts, by discouraging scien-

tific endeavors, Master Xun advocates a state that would be relatively unchanging from generation to generation, with little hope for a better life in the future. The humanism of the *li* would insure that his state could not become a Brave New World, but with no possibility of progress the ancient Confucian's views on history would be self-fulfilling.

This is a forceful objection, but only by postulating a particular economic environment (fairly well-to-do), and a particular set of values (individualistic). If the proffered models of Xunzi and the open society are placed side by side we can see that on the one hand the Chinese model will have maximum security and minimal happiness guaranteed to all. To insure these achievements personal and intellectual freedoms will be restricted somewhat, and the hope of a greatly improved tomorrow will have to be surrendered. On the other hand the open society tolerates greater personal and intellectual freedoms and holds out the hope of an increasing amount of happiness in the future. The price paid for these freedoms and hopes is a loss of security, and the possibility that the future will bring an increasing amount of misery.

If the sides have been correctly drawn it is clear that reasonableness will not be the crucial determinant in choosing between them even under favorable economic conditions. To take a crude analogy, it is like asking whether it is more reasonable to invest in blue-chip stocks or in municipal bonds. The choice in either case will be governed by one's personal preferences, his hopes, fears and goals. In an economically poor environment the analogy does not hold at all, for money will not be invested in stocks or bonds—it will be used to buy food.[124]

In concluding, it cannot be doubted that everyone cherishes certain freedoms, Xunzi as much as anyone else. Freedoms, however, can be ordered, and hence some will have a higher priority than others. In the United States, for example, the freedom to openly carry a deadly weapon is less valued—and usually more sharply curtailed—than the freedom to openly express one's views. At the top of the ordering will be the freedoms from the fear of disease, starvation, and premature death. Without these fundamental freedoms all others are hollow, for without them there is little life and no spirit.

Perhaps it can be said, then, that Xunzi was no less anxious than Popper or any other philosopher to secure freedoms, but not having the good fortune to be born in an affluent society he was forced to start at the top of the list.

Notes

This article, originally published in a festschrift for Helmut Wilhem, is now dedicated to his memory. Three notes on texts and translations. (1) The basic source used is D. C. Lau and Fong Ching Chen, eds., *A Concordance to the* Xunzi 荀子逐字索引 (Hong Kong: The Commercial Press 商務印書館, 1996). I have relied on H. Dubs, *The Works of Hsüntze* (London: Arthur Probsthain, 1928) and on Burton Watson, *Xunzi: Basic Writings* (New York: Columbia Univ. Press, 1963)—hereafter referred to as Dubs and Watson respectively. When the first citation is to the Chinese text, the translation is my own; when Dubs or Watson appears first, it is their translation. (2) I have included both the pagination to Dubs and Watson whenever possible for comparative purposes. It is important to note how seldom the philosophical interpretations offered herein depend crucially on one particular translation. (3) Because of the differences between classical Chinese and modern English it would be misleading to italicize a portion of a translation for emphasis; similarly, in quoting texts a general attempt has been made to provide a context sufficiently large to minimize misrepresentation.

1. As, e.g., the five volumes produced by the Committee on Chinese Thought.

2. Dubs 152, 荀子: 富國 10/42/16.

3. Karl Popper, *The Open Society and Its Enemies*, fourth (revised) edition (London: Routledge and Kegan Paul, 1962) 2 vols. Hereafter referred to as *OSIE* (1) and *OSIE* (2).

4. That it is indeed exemplary has been attested by such people as Bertrand Russell, who said of the work that it "was a vigorous and profound defence of democracy" (*OSIE* (1), from the dust cover).

5. Watson 43, Dubs 132-3, 荀子: 王制 9/38/11.

6. In extolling the virtues of the Zhou sage-kings Xunzi says: "There was no darkened or rustic state which did not hasten to send envoys and joyfully seek peace. Within the four seas it was as if there was one family." Dubs 166, Watson 68, 荀子: 議兵 15/71/15-6. He then exhorts potential sage-kings of the present to follow the Zhou example.

7. Xunzi explicitly notes that the children of different groups are born with similar qualities, and it is their cultural education which accounts for their differences as adults. 荀子: 勸學 1/1/8, Dubs 31-32, Watson 15. Elsewhere he argues, consistent with his anthropological observations, that everyone must have an opportunity to learn and follow the Way. 荀子: 王制 9/35/1-8, Dubs 121-22, Watson 33-34. Thus Xunzi believes in basic human equality through the possibility of education, and not because he believes all men equally evil. For the authenticity of the *Xing'e* 性惡, cf. D. Munro, *The Concept of Man in Early China* (Stanford: Stanford Univ. Press, 1969) esp. 77, where he cites Kanaya Osamu's work on this particular text.

8. Aristotle's arguments are found in *Politics*, 1254a-1256a. The interpretation of Plato is Popper's. Cf. *OSIE* (1) 149-53 for the philosopher-king of the *Republic* as eugenicist (who must lie about his role).

9. Watson 43, Dubs 132-33, 荀子: 王制 9/38/9-11.

10. Watson 44, Dubs 134, 荀子: 王制 9/38/17-8. See also the *Fuguo* 富國, where the same point is made again.

11. Ibid. Cf. also n. 45.

12. 荀子: 解蔽 21/104/16-21/105-1, Dubs 270, Watson 130. Cf. also 荀子: 正論 18/87/12. "All those who rob men must have a reason. If it is not because they do not have enough, then it is because the wealthy have too much. But the Sages . . . did not allow anyone to have too much above what was right." Dubs 204.

13. 荀子: 王制 9/40/1-5, Dubs 140, Watson 48.

14. Homer H. Dubs, *Hsüntze: The Moulder of Ancient Confucianism* (London: Arthur Probsthain, 1927) 263-64. Arthur Waley might disagree with this view because he notes in his *Three Ways of Thought in Ancient China* (Garden City: Doubleday, n.d.) that "Merchants had already been attacked by Xunzi" (170). But the evidence is very strong from numerous other discussions of commerce in his works that Xunzi wanted, if you will, some anti-trust legislation; he did not wish to curb commercial activities as long as they conduced to the well-being of the members of the state. The *Fuguo* reiterates this theme several times.

15. Indeed, the encouragement of regulated, but nevertheless free trade continued well past Xunzi's time. In addition to one of the positions taken in the salt and iron debates, Sima Qian, for example, held economic views almost precisely the same as those discussed above. See Robert Crawford, "The Social and Political Philosophy of the *Shih-chi*," *Journal of Asian Studies* 22:4 (1963) esp. 407-8.

16. For a fuller account of commercial patterns in late Zhou cf. N. L. Swann, *Food and Money in Ancient China* (Princeton: Princeton Univ. Press, 1950).

17. This point is made in anticipation of an objection by Popper to "the Utopian method [which] must lead to a dangerous dogmatic attachment to a blueprint for which countless sacrifices have been made." *OSIE* (2) 163.

18. 荀子: 王制 9/39/20-2, Dubs 138-39, Watson 47.

19. 荀子: 王制 9/35/10, Dubs 122-23, Watson 34-35.

20. 荀子: 正論 18/84/4, Dubs 190 ff. The argument here is that a ruler who does not follow the Way may be replaced by a nobleman who does. Elsewhere Xunzi insists that the gentleman not serve an evil ruler. Cf. n. 91. Further, no pejorative connotations of "ideology" are intended herein; the term is used to mean "pervasive belief-system."

21. 荀子: 禮論 19/97/8. Xunzi is here quoting the *Shijing* 詩經.

22. Cf. n. 19. This is, of course, the "Mandate of Heaven," and hence the word "theoretical" is significant, for the ruler would almost surely have to be deposed by force. But cf. also n. 121.

23. In the *Wangzhi* 王制 chapter Xunzi repeatedly says that the sage-king will gain the allegiance of the feudal lords, but will employ and promote those who follow the Way. See also 66 ff.

24. Dubs 121, Watson 33, 荀子: 王制 9/35/4-6.

25. 荀子: 修身 2/5/18, Dubs 45 ff., Watson 25 ff.

26. 荀子: 王制 9/40/6-7, Dubs 141, Watson 48-49. Cf. also 荀子: 樂論 20/101/6-9, Dubs 256-57, Watson 118-19.

27. Cf. n. 9.

28. Although in regard to military matters, Xunzi implies that the rule of a sage-king will make the military unnecessary: "Men did not build walls and battlements or dig ditches and moats, they did not set up defenses and watch stations or construct war machines, and yet the state was peaceful and safe, free from fear of outside aggression and secure in its position. There was only one reason for this. The leaders illumined the Way and apportioned all ranks fairly, they employed the people at the proper season and sincerely loved them. . . ." Watson 72-73, 荀子: 議兵 15/73/4-6. (Dubs, believing this section repetitive and perhaps spurious, does not translate it.) Cf. also ns. 121 and 123.

29. Watson 34, Dubs 121-22, 荀子: 王制 9/35/7-8.

30. Watson 37, Dubs 125, 荀子: 王制 9/36/6-7.

31. 荀子: 王制 9/35/22-9/36/3, Dubs 124, Watson 36.

32. One of the chief rewards being in the form of honored rites, as seen in the *Lilun* 禮論.

33. 荀子: 王制 9/39/12-3, Dubs 137, Watson 46.

34. Nevertheless, social mobility was not inconsequential. For the Song, cf. E. A. Kracke, Jr., *Civil Service in Early Sung China* (Cambridge: Harvard Univ. Press, 1953). For the Ming-Qing periods, Ho Ping-ti, *The Ladder of Success in Imperial China* (Chicago: Univ. of Chicago Press, 1967).

35. Cf. n. 24.

36. The thesis that the *li* are to affect all aspects of everyone's life will perhaps be challenged. Dubs would concur (*Hsüntze: The Moulder of Ancient Confucianism* 145 ff.), but H. G. Creel certainly would not. In *Confucius and the Chinese Way* (New York: Harper & Bros., 1960) he says: "Xunzi asserted that the people had been divided into 'poor and rich, noble and plebian' by the sage-kings, for their own good. Those of noble status

should be 'regulated by *li* and music,' while the common people should be controlled by the rigors of law." (210) To support his position Creel cites a passage from Dubs' translation from which his conclusion simply does not follow. Indeed, three pages earlier in his work Dubs translates Xunzi as saying: "Develop the common people without waiting to compel them by law" (121). As for the *li* and music being the privileged property of the elite: "Music . . . has the power to make good the hearts of the people, to influence men deeply, and to transform their ways and customs with facility. Therefore, the former kings guided the people with rites and music, and the people became harmonious" (Watson 115, Dubs 251-52, 荀子: 樂論 20/99/24). Rites, of course, were to be governed according to rank; the funeral of a high official would be more elaborate than the funeral of a farmer, but there were explicit rules for both (荀子: 禮論 19/93/11, Dubs 228-30, Watson 97-98). Everyone can learn his public and private norms, and it is one of the functions of the ruler to see that the requisite education is provided (荀子: 性惡 23/116/11, Dubs 313, Watson 166). Further, the sage-kings established the *li* so that everyone could have their desires properly channeled. Cf. n. 45. For more on the universality of the *li* see also ns. 37 and 43. Examples could be multiplied, but the point should be clear: the specific form of the *li* will vary from rank to rank, but the *li* nevertheless apply to all of the people, all of the time; this is a cornerstone of Xunzi's entire philosophy. He says: "Such rules represent the ultimate principle of community harmony and unity" (Watson 108, Dubs 241, 荀子: 禮論 19/97/4).

37. Dubs 44-45, Watson 25, 荀子: 修身 2/5/12-15.

38. 荀子: 王制 9/39/6-7, Dubs 136, Watson 45. Unfortunately, the analysis which follows applies only partially to women, whose subordinate role Xunzi did not challenge.

39. "The Way of the ancient kings." Cf. n. 44.

40. Developing a theme suggested in *Lunyu* 論語 3:12, 17:11.

41. Morton White, *The Age of Analysis* (New York: Mentor, 1955) 55.

42. 荀子: 王制 9/39/4-6, Dubs 136, Watson 45.

43. Dubs 51, Watson 30, 荀子: 修身 2/8/1-2. Cf. also n. 115.

44. 荀子: 禮論 19/92/16-9, Dubs 225, Watson 95. See also my "On Reappraising Ancient Chinese Philosophy," *PEW* 21:2 (1971) 212-3.

45. 荀子: 禮論 19/90/4-5, Dubs 213, Watson 89.

46. Cf. n. 31.

47. Cf. n. 43.

48. One of the themes of the *Zhengming* 正名.

49. 荀子: 王制 9/40/2, Dubs 140, Watson 48. To anticipate Popper's antagonism on this issue: "We can love and hate, especially in art, without

favoring legal measures for suppressing what we hate, or for canonizing what we love," *OSIE* (1) 230.

50. Watson 114-15, Dubs 250-52, 荀子: 樂論 20/99/15-22.

51. 荀子: 禮論 19/92/3, Dubs 223, Watson 94.

52. Cf. ns. 43, 117.

53. 荀子: 天論 17/82/6, Dubs 181, Watson 85. Along not dissimilar lines Vincent Shih says: "The fact that China has no science, though in a sense it is due to our conception of happiness, may also be accounted for by our neglect of what is not of apparent moral consequence." "Hsüntzu's Positivism," *Tsing Hua Journal of Chinese Studies*, New Series 4:2 (1964) 171.

54. 荀子: 天論 17/82/7, Dubs 181, Watson 85. This is also a theme of the *Jiebi* 解蔽. 荀子: 解蔽 21/106/12 ff., Dubs 275 ff., Watson 135 ff. Cf. also n. 105.

55. "Addendum," *OSIE* (2) 369-96.

56. One example, *"There is no return to a harmonious state of nature. If we turn back, then we must go the whole way—we must return to the beasts."* *OSIE* (1) 200-201 (italics in the original).

57. *OSIE* (1) 173, 202, *OSIE* (2) 30-31 and *passim*.

58. Technically, Xunzi's model cannot be a closed society in the historical sense because China had, by his time, long since left its tribal-like and myth-making original social patterns. Hence it is only in the political and social senses that Xunzi's society is "closed." *OSIE* (1) 171 ff. Popper's technical term for the Chinese model would be "arrested." *OSIE* (1) 232. Cf. also n. 98.

59. *OSIE* (1) 124-25. Cf. also n. 22.

60. Ibid.

61. Ibid. 99 ff.

62. Ibid.

63. *OSIE* (2) 224. Because Xunzi claims a Way his system cannot, on Popper's grounds, be rational *by definition*, it can only be "pseudorational." Ibid. 227. We will herein ignore the strict definition because it obviously begs the question at issue.

64. *OSIE* (2) 225.

65. Ibid. 231.

66. Ibid. 232.

67. Ibid. 234.

68. *OSIE* (1) 86-87.

69. *OSIE* (2) 240: "But I believe that the only attitude which I can consider to be morally right is one which recognizes that we owe it to other men to treat them and ourselves as rational."

70. *OSIE* (2) 225.

71. This point applies to contemporary as well as classical China.

72. *OSIE* (1) 8.

73. Ibid. 34: "My attitude towards historicism is one of frank hostility, based upon the conviction that historicism is futile, and worse than that."

74. *OSIE* (2), Chs. 22 and 25. Cf. especially 208-11.

75. Ibid.

76. Ibid. 269 ff.

77. Ibid. 208-11.

78. Cf. n. 45. See also Fung Yu-lan, *A Short History of Chinese Philosophy* (New York: Macmillan, 1960) 144. Fung argues that Xunzi believed everything good and valuable in and for mankind comes from human effort.

79. Watson 79, Dubs 173, 荀子: 天論 17/79/16-21.

80. Ibid. Derk Bodde agrees with this interpretation of Xunzi. Cf. his "Harmony and Conflict in Chinese Philosophy" in A. Wright, ed., *Studies in Chinese Thought* (Chicago: Univ. of Chicago Press, 1967) 28, 36. So does Dubs, *Hsüntze: The Moulder of Ancient Confucianism* 75.

81. *OSIE* (1) 90 ff., 108. *OSIE* (2) 122-24.

82. *OSIE* (1) 159-61.

83. Ibid.

84. Ibid.

85. Cf. n. 9.

86. For more on the ruler's frugality cf. 荀子: 王制 9/41/10, Dubs 146, Watson 52.

87. 荀子: 禮論 19/91/1, Dubs 220, Watson 91.

88. And to hedge his bets Xunzi will have the rulers and their heirs receive the same training given to the scholar-officials, hence they should come to endorse the *li* as their tutors do. Less important, but not insignificant, is the Mandate of Heaven theory as a deterrent to immoral behavior. The ruler does not rule by divine right, and he knows that his tenure is only as secure as the state is well-ordered.

89. Cf. C.O. Hucker, *The Traditional Chinese State in Ming Times* (Tucson: Univ. of Arizona Press, 1961) especially 50-52.

90. Ibid.

91. Watson 169, Dubs 315-16, 荀子: 性惡 23/117/6-8.

92. 荀子: 王制 9/36/10-1, Dubs 125, Watson 37.

93. Watson 53, Dubs 147-48, 荀子: 王制 9/41/19-20.

94. Watson 50, Dubs 143-44, 荀子: 王制 9/40/15-6.

95. Ibid. After the present study originally went to press I learned of Y. P. Mei's "Xunzi's Theory of Government," *Tsing Hua Journal of Chinese Studies* 8:1 and 2 (1970). Therein he notes an important problem of interpreting Xunzi's Daoist-like statement in the *Jundao* 君道:

> Hence the emperor can see without looking, hear without listening, know without listening, know without reflecting, and achieve without stirring. He just sits there by himself... and the people ... obey him like one body, similar to the way the four limbs obey the mind. (55)

If my interpretation of Xunzi is correct, Mei's problem is solved: being a cultural and moral figurehead, the emperor may (should) practice 無為 *wuwei* because he is to *reign*; the officials are to *rule*.

96. For Xunzi, the ruler earns his considerable keep in roughly the same way Elizabeth II earns hers; she is the highest living symbol of the British cultural tradition. Popper, however, does not think too highly of *any* kind of ruler: "I am inclined to think that rulers have rarely been above the average, either morally or intellectually, and often below it." *OSIE* (1) 122. Yet he nowhere even entertains the possibility of a rulerless society.

97. *OSIE* (1) 134-35.

98. 荀子: 修身 2/8/16, Dubs 54, Watson 32.

99. 荀子: 修身 2/8/12, Dubs 53, Watson 32.

100. Cf. n. 88.

101. A significant portion of the *Wangzhi* is devoted to making explicit the duties and responsibilities of the various officials.

102. *OSIE* (1) 135-36. *OSIE* (2) 244.

103. Cf. n. 54. Also, in *Hsüntze: The Moulder of Ancient Confucianism* Dubs says that Xunzi "denied the advisability" of seeking scientific knowledge. (74)

104. Watson 81, Dubs 177, 荀子: 天論 17/80/17-8.

105. Dubs 180, Watson 84, 荀子: 天論 17/81/11-7.

106. Watson 96, Dubs 227, 荀子: 禮論 19/93/6.

107. This distinction is made by K. Baier in "The Meaning of Life" in M. Weitz, ed., *Twentieth Century Philosophy: The Analytic Tradition* (Toronto:

Collier Macmillan Ltd., 1966) 361-80. For Popper's views on the meaning of life, cf. *OSIE* (2) 278.

108. In the 荀子: 議兵 15/70/4 ff., Xunzi can only criticize the tyranny and oppression of the Qin state by appealing to their departure from the Way. Watson 62-63.

109. Admittedly it would not be *impossible* to so derive satisfaction.

110. Cf. n. 36.

111. Cf. n. 37. Also, *OSIE* (2) 275-76.

112. Dubs 225, Watson 95, 荀子: 禮論 19/92/15-7.

113. Watson 35, Dubs 123, 荀子: 王制 9/35/17-9.

114. Watson 148, Dubs 291-92, 荀子: 正名 22/110/14.

115. Dubs 183, Watson 86, 荀子: 天論 17/82/17-8. See also n. 124.

116. *OSIE* (1) 5 and Ch. 10.

117. Dubs 40-41, Watson 22, 荀子: 勸學 1/4/16-20.

118. The point here is analogous to Kierkegaard's "choosing oneself"—by so doing the chooser leaves the aesthetic life for the ethical (in Kierkegaard's senses of those terms). Cf. *Either/Or* (Garden City: Doubleday, 1969), vol. II, 178-81.

119. *OSIE* (1) 107.

120. Cf. n. 108.

121. 荀子: 議兵 15/72/5, Dubs 169-70, Watson 70-72.

122. Watson 152, Dubs 296, 荀子: 正名 22/111/20. It is difficult here to tell whether Xunzi is speaking in terms of self-interest or as an idealist.

123. 荀子: 議兵 15/71/17, Dubs 167, Watson 68.

124. Many of these points apply equally to contemporary China. It would, of course, be foolish to maintain that the present leaders of China are no more than the current recipients of the "Mandate of Heaven"; but it would be no less foolish to ignore the constancy of environmental constraints on Chinese thinkers, and thereby, the continuities between traditional and modern philosophical perspectives on the state and society. Further, it is clear that governments like the United States have unreflectively assumed the universality of Popper's assumptions when dealing (or refusing to deal) with China, which have had numerous untoward consequences for the Chinese. See, for example, *America's Asia*, ed. Edward Friedman and Mark Selden (New York: Random House, 1971).

Two

Ethical Uses of the Past in Early Confucianism: The Case of Xunzi

Antonio S. Cua

The ethical use of the distinction between the past 古 *gu* and the present 今 *jin*, of historical characters, situations, and events, is a familiar and prominent feature of early Confucianism. Henceforth, I shall refer to this feature as "the use of the historical appeal." To a Western philosopher, the use of this appeal, instead of deductive argument, is highly perplexing and problematic. For most Chinese thinkers, "philosophy meant a kind of wisdom that is necessary for the conduct of life, particularly the conduct of government," and "it sought to exercise persuasive power on princes, and . . . resorted, not to deductive reasoning, but to the exploitation of historical examples."[1] More fundamentally, it may be said that "the consideration important to the Chinese is the behavioral implications of the belief or proposition in question. What effect does adherence to the belief have on people? What implications for social action can be drawn from the statement?"[2] This account makes the use of the historical appeal readily intelligible so that it serves as a vehicle for ethical instruction.[3] With such an understanding, however, the perplexity may be eased, but the problematic character of the use of the historical appeal remains. From the point of view of argumentation, it is important to know to what degree, if any, such an appeal can rationally warrant the acceptance of an ethical thesis. That is, how does one appraise the validity of the use of the historical appeal? For averting a negative judgment based on the use of the historical appeal, one should be reminded that although Confucius 孔夫子 regarded himself as a transmitter of ancient wisdom rather than as an innovator,[4] there are still grounds to believe that his own attitude toward the past was not an uncritical one. Moreover, his attitude seemed to have been flexible and was reflected in his conception of paradigmatic individuals—who were cherished for their ability to deal with changing circumstances.[5] In support of the former claim, one may cite this remark of Confucius: "I am able to discourse on the 禮 *li* (rules of proper conduct) of Xia 夏, but the state of Qi 杞 does not furnish sufficient evidence. I am able to discourse on the *li* of Yin 殷, but the state of Song 宋 does not furnish sufficient supporting evidence. This is because there are not enough records of men of erudition. Otherwise I would be able to support what I say with evidence."[6] Whereas evidence for his belief in flexibility as a virtue is contained in this saying: "I have no preconceptions about the permissible and the impermissible."[7] Also it is reported that "There were four things the Master refused to have anything to do with: he refused to entertain conjectures or to insist on certainty; he refused to be inflexible or to be egotistical."[8] The foregoing remarks from the *Analects* suggest that had Confucius reflected upon the value of the historical appeal, he would have maintained that its proper use depends on a careful attention to evidence and to ethical considerations relevant to issues that arise out of changing circumstances.[9] Thus qualified, the use of the historical appeal cannot be considered merely as an "argument from authority," or an appeal to historical sanctions for backing one's ethical conviction. Nor can it be characterized as an "argument from historical examples" if this phrase is intended to convey the idea that its use constitutes a sufficient condition for warranting conclusions in ethical discourse.

The foregoing reminder of Confucius' attitude toward the past, while useful as a caveat against hasty judgment based on the Confucian use of the historical appeal, does not by itself contribute to an answer to the question concerning the validity of such an appeal. However, a just discussion of this question depends on a prior inquiry into its role in exemplary Confucian discourse. The works of Xunzi 荀子 provide us with a good case study.[10] In Xunzi, one finds an extensive use of the historical appeal in contexts that are often illuminating. His philosophical essays, on the whole, evince a respect for argumentation as a disciplined, rather than a haphazard, form of discourse.[11] On this basis, a serious student may concur with Dubs' observation: "While there may not be the vividness of illustration and brilliance of exposition found in Mencius 孟子, yet there is a cogency of argument, a closedness of reasoning, and an analytic power which shows a mind of the first order."[12] Of greater significance, as I have shown elsewhere,[13] the works of Xunzi furnished us excellent materials for a coherent explication of a complex and distinctive Confucian conception of ethical argumentation. Among other things, this conception stresses the desirable qualities of participation, rational and empirical standards of competence, and the compliance with these standards in dealing with difficulties that may arise in the course of argumentation.[14] When Confucian argumentation is construed as a reason-giving activity engaged in by concerned and responsible persons for the exposition and defense of ethical claims, the use of the historical appeal, particularly in different phases of discourse, may be seen to be quite valuable, not as a form of argument, but as an instrument serving a variety of legitimate purposes. Xunzi was the case in point. In what follows, I shall present a critical sketch of four different functions of the historical appeal: the pedagogical, rhetorical, elucidative, and evaluative. It is hoped that this discussion will pave the way toward a general appraisal of the Confucian use of the historical appeal.[15]

I

In charting the principal functions of the historical appeal in Xunzi, I shall confine my attention to two different types of cases: (1) those in which a sharp ethical distinction is drawn between items (for example, between the past (*gu*) and the present (*jin*) or between contrasting types of characters); and (2) those in which some sort of affinity is stressed between distinct items. I shall also attend to Xunzi's extensive use of the notion of former kings 先王 *xianwang*, which is sometimes contrasted with that of later kings 後王 *houwang*. This approach is quite consonant with Xunzi's conception of 道 *dao* (the way) as the unifying perspective implicit in this notion of 道貫 *daoguan* (the thread of *dao*) or 統類 *tonglei* (the unity of classes).[16] More formally, my approach may be characterized by way of Xunzi's distinction between generic 共名 *gongming* and specific terms 別名 *bieming*.[17] Regarding "the historical appeal" as a generic term, its various functions constitute different ways of specifying its significance. The names for these functions are thus specific terms relative to "the historical appeal" as a generic term. However, the distinction between generic and specific terms is a relative rather than an absolute distinction. A term like *li* (rules of proper conduct), for example, may be viewed as a generic term subject to specification in terms of rules of etiquette or religious rites; yet in relation to *dao* as a generic term, *li* is a specific term among others like 仁 *ren* (benevolence) and 義 *yi* (rightness).[18] For my present purpose, I shall set aside the question concerning the degree of generality or specificity of the functions of the historical appeal. In distinguishing these functions I do not intend to suggest a categorical distinction, for in many contexts, these functions overlap. Our classification is given only for convenience of explication.

As in the final analysis, the functions of the historical appeal, in the light of *dao* as a unifying perspective, are but aspects of one thing. To borrow a famous saying of Cheng Yi 程頤, "Substance and function come from the same source 體用同一源 *tiyong tongyiyuan*, and there is no gap between the manifest and the hidden."[19]

The Pedagogical Function

An obvious characteristic of most Confucian writings in general and of Xunzi in particular, is an overriding concern for moral education. Against the background of this concern, the historical appeal may be said to have a pedagogical function. In Xunzi,[20] one finds extensive reference to sage rulers such as Yao 堯, Shun 舜, and Yu 禹 and virtuous rulers such as Tang 湯, Wen 文, and Wu 武 in contradistinction to Jie 桀 and Zhou 紂. This extensive use of historical characters suggests that the appeal is used to promote educational objectives. Before pursuing this suggestion, however, I will preface it with some remarks on Xunzi's conception of moral education.

For Xunzi, the primary aim of moral education is the transformation of man's native but problematic motivational structure (for example, feelings and desires) by way of knowledge of standards of goodness or excellence (for example, *ren* and *yi*) and rules of proper conduct (*li*).[21] One learns for the sake of doing; knowing the right and the good is for the sake of acting in accord with such knowledge. Learning, however, is not equivalent to the mere acquisition of knowledge but more essentially requires understanding and insight. In Xunzi's words:

> Not having learned it [for example, *dao*] is not as good as having learned it; having learned it is not as good as having seen it carried out; having seen it is not as good as understanding it; understanding it is not as good as doing it. The utmost attainment of learning lies in moral performance,[22] and that is its end and goal. He who can carry it out must possess an insight (into the nature of *dao*). If he has such an insight 明 *ming*, he is a sage. The sage founds his conduct upon *ren* and *yi*; he accurately distinguishes right from wrong; he makes his speech and action correspond to each other, not varying the least bit—there is no other reason for that than because he simply carries it out. [荀子: 儒效 8/33/11-4, Dubs 113*]

Thus the ultimate objective of moral learning is to become a sage, one who has "a keen insight (*ming*), which never fails," into the rationale of *dao* and its import for dealing with different sorts 類 *lei* of human situations.[23] *Dao*, as the ideal way of life, is an object of knowledge, and thus learning this way of life consists essentially in comprehending its rationale.[24] "The man who is good at learning is one who can exhaust the rationales of things 盡其理 *jinqili*."[25] [荀子: 大略 27/133/9]

For Xunzi, the basic philosophical issue in moral education pertains to the rational coordination of the intellectual and volitional activities of the mind 心 *xin* by means of the *dao*. Given the autonomy of man's mind, he can choose to accept or reject its guidance. "It is the nature of the mind that no prohibition may be placed upon its selections," [荀子: 解蔽 21/104/13, Watson 129, Dubs 269] but if it is directed by reason 理 *li* and nourished with clarity, and not perturbed by extraneous matters, "it will be capable of determining right and wrong and of resolving doubts."[26] [荀子: 解蔽 21/105/7, Watson 131, Dubs 271]

In the essay entitled "Encouraging Learning" *Quanxue* 勸學, Xunzi points out that learning is an unceasing process of accumulation 積 *ji* of goodness, knowledge, and practical understanding. "If a superior man 君子 *junzi* studies widely and daily engages in self-examination, his intellect will become enlightened and his conduct be without fault." [荀子: 勸學 1/1/5, Watson 14*, Dubs 31] The subject matter of moral education consists of the classics, which were considered by Xunzi to embody in different ways the concrete significance of *dao*. Practical understanding thus involves an appreciation of this concrete significance. For example, "The *Odes* give expression to the will 志 *zhi* or determination (to realize *dao*); the *History* to its significance in human affairs, the *Li* (Rules of Propriety) to its significance in conduct: the *Music* to its significance in promoting harmony; and the *Spring and Autumn* to its subtleties."[27] [荀子: 儒效 8/31/6-7, Dubs 104*] It is important to note, however, that these classics are not self-explanatory. Therefore, the guidance of perceptive teachers is essential. As Xunzi emphatically states: "The *Li* and *Music* present us with models, but no explanations; the *Odes* and the *History* deal with ancient matters and are not always pertinent; the *Spring and Autumn* is terse and cannot be quickly understood." [荀子: 勸學 1/3/20-1, Watson 20, Dubs 38] The point, for our present purpose, is that intellectual and practical understanding of the classics go hand in hand. In the ideal situation, moral teachers are those who, in addition to commanding extensive knowledge, are honorable and clearheaded in explaining the meanings and the concrete significance of the classics. More fundamentally, they must conduct their discourse coherently and with detailed insight into the rationales that underlie different sorts of human affairs 知微而論 *zhiwei er lun*, exemplifying the enlightened intellect of the superior men.[28] [荀子: 至士 14/67/202] Similarly, an accomplished learner or scholar must show not only a single-minded dedication to *ren* and *yi* but also an enlightened knowledge concerning different kinds of human relationships. As Xunzi says, "If a man does not comprehend the unifying significance of different kinds of human relationships and make himself one with *ren* and *yi*, he does not deserve to be called a good scholar." [荀子: 勸學 1/4/12-3, Watson 22*, Dubs 40). Since *dao* provides the unifying perspective, there is a constant need to study and ponder its significance in the process of self-cultivation and experience. Moral learning culminates in the attainment of what Xunzi terms "completeness 全 *quan* and purity 粹 *cui*," that is, a thorough understanding of *dao* and a state of moral integrity 德操 *decao*. As a consequence, one can deploy a resolute will in coping with moral perplexities or exercise one's sense of what is right in responding to changing circumstances 以義應變 *yiyi yingbian*.[29]

The preceding observations of Xunzi's theory of moral education focused on some key elements such as the acquisition of knowledge and critical reflection upon its actuating import in moral life. Given this context, one can readily appreciate the extensive use of the historical appeal for pedagogical purposes. In general, the success of moral education lies in the effective inculcation of the importance of standards and rules of proper conduct, the development of moral dispositions, desires, and abilities for coping with the changing circumstances of personal life. Thus, counsels and admonitions, along with encouragement, exaltation, and edification may at times occupy the center of attention in ethical discourse. Given the appropriate setting, the historical appeal may serve any of these purposes. In general, Xunzi's uses of the historical appeal, in the form of citation of contrasting historical characters, were intended to encourage the adoption of appropriate models for emulation and discourage the imitation of contrary models of evil or depravity. In effect, then, the reader is confronted with a contrast between exemplary moral achievement and moral failure. The historical appeal is a way of presenting "object lessons" in moral learning and conduct. If this suggestion is to be taken seriously, however, it must be qualified by attending to those cases where the affinity between contrasting characters is stressed in terms of their similar capacities for moral achievement. Consider this passage:

Every ordinary person has characteristics in common with others. When hungry he desires to eat; when cold he desires to be warm; when toiling he desires to rest; he is fond of what is beneficial and detests what is harmful—these are native characteristics men have in common and do not depend on learning. In these respects, Yu and Jie were alike. The eyes distinguish white and black, beautiful and ugly; the ears distinguish clear and confused tones and sounds. . . . In these respects also, men normally have the same capacity for discerning distinctions. It does not depend on learning, and Yu and Jie alike possessed it. Anyone can be a Yao or a Yu; he can become a Jie or a Zhi 跖. . . . What he becomes depends on how he manages his life through the accumulation (*ji*) of careful choices and rejections and habitual practices 注錯習俗 *zhucuo xisu*. . . . To be a Yao or a Yu ordinarily brings tranquility and honor; to be a Jie or a Zhi ordinarily brings danger and shame. . . . But most men are the latter and few are the former. Why is this the case? Because their natures are low. Yao and Yu were not born great. They became what they were because of their success in moral transformation, that is, they had exerted their utmost effort in cultivating their capacity for great moral achievement.[30] [荀子: 榮辱 4/15/7-14, Dubs 60-61*]

In this passage, the use of contrasting historical characters, Yu versus Jie, has less to do with presenting "object lessons" than with objects of moral choice. This use is even more important in that it provides *reminders* in a twofold sense. On the one hand, there is a reminder of one's basic capacity for moral achievement and hence the importance of self-cultivation. Instead of historical characters, the distinction between the past (*gu*) and the present (*jin*) is used: for example, "In the past (*gu*) men studied for the sake of self-improvement, today (*jin*) men study to impress others.[31] The superior man studies in order to ennoble himself, the small-minded man studies in order to win attention from others." [荀子: 勸學 1/3/17, Watson 20*, Dubs 37]. In a similar fashion Xunzi utilizes the notion of former kings: "If you want to become like the former kings (*xianwang*) and seek out *ren* and *yi*, then *li* is the very road by which you must travel." [荀子: 勸學 1/4/1-2, Watson 21*, Dubs 38]

On the other hand, within the context of argumentation, we are reminded that self-cultivation and acting in accord with standards and rules of proper conduct are in the *true interest* of the individual, since they give rise to such desirable consequences as tranquility and honor rather than danger and shame. Of course, one is given no guarantee that they will in fact occur; however, in the course of ordinary life, such an expectation is quite reasonable given wise and informed deliberation 知慮 *zhilu*. After all, we engage in ethical deliberation in order to cope with changing circumstances and to resolve perplexities. [荀子: 君道 12/62/19-20] In its reminding function, the historical appeal, with respect to the individual's true interest, has no special connection with historical beliefs concerning the existence of specific historical personages, events, or states of affairs. It is an *implicit* appeal to prudence or the desirability of reflection. It could be characterized as a form of thought-experiment: "If one reflects seriously on the desirable consequences of adopting and acting in accord with standards and rules of proper conduct, he would discover where his true interest lies."[32] The historical appeal, in the context of the desirability of reflection, while valuable, is dispensable in ethical discourse. What is crucial in effective teaching procedure is the appeal to the reflective desirability of accepting and cultivating virtuous dispositions and the desire to act with due consideration of *ren*, *li*, and *yi*, and other associated standards of excellence. In his essay on self-cultivation, we find such an appeal minus the use of historical characters:

> If a person is respectful in his bearing, loyal and sincere, abides by *li* and *yi* and is actuated by affection and *jen*, he may travel all over the world. Even though he may choose to live among the barbarian tribes, people would not fail to honor him.[33] [荀子: 修身 2/6/16-7, Dubs 47-48*, Watson 27*]

In sum, the pedagogical use of the historical appeal points not only to models who are worthy or unworthy of emulation, but more significantly to models functioning as reminders in moral learning and conduct that appeal especially to what is deemed in the real interests of the learner. Notably, gentle suasion rather than coercion is involved, as the individual still retains the freedom to accept or reject it. This constitutes the argumentative value of the pedagogical function of the historical appeal rather than the mere exhibition of moral exemplars. The latter's effectiveness lies primarily in the appeal to paradigmatic individuals (*junzi*).[34] In Xunzi, as in the *Analects*, one finds a recurrent contrast between the superior man (*junzi*) and the small-minded man 小人 *xiaoren*.[35] At any rate, the ultimate value of the historical appeal in pedagogical contexts lies in the effectiveness of the appeal to reflective desires and emotions, rather than to the ability to follow deductive arguments.[36]

II

The Rhetorical Function

Were one preoccupied solely with the arguments Xunzi offered in support of his ethical theses, the use of historical appeal would have merely stylistic interest. As Watson recently maintained: unlike Zhuangzi 莊子, for whom historical anecdotes constitute a form of argument, for Mozi 墨子, Mencius, and Xunzi, the historical anecdotes "serve effectively to vary the tone and pace of discourse. . . . But such anecdotes, lively as they may be, represent no more than ornaments to the argument, momentary detours from the expository highroad."[37] I must confess that until I was engaged in this study, I accepted this view without much qualm throughout more than a decade of preoccupation with Xunzi's ethical theory. This conception of the value of the historical appeal relegates its function to an accessory role, but in reflecting upon its value in ethical argumentation, it can be quite important, not in proffering or arguing for the acceptability of a thesis, but in responding to a recurrent problem of regress in argumentation.[38] As a recent writer on informal logic justly points out, "the answer to this ancient problem depends upon an obvious fact. The activity of arguing or presenting proofs depends upon a shared set of beliefs and upon a certain amount of trust. When I present reasons, I try to cite these beliefs—things that will not be challenged. Beyond this, I expect people to believe me when I cite information that only I possess."[39] Obviously, the historical appeal functions as a technique for *assuring* the audience that the thesis maintained is consonant with shared historical beliefs and obviates having to state reasons for their support. It also constitutes a technique of *discounting* alternative views, shifting the burden of proof to a possible adversary.[40] These uses, of course, are subject to further challenge, for the rational acceptability of the thesis and an assurance that the thesis is not a mere imaginative contrivance to avoid questioning.

In Xunzi, we sometimes find a historical idiom that suggests such an interpretation: "from the ancient times to the present" 自古及今 *zigujijin*. For example, "It is possible to have good laws and still have disorder in the state. But to have a superior man acting as a ruler and disorder in the state—from the ancient times to the present I have never heard of such a thing."[41] [荀子: 王制 9/35/19-20, Watson 35*, Dubs 123] An interesting passage involving historical characters may be cited for closer examination:

In ancient times there were officials who were warped by obsession. Tang Yang 唐鞅 and Xiqi 奚齊 are examples. Tang Yang was obsessed by the desire for power and drove Master Tai 戴子 from the state. Xiqi was obsessed with a desire for the throne and succeeded in casting suspicion on Shensheng 申生. Tang Yang was executed in Sun; Xiqi was executed in Jin 晉. One of them drove a worthy minister into exile, the other cast suspicion upon his brother. They ended by being executed and did not know that this was the misfortune which comes from obsession and closed mind. Is it possible that a man whose conduct is motivated by greed, treason, and struggle for power be freed from the danger of shame and destruction? From ancient times to the present (*zigujijin*), there has never been such a case.[42] [荀子: 解蔽 21/103/1-3, Watson 124*, Dubs 262-263*]

This passage, along with several others involving historical characters and incidents, occurs in Xunzi's essay on dispelling "obsessions" or obscurations 蔽 *bi*.   To expedite the discussion of this passage, something must be said about Xunzi's doctrine of the origin of erroneous beliefs.[43]   In terms of his ethical conception of *dao* as a unifying perspective, a partial grasp of its fundamental rationale 大理 *dali* and significance has a serious repercussion upon conduct. [荀子: 解蔽 21/102/5-10, Watson 121, Dubs 159] More generally, the human mind is liable to be obscured (*bi*) by failure to appreciate the situation because it is partial to one side of a distinction.   Clarity of mind is essential to comprehension of a situation as a whole.   *Bi* (obscuration) is Xunzi's metaphor for factors that obstruct the mind's cognitive task.   Among the distinctions that are potential sources of *bi* are desire and aversion, past (*gu*) and present (*jin*), and distant and immediate consequences of actions 遠近 *yuanjin*.   How can one be impartial, then, in order to avoid that *bi* which may result in harmful conduct?   Earlier, we focused on the role of informal deliberation (*zhilu*) with respect to the consequences of a contemplated course of action.   Informed deliberation must be impartial particularly in weighing 權 *quan* desires and aversions in terms of harmful and beneficial consequences.[44] [荀子: 不苟 3/12/11-3]

Since the passage offers an illustration of Xunzi's doctrine of *bi*, the historical characters and incidents are used for the exposition of a thesis and constitute the *elucidative* use of the historical appeal.   As we have indicated earlier, the historical appeal can have more than one function in the same context.   For our immediate purpose, the passage provides an example of the failure to exercise impartiality in weighing the consequences of actions because their minds were obscured, and they could not see where their true interests were. This recalls one function of the pedagogical use of the historical appeal. Here the appeal to reflective desirability is explicit rather than implicit.

In focusing on the rhetorical function of the locution "from ancient times to the present" (*zigujijin*), the use of historical characters and incidents presupposes a background of shared historical knowledge or beliefs about the past. Given this background, the locution can be considered as an argumentative technique for issuing assurance and discounting possible objections. Its rhetorical force is obvious as it is usually preceded by a rhetorical question. The locution is functionally equivalent to such English phrases as "it is certain that," "it is indisputable," and so forth, and occurs at the end, marking a completion of a train of thought. Thus it can be construed as an emphatic terminating linguistic expression which serves as a reminder of the significance of historical knowledge.

Only a historian can judge whether Xunzi is correct in presuming common historical knowledge. The presumption seems legitimate when viewed as a personal testimony of Xunzi's own historical beliefs. Belief in the testimony of others is a necessary condition of communication, as Austin has pointed out:

> Believing in other persons, in authority and testimony, is an essential part of the act of communicating, an act which we constantly perform. It is as much an irreducible part of our experience as, say, giving promises, or playing competitive games, or even sensing coloured patches. We can state certain advantages of such performances, and we can elaborate rules of a kind for their "rational" conduct (as the Law Courts and historians and psychologists work out the rules for accepting testimony). But there is no "justification" for our doing them as such.[45]

In this light, we can also appreciate the propriety of the use of historical characters and the function of Xunzi's use of the expression "from ancient times to the present" (*zigujijin*). Of course, Xunzi's historical beliefs may well be mistaken, but this is an issue that can only be settled by historians of Chinese antiquity. Much of Confucian argumentation makes use of the presumption of the truth of historical beliefs, which is a plausible presumption in Rescher's sense, where the plausibility of a thesis is not a matter of probability or falsification, but depends on how well it fits in with a conceptual scheme that contains established and operative standards for argumentation. A thesis that employs a plausible presumption can be defeated in context, but it can be warranted so long as there exist no contraindications in common experience.[46]

From a standpoint external to Confucian discourse, the rhetorical function of the historical appeal possesses primarily a psychological value in ethical discourse. We have here an instrument of persuasion, akin to a conjoint use of "persuasive definitions" and "re-emphatic definitions," where the reasons have only a psychological, rather than a logical, connection with the thesis proffered.[47] In the context of Xunzi's rhetorical use of the historical appeal, this interpretation is acceptable only when it is qualified by an acknowledgment of the force of plausible presumptions. At the same time, however, one must also admit that the rhetorical function of the historical appeal pertains primarily to the techniques rather than to the substance of argumentation. Its value belongs to the art of discourse and can neither be regarded as an acceptable substitute for the necessity of arguments, nor can it forestall disputes as to the soundness or validity of arguments. In actuality Xunzi rarely employs the historical idiom. Our excursion to the rhetorical use is interesting mainly for revealing the plausible presumption involved in some of the uses of historical appeal.

III

Before I turn to the elucidative and evaluative uses of the historical appeal, I would like to sketch that aspect of Xunzi's conception of argumentation which governs my interpretation and analysis. Apart from various rational and empirical standards of competence, Xunzi also focuses on what may be termed phases of argumentation, which are centrally concerned with ways of resolving difficulties that may arise in the course of communication.[48] Xunzi is aware throughout that the activity of argumentation is not a facile proceeding. At any moment in discourse, reasonable questions can arise with respect to the clarity of theses and to the reasons offered in their behalf. To these questions, proper answers must be given so that the relevant standard of competence will be satisfied. The four different phases of argumentation are described below:

> When the actualities 實 *shi* referred to by our terms are not understood, one must fix their references 命 *ming*. When the fixing of references is not understood, one must secure concurrence in linguistic understanding 期 *qi*. When one fails

to achieve this concurrence, one must resort to explanation 説 *shuo*. When such an explanation fails, one must embark upon a course of justification 辨 *bian*.[49] [荀子: 正名 22/110/3-4]

Another way to characterize these four phases of argumentation is to view them as four different kinds of speech acts, namely, fixing reference, matching linguistic understanding, explaining, and justifying. The first is necessary whenever the speaker's referential use of terms fails to secure the understanding of his audience due to their ambiguity or vagueness. To fix the reference of a term clearly is to make more precise the use of the term. To assume this responsibility in the context of discourse exhibits the speaker's willingness to engage in successful communication. In cases where there is a failure to understand the fixed reference of terms, the speaker must make an attempt to match his linguistic understanding with that of his audience. Here the concern is not with reference as such, but with the common understanding of the referential function of terms in a particular context. Obviously, at this point in the discourse, questions and answers will be exchanged in an effort by concerned and responsible participants to promote successful communication.

But the matching of linguistic understanding with respect to the referential function of terms may still fail to bring about successful communication. In such cases, explanations must be given as to why the speaker chose such and such a term in this particular context. Here definitions explaining the uses of terms as well as examples of proper use and the description of the situation may help in satisfying the query. Sometimes the giving of such explanatory reasons may not suffice to produce understanding, for in addition to a comprehension of explanation, there must also be an acceptance of the thesis as warranted by appropriate reasons. In this sense, even if one succeeds in explaining one's position in discourse, one must engage in a process of justification, for without such an attempt, one can hardly be said to be engaged in argumentation or to have expended effort in trying to satisfy the standards of competence.

The Elucidative Function

The elucidative and evaluative functions of the historical appeal belong to the explanatory and justificatory phases of discourse. Compared to Xunzi's extensive use of 謂 *wei* (say/call),[50] these functions are quite restrictive. Nevertheless, they are valuable in the exposition and defense of ethical theses. Unlike the pedagogical and rhetorical function, the elucidative one has a direct, argumentative force. It makes explicit the ethical criteria for appraising characters and/or clarifies the general thesis that underlies the ethical distinction at issue. The following example explicates Xunzi's thesis on the importance of impartiality in the weighing of the possible consequences of pursuing certain desires.

> Impartiality gives rise to enlightenment; partiality to obscuration (of the mind): uprightness and honesty give rise to success, deception and hypocrisy to obstacles; sincerity and trustworthiness give rise to marvelous actions 神 *shen*, false pride to perplexity. A superior man is cautious about the causal relation among these six matters, and they are the basis for distinguishing Yu and Jie.[51] [荀子: 不苟 3/12/3-4]

Xunzi goes on to explain his thesis that what presumably distinguishes Yu and Jie lies in part in the method of weighing desirable against undesirable consequences, that is, in clarity of mind versus a mind obscured (*bi*) by an unthoughtful preoccupation with impulses and desires without taking into consideration their possible adverse consequences. Xunzi rightly points out that human beings generally suffer because they are afflicted with partiality.

> When they see something they want, they do not carefully consider whether or not it will lead to something that they detest; when they see something beneficial, they do not consider carefully whether or not it will lead to something harmful. In this way, any action that they perform is bound to entrap them (in their impulses and desires) and to bring about shame. This is the predicament that besets us all—the harm that ensues from the partial view of things 偏傷之患 *pianshangzhihuan*. [荀子: 不苟 3/12/8-9]

In the preceding example, the use of historical characters appears to have both conceptual and pragmatic significance. In general, clarity in conceptual distinction as well as in the articulation of ethical criteria for distinguishing character-types or different grades of moral attainment is a recurrent preoccupation with Xunzi. Much of his efforts are devoted to the elucidation of his general notions of the sage, the superior man, and the scholar. On occasion, however, more specific criteria are proposed for grading characters in terms of one virtue. One interesting passage on different grades of loyalty 忠 *zhong* uses historical characters to illustrate how the criteria set forth may be satisfied.

Loyalty of the highest sort consists in the exercise of virtue 德 *de* to protect and transform the ruler. Loyalty of the intermediate sort consists in the exercise of virtue to harmonize and assist the ruler in his undertakings. Loyalty of the lowest sort consists in the use of what is right as a basis for remonstrating the ruler's wrong conduct but arousing his anger. . . . If one serves his ruler as the Duke of Zhou 周公 served King Wen, he can be said to exemplify loyalty of the highest sort. If one serves his ruler as Guan Zhong 管仲 served Duke Huan 桓公 (of Qi), he can be said to exemplify loyalty of the intermediate sort. If one serves his ruler as Zi Xu 子胥 served Fu Cha 夫差 (of Wu), he can be said to exemplify loyalty of the lowest sort. [荀子: 臣道 13/65/8-11]

The conceptual significance of the use of historical characters in the clarification of a thesis can hardly be questioned, as the historical characters function much like instantiating terms in predicate logic. Theoretically, one can achieve clarity when expounding theses by using purely hypothetical examples, but the use of historical characters in ethical discourse has a dual pragmatic significance in guiding judgment and conduct. First, it shows how an ethical thesis may be applied in practice. Secondly, the historical figures illustrate and embody what otherwise would be an abstract ethical conception. The former enhances one's understanding of the empirical possibility of application, the latter mediates between the ethical thesis as an ideal and the actual world.[52] The historical characters here function as mediating rather than instantiating terms.[53] Obviously, then, the elucidative function of the historical appeal has an important role to play in the explanatory phase of argumentative discourse.

IV

The Evaluative Function

Inherent in the use of historical characters for elucidating and demonstrating the applicability of an ethical thesis is the implicit claim that human history is the proper subject of ethical appraisal. However, this claim is explicit in the evaluative use of the historical appeal. For Xunzi, "*dao* is the proper standard for judging the past as well as the present 古今之正權 *gujinzhi zhengquan*." [荀子: 正名 22/112/2, Watson 153*, Dubs 297] Earlier, in connection with Xunzi's conception of moral education in Section I, I have pointed out that becoming a sage was the ultimate end of learning. When a person becomes a sage, he possesses not only a knowledge of the rationale of *dao*, but also of its significance as a unifying perspective for viewing different sorts of human relationships and affairs, particularly in all matters pertaining to *ren, li,* and *yi.* In light of his knowledge of the unity of different kinds of things (*tonglei*), his discourse is both reasonable and coherent. [荀子: 性惡 23/117/2, Watson 168-169, Dubs 315] Moreover, in discourse, he does not engage in any prior deliberation or planning. [荀子: 非相 5/21/1-2] With this knowledge, the sage can deal with the present through the past 以古持今 *yiguchijin* or with the past through the present 以今持古 *yijinchigu.*[54] In the words of Xunzi:

> The sage considers himself as a measure for appraising things. Hence, by means of (his knowledge of) men in the present, he can judge men in the past. By means of (his knowledge of) conditions of the present, he can judge conditions of the past. By means of (his knowledge of) different kinds of things (*lei*), he can determine the kinds to which things belong. By means of speech, he can assess accomplishments. By means of *dao*, he can command a comprehensive view of things. The same standard applies to both the past and the present. So long as different kinds of things are not confused, although they might have persisted for a long time, the rationales (underlying their respective classifications) remain the same 雖久同理 *suijiu tongli.* [荀子: 非相 5/19/2-4]

Unlike the sage, the superior man (*junzi*) has no such comprehensive and systematic knowledge. While he is aware that *dao* is the ultimate standard for thought and action (as a commitive agent), he cannot claim to understand how it guides action without first expending effort in intelligent and informed reflection. Similarly in discourse, we would expect a reasonable and conscientious person to engage in inquiry and deliberation before pronouncing any ethical judgment.[55] [荀子: 非相 5/20/16] As Xunzi succinctly states, "In argumentative discourse, one must give an exhaustive account of one's reasons 辨則盡故 *bian ze jingu.*" [荀子: 正名 22/110/9, Watson 147-148, Dubs 291] Of special interest to moral philosophy is the kind of reasoning involved in judging the present through the past (*yiguchijin*) as distinct from judging the past through the present (*yijinchigu*). The distinction is not based on logical structure but has to do with two different kinds of ethical justification.[56]

For purposes of discussion, I shall use the term "retrospective" to refer to the use of the appeal to the past for judging the present (*yiguchijin*), and "prospective" to indicate its converse (*yijinchigu*).[57] In the context of argumentation, Xunzi's expression *yiguchijin* can be perspicuously rendered as "to use one's knowledge of or beliefs about the past in order to maintain a view about the present." Xunzi is clearly recommending the adoption of a standpoint based on historical knowledge or beliefs for the purpose of maintaining or assessing the adequacy of current beliefs. Both the retrospective and prospective uses of the historical appeal are essentially *critical*, and can be used either in the positive defense of one's thesis or in the negative evaluation of another's thesis or both. In Xunzi, the retrospective use is far more frequent and wide-ranging than the prospective one. In attacking the current persuasive view that physiognomy can foretell fortune and misfortune as well as indicate human character, Xunzi uses examples of historical characters to show that a man's fortune or misfortune has no intrinsic connection with his height or weight and handsomeness or ugliness. Rather the crux of the matter lies in the way in which the man employs his mind and his method of choice 擇術 *zeshu*. "When a person's method is upright and his mind follows it without reservation, although his physiognomy be repulsive, yet if his mind and method of choice are directed toward the attainment of moral excellence 善 *shan*, his physiognomy will not hinder him from being a superior man (*junzi*)."[58] [荀子: 非相 5/17/12-3, Dubs 67*]

In discussing the retrospective use of the historical appeal, however, I shall focus on the following passage, which illustrates more clearly the kind of justification involved in the defense of an ethical thesis as a response to challenge.

Chen Xiao 陳囂 said to Xunzi, "When you talk about the use of arms, you always insist on *ren* (benevolence) and *yi* (rightness) as the basis of justification 本 *ben*. A man of *ren* loves others; a man of *yi* does what is right and reasonable 循理 *xunli*. Why, then, would they have any recourse to arms in the first place? Those who take up arms do so only in order to contend with others and seize some spoil!"

Xunzi replied, "This is not something that you would understand. The man of *ren* indeed loves others, and because he loves others, he hates what brings harm to others. The man of *yi* indeed does what is right and reasonable, and for that reason he hates those that lead others astray. He takes up arms in order to put an end to violence and to do away harm, not in order to contend with others for spoil. Therefore, where the soldiers of the man of *ren* encamp they command a godlike respect; and where they pass, they transform the people. They are like the seasonable rain in whose falling all men rejoiced. Thus Yao attacked Huan Dou 驩兜, Shun attacked the rulers of the Miao 苗, Yu attacked Gonggong 共工, Tang attacked the ruler of Xia, King Wen attacked Chong 崇, and King Wu attacked Zhou. These four emperors and two kings all marched through the world with their soldiers of *ren* and *yi*. Those nearby were won by their goodness, and those far off were filled with longing by their virtue. They did not stain their swords with blood, and yet near and far alike submitted; their virtue flourished in the center and spread to the four quarters." [荀子: 議兵 15/71/21-7, Watson 69-70*, Dubs 107-8]

Although Xunzi considers *dao* to be the ultimate standard for all ethical judgment, justification of an ethical view or judgment appeals to one or more of its basic specifications, that is, to *ren*, *yi*, or *li*, more often to the conjoined appeal of *li* and *yi*. In the present case, Xunzi appeals to *ren* and *yi* as a justification for the permissibility of the use of arms. The appeal consists essentially in invoking certain established or accepted applications of ethical notions attested to by the historical incidents presumed to be common knowledge. In the present instance, the appeal does involve plausible presumptions discussed earlier in Section II. One distinctive feature of the retrospective use of the historical appeal, however, may be said to be *standard-invoking* as contrasted with the *standard-setting* aspect of the elucidative use.[59] In effect, it constitutes an appeal to an established framework with its operative criteria or standards for justification of ethical judgments. Of course, one can always raise external questions about an established practice, but a discussion of this question, as important as it is to moral epistemology, goes beyond the scope of this paper.[60]

From a point of view internal to the practice of ethical justification, the invocation of accepted standards of conduct and their applications amounts to an appeal to rules. Perhaps, for this reason, Xunzi often couples *li* (rules of proper conduct) and *yi* (rightness) in order to emphasize that the rules of proper conduct are the right sort of rules to employ in justifying one's ethical judgments with regard to conduct. In the context of argumentation, such an appeal to established rules is legitimate unless it can be shown that what is at issue falls outside their purview. These practice-rules are authoritative in that they command obedience irrespective of one's wishes or desires, for they have been, explicitly or tacitly, acknowledged to be legitimate constraints upon one's freedom of thought, speech, and action.[61] It is in this light that one can appreciate Xunzi's insistence on the key role of learning the classics, particularly the ones pertaining to history and the rules of proper conduct (*li*). Mastering ethical justification is thus learning how to apply established standards of conduct, and must rely on teachers who possess extensive knowledge of the existing ethical framework and its history of application. Thus an uninformed moral agent must rely on those who have the expertise in and knowledge of an ethical practice and its history. Retrospective use of the historical appeal is thus *conservative* in that it attempts to preserve the continuity of an ethical practice. If the appeal is deemed problematic, the relevant inquiry is more a search of the historical memory than an exploration of new avenues for resolving ethical problems. The historical memory, however, is not always reliable and often requires ethical interpretation. It is this reason that the retrospective use of the historical appeal in problematic cases cannot offer a sufficient basis for ascertaining the adequacy of ethical judgments. Its value for argumentation lies primarily in its focus on the importance of complying with the normal practice of ethical justification.

The prospective use of the historical appeal reverses the standpoint of the retrospective one. Human history is seen as a subject-matter rather than as a basis for ethical judgment. In adopting this standpoint, one can no longer avail oneself of the presumption of the truth of historical beliefs (without critical examination), nor can one presume the existence of shared historical knowledge. The key issue here lies in the present evidential grounding of ethical claims. Xunzi is emphatic concerning this requirement: "Those who are good at discussing matters pertaining to the past (*gu*) must support their claims by an appeal to matters pertaining to the present (*jin*). . . . In any discussion, what deserves our esteem are clarity in conceptual distinction, consistency and coherence 辨合 *bianhe*, and accord with evidence 符驗 *fuyan*."[62] [荀子: 性惡 23/115/10] Also, Xunzi is quite sensitive to the difficulty of acquiring accurate information about the past, although he does not doubt that such a difficulty could not arise for a sage who possesses comprehensive knowledge of things. His own answer to this difficulty, however, poses a problem for the coherent interpretation of a central thesis in his political philosophy, namely, that an ethically responsible ruler must follow the sage kings 法聖王 *fashengwang* or former kings 法先王 *faxianwang* who embodied *dao*, or *ren*, *li*, and *yi*.[63] In response to the question as to which specific *li* to follow among the existing diversity of *li* (rules of proper conduct) among the sage kings, Xunzi avers:

When the rules of proper conduct (*li*) are preserved too long, they are lost. There are officials to preserve the arts and rules of proper conduct; but if preserved to a great age, they become negligent (in recording their significance). Hence, it is said that if one wants to see the footprints of (the *dao* of) the sage kings, then look where they are most clear, that is to say, at the later kings (*houwang*). Hence, it is said that if you wish to know a thousand years, then consider today. . . . By the present you can understand the past, by means of the one, you can deal with diversity; by the subtle you can understand the clear—this saying expresses what I mean.[64] [荀子: 非相 5/18/18-22, Dubs 72-73*]

Xunzi goes on to point out, "The longer things have been handed down, the more sketchy they are; the more recent they are, the more detailed they are."[65] [荀子: 非相 5/19/6-7, Dubs 74-75*]

This passage seems to confuse the distinction between the earlier and later kings with the distinction between the past and the present. The former pertains to the historic past rather than a distinction between past and present. Such a passage also seems to contradict Xunzi's recurrent emphasis on following the former kings (*xianwang*). One way of resolving this problem is to suggest that when Xunzi uses the notion of former kings (*xianwang*), it is functionally equivalent to that of sage kings. When "former kings" occurs singly, it is basically to be construed as a generic term (*gongming*) for which the distinction between earlier and later kings are proper specifications (*bieming*). Further, where Xunzi uses the notion of later kings (*houwang*), what he means to emphasize is the importance of the critical consideration of evidence in assessing any claim about historic events or states of affairs. As for following the sage kings, Xunzi is clear that the following (*fa*) at issue is not a matter of imitation, but a matter of doing what is required by *ren*, *yi*, or *li*, given critical reflection on the significance of these requirements. "If a person wants to discuss following the sage kings (*fashengwang*), he must know what they valued. If he uses *yi* to regulate all his undertakings, then he may know what is truly beneficial to the state. If he wants to discuss what they valued, then he must know why they engaged in self-cultivation." [荀子: 君子 24/119/8] However one resolves the issue of a coherent interpretation, Xunzi is clear in his insistence on the need for evidential support in making ethical judgments about the past. For my immediate purpose this is an important feature of the prospective use of the historical appeal. Before I elaborate this and other features, let me turn briefly to Xunzi's own prospective use of the historical appeal.

For the most part, Xunzi's prospective use of the historical appeal takes the form of ethical explanations of historical events, that is, historical explanations involving the use of ethical notions. For example, in attacking the view that Jie and Zhou were the legitimate rulers of the empire, and that Tang and Wu rebelled and usurped the throne by force, Xunzi points out, among other things, that:

> Tang and Wu did not capture the empire; they cultivated their ways (*dao*); they practiced *yi* (rightness); they rigorously promoted common benefits and did away with common sources of harm; and so the whole world professed allegiance. Jie and Zhou did not abandon the whole world; they perverted the virtues of Yu and Tang; they confused the distinction between rules of proper conduct (*li*) and righteousness (*yi*); their bestial actions heaped up misfortune for them, completed their evil destiny, and the whole world dismissed them.[66] [荀子: 正論 18/84/6-8, Dubs 190-191*]

As I understand it the historical explanations proffered are essentially ethical judgments or verdicts about historical events rather than attempts at objective historical explanations. Although I am in no position to decide the truth of Xunzi's historical accounts, I assume that given his own requirement of accord with evidence, Xunzi must have had some factual basis for his claims. At issue is the question of historical objectivity when ethical or value judgments enter into the historian's causal explanation or characterization of an action. It is not possible to pursue this problem in the philosophy of history in this paper. However, on behalf of Xunzi, one may point out that, although his ethical explanation of history is reminiscent of the Chinese praise-and-blame theory of history, there is no evidence to suggest that he holds such a theory in its naïve form. He does offer ethical judgments of history, but the crux of the matter is whether these judgments would then influence his account of ancient Chinese history, if he were writing a historical account thereof. Given his requirement of accord with evidence, it is not likely that he would have allowed himself to distort evidence to support his ethical theses.[67] Needless to say, Xunzi is a moral philosopher and not a historian. Thus my main interest here lies in explicating the prospective use of the historical appeal and its argumentative value, rather than establishing the accuracy and legitimacy of ethical explanations of history as a thesis in the philosophy of history. More specially, I am interested in the form of ethical justification that contrasts it with the retrospective use of the historical appeal.

Returning to the form of ethical justification, let us recall the passage which expresses Xunzi's view in response to the question concerning the diversity of *li* (rules of proper conduct). In his response, Xunzi speaks of the "footprints" or "traces" of the *dao* of the sage kings. [非相 5/18/19, Dubs 74-75] This metaphor of footprints indicates that in problematic cases of ethical judgment, evidence is a product of the reconstruction of the past application of *dao* in light of what a reflective person deems to be an *acceptable* application on the basis of his present knowledge about the past. Evidence is factual information that is present-at-hand, rather than something which is presumed. For the realization of the practical import of ethical notions or their applicability to the issue-at-hand requires the addition of imaginative reconstruction. The prospective use of the historical appeal, unlike the retrospective one, does not rely on an established practice of ethical justification, but rather on the *acceptability* of one's ethical judgments about the past, that is, on the strength of one's reasons supported by argument and relevant matters of fact. While the retrospective use of the historical appeal is conservative, the prospective use implies a creative form of ethical judgment, though essentially contestable, in response to exigent and changing circumstances. Its argumentative value lies in laying the ground for a possible reasonable acceptance rather than invoking the support of an established framework of ethical justification. This interpretation is plausibly suggested in Xunzi's remark:

> Where there are established rules of conduct 法 *fa*, comply with them. Where there are no such rules, act in the spirit of analogy (*lei*). Know the branches through the root, the right from the left. In general, the hundred human affairs have their different rationales (*li*), yet they all abide by the same *dao*.[68] [荀子: 大略 27/131/8-9]

Finally, in view of Xunzi's conception of the holistic character of *dao* as a unifying perspective, both the retrospective and prospective, as well as the pedagogical and rhetorical uses of the historical appeal, are liable to abuse, for the distinction between the past and the present is a potential source of erroneous ethical beliefs (Section II). In this essay, I have merely offered a sketch of the various functions of the historical appeal. I hope this discussion of an aspect of Xunzi's thought has provided some materials which might aid in a general evaluation of the Confucian use of history and promote an understanding of some aspects of ethical discourse which may be relevant to contemporary moral philosophy.

Notes

1. Herbert Butterfield, "Historiography," in Philip P. Weiner, ed., *Dictionary of the History of Ideas*, vol. 2 (New York: Charles Scribner's Sons, 1973) 480. More fully, one may contrast the social conditions of the ancient Chinese thinkers and their Greek counterparts. Unlike Greek philosophers, who lived in democratic city-states, the Chinese thinkers lived in proto-feudal states. According to Stange, given his situation, the Chinese "could not like his Greek counterpart discuss his ideas on a political situation with an assembly of men of equal rights on the same level as himself, he could only bring his thoughts to fruition in practice by gaining the ear of a prince. The democratic method of logical argumentation was not feasible in discussions with an absolute ruler, but an entirely different method, the citation of historical examples, could make a great impression. Thus it was that proof by historical examples prevailed very early in Chinese history over proof by logical argument." [quoted in Joseph Needham, *Time and Eastern Man* (Royal Anthropological Institute Occasional Paper, no. 21, 1965) 15]

2. Donald J. Munro, *The Concept of Man in Early China* (Stanford: Stanford Univ. Press, 1969) 55.

3. Throughout this essay, I use the term "moral" (as distinct from "non-moral") in the broad sense as inclusive of principles/rules and ideas/virtues. The term "ethical" is sometimes used interchangeably with "moral" in the broad sense. For justification of this proposal, see my "Tasks of Confucian Ethics," *JCP* 6:1 (1979).

4. D. C. Lau, *Confucius: The Analects* (New York: Penguin Books, 1979) 7:1.

5. For fuller discussion on the notion of paradigmatic individuals, see my *Dimensions of Moral Creativity: Paradigms, Principles, and Ideals* (University Park, Pennsylvania: Pennsylvania State Univ. Press, 1978) chap. 5; See also *Mencius*, 5B1.

6. *Analects*, 3:9.

7. Ibid. 18:8.

8. Ibid. 9:4.

9. For other relevant remarks of Confucius, see *Analects*, 2:11, 2:15, and 13:5. On Confucius' attitude toward antiquity, Ames justly said that he "tempers this respect for antiquity with the practical consideration that this inherited knowledge must be made relevant to prevailing circumstances," though it is misleading to claim, as Ames does, that Confucius has a philosophy of history. See Roger Ames, *The Art of Rulership: A Study in*

Ancient Chinese Political Thought (Honolulu: Univ. of Hawaii Press, 1983) 5.

10. For convenience of discussion of the uses of the historical appeal in the *Xunzi*, I have throughout referred to Xunzi as the author of this work, well aware of the problem of authorship. My interest lies primarily in the coherence of basic philosophical views expressed in such essays as *Tianlun* 天論, *Jiebi* 解蔽, *Zhengming* 正名, *Fuguo* 富國, *Zhenglun* 正論, and *Xing'e* 性惡. The problem of textual authenticity does not affect the issue of philosophical explication. References to the *Xunzi* are taken from the following: D. C. Lau and Fong Ching Chen, eds., *A Concordance to the* Xunzi 荀子逐字索引 (Hong Kong: The Commercial Press 商務印書館, 1996); H. H. Dubs, *The Works of Hsüntze* (Taipei: Chengwen, 1966); and Burton Watson, *Hsün Tzu: Basic Writings* (New York: Columbia Univ. Press, 1963). Whenever available, a third reference is given for comparative purposes only. Emendations of translations are marked by asterisks. When only the Chinese text is cited, this indicates either my translation or reference to a passage not found in both Dubs' and Watson's works. For a detailed discussion of textual problems, see Yang Yunru 楊筠如, *Xunziyanjiu* 荀子研究 (Taipei: Commercial Press, 1974) chap. 1.

11. I have in mind the essays cited in the preceding note.

12. It must be admitted, as Dubs points out, that Xunzi's style is "terse and sententious." This style often creates problems for systematic presentation of his theses in standard Western philosophical form. For example, see my "The Conceptual Aspect of Hsün Tzu's Philosophy of Human Nature," *PEW* 27:4 (1977). For similar appreciation of Xunzi's philosophical stature, see Fung Yu-lan, *A History of Chinese Philosophy*, vol. 1, Derk Bodde, trans. (Princeton: Princeton Univ. Press, 1952) 280; E. R. Hughes, *Chinese Philosophy in the Classical Times* (New York: E. P. Dutton, 1942) 226; Frederick Mote, *Intellectual Foundations of China* (New York: Alfred A. Knopf, 1971) 61; Liu Wu-chi, *A Short History of Confucian Philosophy* (New York: Delta Books, 1955) 65; and H. G. Creel, *Chinese Thought from Confucius to Mao Tse-tung* (Chicago: Univ. of Chicago Press, 1953) 115-116.

13. A partial profile of argumentation is given in my "Hsün Tzu's Theory of Argumentation: A Reconstruction," *Review of Metaphysics* 36:4 (1983); hereafter cited as Cua, "Hsün Tzu's Theory of Argumentation." For a full explication of this profile, see my *Ethical Argumentation: A Study in Hsün Tzu's Moral Epistemology* (Honolulu: Univ. of Hawaii Press, 1985).

14. This last topic, followed by others, such as the nature of ethical reasoning, the uses of definition, and diagnosis of erroneous ethical beliefs, is extensively discussed in chap. 2 of my *Ethical Argumentation*.

15. An adequate appraisal of the value of the historical appeal, I believe, depends on considerations that are functionally equivalent to the elements of the profile elaborated in my *Ethical Argumentation*. Seen in light of this

book, my present aim is quite limited, being an exercise in application of the Confucian conception of ethical argumentation. Thus I have often made use of materials from the book without explicit reference.

16. For *daoguan* (the thread of *dao*), see 荀子: 天論 17/82/20, Dubs 183-184, Watson 87. For *tonglei* ("unity of classes"), see 荀子: 非十二子 6/22/13; 荀子: 儒效 8/33/4, Dubs 112, and 荀子: 儒效 8/34/16, Dubs 117-118; 荀子: 儒解蔽 21/106/23, Dubs 276-277, Watson 136; and 荀子: 性惡 23/117/2, Dubs 315, Watson 168-169. For an incisive discussion of the notion of *tonglei* see Wei Zhengtong 韋政通, *Xunziyugudaizhexue* 荀子與古代哲學 (Taipei: Commercial Press, 1974), chap. 1. See also Cua, *Ethical Argumentation*, chap. 2 (2.8).

17. See 荀子: 政名 22/109/7-9, Watson 143-144, Dubs 286.

18. Throughout this paper, I focus on *dao* as an ideal way of life, rather than *dao* of heaven or earth. An explicit passage runs: "The *dao* of the former kings is the magnifying of *ren*. Follow the mean 中 *zhong* in acting it out. What is meant by the mean? It is *li* and *yi*. *Dao* is not primarily the *dao* of heaven 天 *tian*; it is not the *dao* of earth; it is the *dao* man acts, the *dao* the superior man acts." [荀子: 儒效 8/28/15-6] For discussion of *li* (rules of proper conduct) as a generic term, see my "Dimensions of *Li* (Propriety): Reflections on an Aspect of Hsün Tzu's Ethics," *PEW* 29:4 (1979). For the relation between *li* and *dao*, see Cua, "Conceptual Aspect," 383-385, and Cua, *Ethical Argumentation*, chap. 4 (4.4).

19. Or more perspicuously, Wang Yangming's 王陽明 comment on Cheng I's saying: "When we speak of substance as substance, function is already involved in it, and when we speak of function as function, substance is already involved in it." [Wang Yangming, *Instructions for Practical Living and Other Neo-Confucian Writings*, translated with notes by Wing-tsit Chan (New York: Columbia Univ. Press, 1963) 69] For Cheng I's remark, see Wing-tsit Chan, trans. and ed., *A Source Book in Chinese Philosophy* (Princeton: Princeton Univ. Press, 1963) 570.

20. See, for example, 荀子: 不苟 3/12/3-4, and 荀子: 榮辱 4/15/7-14, Dubs 62-63 passim. As Watson points out, "Xunzi frequently harks back to the golden ages of the past—the reigns of sage rulers Yao, Shun, Yu, King Tang of the Shang dynasty, and King Wen and Wu of the Zhou—as examples of such periods of ideal peace and order." [Watson 5-6] While Xunzi accepted much of the traditional account of Chinese history, he is quite aware of the issue of evidence. See 荀子: 非相 5/18/24-19/8, Dubs 74-75, and 荀子: 性惡 23/115/10, Dubs 309, Watson 163.

21. For an explication of the problematic character of man's basic nature, see Cua, "Conceptual Aspect." For a clearer and more plausible articulation of the connection between moral knowledge and action, see my *The Unity of Knowledge and Action: A Study in Wang Yang-ming's Moral Psychology* (Honolulu: Univ. of Hawaii Press, 1982).

22. In 荀子: 正名 22/107/25, 行 *xing* (moral conduct) is defined as "action that is performed for the sake of righteousness (*yi*)." Confer Dubs 282, Watson 140.

23. 荀子: 勸學 1/3/10, Dubs 36, Watson 19, and 荀子: 修身 2/7/18-9, Watson 30, Dubs 51. For stress on comprehending the rationales of changing circumstances in terms of a unifying perspective, see 荀子: 大略 27/131/8.

24. As Xunzi remarks, if a person's "words are reasonable, you may discuss with him the *li* (rationale) of *dao*." [荀子: 勸學 1/4/7, Watson 21*, Dubs 39]

25. For the morally superior person, completeness and purity are basic values. For this reason, says Xunzi, "he reads and listens to explanations in order to penetrate the Way (*dao*), ponders in order to make it part of himself, and shuns those who impede it in order to sustain and nourish it." [荀子: 勸學 1/4/16-7, Watson 22, Dubs 40]

26. For further discussion, see Cua, *Ethical Argumentation*, chap. 4 (4.1-4.2).

27. For a different passage of similar purport, see 荀子: 勸學 1/3/7-12, Dubs 36-37, Watson 19-20.

28. In this passage 荀子: 至士 14/67/70-2, other qualifications for moral teachers are also mentioned, for example, sternness, trustworthiness, and awe-inspiringness.

29. See 荀子: 勸學 1/4/19-21, Watson 22, Dubs 40-41; 荀子: 儒效 8/31/5-10, Dubs 104; 荀子: 不苟 3/10/1; and 荀子: 至士 14/67/8-11. For rendering *decao* as moral integrity, I follow Mei. See Y. P. Mei, "Hsün Tzu's Theory of Education with An English Translation of the *Hsün Tzu*, Chapter I, An Exhortation to Learning," *Tsing Hua Journal of Chinese Studies*, n.s. 2, n. 2 (1961) 375.

30. For similar passages involving contrast between Yu and Jie, see 荀子: 非相 5/18/13-7, Dubs 71, and 性惡 23/115/22-7, Watson 164-165, Dubs 310-311. For the notion of proper objects of the senses, see 荀子: 天論 17/80/9-15, Dubs 175-176, Watson 80-81; 荀子: 正名 22/108/14-109/3, Dubs 284-285, Watson 142. For a discussion of the general capacity for making distinctions, see Cua, "Hsün Tzu's Theory of Argumentation," 886-891.

31. As Watson points out, this is actually a quotation from the *Analects*, 14:25 (Watson 20, note).

32. In Xunzi, such thought-experiments are, I believe, plausibly deployed in supporting his famous thesis on the problematic character or badness of man's basic nature. See my "The Quasi-Empirical Aspect of Hsün Tzu's Philosophy of Human Nature," *PEW* 28:1 (1978). For the general form of appeal to reflective desirability in the vindication of the Confucian vision of *dao*, see Cua, *The Unity of Knowledge and Action*, 79-100.

33. For the importance of developing second-order reflective desires, see Cua, "Dimensions of *Li*," 380-381.

34. For a discussion of the role of this and other appeals in argumentation, see my "Reasonable Action and Confucian Argumentation," *JCP* 1:1 (1973).

35. I have discussed this notion of paradigmatic individuals in Cua, *Dimensions of Moral Creativity*, chaps. 3 and 5.

36. With qualification in terms of the role of reflection, Xunzi would concur with this assessment of Hume on sentiment in ethical discourse:

> The end of all moral speculations is to teach us our duty, and, by proper representations of the deformity of vice and beauty of virtue, beget correspondent habits, and engage us to avoid the one, and embrace the other. But is this ever to be expected from inferences and conclusions of the understanding, which of themselves have no hold of the affections or set in motion the active powers of men? They discover truths. But where the truths which they discover are indifferent and beget no desire or aversion, they can have no influence on conduct and behavior. What is honorable, what is fair, what is becoming, what is noble, what is generous takes possession of the heart and animates us to embrace and maintain it. [David Hume, *An Inquiry Concerning the Principles of Morals* (Indianapolis: Bobbs-Merrill, 1957) 5-6]

37. Burton Watson's Foreword to *Experimental Essays on Chuang Tzu*, ed. Victor H. Mair (Honolulu: Univ. of Hawaii Press, 1983). It must be noted that Mozi explicitly espouses the appeal to the deeds of the sage kings of antiquity as one of the three criteria for the acceptability of theories—a thesis explicitly rejected by Xunzi. See Watson, *Mo Tzu: Basic Writings* (New York: Columbia Univ. Press, 1963) 118; and 荀子: 性惡 23/115/10, Watson 163, Dubs 309. I shall later consider Xunzi's view in connection with the evaluative function of the historical appeal.

38. Arguably, the infinite regress argument is valuable in philosophical discourse because of its function as a reminder, rather than as an argument that validates philosophical theses. See John Passmore, *Philosophical Reasoning* (London: Gerald Duckworth, 1961), chap. 2.

39. Robert J. Fogelin, *Understanding Arguments: An Introduction to Informal Logic* (New York: Harcourt Brace Jovanovich, 1978) 41.

40. Ibid. 41-43.

41. For a similar passage, see 荀子: 至士 14/66/23-7. See also the following relevant occurrences of *zigujijin*: 荀子: 儒效 8/31/10, 王制 9/35/19, 君道 12/63/10, 至士 14/66/26, 至士 14/67/17, 解蔽 21/103/3, 解蔽 21/105/11, and 哀公 31/148/8. My following observations also apply to such expressions as "from the ancient times to the present, it has always been

the same" 古今一也 *gujinyiye*. See 荀子: 議兵 15/74/17, 彊國 16/76/5, 正論 18/87/4, and 君子 24/119/12.

42. The translation of the last two sentences is my own, with the deletion of 故 *gu* (hence) in order to bring out the rhetorical force of the historical idiom. For informative notes on the historical characters and incidents, see Watson 124, note.

43. For a fuller treatment of Xunzi's doctrine of erroneous beliefs, see Cua, *Ethical Argumentation*, chap. 4. A briefer version was presented at the Conference of the International Society for Chinese Philosophy, held in Toronto, Canada, August 1983.

44. See note 33 preceding.

45. J. L. Austin, "Other Minds," in *Philosophical Papers* (Oxford: Oxford Univ. Press, 1961) 83.

46. See Nicholas Rescher, *Dialectics* (New York: SUNY Press, 1977) 38; and *Skepticism* (Totowa, New Jersey: Rowan and Littlefield, 1980), chap. 7.

47. C. L. Stevenson, *Ethics and Language* (New Haven: Yale Univ. Press, 1944) 290-294.

48. The following remarks are mostly taken from the preliminary summary of a lengthy treatment of phases of argumentation in chaps. 2 and 3 of my *Ethical Argumentation*.

49. This translation is my own. A full justification for this rendering is given in the work cited in the preceding note. For Watson's and Dubs' translations, see Watson 147 and Dubs 290.

50. In the *Xunzi*, there are around four hundred occurrences of *wei* in such constructions as 所謂 *suowei*, 可謂 *kewei*, 之謂 *zhiwei*, and 謂之 *weizhi* that can be construed as quasi-definitional formulas. An extensive analysis of these constructions is given in chap. 3 of my *Ethical Argumentation*.

51. Yu was one of the three early sage kings, and Jie was a legendary tyrant. For passages of similar purport but pertaining to other fundamental theses, for example, king 王 *wang* versus hegemon 霸 *ba*, see 荀子: 王制 9/36/15-37/17, Watson 37-42, Dubs 126-130; 荀子: 王霸 11/49/15-50/10.

52. I owe this conception of mediation to Paul Dietrichson's interpretation of Kant's notion of a typic of the moral law. See Dietrichson, "Kant's Criteria of Universalizability," in *Kant: Foundations of the Metaphysics of Morals: Text and Critical Essays*, ed. Robert Paul Wolff (Indianapolis: Bobbs-Merrill, 1969).

53. Such a mediation, of course, may be accomplished by the use of fictional rather than historical characters, as in the case of Classical Taoism. See my "Opposites as Complements: Reflections on the Significance of *Tao*," *PEW* 31:2 (1981).

54. The expression *yiguchijin* occurs in 荀子: 儒效 8/33/2-3, Dubs 111-112, where a similar point is made.

55. See also 荀子: 解蔽 21/106/18-107/8, Watson 136, Dubs 276-277; and 荀子: 不苟 3/11/14-8.

56. Again, my explication that follows is an application of a highly condensed account of Xunzi's conception of ethical justification based on a reconstruction of extant materials given in Cua, *Ethical Argumentation*, chaps. 2 and 3.

57. For an elaboration of this distinction, see my "Introduction," in Cua, *Dimensions of Moral Creativity*.

58. Lengthy examples are noteworthy in such essays as *Wangzhi* (Regulations of kings), *Yibing* (Discussion on military affairs), and *Zhengming* (Correction of errors). I have chosen for discussion one passage, among many others, from *Yibing*. But notably, Xunzi sometimes explicitly states the distinction between the past (*gu*) and the present (*jin*) in the retrospective sense. See, for example, 荀子: 非十二子 6/24/4-10; 荀子: 富國 10/43/11-44/13; 荀子: 君道 12/60/25-61/11.

59. This distinction is indebted to Urmson but perhaps employed in a context that may be alien to his intent. Also, while the distinction is important in elucidating some aspects of Xunzi's ethical theory, as Urmson points out, the distinction may be blurred in practice, especially in situations "where standards are gradually evolved and gradually changed." I believe that Xunzi was quite sensitive to this issue of changing and evolving standards, as shown, for example, in his insistence on distinguishing different grades of Confucians in his essay on the merits of Confucians (*Ruxiao*). This effort may be regarded as a response to the shifting and changing conception of being a Confucian in his own times. And it may be quite properly construed as an effort directed to standard-setting guided by the ideal of *dao*. See J. O. Urmson, *The Emotive Theory of Ethics* (London: Hutcheson Univ. Library, 1968) chap. 6.

60. My defense of Xunzi's view of ethical justification is found in the first three sections of chap. 3 in *Ethical Argumentation*.

61. This feature of Xunzi's ethics is the basis of some scholars' complaint about his authoritarianism. But if I have not been mistaken in my presentation thus far, this complaint is more a Western "democratic" reaction than one found in the works of Xunzi. See, for example, Dubs, *Hsüntze: The Moulder of Ancient Confucianism* (London: Arthur Probsthain, 1927) 109 passim; and H. G. Creel, *Chinese Thought from Confucius to Mao Tse-tung* (Chicago: Univ. of Chicago Press, 1953) 133.

62. This is my interpretive translation for the present purpose of discussing the prospective use of the historical appeal. Actually the notion of *he*, which I elsewhere rendered as "concordance," involves also respect for linguistic practices and accord with *li* (reason). Together these requirements

constitute what I call "standards of competence." A preliminary sketch is given in Cua, "Hsün Tzu's Theory of Argumentation." Fuller discussion is given in chap. 1 of Cua, *Ethical Argumentation* (confer Watson 163, Dubs 309).

63. For identification of relevant passages on "following the former kings," see 荀子: 非相 5/19/10, 非十二子 6/22/4, 非十二子 6/22/8, 儒效 8/27/26, 儒效 8/33/2.

64. See also 荀子: 儒效 8/34/20-4, Dubs 118.

65. Or more generally, "In discussing small and intricate matters, one must exercise care in inquiry. When the clues for dealing with them are seen, one can then deal with them with understanding and appreciate the rationales (*li*) underlying the fundamental distinctions involved." [荀子: 非相 5/20/16]

66. According to traditional Chinese history, Tang was the first ruler of the Shang dynasty; Wu, founder of the Western Zhou dynasty, who defeated Zhou, the last ruler of the Shang dynasty. Jie was the last ruler of Xia, and Yu established the Xia dynasty (see note 20 preceding). For other examples, see 荀子: 王制 11/54/23-55/5, and 荀子: 臣道 13/64/7-9 passim.

67. Arguably, as Dray points out, the notion of history is a quasi-evaluative notion, for the notion pertains not just to the past, but to significant past. And the issue of the praise and blame theory of history is incisively stated by Max Fisch:

> The historian is not blamed for praising or blaming, and praised for doing neither, but blamed if antecedent judgments of value blind him to contrary evidence, and praised if his selection and treatment of evidence is clearly not unbalanced by the desires to support judgments formed in advance of the search for evidence. . . . The historian of art is a critic of art, the historian of science a critic of science, and similarly the historian of economic, social and political institutions is a critic of those institutions. Objectivity is not the absence of criticism, but unreserved submission to further criticism, complete openness, withholding nothing from judgment.

This notion of objectivity is present in Xunzi's requirement of impartiality in argumentation. See William H. Dray, *Philosophy of History* (Englewood Cliffs: Prentice-Hall, 1964) 28 and 40-55. See also Dray, *Perspectives on History* (London: Routledge and Kegan Paul, 1980) 42-46. For Xunzi's view, see Cua, "Hsün Tzu's Theory of Argumentation," 873-975.

68. See also 荀子: 王制 9/35/18, Dubs 123, Watson 35.

Three

Virtues in Xunzi's Thought

Jonathan W. Schofer

1. Introduction

Xunzi 荀子 (c. 310-219 B.C.E.),[1] one of the great early Confucian thinkers, offers a profound and subtle picture of ethical development and flourishing. My study of virtues in Xunzi's thought will begin with a review of his understanding of human nature and the process by which people attain virtue.

Xunzi is known for holding that "human nature is bad" 性惡 xing'e, a position which opposes that of his predecessor, Mencius. Although there has been much debate over what Xunzi means by this claim, we can at least take Xunzi to believe that people do not have innate tendencies that can guide them toward developing virtuous qualities. While it is incorrect to attribute to Xunzi an Augustinian view that people are "evil," [2] it is fair to say that Xunzi saw people's spontaneous desires as being at best "simply and rather foolishly selfish"[3] and as leading at worst "to strife and disorder."[4]

Desires cannot be eliminated, but they can be directed through study and practice of the teachings and rituals that define the Confucian Way.[5] Xunzi calls this process "learning" 學 xue:

> Where does learning begin and where does it end? I say that as to program, learning begins with the recitation of the Classics and ends with the reading of the ritual texts; and as to objective, it begins with learning to be a person of breeding, and ends with learning to be a sage. If you truly pile up effort over a long period of time, you will enter into the highest realm. Learning continues until death and only then does it cease.[6]

Learning is a process of study and practice through which people do more than develop intellectually; they re-form their characters. Xunzi describes people who represent distinct levels of ethical development, including the person who lives according to selfish innate desires, the person of breeding, the refined person 君子 junzi, and the sage.[7] The nature and goals of learning change as one progresses: initially, one recites relatively accessible texts with the aim of becoming a person of breeding. Only later does one read more difficult texts and aim to attain the qualities of the sage, who represents the highest level of development. Only by sustained effort over one's lifetime can one "enter into the highest realm."

The process of learning requires people to have the correct engagement of the "mind" 心 *xin*. Xunzi calls this engagement "conscious activity" 偽 *wei*. Conscious activity is not simply a matter of reflection. In fact, Xunzi sees pure reflective thought as having little value for learning. He writes, "I once tried spending the whole day in thought, but I found it of less value than a moment of study." [Watson 16] Xunzi defines conscious activity in his chapter entitled "Rectifying Names": "When the mind conceives a thought and the body puts it into action, this is called conscious activity. When the thoughts have accumulated sufficiently, the body is well trained, and then the action is carried to completion, this is also called conscious activity." [Watson 139-40] Conscious activity, then, refers both to individual intentional actions and to a person's capabilities and tendencies that result from repeated intentional actions.[8] Conscious activity as part of learning includes studying texts, practicing ritual, being conscious of good and bad qualities in oneself and others, following the instructions of a teacher, associating with good and learned people, and concentrating on attaining the qualities exhibited by a Confucian sage. A person's environment is crucial to this process. One needs to have the right teachers and friends, and to be in a society that has the appropriate practices, rituals, and etiquette. Xunzi writes that a refined person "must be careful where he takes his stand." [Watson 17; see also 15-23, 24, 89-90, 150-56, 157-58][9] It is important to note that the learning process likely requires resources and leisure time that only elite members of the society can afford.

Xunzi thinks that people at the early stages of ethical development may neither understand nor be motivated by good order or rituals in themselves—they may simply desire to avoid patterns that lead to "wrangling and strife," "violence and crime," "license and wantonness," and so on. [Watson 157] Xunzi, however, believes that people can eventually realize the intrinsic values of virtuous qualities and ritual. He writes, "[A refined person] trains his eyes so that they desire only to see what is right, his ears so that they desire to hear only what is right, his mind so that it desires to think only what is right." [Watson 22] He also writes, "Heaven and earth are the beginning of life, ritual principles are the beginning of order, and the refined person is the beginning of ritual principles. Acting on them, practicing them, guarding them, and loving them more than anything else—this is the beginning of the refined person." [adapted from Watson 44; see also 20-23, 24, 26-27, 86, 94-96] An important part of learning is that people come to value the process, the objects of their study, and the forms they practice as inherently good.

In Xunzi's view, then, we begin with selfish, immediate, unlimited and often inappropriate desires. However, because we have the capability to re-form that nature through a sustained learning process, we can attain states of character that are beyond anything we initially could understand.

2. Modern Western Categories

2.1 Attaining virtue

Recent work in comparative ethics offers conceptual tools that can help us understand Xunzi's view of how people attain virtue, though the categories must be modified in order to do so.

In contrasting the views of Mencius and a much later Confucian thinker, Cheng Yichuan (c. 1033-1107 C.E.), A. C. Graham makes a distinction between developing benevolent qualities and discovering benevolence in one's nature.[10] The distinction has been elaborated by Lee Yearley and P. J. Ivanhoe into the constructs of a "development model" and a "discovery model."[11]

A discovery model of attaining virtue is based on ontological notions that people have a "fundamental nature" or "true self" that is covered or obscured. In a discovery model, attaining virtue consists in touching or realizing that true self. The person thus *discovers* a true essential self. Xunzi's view of how people attain virtue is clearly not a discovery mode. He does offer a notion of human nature, and within the framework of his thought it is possible to speak in some sense of a "true self"; however, his goal is to change that nature, not to come into contact with it.

In contrast, a development model is based on an agricultural image of growth. People are born with capacities to develop certain virtuous dispositions. If these capacities are nurtured and unhindered, they can grow into virtuous dispositions. A person thus *develops* a full or cultivated self.

The process of attaining virtue described by Xunzi is compatible with the development model in that virtuous dispositions do develop through a process that includes attention to one's behavior, emotions, and so on. However, the organic image is inaccurate. Xunzi does not have a picture of natural capacities that "grow" into virtuous dispositions.   While Mencius often refers to agricultural images in describing ethical development,[12] Xunzi's images are quite different: "Thus, if wood is pressed against a straightening board, it can be made straight; if metal is put to the grindstone, it can be sharpened; and if the refined person studies widely and each day examines himself, his wisdom will become clear and his conduct without fault." [adapted from Watson 15; see also 157-58, 164]   People's desires and conduct, then, are re-formed—straightened, sharpened, and so on—by the process of learning through conscious activity.   Moreover, Xunzi states explicitly that rituals, the principles embodied in ritual, and the process of conscious activity are not "natural"—that is, they are not part of people's innate or spontaneous nature.   The ancient sages created rituals and their underlying principles as a potter molds pots out of clay. [Watson 164]

One might argue that Xunzi does have a sense of inborn capacities that develop into virtues, for he writes that all people have the "essential faculties" needed to understand necessary ethical principles and the "potential ability" to put them into practice. [Watson 166-67]   However, the "essential faculties" to which Xunzi refers enable people to engage in a process that leads them to redirect, not build upon, their natural tendencies.

One might also argue that Xunzi's rejection of agricultural or growth images is primarily rhetorical.   However, Xunzi's images are significant in that they help distinguish his views from those of Mencius.   For Xunzi, people cannot trust their spontaneous impulses and desires to guide them in their ethical development.   Instead, they have to rely on wisdom and practices that are external to the individual.   The true understanding of the Way is *learned*; it is not attained through attention to intuitions.   Correct emotional responses are products of focused *practice*; they are not expansions or extensions of spontaneous desires. The process relies on engagement with the correct *social forms*; it does not rely on appropriate motivation.   People *re-form* their nature; they do not cultivate it.

The notion of a development model, then, is relevant in describing Xunzi's picture of how people become virtuous, but the notion is distorting to the extent that it is connected to agricultural images of growth.   The model can be amended to take account of and differentiate the notions of re-formation and cultivation as subsets of development.   A re-formation model refers to ethical development that depends on the overcoming of natural or spontaneous impulses; a cultivation model refers to ethical development that depends on extension and expansion of those impulses.

2.2 Virtue

The project of discussing virtues in Xunzi's thought turns on some conception of a "virtue." Xunzi, however, does not employ a corresponding term, so we are required to find an appropriate, though alien, category of analysis. Modern Western ethicists offer a variety of definitions of virtue.

Edmund Pincoffs makes cogent criticisms of several overly restrictive definitions of virtue in his insightful survey.[13] His own definition of virtues and vices as "dispositional properties that provide grounds for preference or avoidance of persons," however, is not very useful in relation to Xunzi's thought.[14] I agree with Bryan Van Norden in his general criticism of this definition as overly vague.[15] In addition, such a definition would be misleading if applied specifically to Xunzi, who believes that virtues have intrinsic value for both the virtuous individual and for the society. One comes to love virtue because it is good in itself; virtues are not merely grounds for being preferred or avoided.

Alasdair MacIntyre offers an influential, if controversial, definition of virtue in terms of practices, narratives, and traditions.[16] This definition could be fruitfully applied in relation to Xunzi's thought. For example, one virtue I describe below (section 3.2) can be seen as a quality that enables people to attain goods internal to educational and ritual practices that occur in the context of the Confucian tradition. However, MacIntyre's account has a number of problematic ambiguities, as pointed out by J. B. Schneewind and others.[17] Also, this definition cannot capture important aspects of Xunzi's thought, such as the transformation that distinguishes a sage from a refined person (see section 3.4)

Yearley's comparative study *Mencius and Aquinas* is particularly relevant for my project in that he examines the thought of a classical Confucian thinker who was contemporary with Xunzi.[18] The definition of virtue that Yearley offers is both accurate and useful in discussing Xunzi's outlook. Like Pincoffs and Bernard Williams, Yearley defines virtues as being types of dispositions.[19] Virtuous dispositions, on this view, are tendencies toward actions that rely on natural or acquired capabilities and involve an element of choice or judgment. Dispositions can be created through training, and the formation of a disposition can add to or change a person's character, motivations, and actions in significant ways.[20] A virtue, then, is "a disposition to act, desire, and feel that involves the exercise of judgment and leads to a recognizable human excellence or instance of human flourishing. Moreover, virtuous activity involves choosing virtue for itself and in light of some justifiable life plan."[21]

Xunzi's descriptions of people who have attained the higher levels of ethical development—refined people and sages—show them as having acquired, through training, tendencies toward good desires, emotions, and actions. These tendencies are not habits but are results of choice and assessment of what is good. As I have shown above, such people come to find intrinsic value in what is good and choose it for itself. Moreover, they do so in light of a "life plan" defined in terms of Confucian practices, teachings, and the models of the sages. This process is one that pervades a person's activities and continues throughout a lifetime.

Yearley's definition of virtue is closely connected to a number of other terms, most of which are useful in relation to Xunzi's thought. He writes that discussions of virtue center on the "good person criterion," in that the good or flourishing person is the standard by which to judge evaluations of goodness and wretchedness.[22] In Xunzi's case, the standard of human excellence is the sage. He often describes exemplary people in order to show qualities that people should strive to create in themselves, and he describes unformed, weak, and bad people in order to show qualities that people should avoid or work to diminish in themselves.

Drawing on the work of Philippa Foot, Yearley writes that virtues are "corrective." Virtues are connected to views of human weakness, need, and difficulties. They correct "some difficulty thought to be natural to human beings, some temptation to be resisted, or some deficiency of motivation to be made good."[23] While Xunzi holds that virtue is good in itself, he also clearly believes that ethical development and virtuous qualities correct people's errant natural tendencies. In addition, Xunzi describes virtues needed to correct or balance decadent tendencies engendered by a person's specific and immediate condition (see section 3.3). Neither Yearley nor Foot writes explicitly about this latter sense of "corrective" virtues.

Yearley distinguishes between "inclinational" or "motivational" virtues that define appropriate goals and "preservative" virtues that overcome internal desires and weaknesses that are obstacles to attaining those goals.[24] Xunzi is concerned that people develop both motivational and preservative virtues, and the distinction helps clarify the difference between the refined person and the sage (see section 3.4).

Virtues, in Yearley's view, are to be contrasted with counterfeits and semblances of virtue. Counterfeit virtues are apparently virtuous actions done with the intention of deceiving others. Semblances, or simulacra, of virtue are actions that appear to be virtuous but are done out of habit, are based on incorrect motivation, or are results of simply following rules. A concern with counterfeits and semblances of virtue highlights the importance of intention and motivation in distinguishing between virtues and vices that appear to be virtues.[25] Xunzi is very concerned with counterfeits and semblances of virtue (see section 3.5), but not in the sense described by Yearley. Xunzi is more critical of people who promote incorrect and misleading conceptions of the Way than of those who do correct actions without correct motivation.

3. Virtues in Xunzi's Thought

Xunzi does not allow us easily to apprehend in any sophisticated way his understanding of the higher forms of ethical development. He often describes virtuous qualities in his analyses of subjects such as education and language, but he offers neither an explicit theory of virtue nor systematic and clearly defined analyses of particular virtues and how they relate to each other. In addition, many of Xunzi's most profound discussions of human excellence involve unconventional terms of art that are only indirectly defined, such as "oneness" and "subtlety."

A. S. Cua has done considerable scholarly work on aspects of Xunzi's understanding of virtues, and his analysis is worthy of careful attention.[26] This essay differs from Cua's work in two respects. First, I examine modern ethical categories and their relevance to Xunzi in ways that Cua does not. Second, Cua focuses his analysis on the Confucian virtues of 仁 *r e n* (benevolence), 義 *yi* (righteousness), and 禮 *li* (propriety). He treats these virtues as something like hinge virtues, and he refers to virtues such as filial piety, loyalty, fidelity, kindness, and generosity as "varying expressions, in appropriate contexts, of the concern for *ren, yi,* and *li*."[27]

I hold that Cua's approach is overly narrow for understanding Xunzi's conception of virtue. Treating virtues such as "endurance" and "subtlety" as subordinate to, or parts of, *ren, yi,* and *li* may shed light on how these virtues are connected, but this approach does not lead to a nuanced understanding of the specific virtues themselves. Moreover, one cannot create a full description of virtues in Xunzi's ethical outlook by examining only, or even primarily, Xunzi's discussions of *ren, yi,* and *li*. Passages in which Xunzi describes virtuous qualities using unconventional terms of art are crucial for understanding the subtleties of his thought; in fact, they may be more important than his discussions of *ren, yi,* and *li*. Below, I will discuss three such passages and show how they provide detailed descriptions of specific virtues as well as inform us about Xunzi's general conception of virtue.

3.1 Xunzi's use of "de"

The Chinese word 德 *de*, which is generally rendered as "virtue," often occurs in Xunzi's writings. As with the words *arete, virtus*, and "virtue" in Western traditions, the Chinese term has a long history of changing meanings, and I will not attempt to summarize that history here.[28] Xunzi generally uses *de* to refer to the state or power of a person who has a high degree of ethical development. Thus, *de* resembles the sense of "virtue" in "Yao's actions display virtue." Xunzi does not use the term to refer to specific virtues, so *de* does not resemble the sense of "virtue" in "compassion is a virtue."

A large proportion of Xunzi's uses of the term *de* occur in his discussions of kings. Xunzi is particularly concerned with the *de*, or lack thereof, of the rulers of society; in his ideal state, the leaders are sages. Xunzi calls the practice of good government "the *de* of Heaven." Kings with *de* are benevolent and righteous, and they honor and support virtuous people in the kingdom.[29] It is important to note that the hierarchical society advocated by Xunzi may not provide all people with opportunities to attain *de*.

De is created through the practice of rites and good acts, and *de* allows people to do actions and attain states that would not be possible without *de*. *De* is connected both to mental activity and to emotions. People with *de* are free from obsession, the clouding of understanding that comes from following a false doctrine; they may attain "godlike understanding," an accurate and comprehensive understanding of the world. Such people also have correct desires and are not swayed by false goods such as profit and power. [Watson 17-8, 22-3, 83, 91, and 126]

Xunzi also describes *de* as the virtuous king's power to affect and move others. This active sense of *de* seems related to what David Nivison describes as a sense that was present in the earliest Chinese texts, the "energy in the ruler that enables him to found or continue a dynasty."[30] People are attracted to and wish to be ruled by a virtuous king, and kings can come to rule a state simply through their *de*. People follow and obey virtuous kings without the need for coercion or other forms of control. Xunzi, like Confucius, sees the effect of *de* as the only legitimate and effective way to take control of a state. In a related sense, *de* inspires a sense of debt and gratitude in people toward the virtuous person. This effect allows kings to be secure in relation to powerful people in and near their states.[31]

Interestingly, Xunzi refers to *de* in his discussion of music. He sees music as being closely connected with joy, and he plays on the fact that both words are represented by a single Chinese character to say "music is joy." Music is also connected with *de*. Xunzi writes that musical instruments are "the means of guiding *de*," and a person with *de* realizes and shows others the importance of music. [Watson 112-20]

An understanding of *de* and the relation between *de* and specific virtues is necessary for understanding Xunzi's picture of human excellence. However, a study of his use of *de* cannot substitute for examination of specific virtues described in his writings. His references to *de* generally do not involve detailed descriptions of specific virtues, and the word does not play a significant role in most of his accounts of human re-formation and excellence. The term *de* (as well as other common virtue terms such as *ren, yi, li,* and *zhi*) is absent in a number of significant places, most notably in the beginning of the chapter entitled "Rectifying Names," where he defines important terms of art. In this section he defines neither the word *de* nor words that describe virtuous qualities (though he does define "conscious activity" and "moral conduct").

3.2 Virtues required for learning

In the first two chapters of the *Xunzi*—"Encouraging Learning" and "Improving Yourself"—Xunzi describes a number of virtues required in the formative stages of ethical development. The process of learning and improving oneself requires particular virtues. These virtues are necessary for people in the early stages of ethical development (that is, most people) as well as for those who have reached the level of a refined person.

In his chapter entitled "Encouraging Learning," Xunzi quotes a passage in the *Odes* that describes a dove assiduously searching for food for its seven offspring. He then writes that a refined person likewise "binds himself to oneness — *yi*."[32] He does not give a formal definition of "oneness," but the preceding passage reads:

> . . . unless you pile up little steps, you can never journey a thousand *li*; unless you pile up tiny streams, you can never make a river or a sea. The finest thoroughbred cannot travel ten paces in one leap, but the sorriest nag can go a ten days' journey. Achievement consists in never giving up. If you start carving and then give up, you cannot even cut through a piece of

rotten wood, but if you persist without stopping, you can carve and inlay metal or stone. Earthworms have no sharp claws or teeth, no strong muscle or bones, and yet above ground they feast on the mud, and below they drink at the yellow springs. This is because they keep their minds on one thing. Crabs have six legs and two pincers, but unless they can find an empty hole dug by a snake or water serpent, they have no place to lodge. This is because they allow their minds to go off in all directions. Thus, if there is no dark and dogged will, there will be no shining accomplishment; if there is no dull and determined effort, there will be no brilliant achievement. He who tries to travel two roads at once will arrive nowhere; he who serves two masters will please neither. The wingless dragon has no limbs and yet it can soar; the flying squirrel has many talents but finds itself hard pressed. [Watson 18, compare to Knoblock 1.6]

Learning is a continuing process consisting of many small actions. As a long journey is made up of many small movements, re-forming oneself consists of many small actions and thoughts. The process is long and difficult, and even the most gifted people (the finest thoroughbreds) cannot complete it in "one leap." What is needed is continued, focused effort. Neither great natural ability nor intense but unsustained spurts of activity are sufficient to realize the goals of learning.

In this passage, Xunzi describes a virtue that is necessary for the process of learning. The virtue has two aspects. (1) The first aspect of the virtue, Xunzi's concern with "not giving up," is a disposition to endure or carry on with the process of learning. The process of learning is a long-term undertaking that is difficult and tiresome. It involves shaping and guiding powerful desires that stand in the way of the process itself. Endurance is crucial for this learning and is far more important than great power or effort that does not endure. (2) The second aspect of the virtue, Xunzi's concern with keeping one's mind on one thing, is a disposition to focus on one's activities and the ultimate goal of one's projects. In the process of learning, there are many ways that people can be distracted, and there are many apparent but false goods to which people can be drawn. If people let their minds "go off in all directions" and do not concentrate on what they are doing, as well as their reasons for doing it, they will never accomplish or develop toward anything.

Oneness, then, refers to a disposition toward sustained, focused concentration and activity. Oneness results in "dark and dogged will" or "dull and determined effort." This virtue is a *preservative* virtue; it is concerned with overcoming obstacles that stand in the way of the goals of learning. Xunzi's imagery—"dark and dogged" and "dull and determined"—is a reminder that the process of learning and the virtues needed are neither glamorous nor exciting.

3.3 Virtues of a refined person

The refined person must develop and act upon virtues beyond those required for learning. Xunzi writes that a refined person "practices the good order 理 *li* of the Way with courage." [adapted from Watson 31] He then describes a number of a refined person's virtues:

> Though poor and hard pressed, a refined person will be broad of intentions. Though rich and eminent, he will be respectful in his manner. Though at ease, he will not allow his spirit to grow indolent; though weary, he will not neglect his appearance. He will not take away more than is right because of anger, nor give more than is right because of joy. Though poor and hard pressed, he is broad of intentions because he honors benevolence. Though rich and eminent, he is respectful in manner because he does not presume upon his station. Though at ease, he is not indolent because he follows what is right. Though weary, he does not neglect his appearance because he values good form. He does not take away too much in anger nor give too much in joy because he allows law to prevail over personal feeling. [adapted from Watson 31-32, compare Knoblock 2.13]

In this passage, Xunzi describes six different conditions in which a person may be. These six conditions are presented as three pairs of contrasts—being poor and being rich, being at ease and being weary, being angry and being joyful. For each condition, Xunzi describes a virtue that balances, or *corrects*, destructive or decadent tendencies engendered by the refined person's condition. He also describes the good or quality that refined people value and develop in themselves in order to attain that virtue.

Thus, when Xunzi writes, "Though poor and hard pressed, a refined person will be broad of intentions," the point is that a refined person's range of awareness and concerns is not dependent upon wealth. While it is relatively easy for people who are wealthy to have broad concerns, those who are hard pressed may be led to focus on little more than their basic needs and easing their condition. Refined people, however, maintain a wide range of awareness and concerns even if they are poor or otherwise in conditions that would lead people to ignore less immediate concerns. This awareness includes both relations with other people and care for oneself. Despite difficult conditions, refined people are able to maintain an awareness of "larger" concerns such as the condition of their family members, neighbors, or country, as well as their own spiritual state, education, and religiously significant practices. Refined people attain the virtue of being broad of intentions by "honor[ing] benevolence." In their learning, they focus on identifying and valuing benevolence as a quality of good people, and they work to shape their desires so that they will become benevolent themselves.

When Xunzi writes, "Though rich and eminent, he will be respectful in his manner," the point is that a refined person's respect for others is not based on their social status in relation to his own. While people who are rich and eminent do not find it hard to have broad intentions, being rich may lead people to lack respect for others, especially those who are neither rich nor powerful. Refined people, however, will be respectful of other people whether or not they are rich and eminent. A refined person attains the virtue of being appropriately respectful "because he does not presume upon his station." In learning, a refined person focuses on developing the sense that respect is not grounded in wealth or social status.

In a similar manner, being at ease would lead many people to be indolent or lazy. Refined people are not indolent, even if they are at ease, because they have trained themselves to be hard working in their pursuit of what is right. The contrasting condition of being weary would lead many to neglect their appearances. However, refined people attend to their appearances, even if they are weary, because they have trained themselves to value good form. Being overly angry or overly joyful can lead many to be unfair in their transactions, and they may take or give more than is correct. Refined people do not do so, even if they are angry or joyous, because they have trained themselves to act according to rules and laws in their transactions, and not to be swayed by their feelings.[33]

The virtues that people must attend to and strive to develop, then, are dependent upon their conditions and situations. People must be aware of the ways in which their circumstances can corrupt or weaken their characters, and they must be sure to develop virtues that overcome the corrupting influence.

3.4 Virtues of a sage

In his chapter entitled "Dispelling Obsession," Xunzi writes that Confucius' disciple Youzi, in order to avoid falling asleep while studying, burned the palm of his hand. Xunzi comments, "This shows remarkable endurance, but does not reach what is good 好 *hao.*" [adapted from Watson 133] Given Xunzi's strong emphasis on the need to develop preservative virtues, it may seem striking that Xunzi does not applaud Youzi's efforts. However, Xunzi refers to Youzi among several examples that he contrasts with the "subtlety" 微 *wei* of a sage:

> True subtlety is the quality of the perfect man. What has he to do with strength of will, endurance, and guardedness? Dull brightness shines on the outside. Clear brightness shines on the inside. The sage follows his desires, satisfies all his emotions, and what regulates him in doing this is proper order. What has he to do with strength of will, endurance, or guardedness? The benevolent man practices the Way through inaction; the sage practices the Way through non-striving. The thoughts of the benevolent man are reverent; the thoughts of the sage are joyous. This is the way to govern the mind. [adapted from Watson 133]

A harmony of desires and an ease of movement along the Confucian Way are features of the subtlety that is distinctive to the character of a sage. A sage has gone through a significant transformation that makes irrelevant many of a refined person's most important virtues. "Strength of will," "endurance," and "guardedness" are preservative virtues needed by people who are in the process of shaping their desires and emotions. Since sages have reached a state in which their desires and emotions are fully re-formed, they desire and do what is good with no need of preservative virtues.

Sages act appropriately without effort, and they think appropriately with joy. Their virtue does not require great effort or show, in contrast with people like Youzi, who still must overtly struggle to do what is good. The sages' excellence, or "brightness," is internal. They follow their desires and their own sense of "proper order;" they no longer have to rely on external guides and prods, such as teachers and a burning stick, to know and do what is good. In other words, the sages have fully acquired virtuous dispositions.

It is worth noting the similarity between the sage's subtlety and the refined person's oneness. Both dispositions enable a person to focus full attention on the Confucian Way. However, within that similarity lies a crucial difference: people with oneness have focused attention through discipline and overcoming of desire, while people with subtlety have a quiet ease, a unity of intention and desire.

3.5 Failures to be virtuous

Xunzi presents two general sets of reasons for people's failure to develop the virtuous dispositions of sages. First, people may be distracted from the Confucian Way, and from the task of developing real virtues, by false understandings of the world and the Way. Or, second, they may have a correct conception of the Way but fail to form themselves sufficiently in relation to it.

Xunzi holds that people must be guided by particular teachings, rituals, and conceptions of the Way. Developing a correct understanding of these guides is a necessary, though not sufficient, condition for becoming a refined person and later a sage. Xunzi criticizes two types of false understandings of the world. The first type is manifest in popular religious beliefs of his time—beliefs that there exist spirits and ghosts that cause unusual events in the natural world and that may help or harm people. These beliefs, according to Xunzi, cause unnecessary fear, lead to practices that waste materials and people's energy, and distract people from the important concerns in life. He writes, "Useless distinctions, observations which are not of vital importance—these must be left aside and not tended to."[34]

The second type of false understanding criticized by Xunzi is exemplified by the views of philosophers with whom he disagrees, such as Mozi and Zhuangzi. "These various doctrines," he writes, "comprehend only one small corner of the Way." [Watson 126] People who subscribe to and promote them are "obsessed by a small corner of the truth and fail to comprehend its over-all principles." [Watson 121] Thus, "Mozi was obsessed by utilitarian considerations and did not understand the beauties of form," and "Zhuangzi was obsessed by thoughts of Heaven and did not understand the importance of man." [Watson 125] Such doctrines and theories "bring disorder to the age." [Watson 137] They lead their followers falsely to believe they are developing themselves to become good and falsely to deny the necessity of the Confucian Way.

Even if people do direct themselves toward the correct rites, texts, manners, and so on, Xunzi is not confident that they successfully will re-form themselves. People have powerful desires, and the world presents many sources of obsession and distraction. Few people have the power of mind and live in the supporting environment necessary for them to re-form themselves as sages. [Watson 121-2] Moreover, the process of re-formation itself requires a number of virtues that are necessary to endure the process and focus on the proper concerns. Xunzi describes two ways people may partially but insufficiently re-form themselves. First, people may insufficiently develop necessary virtues: they may have some understanding of ethical principles but fail to incorporate these principles into practical action. Second, people may develop some virtues and lack other necessary virtues: they may be very perceptive or courageous but fail to have a full understanding of the regulations of society. [Watson 135-36]

Xunzi is concerned that people develop correct motivations for their actions, and the fully formed person, the sage, does choose and follow the Way with correct motivations. However, unlike Mencius, he does not view actions that appear to be virtuous, but that are done with incorrect motivation, as threatening and misleading distortions of virtuous action. In fact, for Xunzi, the state of being able to act correctly without correct motivation may be a necessary stage in the process of ethical development. For this reason, Yearley's notions of counterfeit virtues and semblances of virtues, defined in terms of flawed motivation (section 2.2), do not fit the states of character that Xunzi most extensively criticizes.[35]

Xunzi does give a great deal of direct attention, though, to criticizing semblances or counterfeits of virtue in the sense of actions that are mistakenly considered to be virtuous by many people because of the influence of false understandings of the world. He does see these actions as threatening and misleading distortions of virtuous action. In other words, he is not as worried about people who do correct actions with wrong motivations as he is about well-motivated people who choose false teachings to guide them. His worry is more about ethos and ways of life than about motivation. This worry is understandable given that his view of ethical development relies on people engaging with the appropriate teachings, practices, and models. A person who does the correct actions with improper motivations may come to have correct motivation, but a person who is guided by the wrong teachings is lost.

3.6 The absence of a systematic analysis of specific virtues

Xunzi's ethical outlook has sophisticated accounts of human excellences, how those excellences are created in ethical development, and how they are necessary for that development. A significant question, then, is, Why does Xunzi not present a clearly defined and systematic analysis of virtues? He clearly has the ability to do so. This question concerns Xunzi's reasons for choosing his form of presentation. Of course, any attempt to answer this question is speculative, but such attempts can be illuminating.

One probable reason Xunzi does not present a systematic analysis of virtues is that he, like Mencius, is concerned with the process of ethical development and does not seem to think that a systematic analysis of virtues contributes a great deal to that process.[36] Much of Xunzi's writing concerns the process of re-formation and descriptions of the actions of good as well as bad people. This answer provides some insight, but it does not explain two things. First, it does not explain an important difference between Mencius's and Xunzi's writings about virtues. Though Mencius does not offer systematic analyses of virtues in the manner of Aristotle or Aquinas, he does have passages in which he clearly defines particular human excellences (*ren, yi, li,* and *zhi*) that he sees as central to any person's ethical development.[37] Xunzi, however, does not present any equivalent list of virtues. Second, this answer does not explain a difference between Xunzi's writing about virtues and his writing about issues such as Heaven, rites, music, obsession, language, and human nature. He does address these latter issues using description and (often extensive) argumentation. He does not, however, directly address the topic of virtue or human excellence in the same manner.

A second possible reason Xunzi does not present a systematic analysis of virtues—one which addresses the two issues noted above—is that he does not want people to think that they can have a clear sense of what virtue is without re-forming themselves through ritual and study; he does not want them to think that they have innate potentials or tendencies to become virtuous. Xunzi believes that the process of re-formation is a long, arduous process in which people do not fully understand why they do what they do, or what they are trying to become, until they are far into the process. Perhaps Xunzi is afraid that if he were to give focused attention to human excellence itself, he would lead people to think that they know what virtue is before they reach a state where they are truly able to have that knowledge. If people think they know what virtue is, they may try to re-form themselves without giving appropriate attention to learning.[38] This view of Xunzi is supported by his criticism of Mencius's view that people are capable of learning because their natures are good; Xunzi emphasizes the importance of ritual in the process of re-formation. [Watson 158-59, 162-63] He likely believes that Mencius's outlook leads people not to give sufficient attention to learning, teachers, and the rites. It makes sense, then, that Xunzi would present his views in a way that would make sure to focus people's attention on the importance of learning.

4. Conclusion

The comparative project of examining modern Western categories and applying them to Xunzi's thought helps us to see and understand aspects of his outlook we would otherwise find less clear. Xunzi does not give explicit attention to analysis of specific virtues, and he does not even use a category that corresponds to "a virtue." Drawing on an appropriate modern Western definition of virtue as a type of disposition that leads to human excellence and flourishing, we can identify and analyze descriptions of specific virtues in Xunzi's discussions of topics such as human nature and character development. In addition, the related categories of motivational and preservative virtues, and of virtues being corrective, help bring to light features of specific virtues such as oneness, having broad intentions, being respectful, and subtlety.

The language of modern virtue ethics also makes possible the worthwhile project of a broad and detailed analysis of virtues in Xunzi's thought. Such a project would include analysis of the virtues Xunzi describes, how they are connected and ranked, and how they relate to each other and to different stages of ethical development.

The comparative project also requires us to re-examine our modern categories of analysis. Xunzi's view that one can re-form one's character through focused study and practice of ritual contrasts with modern notions of character development that focus on cultivating innate capacities or on realizing a hidden true self. Also, Xunzi's relative lack of concern with appropriate motivation during much of the process of learning challenges modern concerns with semblances of virtue defined in terms of inappropriate motivation. Consideration of Xunzi's views leads us to expand the construct of a development model of attaining virtue and also to question the significance of semblances of virtue as we understand them.

Notes

1. I follow the dates proposed in John Knoblock, "The Chronology of Xunzi's Works," in *Early China* 8 (1982-3) 34. Xunzi's name is written "Hsün Tzu" in the Wade-Giles Romanization system. I will use the Pinyin system throughout this paper, except in direct citations or when referring to the names of Mencius (Mengzi) and Confucius (Kong Fuzi).

2. Homer Dubs, "Mencius and Sün-dz on Human Nature," *PEW* 6 (1956) 213-22.

3. Lee Yearley, "Hsün Tzu on the Mind: His Attempted Synthesis of Confucianism and Taoism," *Journal of Asian Studies* 39:3 (1980) 466.

4. D. C. Lau, "Theories of Human Nature in *Mencius* and *Xunzi*," chapter nine in this volume, pp. 201-5.

5. On Xunzi's understanding of the Way, see P. J. Ivanhoe, "A Happy Symmetry: Xunzi's Ethical Thought," *JAAR* 59:2 (1991) 309-22.

6. Translation adapted from Burton Watson, *Hsün Tzu: Basic Writings* (New York: Columbia Univ. Press, 1963) 19. For a different interpretation of this passage, see John Knoblock, *Xunzi: A Translation and Study of the Complete Works*, vol. 1 (Stanford: Stanford Univ. Press, 1988) 1.8. Further references to these two translations will be in the text in brackets.

7. The term *junzi* originally denoted a rank and later was used to refer to a person who had attained a high level of ethical development. Scholars have had difficulty finding an adequate translation for the term. It has been rendered in many ways, including "gentleman," "cultivated individual," "superior man," "noble person," and "paradigmatic individual." A. S. Cua reviews attempts to translate *junzi*, though he does not offer a solution to the problem. See "Review of Xunzi: A Translation and Study of the Complete Works, vol. 1, books 1-6, by John Knoblock," *PEW* 41:2 (1991) 215-27. My choice is "refined person." The adjective "refined" is appropriate in that it implies intentional action by a person that shapes and improves an object (in the *junzi's* case, the object is himself).

8. P. J. Ivanhoe pointed out to me these two senses of conscious activity. For a fuller treatment of Xunzi's picture of the mind, see Lau, "Theories of Human Nature in *Mencius* and *Xunzi*;" Yearley, "Hsün Tzu on the Mind: His Attempted Synthesis of Confucianism and Taoism;" and Bryan Van Norden, "Mengzi and Xunzi: Two Views of Human Agency," chapter five in this volume.

9. Note that the case of the sage-king Shun, as described by Mencius, presents a difficulty for Xunzi's views here. According to Mencius, Shun grew up in an extremely hostile environment that made it all but impossible to develop virtuous qualities, yet he became a sage. See D. C. Lau, *Mencius* (Baltimore: Penguin Books, 1970) 5A2. All further references to the *Mencius* will be to this translation and will be cited by Book, Part, and Section following Lau's numbering.

10. A. C. Graham, *Two Chinese Philosophers: Ch'eng Ming-tao and Ch'eng Yi-ch'uan* (La Salle, Ill.: Open Court Press, 1992) 54.

11. See Lee Yearley, *Mencius and Aquinas: Theories of Virtue and Conceptions of Courage* (New York: SUNY Press, 1990) 58-60, 79, and P. J. Ivanhoe, *Ethics in the Confucian Tradition: The Thought of Mencius and Wang Yang-ming* (Atlanta: Scholars Press, 1990) 73-90.

12. *Mencius* 2A2, 2A6, 6A7, 6A8.

13. Edmund Pincoffs, *Quandaries and Virtues* (Lawrence, Kansas: The Univ. Press of Kansas, 1986) 73-100.

14. Ibid. 82.

15. Bryan Van Norden, *Mencius, the Philosopher* (unpublished manuscript).

16. Alasdair MacIntyre, *After Virtue*, 2d ed. (Notre Dame: Univ. of Notre Dame Press, 1984) 181-225.

17. See J. B. Schneewind, "Virtue, Narrative, and Community: MacIntyre and Morality," *Journal of Philosophy* 79 (1982) 653-63, and "Moral Crisis and the History of Ethics," in *Contemporary Perspectives in the History of Philosophy*, edited by P. French, T. Uehling, Jr., and H. Wettstein, *Midwest Studies in Philosophy*, vol. 8 (Minneapolis: Univ. of Minnesota Press, 1983) 525-39.

18. Lee Yearley, *Mencius and Aquinas: Theories of Virtue and Conceptions of Courage* (New York: SUNY Press, 1990).

19. Bernard Williams, *Ethics and the Limits of Philosophy* (Cambridge: Harvard Univ. Press, 1985).

20. Yearley, *Mencius and Aquinas*, 102-9.

21. Ibid. 13. See also Williams, *Ethics and the Limits of Philosophy*, 35-7. Note that the concept of flourishing employed here is not the narrow biological definition criticized by Pincoffs, *Quandaries and Virtues* 98-99. For a useful discussion of flourishing, see Van Norden *Mencius, the Philosopher*.

22. Yearley, *Mencius and Aquinas*, 14, 71, 218 n. 26.

23. Ibid. 16-7. See also Philippa Foot, "Virtues and Vices," in *Virtues and Vices and Other Essays in Moral Philosophy* (Berkeley: Univ. of California Press, 1978) 8-14. Note the criticisms by Robert C. Roberts, "Will Power and the Virtues," *Phil Rev* 93:2 (1984) 232-3.

24. Yearley, *Mencius and Aquinas*, 13-4, and Roberts, "Will Power and the Virtues," 228-33.

25. Yearley, *Mencius and Aquinas*, 19-21, 67-72. See also Van Norden, *Mencius, the Philosopher*, and MacIntyre, *After Virtue*, 182-3, 239-43.

26. A. S. Cua, *Ethical Argumentation: A Study in Hsün Tzu's Moral Epistemology* (Honolulu: Univ. of Hawaii Press, 1985), and "Hsün Tzu and the Unity of Virtues," *JCP* 14 (1987) 381-400. See also Kwong-loi Shun, "Review of *Ethical Argumentation: A Study in Hsün Tzu's Moral Epistemology*, by A. S. Cua," *PEW* 41:1 (1991) 111-17.

27. Cua, "Hsün Tzu and the Unity of Virtues," 381. Also see Cua, *Ethical Argumentation*, 163.

28. See Donald Munro, *The Concept of Man in Early China* (Stanford: Stanford Univ. Press, 1969) 185-97; David Nivison, "Tao and Te," in *The Encyclopedia of Religion*, edited by M. Eliade (New York: Macmillan Publishing, 1987) 283-86; and Yearley, *Mencius and Aquinas*, 54-6.

29. Watson 33-4, 42, 75. See also Henry Rosemont, Jr., "State and Society in the *Xunzi*: A Philosophical Commentary," chapter one in this volume.

30. Nivison, "Tao and Te," 284. See also Yearley, *Mencius and Aquinas*, 54.

31. Watson 40, 69-70, 74, 76-77. See also D. C. Lau, *Confucius: The Analects* (Baltimore: Penguin Books, 1979) 2:1.

32. Knoblock renders *yi* as "constancy." [Knoblock 1.6]

33. The virtues described in this passage resemble virtues described by Western thinkers, such as generosity, good will, diligence, humility, justice, and temperance. However, I have refrained from using these terms in my analysis because meaningful comparisons would require both more extensive study of Xunzi's virtues and a detailed account of the specific Western virtues.

34. Watson 83-5, 134-5. See also Lee Yearley, "Hsün Tzu: Ritualization as Humanization" (unpublished manuscript).

35. Note that Xunzi never discusses the "village honest man" in his writings. Mencius claims that the village honest man is the "thief of virtue" because he does correct actions with false motivation. See *Mencius* 7B37. Also Lau, *Confucius*, 17:13, and Yearley, *Mencius and Aquinas*, 20, 67-68, 217 n. 21.

36. Yearley makes this comment concerning Mencius. See Yearley, *Mencius and Aquinas*, 170.

37. *Mencius* 2A6, 6A6.

38. P. J. Ivanhoe, "Thinking and Learning in Early Confucianism," *JCP* 17:4 (1990) 473-93.

Four

Xunzi: Morality as Psychological Constraint

Joel J. Kupperman

The stereotyped, simple version of early Chinese philosophy portrays Xunzi 荀子 as the opposite of Mencius 孟子. Mencius argues that human nature is good; Xunzi portrays it as evil. A number of recent scholarly studies have rejected this simple opposition, and it is very clear that Xunzi's view is far more complex than the stereotype would suggest.[1]

It may be misleading to summarize Mencius as holding that human nature is good. A more accurate summary would be that he holds that human nature contains an element that is good, and perhaps it would be more accurate still to speak of him as holding that human nature contains the seeds or sprouts of goodness. What does Xunzi believe about human nature? The very form of this question, I will argue, is misleading, because it suggests that there is something fixed (good, evil, or some mixture of the two) about human beings in general. To speak of someone as having a view of human nature is to suggest a claim of something that (at least in normal cases) is fixed, remaining in place from early childhood to advanced old age. Mencius in this sense has a view of human nature, namely that tendencies toward benevolence are a normal element of being human. Xunzi rejects this claim and counters with a bleak view of what humans are like in the opening stages of life (and remain like, absent culture and good education). But does he have his own view of human nature—in the sense of fixed tendencies normally involved in being human? My judgment is that this is doubtful.

The thesis of this chapter is that Xunzi is best read, not in terms of any ascription of fixed elements of being human, but rather in terms of a model of possible stages of the development of moral awareness. The modern psychological counterpart of this model is to be found in Jean Piaget. To say this invites comparison between Xunzi and someone else who produced a model of possible stages of moral development, namely Lawrence Kohlberg.

Detailed comparison would take me too far from the main subject, namely Xunzi, by giving too much space to discussion of Kohlberg. Let me remark though that Kohlberg's system seems to me to be driven by a somewhat simplistic Kantianism in ethics (which then is used to organize empirical data), whereas Xunzi's view I think is genuinely empirically driven.[2] Some further comments will be made in the course of examination of Xunzi's view.

Morality

Xunzi's account of what humans are like centers on the gap between what they are at birth, on one hand, and moral virtue on the other. Are humans at birth evil? Given the ordinary meaning of the English word, this seems most implausible.[3] A prerequisite for evil is some sense of what is morally appropriate, which the evil person then goes against. Whether Mencius thought that humans at birth had such a sense is a complicated and difficult question: the innate benevolence that he posits comes close to what David Hume called the "natural" virtues (such as kindness and compassion) but cannot be equated with them. In any case Xunzi clearly rejects the thesis of innate benevolence. So no one, in his view, can be born evil. By 惡 *e*, which is generally translated as evil, he has to mean something like "ignoble in a way that lacks the support necessary for an adequate society or personal life." "Not inclined toward goodness" might seem a tempting translation, but as we will see Xunzi did think that there *are* respects in which humans at birth are inclined in the direction of goodness.

We can appreciate Xunzi's view of the gap between ethical development at birth and moral virtue if we understand what is required for moral virtue. This will also help us to see that there is a somewhat (but not entirely) similar gap for Mencius. Both Xunzi and Mencius hold what is after all a standard Confucian view, that moral virtue goes beyond adherence to learned norms, and requires that moral commitment be internalized and consistent.

In Mencius' view benevolence is at the root of moral virtue, but for most people benevolence is a sporadic force, usually directed without much intelligence when it occurs. The well-known Mencian story of the king who spared the sacrificial ox because he saw its fear of death is a perfect example.[4] Because the ceremony required a sacrificial animal, a lamb (which the king presumably did not look at) was substituted for the ox. More importantly, as Mencius points out to the king, his policies allow many of his people to sink into conditions of misery. Presumably he hardly looks at this either. Viewed against this background, the king's rescue of the ox—while perhaps a hopeful sign of his potentialities—hardly represents moral virtue or anything close to it. If someone from benevolent impulses prevents doctors from administering painful inoculations to children, or kindly rescues a mass murderer like Charles Manson from his painful confinement, this hardly approaches moral virtue. Mencius gives another nice example of unintelligent benevolence elsewhere, in the case of the high official who on occasion lends his carriage to people wishing to ford local rivers. He could build footbridges, Mencius observes.[5]

Moral virtue for Mencius requires the transformation of benevolent impulses into committed and intelligent policies of benefitting people. Benevolence needs to be "extended," so that it is reliable rather than sporadic and also is directed in a reasonable way. Someone for whom this happens will be different from the great majority of people. Such a person will have strong and reliable inner sources of satisfaction, so that unexpected vexations will not seem truly disturbing.[6] Further, the benevolence will be visible, to those who know how to see, in the face and the back and even in the limbs.[7]

Xunzi's model of moral virtue is not keyed to extended and rationally directed benevolence in the way that Mencius' is. Conversely, there is a strong explicit emphasis in Xunzi on loyalty to (and adequate performance in) social roles, which in a hierarchical society imply proper deference to those in superior positions.[8] [Knoblock 23.1e] One's station generates ritual and moral duties, and it follows that moral virtue is the successful absorption of these principles. In the process, desires that stem from original human nature will possibly not go away; but they will be transformed, and also will be channeled in appropriate ways. [Knoblock 22.5a][9]

It is worth pointing out that Mencius too believes in social hierarchy, and that one's station generates duties.[10] The major difference between Mencius and Xunzi is that Mencius introduces something (innate benevolence) into Confucianism, which Xunzi takes back out. There are certainly other differences, notably in Xunzi's treatment of law. But the difference about innate benevolence seems to me the main one.

How do humans get to morality? Two answers that have had great influence in the West are Hobbes' and Hume's. For Hobbes the crucial transition is a social contract, negotiated out of a shared sense of perceived self-interest. (Hobbes' story though turns out to be less simple than this sounds, because he observes that actually there may never have been humans in the state of nature that would have preceded a social contract.[11] So it is *as if* humans had made a brilliant guess that they would be happier and more secure if they invented law and morality.) For Hume, morality develops through the sophistication of an original good-tending element (benevolence or sympathy) in human nature. A crucial step is the development of a special form of discourse which locates sentiments in a perspective that is not purely personal but rather purports to be anybody's.[12]

It may be tempting to assimilate Xunzi to Hobbes and Mencius to Hume. Xunzi like Hobbes refuses to be upbeat about original human nature. There also are some interesting Hobbes-like passages in Xunzi that encourage the notion that much of human development is colored and influenced by the general persistence of desire. [Knoblock 19.1a, and also 21.1] The persistence of desire, if it is without measure, leads to social disorder; and Xunzi, like Hobbes, links disorder to poverty. [Knoblock 19.1a] Hume has a thought experiment to demonstrate inner benevolence (imagine that you could step on someone's gouty toes or alternatively step out of the way, without penalty for you in either case) like Mencius' of the child about to fall into the well.[13] He also, like Mencius, has ways of dealing with the apparent counter-examples of humans who are totally lacking in benevolence. Mencius has the elaborate metaphor of Ox Mountain, which (against its original nature) is made bald, first by wood cutters lopping its trees and then by cattle and sheep being brought to nibble on whatever grows.[14] Hume defends the view that benevolence is essential to humanity by the simple expedient of insisting that the Emperor Nero and also the ancient Scythians (who took scalps) had lost their humanity.[15] Hence they do not count.

The parallels however do break down, especially when one looks at the context of inquiry. Both Mencius and Xunzi are preoccupied—practically as well as theoretically—with the moral psychology of the transition from what one was born with to moral virtue—in a way in which their Western near-counterparts are not. Conversely, there is nothing in Mencius that closely corresponds to Hume's preoccupation with the rival claims of reason and the sentiments to be decisive in ethical judgment. The divergence between Xunzi and Hobbes is perhaps most striking. Hobbes scarcely bothers to examine how human psychology is transformed, if at all, by the transition marked by the introduction of law and morality. These still loom in his account as external constraints, and Hobbes enjoys remarking on how the selfish, appetitive nature of human beings is still visible despite these constraints. Perhaps Hobbes believed in the inner nastiness of all puritans? For Xunzi, in contrast, it is clearly possible for human beings to transform what they are, even if most people do not travel very far along that route. There are, or at least have been, sages.

Stages of Becoming Moral

In the end any significant thinker cannot be entirely paralleled by, or reduced to, any collection of others. This is certainly true of Xunzi. Parallels can be useful, not as thoroughgoing explication, but as heuristic devices. They can get us to see what we otherwise might overlook. Or they may get us to eliminate from our image of a thinker some element that it was (or would be) a mistake to include.

In this spirit I think that reference to Piaget's psychology is useful in eliminating, from our image of Xunzi, the mistaken notion that he has a view of human nature that is comparable (although opposite) to Mencius'. Mencius famously does claim that there is an element of benevolence in human beings (except for those who have undergone a psychic transformation akin to what happened to Ox Mountain) throughout their lives. (This is the received view of what Mencius' position is; and in this case the principle of interpretative charity supports, rather than undermines, the received view, because there is modern psychological evidence that supports something like the Mencian position.)[16] While this never claims to be a *complete* picture of human nature, what it posits is sufficiently ongoing and entrenched that we may say "Yes: Mencius has a view of human nature, namely that it includes an element of benevolence."

In this sense Xunzi does *not* have a view of human nature. The *e* with which we are born is normally subject to transformation, the degree of transformation depending greatly on circumstances, social influences, and personal effort. One of the merits of John Knoblock's translation is that he renders Xunzi's *xing* as "original human nature." One could alternatively have "opening stage human nature."

In place of a fixed human nature, Xunzi offers us stages of development. The obvious comparison is with Jean Piaget's cognitive psychology of childhood. Piaget's stages represent an invariant sequence, in which earlier stages become integral parts of the structures of those that follow.[17] One might imagine an explicitly Piagetian version of Xunzi in which, say, mastery of ritual becomes part of the structure of the steps of becoming a genuinely virtuous person. A stage, according to

Piaget, includes a level of preparation on one hand, and of completion on the other.[18]

This implies the importance of readiness for the next stage. Readiness, it should be noted, cannot be rushed. In experiments performed in Geneva in the late 1950s it turned out that a carefully designed training program did not markedly accelerate cognitive development.[19] It is not farfetched to suppose, especially in relation to stages of ethical development, that this readiness for the next stage could be felt as desire to move in that direction. This sheds interesting light on Xunzi's comment (particularly striking in relation to the traditional image of his philosophy) that "As a general rule, the fact that men desire to do good is the product of the fact that their nature is evil. Those with very little think longingly about having much . . . indeed whatever a man lacks within himself he is sure to desire from without." [Knoblock 23.2b]

The bulk of Piaget's work of course was concerned with cognitive development. Is there any significant difference between stages of ethical development and those of (non-ethical) cognitive development? One might think of Plato's insistence that, in knowledge of the good, the knower becomes the known: the knowledge, in other words, is not some detached thought module, but rather permeates the self of the person who has it. Kierkegaard makes a similar point in *Concluding Unscientific Postscript* about the special characteristics of ethical or ethico-religious knowledge.[20]

This is relevant to a distinction that some admirers of Piaget make between "hard" and "soft" stages of development. Hard structural stage theories, it is said, rely on abstraction from the concrete self to the perspective of an "epistemic self" or "rational moral self."[21] Why, one might wonder, bearing Plato and Kierkegaard in mind, would a theory of ethical development abstract from the concrete self? There is an important point here, and it is not always clear whether or not the Kohlbergians get it. It is in any case probably fruitless to try to decide whether Xunzi's stages of ethical development would count as "hard" or "soft." In the version of the distinction just cited they look soft. There is another version in which they look hard.[22]

In any event the crucial point in relation to our investigation is that any generalization about human nature to which Xunzi is committed is development stage-sensitive. Indeed we can go further: generalization is possible only for the opening stage. Opening stage human nature is *e*. After that, it depends.

Becoming Moral as External
and Internal Constraint

The *Xunzi* begins with the metaphor of opening stage human nature as warped (at least in relation to any desirable nature). Learning is a process of correcting the warping, like steaming wood to change its shape. [Knoblock 1.1] We all have needed this: "The gentleman by birth is not different from other men." [Knoblock 1.3] Besides self-shaping there will be shaping by environmental influences. Hence one needs to take care in selecting the community one lives in. The process of properly shaping up our natures is not a matter of fits and starts, but rather needs to be constant. [Knoblock 1.6; see also 2.8]

It is possible to read all of this in terms of persistent willed effort (encouraged and facilitated by environmental influences) on the part of the would-be gentleman to improve his nature. No doubt some will to improve is necessary at any stage, and becomes crucial as one grows older. However, realistic reflection suggests that in the earlier stages the impetus to reshape opening-stage nature will come largely from outside: from parents and teachers especially. Part of this becomes explicit in Book 23.1b, which returns to the theme of original nature's being like warped wood, and notes that the "instructions of a teacher" are needed for the required work to take place.

Clearly the reshaping of original nature is for Xunzi not wholly a comfortable or entirely appealing process for the person who needs it. The influence of habits and customs [Knoblock 4.9] is crucial. But how will someone acquire the new habits and customs that contribute to reshaping her or his nature? The answer surely is that such a person needs to be pressured, or at least steered, in the direction of the new patterns of behavior. 4.10 mentions the importance of a teacher, and also the influence of a model (which the teacher may provide) of behavior to be imitated.

To a degree all of this concerns constraints which are at least partly external in their origin. The original nature left to itself, without constraints, will remain *e*. If one acquires chaotic customs in a chaotic age, something close to this also will be true.

Good teaching, which presumably involves pressure as well as encouragement, matters a great deal. But external constraints in the form of rewards, commendations, punishments, and penalties handed down by political authorities also can affect people's habits and motivations. [Knoblock 15.5] Xunzi takes this seriously, and it seems likely that he would have been more sympathetic than Confucius or Mencius would have been to something like Aristotle's insistence that law is an important factor in the early development of character.[23]

Both Aristotle's and Xunzi's views on the role of law in the shaping of character (especially in the early stages) can be given a minimalist or a maximalist interpretation. The minimalist reading is that laws (along with parental and informal community encouragements and sanctions) have an important role in shaping the habits that are so important, especially in the early stages. One is very likely to develop the habit of not doing what is forbidden. A maximalist reading is that laws also embody ethical instructions, and in this are a form of modeling of what is desirable that normally will have ethical influence. On either reading laws represent important constraints on a developing character, constraints that are external in origin but may well be internalized. (The degree to which these constraints are internalized of course depends on the ethical progress of the individual.) In the maximalist reading the process of internalizing is more strongly emphasized.

Xunzi clearly takes this seriously. But he is enough of a Confucian that he does insist that the influence of rewards, commendations, punishments, and penalties is—especially in the long run—limited in comparison to the attraction generated by moral force. [Knoblock 15.5] On the other hand, moral force does not seem to work for some people. Even in a well-managed society, Xunzi insists, there can be incorrigibly bad people. Reforming them is a hopeless task and we need laws to punish them. [Knoblock 9.1] Even a good ruler may need to execute some men, such as officers negligent in the performance of their essential duties. [Knoblock 11.7b]

Xunzi attempts to strike a balance in what he says about law and about political power. On one hand, sheer force, no matter how brutal and efficient, has its limitations, which may be crucial in the long run even if not in the short run. This is evident in his skepticism about the long-run political prospects of the Qin authoritarian government. [Knoblock 15.3, 16.5] In the end moral force is far more effective than rewards, punishments, and threats.[24] On the other hand, sheer force has its uses. This is linked not only to Xunzi's view that opening stage human nature is *e*, but also (more importantly) to his skepticism about hopes that the vast majority of people can transform themselves significantly beyond that stage.

Above and beyond its necessity, law plays a constructive role. By regulating such things as types of clothing and other marks of status, it can contribute to a stable and harmonious social infrastructure that plays a part in the development of goodness. [see Knoblock 12.6] The foundation of government education is first and foremost to see that there are appropriate laws.

We have seen that it is reasonable to suppose that the constraints that gradually reshape the misshapen wood of original nature are, in early life, largely external in origin. The child at the very least needs direction, and also will need some sense of the boundaries of what is permissible. It is reasonable also to suppose that in favorable cases, when the child is making real progress and shows signs of being able to become a genuinely good person, the impetus will gradually shift from the external to the internal, as the development becomes more self-directed.

Nevertheless there still will be constraints, even if these become more self-imposed. Ritual plays an important role in this transition. Xunzi's account of ritual is especially interesting in two ways. It gives a nuanced picture of the differences between the early and late stages of acquisition of ritual. And it deftly connects ritual to what Xunzi sees as its social prerequisites, most fundamentally to social inequality. [see Knoblock 19.1c and 9.3]

Why, one might wonder, could not a thoroughly egalitarian society have rituals? People could still thank others for presents, and the first person in a group to reach a door could hold it open for the others. My guess is that Xunzi's response to this challenge would be something like the following. In some cases temporary imbalances of position or of kindness give rise to little rituals. For a few seconds the people for whom the door is being held open are not equal to the one holding it for them, although reasonable people would hardly care about this. (If the same person were always in the position of holding open the door, though, this might begin to register.) An egalitarian society then could generate little rituals from temporary inequalities. A system of ritual, though that has a profound effect on people's development, doing a great deal to reshape their natures, must include more than merely a few little rituals. Inequality that is more than temporary will be required for this.

Certainly the system of ritual that Xunzi was familiar with would start from the differences in behavior that corresponded to the fundamental inequalities of parent/child or of ruler/high official/low-ranked official/subject. Perhaps in a world of extreme equality one could imagine oneself anywhere, in any position; the consequent sense of self and of the world would seem to Xunzi to be chaotic. [cf. Knoblock 4.10] The Confucian world in contrast generates rituals that strongly shape one's nature in part because they are repeated: one's positions in a family or in society do not change that quickly.

Xunzi gives us a rather Hobbesian view of humans at the earliest stage of the process of mastering ritual. "Men are born with desires which, if not satisfied, cannot but lead men to seek to satisfy them." The risk is that these men (close to the opening stage nature that includes *e*) will observe no measure. This will lead to contention, disorder, and poverty. [Knoblock 19.1a] We get the same bleak view of the lowest level in the remark that "All rites begin with coarseness . . .". [Knoblock 19.2c]

One might imagine a dancing class for thugs. But probably a more accurate image of what Xunzi has in mind is of the first steps in teaching very young children the rudiments of good manners: such things as asking nicely for what one wants, thanking someone for a favor granted, and excusing oneself instead of simply running out of the room. No one expects much elegance in even the better performances.

However, Xunzi does insist that the emotional elements of any ritual come from inborn nature, so that at least in this respect the *e* of original nature includes markers that point in the direction of the ritual that will improve it. The crucial sorrow and happiness, in particular, "inherently have their beginnings in man's inborn nature." [Knoblock 19.5b] More specifically, "sacrifice originates in the emotions stirred by remembrance and recollection of the dead." [Knoblock 19.11] Hence "inborn nature is the root and the beginning." [Knoblock 19.6] This point is broadened when Xunzi later observes that "As a general principle, the faculty of knowing belongs to the inborn nature of man." [Knoblock 21.9]

When Xunzi claims [Knoblock 23.2a] that ritual principles and moral duty "are not the product of anything inherent in man's inborn nature," this needs to be read in the context of the statements just quoted. Xunzi certainly holds that there is nothing in inborn nature that by itself would incline someone to be benevolent or morally virtuous, or to perform rituals in a satisfactory way. But he also holds that there are emotions and faculties in inborn nature that can lead in these directions.

After remarking that rites begin with coarseness, Xunzi continues more hopefully with "are brought to fulfillment with form, and end with pleasure and beauty." He goes on to say that "Rites reach their highest perfection when both emotion and form are fully realized." At the coarse stage the child carries on normally because life would be made uncomfortable if it did not. Saying a gruff "Thanks" typically does not bring that much joy. Later on, given a good deal of practice or more maturity, the child can feel fairly comfortable in its performance of elementary rituals. Conversely it can be uncomfortable if it realizes that it has omitted one of them. At this point the external constraint of mastering rituals under pressure is being transformed into an internal constraint. The civilized adult has to express gratitude because it wouldn't feel right if one didn't.

Also if the process of mastering rituals ends "with pleasure and beauty," this strongly suggests that the ritual performances in time will have their own appeal. Beauty typically is experienced as a form of attraction, and some philosophers have suggested that one of the marks of pleasure, at least of what we will decide was a pleasure, is that it contains motivation to have it repeated. So that ritual, really well mastered, has a hold on us, generating its own attraction. Something like this is true of what Xunzi sees as another important element of psychic reshaping, namely really good music, which is "joy." [Knoblock 20.1] As joy it draws us toward the experiences it provides, and makes the people who appreciate it harmonious. [Knoblock 20.2]

It scarcely need be emphasized that there are Confucian echoes in much of this. The original sequence of refinement, according to Confucius, is "Let a man first be incited by the *Songs*, given a firm footing by the study of ritual, and finally perfected by music."[25] It seems to me that Mencius does not pay as much attention to the *Songs* as he does to music.[26] The three sources of cultivation are all present in Xunzi's account.

Finally there are the inner constraints associated with moral duty. One needs to force oneself to control one's desires and the related balance of one's mind. The mind can become obsessed by desire or aversion, or by any one of the myriad things. [Knoblock 21.2] The sage avoids blindness by being "without desires and aversions." [Knoblock 21.5a]

What does Xunzi mean by this? Clearly he does not mean that the sage will not have a negative view of social disorder or of rapacious behavior, or that the sage will not seek the improvement of society. The context of 21.5a suggests that what the sage will lack will be desires and aversions that are out of proportion, and especially those that take over the mind ("obsession") in an unwholesome way.

It is important to observe proportion, but also not to have fixed ideas to which one is wedded. Xunzi praises an "emptiness," which perhaps could have been translated "openness." It centers on "not allowing what has previously been stored to interfere with what is received in the mind." [Knoblock 21.5d]

In the end, Xunzi expects that there will be few sages, and that most people will not become reliably virtuous. He suggests the thought experiment of imagining a world (somewhat like Hobbes' state of nature) without the authority of superiors, and without influence of ritual and morality. The prospects for human behavior in this world, he thinks, would be very bleak. Presumably if the structures of society crumbled, we could see this for ourselves. The implications of this, in relation to the "virtue" of people in the world we presently inhabit, is that most of the good behavior is what contemporary psychologists term "situational" and in this respect not reliable if contexts change. Experiments such as those of Stanley Milgram and the Stanford prison experiment bear Xunzi out in this view.[27] Xunzi's cry of "It is the environment that is critical!" [Knoblock 23.5b] would be joined in by many psychologists today.

Notes

1. See, for example, Philip J. Ivanhoe, "Human Nature and Moral Understanding in the *Xunzi*," chapter eleven in this volume; Antonio S. Cua, *Ethical Argumentation: A Study of Hsün Tzu's Moral Epistemology* (Honolulu: Univ. of Hawaii Press, 1985).

2. A good source for Kohlberg is his *The Philosophy of Moral Development: Moral Stages and the Idea of Justice* (San Francisco: Harper & Row, 1981). Detailed criticism of the Kantian model that guided Kohlberg's research would take us too far afield from the topics of this chapter. But it should be noted that Kohlberg makes becoming virtuous seem a conceptual skill rather like becoming good at mathematics, thus slighting the factor of the "good will" which plays such a major role in Kant's Kantianism. This is linked to an astonishing weakness in the empirical research, namely that it relies on responses to questions. As a method this does not provide a reliable way of distinguishing between what someone would like to think his or her principles are, on one hand, and, on the other hand, what those principles operationally actually are.

3. This of course adds support to the view that "evil" is an exceedingly inexact translation of Xunzi's *e*.

4. *Mencius* 1A7.

5. Ibid. 4B2.

6. Ibid. 4B28.

7. Ibid. 7A21.

8. John Knoblock, *Xunzi: A Translation and Study of the Complete Works* (Stanford: Stanford Univ. Press, 1994) 23.1e. References to Xunzi will be to this work following Knoblock's own section numbers, and after this will be parenthetical in the text.

9. I am indebted to P. J. Ivanhoe for calling this passage to my attention, and for other helpful comments.

10. Cf. *Mencius* 3A4.

11. *Leviathan*, ed. Michael Oakeshott (Oxford: Basil Blackwell, 1957) 83.

12. *Treatise of Human Nature*, ed. L. A. Selby-Bigge, 2nd ed. rev. P. H. Nidditch (Oxford: Clarendon Press, 1978) Book III, Part I, II, p. 472; Book III, Part III, I, p. 591; *Enquiry Concerning the Principles of Morals*, in *Enquiries*, ed. L. A. Selby-Bigge, 3rd ed. rev. P. H. Nidditch (Oxford: Clarendon Press, 1975) Sect. V, Part II 186, p. 229.

13. See Hume, *Enquiry Concerning the Principles of Morals*, Sect. V, Part II 183, p. 226; *Mencius* 2A6.

14. *Mencius* 6A8.

15. *Enquiry* Sect. V, Part II 184, p. 227; Sect. VII 205, p. 255.

16. See Martin L. Hoffman, "Interaction of Affect and Cognition in Empathy," in *Emotions, Cognition, and Behavior*, eds. Caroll E. Izard, Jerome Kagan, and Robert Zajonc (Cambridge: Cambridge Univ. Press, 1984).

17. *The Essential Piaget*, eds. Howard E. Gruber and J. Jacques Voneche (New York: Basic Books, 1977) 815.

18. Ibid. 816.

19. Ibid. xxv. As part of an ongoing attempt to undermine simple contrasts between major philosophers, let me point out the similarity of this result to the point of Mencius' joke (2A2) about the farmer who pulled at his plants to encourage their growth. Mencius may believe in an innate element of human nature, but he too—like Xunzi—is preoccupied with stages of ethical growth.

20. Søren Kierkegaard, *Concluding Unscientific Postscript*, trans. David F. Swenson and Walter Lowrie (Princeton: Princeton Univ. Press, 1941) 176-7.

21. Lawrence Kohlberg, Charles Levine, and Alexandra Hewer, *Moral Stages: A Current Formulation and a Response to Critics* (Basel: S. Karger, 1983) 36.

22. Ibid. 139.

23. See *Nicomachean Ethics* in *The Complete Works of Aristotle*, vol. 2, ed. Jonathan Barnes (Princeton: Princeton Univ. Press, 1984) Book X, 9, 1864-5.

24. This chapter does not go much into the topic of moral force, even though it clearly is important to Xunzi. There is a rich and interesting discussion of moral charisma, especially in relation to ritual efficacy, in T. C. Kline III, "Moral Agency and Motivation in the *Xunzi*," chapter seven in this volume.

25. *The Analects of Confucius*, trans. Arthur Waley (New York: Vintage Books, 1938) 8.8.

26. Mencius held that there are kinds of music that can be associated with benevolence. See 7A14.

27. See Stanley Milgram, *Obedience to Authority* (London: Tavistock, 1974); Craig Haney, Curtis Banks, and Philip Zimbardo, "Interpersonal Dynamics in a Simulated Prison," *International Journal of Criminology and Personology* 1 (1973), 69-97.

Five

Mengzi and Xunzi: Two Views of Human Agency

Bryan W. Van Norden

What do Mengzi (Mencius) 孟子 and Xunzi (Hsün Tzu) 荀子 disagree about? The simple answer, familiar to anyone who has taken even an introductory course in Chinese philosophy, is that Mengzi thinks human nature is good, while Xunzi thinks human nature is evil. But what is the "cash value" of this disagreement? What is the difference that makes a difference between claiming that human nature is good and claiming that it is evil? The noted translator of ancient Chinese philosophic works, D. C. Lau, has taken the line that there is no real difference of opinion between Mengzi and Xunzi on this point, because the two thinkers mean different things by the word 性 *xing* (which we commonly render by "nature" in English). Lau claims that, for Mengzi, the "nature" of something is primarily what is distinctive of it. Hence, what is definitive of the nature of humans are "the incipient moral tendencies in the human heart," since only people have these, as opposed to our desires for food, sex, etc., which we share with lower animals.[1] For Xunzi, on the other hand, the nature of something is what cannot be "learned or acquired by effort," what something is just by being the kind of thing it is.[2] According to Lau, Xunzi thinks this rules out our moral impulses as part of our nature, as these impulses must be self-consciously cultivated.[3] Hence, on this reading, Mengzi and Xunzi are simply speaking at cross-purposes.

A. C. Graham agrees with Lau that ". . . Xunzi[4] criticizes the doctrine of natural goodness from a definition of human nature which is not that of Mengzi, so that his objections although lucidly argued are not quite to the point. It is indeed far from easy to locate any issue of fact on which they disagree."[5] Another distinguished scholar, Donald Munro, is also at pains to point out the number of areas of agreement between Mengzi and Xunzi, and takes seriously the possibility that parts of

103

Xunzi's essay, "[Human] Nature is Evil," are not authentic.[6] Indeed, Munro goes as far as to say that one should be "extremely wary of attributing great significance to the notion of an evil human nature in any examination of the thought of Xunzi."[7]

Likewise, Antonio Cua, who has written extensively on Xunzi, asserts that ". . . Xunzi's remark that 'human nature is bad,' . . . is quite inadequate as it stands for distinguishing his view from that of Mengzi."[8] Specifically, Cua holds that "Xunzi's thesis is rooted in a picture of man as beset by a conflict of desires, whereas Mengzi's is a picture of man as a moral agent with inherent tendencies toward the fulfillment of moral excellence. . . . In this way, not only are their theses consistent with one another, they are also complementary in focusing upon two aspects of moral experience."[9] This downplaying of Xunzi's explicit stand on human nature is not confined to contemporary scholars. The Qing Dynasty commentator Wang Xianqian writes, "I say that the doctrine that [human] nature is evil is not Xunzi's fundamental idea."[10]

We must be grateful to these eminent scholars for highlighting the similarities between Mengzi and Xunzi. Furthermore, none of them suffers from the illusion that Mengzi and Xunzi have no points of difference.[11] But the received view is unsatisfying for the following reason. Xunzi thought that human nature was what humans have from birth, what we have without requiring any effort. Furthermore, it is the case either that Xunzi thought humans were born with at least incipient moral impulses or that he thought they were not born with incipient moral impulses. If Xunzi thought that humans were *not* born with incipient moral impulses, then he was right in thinking that he had a significant disagreement with Mengzi, because Mengzi insists that even "babes in arms" have incipient moral impulses.[12] On the other hand, if Xunzi agreed with Mengzi that humans are born with incipient moral impulses, then it is not clear why he thinks he disagrees with Mengzi at all. Even if Xunzi thinks that Mengzi is being too optimistic in declaring human nature (in Xunzi's sense) good, why does Xunzi not just say that human nature is morally neutral?

In this paper, I have a minimal and a maximal goal. My minimal goal is to convince the reader that Mengzi and Xunzi disagree over a significant thesis about human agency, and that this disagreement plays a crucial role in distinguishing their positions. My maximal goal is to convince the reader that this disagreement explains what Xunzi means by saying that human nature is evil, and what Mengzi means by saying that human nature is good. My main piece of evidence for thinking that Mengzi and Xunzi disagree about human agency is a comparison of two passages, *Mengzi* 6A10 and a section from Xunzi's "Essay on Rectifying Names" *Zhengming* 正名. Lau has argued that the latter passage turns on an ambiguity and hence is merely a fallacious argument,[13] but I shall argue that it is unambiguous and a clear attack on the sort of position Mengzi advocates in 6A10.

Now, to distinguish these positions from one another: Mengzi said that human nature was good, Mengzi's contemporary Gaozi held that human nature was morally neutral, and Xunzi claimed that human nature was evil. But the fundamental disagreement among the three seems to have been over issues of human agency. Hence, I suspect that this disagreement over human agency was what the discussion of human nature's goodness amounted to.[14] This is my more ambitious claim.

I. Graham's Interpretation

Before presenting my own interpretation, though, it behooves me to respond to the analysis offered by the redoubtable A. C. Graham.[15] Graham says that there are "three steps in [Mengzi's] argument" for the thesis that human nature is good. Graham never states what the logical relation is between these three "steps." For now, I shall treat them as three independent premises which are jointly sufficient to establish the intended conclusion (but see my comments at the end of this section).

Premise 1 is that "Moral inclinations . . . germinate spontaneously without having to be learned or worked for, they can be nourished, injured, starved, they develop if properly tended but their growth cannot be forced."[16] In other words, premise 1 is that moral inclinations are part of our nature. But, as Graham notes, this is not sufficient to establish that human nature is good, since there might be evil inclinations in human nature as well. Hence, Graham suggests that "[i]n order to find out the distinctive nature of a living thing one must discover the capacities which it realizes if uninjured and sufficiently nourished. In the case of man these include his term of life and the moral perfection of the sage, and it is above all the latter which distinguishes him from other species."[17] To use Graham's own analogy, we might say that the natural life span of a human is 70 years, in the sense that "[t]he possibility of living to 70 and not very much longer is inherent in the human constitution, and is one of the characteristics which distinguish man from the tortoise and the mayfly."[18] Premise 2, then, is that the possibility of becoming good is distinctive of human beings (as compared with other creatures). Nonetheless, we may ask: "Granted that [premise 1] the moral inclinations belong to our nature and are [premise 2] what distinguishes us from animals, are not the appetites which conflict with them natural as well?"[19] Graham rejects the suggestion (offered, as we saw above, by D. C. Lau) "that Mengzi eludes this difficulty by simply confining the scope of *xing* to the exclusively human."[20] Instead, Graham suggests that "[i]n making the stronger claim that human nature is good Mengzi implies . . . that it is *natural* to prefer the moral to other inclinations."[21] Graham expands this point, premise 3, as follows:

> Our natural inclinations, physical and moral, belong to one whole, within which we prefer the major to the minor [the same] as we judge between members of the body. . . . Consequently it is not a matter of fighting the bad in our nature in order to promote the good; when we reject the minor for the major desire we accord with our nature as a whole, just as by defending the shoulder rather than a finger we protect the body as a whole.[22]

Now, admittedly, Graham is not endorsing Mengzi's argument; he is merely explaining what he takes it to be.[23] But the position he attributes to Mengzi is notably uncompelling. Why is human nature good? Because "it is *natural* to prefer the moral to other inclinations."[24] But what does "natural" mean here? If it means, "in accordance with human nature," then the argument becomes, "Human nature is good because it is in accordance with human nature to be good." This is not a persuasive argument. Of course, Graham does not assert that "natural" does mean "in accordance with human nature" in this context, but if it does not, then we are in the dark about what it does mean.

It is also unclear what role premise 2 plays. Premise 2 asserts that the moral inclinations are what is distinctive of human beings as a species. Graham denies, however, that this is sufficient to establish that human nature is good, since Mengzi admits that "physical appetites belong to our nature" as well.[25] It seems, though, that premise 2 is also unnecessary for establishing the conclusion that human nature is good. The conclusion follows from premises 1 ("the moral inclinations are part of our nature") and 3 ("it is natural to prefer that part of our nature which is constituted by the moral inclinations") alone.

In short, although it is not impossible that the argument Graham devises is the one underlying Mengzi's position, the argument Graham attributes to Mengzi is embarrassingly weak. And although it is not Graham's fault if Mengzi's reasoning is weak, the principle of charity tells us to attribute a stronger position to Mengzi, if we can find one that is consistent with the textual evidence. I submit that the explanation of what Mengzi means by claiming that human nature is good, which I develop below, both (1) makes better sense out of some of Mengzi's explicit statements on human nature and human agency than does Graham's, and (2) does not attribute as weak an argument to Mengzi as does Graham's.

II. Preliminary Observations

Before proceeding, I will offer two preliminary comments about what I am attempting to do, in order to head off any possible misunderstandings. First, I am attempting to *explain* what Mengzi meant by claiming that human nature was good, what Gaozi meant by claiming that human nature was morally neutral, and what Xunzi meant by claiming that human nature was evil. Although I may occasionally suggest lines of defense for various claims which Mengzi and Xunzi advance, I am *not* primarily concerned in this paper with *defending* what these thinkers have said. It is, therefore, *not* an objection to anything I have written if it turns out, say, that Mengzi's view of human agency is wrong, or that Xunzi has not adequately addressed Mengzi's argument.

On the other hand, as the principle of charity states, if it turns out that there is another interpretation which explains the text of the *Mengzi* as well as mine does, and which attributes to the *Mengzi* a more persuasive position than the one I attribute to it, then (all else being equal) we should adopt this other interpretation. I am not aware, however, of any such interpretation.

Second, it is tempting to begin an inquiry such as ours by asking, "What do *we* mean by the claim that human nature is good?" and then try to locate in the *Mengzi* what seems to us to be a plausible answer. This is not the proper methodology, though. What we have to do is to find out how thinkers like Mengzi, Xunzi, and Gaozi used phrases like 性善 *xingshan*, 性惡 *xing'e*, 性無善無不善 *xing wushan wubushan*. It may turn out that their use of these phrases does not map very well onto our use of "human nature is good," "human nature is evil," and "human nature is morally neutral." But that serves only to remind us that these English phrases are no more than the closest English equivalents for the phrases in ancient Chinese.

III. Mengzi

So how does Mengzi use the phrase *xingshan* ("human nature is good")? Fortunately, Gongduzi asked him outright what he meant by this claim. Mengzi responded: "As for one's essence 情 *qing*, one can become good. This is what I mean by calling it good. As for becoming not good, that is not the fault of one's native endowment." (6A6)[26] This might strike us as a disappointing answer, for it seems to reduce the claim that human nature is good to the assertion that human beings, as part of their essence, are capable of becoming good. Why should Mengzi bother to assert that humans are capable of becoming good? Surely, no one would deny that? But in fact, Mengzi seems to have been deeply troubled by the problem of individuals who thought that some humans are incapable of becoming good. Witness the following quotations:

> People's having these four sprouts [of virtue] is like their having four limbs. One who has these four sprouts and says of himself that he is *unable* [sc. to be virtuous] is a thief of himself. One who says that his lord is *unable* [sc. to be virtuous] is a thief of his lord. (2A6)

> One who taxes one's lord to do what is [morally] demanding is called respectful. One who discourses on what is [morally] good and represses what is evil is called reverential. [One who says,] "My lord is *unable* [sc. to do what is morally demanding]" is called a thief. (4A1)

> One cannot work together with those who throw themselves away. . . . [Those who say,] "I myself am *unable* to dwell in benevolence and follow righteousness 義 *yi*," are said to throw themselves away. (4A11)

Consider also Mengzi's extended interaction with King Xuan of Qi. In 1A7, the lengthy and fascinating discussion begins with the King asking "Is one such as I *capable* of protecting the people?" Mengzi then attempts to prove that the King's spontaneous act of kindness to an ox being led to sacrifice shows that he is so capable. Likewise, in 1B5, Xuan suggests that his "passions" (likings for wealth and beauty) prevent him from putting into practice Mengzi's advice, but Mengzi argues that Xuan *is* capable of "kingly government" because these very passions can be put to the service of morality.

So the claim that humans are capable of becoming good, although it may sound trivial to us, was anything but trivial to Mengzi, since he seemed to think that he was awash in people who thought they really were incapable of becoming moral. Still, this cannot have been all Mengzi meant by the claim that human nature was good, because other thinkers (like Gaozi, whom we shall look at in more detail below) also thought that humans were capable of becoming good, but did not sub-

scribe to the *xingshan* doctrine.   What distinguished Mengzi's position
from others who thought that humans could become moral?
In order to answer this question, let us consider *Mengzi* 6A10:

> Fish is what I desire 欲 *yu*; bear's paw [a Chinese delicacy] is
> also what I desire.   If I cannot have both, I would select bear's
> paw and forsake fish. Life is what I desire; integrity is also what
> I desire.   If I cannot have both, I would select integrity and
> forsake life.   On the other hand, though life is what I desire,
> there is something I desire more than life.   Hence, I will not do
> anything just to obtain life.   On the other hand, though death is
> what I hate 惡 *wu*, there is something I hate more than death.
> Hence there are troubles I do not avoid.   If it were the case that
> someone desires nothing more than life, then how could one not
> use whatever means will obtain life for one?   If it were the case
> that someone hates nothing more than death, then how can one
> not do whatever will avoid trouble for one?   From this we can
> see that there are ways of obtaining life that one will not
> employ.   From this we can [also] see that there are things which
> would avoid calamity that one will not do.   Therefore, there are
> things one desires more than life and there are also things one
> hates more than death.   It is not the case that only the moral
> person has this heart.   All humans have it.   The moral person
> simply never loses it.

What exactly is Mengzi claiming here?   Consider the following
propositions:

1) Person A desires nothing more than life.
2) Person A hates nothing more than death.
3) Person A will choose life over anything else.
4) Person A will choose anything else over death.

It seems, then, that what Mengzi is arguing for in 6A10 is the claim that
(1) implies (3), and (2) implies (4).   In other words, Mengzi is asserting
a thesis about human agency, claiming that a human must seek that
which she desires the most.   So Mengzi is at pains to assert that every
human is capable of becoming moral, but he also holds that a human
must seek that which he desires the most.   Are these claims consistent?
What about a person whose strongest desires are selfish?   Is such a
person really capable of becoming good?   And if so, how?
    There is one family of ethical views according to which there is no
inconsistency between acting morally and acting on selfish desires.   We

might refer to these as the views of morality as enlightened self-interest. Hobbes seems to hold such a view. If Mengzi also holds such a view, then there is no inconsistency between his claim that every human is capable of becoming good, and his claim that a person must seek that which she desires the most. For on a view of morality as enlightened selfishness, the demands of morality and self-interest coincide. Herrlee Creel seems to attribute such a view to Mengzi, for he writes that "[w]hat Mengzi is preaching here is really a doctrine of enlightened selfishness—which is, of course, quite utilitarian."[27] And, indeed, there is textual evidence to support such an interpretation. Thus, in 7B25, we find a line which could be translated as "The good is the desirable."[28] Furthermore, in 1A7 Mengzi tries to persuade King Xuan to change his form of government on the grounds that "[t]o seek such things as you desire, by means of such methods as you employ, is like climbing a tree in search of a fish." In other words, Mengzi tells Xuan that he merely misperceives what will satisfy his desires and what is in his own interest.

As attractive and powerful as the "enlightened self-interest" reading is, however, it cannot be the whole story. For Mengzi holds that we must not only do the moral act, but do it with the right motivation. For example, in describing a spontaneous benevolent reaction in 2A6, Mengzi specifically rules out selfish motivations. He claims that anyone who sees a child about to fall into a well "would have a feeling of alarm and compassion—not because one sought to get in good with the child's parents, not because one wanted fame among one's neighbors and friends, and not because one would dislike the sound of [the child's] cries." Furthermore, in a number of other passages Mengzi distinguishes invidiously between genuine virtues and their *semblances* (2A3, 4B6, 4B16, 7B11), and where the *differentia* is made apparent, it seems to be that possession of the genuine virtues involves having the appropriate (non-selfish) motivation.

That Mengzi does not merely want us to follow our desires (whether enlightened or not) can be seen from 6A10 itself, for the passage continues:

> A basket of food and a bowl of soup – if one gets them then one will live; if one doesn't get them then one will die. [But] if they're given with contempt, then [even] a wayfarer will not accept them. If they're trampled upon, then [even] a beggar won't take them. [However,] when it comes to 10,000 bushels [of grain], then one doesn't notice ritual propriety and integrity and accepts them. What do 10,000 bushels add to me? [Do I

accept them] for the sake of a beautiful mansion? for the obedience of a wife and concubines? to have poor acquaintances be indebted to me? In the previous case, for the sake of one's own life one did not accept [what was offered]. In the current case, for the sake of a beautiful mansion one does it. In the previous case, for the sake of one's own life one did not accept [what was offered]. In the current case, for the obedience of a wife and concubine one does it. In the previous case, for the sake of one's own life one did not accept [what was offered]. In the current case, in order to have poor acquaintances be indebted to oneself one does it. Is this indeed something that one can't stop [doing]? This is what is called losing one's fundamental heart.

As I read this passage, Mengzi's point is that often one's desires are foolish, since one is willing to sacrifice integrity and propriety for "secondary" goods such as a nice house, although even a beggar would rather die than sacrifice integrity for as important a good as food.[29] Consequently, Mengzi holds that it makes sense to transform one's desires according to some moral standard. The moral person, then, is the one whose desires are always of the appropriate sort—that is, the one who never loses her "fundamental heart." Mengzi described his own project well, then, when he said, "I . . . desire to rectify people's hearts" (3B9).

So let us recapitulate. Mengzi holds that (1) every human being is capable of being virtuous and (2) every human being must do that which she believes will get for her what she most desires, but (3) virtue is not just enlightened self-interest, since it requires non-selfish motivation. Are these claims consistent? They are if either (a) all humans are virtuous already (and, hence, already have the right motivations) or (b) humans can alter their desires in some way so as to acquire the appropriate motivations. Mengzi does not hold (a); he is aware that some humans are vicious (6A7). Instead, as David S. Nivison has pointed out, Mengzi believes that humans are capable of, and responsible for, the management of their moral motivations.[30]

But how is it possible for people to alter their desires? The answer depends upon the fact that all humans have incipient moral impulses. Let us take another look at 2A6, where our philosopher asks us to perform the following thought experiment:

Suppose someone suddenly saw a child about to fall into a well: everyone [in such a situation] would have the heart [i.e., "feeling" 心 *xin*] of alarm and compassion—not because one sought to get in good with the child's parents, not because one wanted fame among one's neighbors and friends, and not because one would dislike the sound of [the child's] cries. From this we can see that if one is without the heart of compassion, one is not a human. If one is without the heart of disgust, one is not a human. If one is without the heart of deference, one is not a human. If one is without the heart of right and wrong, one is not a human. The heart of compassion is the sprout 端 *duan* of benevolence. The heart of disgust is the sprout of integrity. The heart of deference is the sprout of ritual propriety. The heart of right and wrong is the sprout of wisdom.

Hence, Mengzi ties each of his four cardinal virtues—benevolence, righteousness, ritual propriety, and wisdom—to innate but incipient moral senses (or "hearts"). In addition, he refers to these incipient moral hearts as "sprouts" *duan*. The use of this word is not a random rhetorical flourish. Mengzi has deliberately chosen an agricultural metaphor to stress the fact that the feelings begin only as incipient dispositions that must be carefully nurtured in order to reach maturity. How does one nurture these sprouts? According to Mengzi, one engages in an activity called "concentration" 思 *si*.[31] Thus, we find Mengzi saying, "Benevolence, integrity, ritual propriety, and wisdom are not welded on to me from without. I definitely have them. It's just that I haven't concentrated *si* upon them. Hence, it is said, 'Seek and you will get it. Abandon it and you will lose it.'" (6A6) Since *si* is obviously important for Mengzi, we would like to know more about what exactly this psychological act involves. Unfortunately, Mengzi does not use the term in its technical sense very often. In the *Mengzi*, *si* is used 16 times as part of a proper name. Of the 28 other occurrences of *si* in the text, there are 8 occurrences in which *si* clearly is a technical term of Mengzian psychology referring to the psychological act that I label "concentration": 4A1, 6A6, 6A13, 6A15 (four occurrences), and 6A17. Then there are two other occurrences in which *si* could refer to concentration, but it is hard to tell: 4A13 and 4B20.[32] None of these passages tells us very much about *si*. We would expect, however, that Mengzi's technical use of *si* is related to the standard non-technical uses of the word. Among its other uses, *si* can mean "to recall," "to long for," "to think fondly of," or "to think anxiously about."[33] Consequently, we can hazard a guess that to *si* the sprouts involves at least (1) an awareness that they exist within oneself, and (2) a concern for their nurturing.

The result of this process of concentrating is that one "extends" one's moral actions and reactions to more and more situations. Hence, in a discussion of benevolence, Mengzi writes, "That wherein the ancients greatly surpassed other people, was no other than the fact that they were good at extending 推 *tui* what they did" (1A7). Again, he states, "Humans all have things which they cannot bear. Extending 達 *da* it to what they can bear is benevolence. Humans all have some things that they will not do. Extending *da* it to what they will do is integrity." (7B31) Thinking back to 6A10, we recall that a beggar manifests his sprout of integrity in refusing to accept food contemptuously offered. But the person who compromises his principles in exchange for 10,000 bushels of grain has "lost" his heart of integrity, in the sense that it is not properly manifesting itself. By concentrating, one extends one's moral feelings, so that instead of just maintaining one's integrity in some things, such as not accepting food contemptuously offered, one maintains one's integrity in all situations.

Why should anyone undergo the process of self-cultivation necessary in order to become a sage? Mengzi's answer is that there are certain goods which accrue only to one who is genuinely benevolent. For example, for a ruler to win the loyalty of the people, reunify China, and enjoy stable government, it is a necessary (although apparently not sufficient) condition that he be benevolent. Thus, Mengzi writes: "If a lord be benevolent, no one [else] will fail to be benevolent. If a lord manifest integrity, no one [else] will fail to manifest integrity." (4B5) And Mengzi held that it is necessary for a ruler to inspire morality among his subordinates and the common people, for otherwise he could never be secure. If everyone is concerned solely with personal profit, then "those above and those below will contest with one another and the country will be in danger" (1A1). Furthermore, "If people put righteousness last and profit first, then they will not be satisfied without stealing. There has never been one who was benevolent who neglected one's parents. There has never been a righteous person who put one's lord last." (1A1)

Mengzi also thinks that the life of benevolence and integrity is intrinsically appealing. He makes the following comment, which is brief but profound:

> The desire to be esteemed is the common heart of humans. All humans have what is esteemed within themselves, they have not concentrated upon it [sc., their innate moral feeling], that is all.[34] The esteem given by humans is not true esteem. He whom Zhao Meng [a "kingmaker" in the state of Jin] esteems,

Zhao Meng can debase. The *Odes* say, "Already drunk with his wine, already satiated with his virtue." This means that being satisfied with benevolence and integrity, one does not covet the taste of others' fine food and grain; having a good reputation and broad praise accorded oneself, one does not covet the official rainments of others. (6A17)

Mengzi's point here, it seems to me, is a deep one. It is that humans are, intrinsically, evaluative animals. We are not just creatures who desire to satisfy our desires for food, sex, etc. We are creatures who desire to feel worthy, to be esteemed, to lead lives which have moral value.

Compare 1A7, in which Mengzi asks King Xuan what his greatest desire is, for which the king raises armies and wars with the other states. Mengzi suggests, as possibilities, that the king does not yet have enough fine foods to please his palate, enough warm clothing to wear, enough pretty things to look at, enough melodious music to hear, enough servants to get him what he wants. But the king denies that he does what he does for any of those reasons. Mengzi concludes that the king acts because he desires to subdue all the other statelets of China and reunify the country. I submit that it is deeply significant that the king's motivating desire is not any of the bodily desires. What the king wants is to be esteemed.[35]

Hence, whereas for Aristotle humans are "rational animals," for Mengzi humans are essentially "evaluative animals." There is a certain good, what we might call "moral esteem," which only the truly moral human can obtain. That is why one should undergo the course of self-cultivation outlined by Mengzi.

But now we are in a position to see a difficulty. The claim is that, for Mengzi, we must do what we most desire to do. This, however, does not limit Mengzi to a conception of morality as enlightened self-interest, for he also holds that humans intrinsically have "moral desires" as well. These moral desires are strengthened by the psychological act of concentration, and Mengzi offers explanations of why one ought to cultivate oneself via concentration. The problem, however, is that now we are led to wonder why it is, if Mengzi is right in what he says, that some people are persuaded by him and others are not.

This difficulty seems to have been felt by at least some of Mengzi's contemporaries, for one of his disciples asks him, "All of us are humans, but some of us become great humans, while some of us become petty humans. Why is this?" Mengzi responds, "Those who follow the greater part of themselves become great humans. Those who follow the lesser part of themselves become petty humans." His disciple persists by asking why some people follow the greater part of themselves while some follow the lesser part. Mengzi explains: "The faculties of hearing and sight do not concentrate *si* and are misled by external objects. Objects interact with other objects, so they just lead them [i.e., the senses] along. The faculty of the heart [on the other hand] concentrates. If you concentrate then you'll get it; if you don't concentrate then you won't get it." (6A15) This passage is interesting because it confirms the importance of concentration in Mengzi's picture of self-cultivation, but it fails as an altogether satisfactory answer to the question raised, since we may go on to ask why some people concentrate and others do not.[36]

Mengzi seems willing to say that to some extent, at least, our moral cultivation is the product of our environment. Thus, in 6A7, he writes: "In years of plenty, the young men are mostly good; in years of famine, the young men are mostly bad. It is not that the endowment which Heaven sends down is different. It is that which drowns their heart being so." Furthermore, in 6A8, Mengzi speaks of the 氣 *qi* of the night and morning as having the effect of restoring or preserving an individual's moral sense.[37]

Mengzi also seems to have the sense that some events are due to the opaque operations of Heaven and Destiny. When Duke Ping of Lu is dissuaded from going to pay a visit to Mengzi by his favorite Zang Cang, Mengzi comments: "When someone advances, something causes it. When someone stops, something prevents it. Advancing and stopping are not things which humans are capable of [sc., by themselves]. My not meeting the Marquis of Lu is due to Heaven. That son of the Zang clan, how could he cause me not to meet [the Marquis]?" (1B16) Elsewhere, Mengzi notes, "Nothing is not Destiny." (7A2).

To some, it may seem very unsatisfactory that Mengzi, insofar as he has an explanation, must attribute moral failure to Destiny or to environmental influences. We might be led by the standard translations of the *Mengzi* to believe that there was some third faculty in Mengzian psychology, distinct from the senses and the heart, which is responsible for moral success or failure. Specifically, the translations of D. C. Lau and James Legge render the Chinese word 志 *zhi* by the English word "will." The will seems tailor-made for the kind of problem we have found in Mengzi. Augustine was the first to apply the notion of will (or *voluntas* in Latin) to human beings, using it to designate a faculty that is responsible for the orientations of the cognitive and appetitive faculties. Whether cognition and appetition were directed toward things Heavenly or things mundane was the responsibility of the will. Now, the distinction between the senses and the heart in Mengzi is not the same as the distinction between cognition and appetition. But if *zhi*, like "will," designates some independent faculty, we might be encouraged to look for evidence that it is responsible for the relative dominance of the senses and the heart, and for whether or not the heart engages in concentration. I shall argue, however, that the *zhi* is not a distinct faculty at all, but is instead the heart *xin* when it is regarded as having a specific orientation. The translation of *zhi* I shall recommend is "intention."

Note that, in all of the *Mengzi*, the *zhi* is never spoken of as affecting the heart. This makes perfect sense if, as I suggest, the *zhi* just is the heart, thought of as having some intent or orientation. Furthermore, in one crucial passage, the *zhi* seems to be implicitly equated with the motion of the heart. Thus, in 2A2, Gongsun Chou asks Mengzi whether the *zhi* is always dominant over the *qi*, or whether the *qi* can also affect the *zhi*.[38] Mengzi responds: "The *zhi* when unified 壹 *yi*[39] moves the *qi*. The *qi* when unified moves the *zhi*. Now, stumbling and running, this is [a matter of] *qi*, but nonetheless it moves the heart." Here, Mengzi begins by discussing the mutual influence of the *zhi* and the *qi*, and then illustrates what he means by citing the influence of the *qi* on the heart. Again, this makes perfectly good sense if the *zhi* is just the heart, considered under a certain aspect.

Furthermore, translations using "intention" for *zhi* seem to yield sensible English equivalents. Consider some examples. In 2B14, the ever-impertinent Gongsun Chou asks why Mengzi stayed in the state of Qi despite his failure to persuade the King there. Mengzi responds, "It was my *intention* to leave," but explains that the military situation prevented him from acting on his intention. In 6B4, Mengzi discovers that Song Keng is about to attempt to dissuade the kings of Qin and Qu from fighting a war by appealing to the unprofitability of war. So Mengzi tells him, "Your *intention* is grand, but your advice is unacceptable."

To summarize, Mengzi claims that (1) all humans are capable of becoming good. But he is also committed to a thesis about human agency, to the effect that (2) humans must do that which they believe will obtain for them what they most desire. In addition, Mengzi holds that (3) genuinely virtuous acts cannot be motivated by selfish desires. Since Mengzi admits that (4) not everyone is already virtuous, the doctrine of the "four sprouts" takes on immense significance. For given (2), (3), and (4), thesis (1) is true only if non-virtuous humans are capable of altering their current desires in some way. Mengzi's explanation for how we can alter our desires is that (5) all humans have incipient virtuous dispositions which they are capable of bringing into play via a psychological act labeled "concentration." Thesis (5), then, explains how (1), (2), (3), and (4) can all be true.

Which thesis (or theses) is to be identified with Mengzi's slogan that "human nature is good"? Judging from 6A6, Mengzi most closely identified his slogan with thesis (1). Thesis (1), however, does not distinguish Mengzi's position from that of many of his contemporaries (such as Gaozi).[40] My guess is that Mengzi saw the five theses as closely related and did not carefully distinguish between them in his own mind. As we have seen, all of them are important to Mengzi's position.

IV. "Rectifying Names"

Compare now *Mengzi* 6A10 with the following passage from Xunzi's "Essay on Rectifying Names":

> Desires do not await being satisfiable, but what is sought follows upon what is approved of 所可 *suoke*. That desires do not await being satisfiable is what is received from Heaven. That what is sought follows upon what is approved of is received from the heart *xin*. . . .
>
> Of the things which a person desires *yu*, life *is* foremost. Of the things which a person hates *wu*, death *is* foremost.[41] Nonetheless, there are those who abandon life and follow death—not because they don't desire life and desire death, but [because] it is improper 不可以 *bukeyi* to live but proper 可以 *keyi* to die. Hence, if the desires exceed it [the proper standard] but the actions don't go that far, this is the heart restraining it. If that which the heart approves hits the mark of principle, then although the desires are numerous, how is this harmful to governing? If the desires don't go that far but the actions exceed it [the proper standard], this is the heart commanding it. If that which the heart approves of misses the mark of principle, then although the desires are few, how can it stop even at chaos?
>
> Hence, order and chaos reside in that which the heart approves of. They are not in that which the essence desires. If you do not seek them [order and chaos] where they are, but seek them where they are not, although you say, "I've found them!"—you've lost them.[42]

The phrasing at the beginning of this passage is too close to that of *Mengzi* 6A10 to be a coincidence. Xunzi is explicitly denying what

Mengzi had asserted in 6A10, and he is doing that by drawing a distinction between what one "desires" *yu* and what one "approves of" *ke*. Whereas Mengzi had claimed that a human must seek that which she desires the most, Xunzi asserts that a person's actions are determined, not by what he desires, but by what he approves of.[43]

In order to see what Xunzi is getting at, let us focus on the following line: "If that which the heart approves of misses the mark of principle then although the desires are few, how can it stop even at chaos?" A contemporary example of what Xunzi has in mind might be the case of a man in our society who is promiscuous, not because he wants casual sex per se, but because there is a "macho" ideal of a promiscuous man which he happens to *ke*. It is not, Xunzi would say, that this man's desires are out of control. Rather, it is that he "approves of" a bad ideal of masculinity. Phrased in Freudian terms, Xunzi's point is that bad behavior can just as easily be the result of a misguided superego, as of an id run amok. Another example would be the bulimic, who does not desire to binge-eat and induce vomiting, but who does so because she *ke*'s an ideal of emaciated, thin women.

The other side of the coin is a bit trickier, though. For Xunzi asks, "If that which the heart approves hits the mark of principle, then although the desires are numerous, how is this harmful to governing?" I say that this is trickier, for we may doubt the quality of a society in which people have numerous antisocial desires which they only manage to suppress.[44] But Xunzi's position is deeper than this, for he (like Mengzi) holds that there are stages along one's path toward perfect moral cultivation.

> (1) He who acts from a love of the model is a scholar. (2) He who embodies it with a firm sense of purpose is a gentleman. (3) He who has an understanding of it that is acute without limit is a sage. (1') If a man lacks the model, he acts with rash and aimless confusion. (2') If he possesses the model, but has no recognition of what is congruent with it, he nervously looks about, anxiously wondering what to do. (3') Only after he has come to rely on the model and then gone on to penetrate deeply into its application through analogical extension to other categories and types of things does he act with gentle warmth and calm confidence.[45]

Interestingly, Xunzi's levels of self-cultivation seem to correspond (at least roughly) to those of Aristotle (as reconstructed by M. F. Burnyeat). We must begin by cultivating a love for what is noble. But Aristotle's beginner (like Xunzi's "scholar") will not yet succeed in being steadfastly noble: "He wants to do noble things but sometimes does things that are disgraceful, ignoble . . ."[46] Eventually, however, one comes to do consistently what is noble,[47] and has become the sort of person who "already wants and enjoys virtuous action and needs to see this aspect of his life in a deeper perspective."[48] After having gained this deeper perspective (either by studying the *Nicomachean Ethics* or by reading Xunzi's essays) one has reached the highest level of moral development (which Xunzi labels the "sage," and Aristotle calls the man of practical wisdom.[49]

Xunzi (again like Mengzi) also holds that at the highest level of moral development, one no longer has any desire to do what is evil. He writes: "[the noble] makes his eyes be without desire to see what is not correct. He makes his ears be without desire to hear what is not correct. He makes his mouth be without desire to speak what is not correct. He makes his heart be without desire to ponder what is not correct."[50] What the "Rectifying Names" passage shows us, however, is that Xunzi differs from Mengzi in that Xunzi claims that the process of self-cultivation begins with our self-consciously overriding our desires, when they would lead us to do evil.

> Now it is the nature of man that when he is hungry he will desire satisfaction, when he is cold he will desire warmth, and when he is weary he will desire rest. This is his emotional nature. And yet a man, although he is hungry, will not dare to be the first to eat if he is in the presence of his elders, because he knows that he should yield to them, and although he is weary, he will not dare to demand rest because he knows that he should relieve others of the burden of labor.[51]

Furthermore, Xunzi claims that every human is capable of doing this, because (contrary to what Mengzi had thought) a person does, not what she most desires to do, but what she approves of.

But what makes someone approve of a course of action? And what does Xunzi believe one ought to approve of? Reading in isolation from the rest of Xunzi's writings, one is tempted to give a "conventionalist" reading of Xunzi's "Essay on Rectifying Names." Chad Hansen apparently subscribes to such an interpretation. Focusing on Xunzi's attitude toward the adoption of a linguistic scheme, Hansen reads Xunzi as claiming that

> . . . the sage provides a single model which can coordinate and harmonize the way people make evaluative distinctions,

cultivate attitudes, make choices, and act. The objection to [the] nontraditional use of names is not simply that they are wrong, but that they confuse, complicate, and disorder the society. Implicitly, the argument seems to allow that *any* way of assigning names that was universally adopted (and met survival and effectiveness criteria) would be acceptable.

Confucian and Burkian traditionalism have in common this appeal to an argument from anarchy. They do not claim that the traditional values are rationally justified, but that messing with it [sic] will create chaos.[52]

Hansen carries his conventionalist interpretation to the point where he makes the startling claim that, according to Xunzi, ". . . the assertability[53] of an utterance (a judgment or distinction) was only a function of community acceptance."[54]

But Xunzi writes, "The noble makes clear [the nature of] music. This is his Virtue. [But] a chaotic age hates what is good and does not listen to him. Alas!"[55] The very notions of "a chaotic age" and of someone who was both ethically exemplary (i.e., a noble) and at odds with his age would not make any sense if Hansen were correct in claiming that approval is solely a function of community acceptance. How can an age be chaotic if what is good is determined simply by what the age approves of? How can an individual be virtuous but at odds with his age if virtue is just what the age says that it is?

As attractive as a conventionalist reading might be in some ways, numerous passages in the *Xunzi* demonstrate that this philosopher is an objectivist and "monist" about ritual, music, the Way, and at least some aspects of language use.[56]

In the world there are not two Ways. The sage is not of two minds.[57]

Through rites Heaven and earth join in harmony, the sun and the moon shine, the four seasons proceed in order, the stars and constellations march, the rivers flow, and all things flourish. . . . When they [i.e., the rites] are properly established and brought to the peak of perfection, no one in the world can add to or detract from them.[58]

Music is unalterable harmonies. The rites are unexchangeable patterns.[59]

The Way is the proper standard for past and present.[60]

That which everyone in the world, past and present, calls "good," is that which is correct, well-patterned, peaceful, and well-ordered. That which they call "evil" is prejudiced, dangerous, perverse, and chaotic.[61]

But how do we reconcile Xunzi's belief that the rites, ethics, and (in general) the Way of the sage kings are inventions, with these seemingly objectivistic remarks? The answer is simple.[62] Xunzi does hold that the Way had to be invented, but he also holds (rather naively) that the Way of the sage kings is the uniquely optimal way for structuring a society. Xunzi holds that this particular Way is the *one* that does best the many things which such schemes are supposed to do: making clear hierarchical distinctions, retraining and providing expression for human desires and emotions, and, in general, creating and maintaining social order.[63]

Note that among the purposes I list for ritual is the retraining of desires. As some of the passages we looked at above show, Xunzi clearly thought that an essential part of self-cultivation was the sublimating of old desires and the acquisition of new desires. But why should one seek to alter recalcitrant desires and acquire new ones? Why bother to undergo the process of self-transformation? Xunzi holds that, on balance, the Confucian way is the most profitable: "To follow the [Confucian] Way is like exchanging one thing for two. How could it be a loss? To depart from the Way and choose subjectively by oneself, however, is like exchanging two for one. How could it be a gain? To exchange the accumulated [satisfaction of the] desires of a hundred years [of life] for one moment of contentment—in such a case to act so, is not to understand arithmetic."[64] But why is the Confucian way so profitable? The surprisingly Hobbesian answer Xunzi gives is that everyone would be worse off without ritual:

What is the origin of ritual? I reply: man is born with desires. If his desires are not satisfied, he cannot but seek to satisfy them. If there is no measure or limit to his seeking, then he will be unable not to fight [with others]. From fighting comes disorder and from disorder comes poverty. The former kings hated such disorder, and therefore they established ritual and righteousness in order to establish [social] divisions, in order to cultivate peoples' desires, and to provide for what people sought. They brought it about that desires were never lacking in regard to their objects, and that the objects [of desire] were never exhausted by desires. [Thus] these two [i.e., desires and their objects] support each other and flourish. This is the origin of the rites. Hence, the rites are for cultivation.[65]

Xunzi differs on several counts from Hobbes, however. First, as we have seen, Xunzi is an objectivist about values. The practices of the ancient sage kings are, Xunzi holds, uniquely optimal for producing social organizations which are "correct, well-patterned, peaceful, and well-ordered." And it is just these properties that are definitive of a social order's being "good." Hobbes, on the other hand, claims that ". . . whatsoever is the object of any man's Appetite or Desire; that is it, which he for his part calleth *Good*: And the object of his Hate, and Aversion, *Evill*. . . ."[66] Second, Hobbes nowhere advises us (as does Xunzi) that a transformation of our desires is needed and, consequently, does not give us advice (as does Xunzi) about the proper program for self-cultivation. Third, Hobbes holds (again contra Xunzi) that we are not capable of acting against our desires, as is evident from his definition of "Will" as simply "the last Appetite in Deliberating."[67]

The main difference, then, between the ethical philosophies of Xunzi and Mengzi is in the details of their programs of self-cultivation. Mengzi, as we have seen, holds that self-cultivation occurs via concentrating upon, and thereby strengthening, one's innate moral dispositions. Xunzi denies that humans have innate moral desires, and, consequently, assigns no role to them in self-cultivation. Rather, he thinks that we must submit ourselves to the discipline of ritual practice, and to the transforming effect of a good teacher, so that we gradually come to love ritual practice (and hence, virtue) in itself. Thus, Xunzi writes: "Where does learning begin and where does it end? I say that as to program, learning begins with the recitation of the Classics and ends with the reading of the ritual texts; and as to objective, it begins with learning to be a man of breeding, and ends with learning to be a sage."[68] And lest one think that rote learning is enough to reach real understanding, Xunzi adds:

> In learning, nothing is more profitable than to associate with those who are learned. Ritual and music present us with models but no explanations; the *Odes* 詩 and *Documents* 書 deal with ancient matters and are not always pertinent; the *Spring and Autumn Annals* 春秋 is terse and cannot be quickly understood. But if you make use of the erudition of others and the explanations of gentlemen, then you will become honored and may make your way anywhere in the world. Therefore I say that in learning nothing is more profitable than to associate with

those who are learned, and of the roads to learning, none is quicker than to love such men. Second only to this is to honor ritual. If you are first of all unable to love such men and secondly are incapable of honoring ritual, then you will only be learning a mass of jumbled facts, blindly following the *Odes* and *Documents* and nothing more.[69]

It is through ritual that the individual is rectified. It is by means of a teacher that ritual is rectified. If there were no ritual, how could the individual be rectified? If there were no teachers, how could you know which ritual is correct?[70]

To summarize, for Xunzi, the process of self-cultivation begins with performance of ritual activities which one does not yet delight in, and in the study of ritual, literary, and historical texts which one cannot yet appreciate or fully understand. Through determined and prolonged effort, one eventually comes to delight in the ritual practices for their own sakes, and to understand and appreciate the canonical texts. According to Xunzi, one must be *trained* to delight in ritual and morality. In contrast, for Mengzi, one begins the process of self-cultivation by performing moral acts and by taking part in ritual practices *which one delights in even from the start*. Mengzi explicitly holds that because one delights in the performance of these acts, the virtues of which they are the expression "grow" (4A27). Furthermore, as Mengzi suggests using the "man from Song" parable (2A2), to attempt to perform ritual or moral acts for which one does not yet have the appropriate motivation is positively detrimental to moral development. Consequently, for Mengzi, the rituals of the Zhou are the expression and product of our moral impulses. For Xunzi, on the other hand, rituals are the cause of the development of moral impulses in human beings.

Hence, Mengzi seems to de-emphasize slightly the importance of ritual and tradition. Xunzi notes this de-emphasis and criticizes Mengzi for it, for one of the distinguishing features of Confucianism had been its insistence upon the importance of learning the ritual and historical texts: "If the nature of man were good, we could dispense with sage kings and forget about ritual principles. But if it is evil, then we must go along with the sage kings and honor ritual principles."[71] Xunzi also asks the rhetorical question, if Mengzi is right about human nature, "then what reason is there to pay any particular honor to [the sage kings] Yao, Yu, or the gentleman?"[72]

We might raise an objection here to Xunzi's attack on Mengzi.[73] Mengzi says that one does good because one desires to do good. Xunzi says that one does good because one "approves of" doing good. Is this disagreement anything other than terminological? Xunzi does not explicitly address this issue. Furthermore, it is crucial to bear in mind that my aim in this paper is to explicate Xunzi, not to defend him. It is enough for my purposes that Xunzi *thought* there was a crucial distinction to be drawn between *yu* and *ke*. The passage I quoted at the beginning of this section (from "Rectifying Names") demonstrates conclusively that Xunzi *did* want to draw such a distinction. It is interesting, however, to speculate on what Xunzi might have said had someone offered the objection that there is no real distinction between the psychological states which I have labeled "desire" and "approval."

The first reason for thinking that approval is distinct from desire is that the two do not seem to be commensurable.[74] They are not to be weighted one against the other. As Xunzi makes clear,[75] no amount of desire can override approval. Approval simply trumps desire.

The second feature distinguishing Xunzi's "approval" from Mengzi's "desire" has to do with the enjoyment of moral acts. As we have seen, both thinkers agree that the sage delights in doing what is good. Mengzi, however, associates enjoyment with following one's moral desires in the early stages of cultivation: "When one delights in them [sc. benevolence and integrity] they grow" (4A27). Xunzi mentions no such delight associated with approval in the early stages of cultivation.

Finally, we can distinguish approval from desire based on the phenomenological differences between the two states. In other words, it seems simply to feel different to be in the two states. This is a highly speculative claim, since trying to surmise what individuals from an ancient culture may have felt is risky. But perhaps the distinction I draw will seem compelling. Consider the phenomenological difference between feeling morally compelled to perform (or refrain from performing) some action,[76] and performing (or refraining from performing) some action in order to satisfy some desire. For example, consider having to give a bad grade to a hard-working and sincere but untalented student. Here, a feeling of compulsion to perform the act because it is proper to one's role seems far easier to muster than a desire to do it, even if one knows it is the right thing to do. Contrast this with spending extra time with one's daughter to help her on a school project. In this case one simply and wholeheartedly desires to help her. This is not to deny that the sense of appropriateness and compulsion cannot coexist with positive desires. Indeed, Xunzi thinks that they do coexist in the sage. Still, the phenomenological difference is brought out best in cases where only one of the two mental states is present.[77]

V. Xunzi versus Gaozi

In "Rectifying Names," then, Xunzi denies the thesis about human agency that Mengzi had asserted in 6A10. Consequently, Xunzi is not required (as is Mengzi) to attribute to human beings incipient moral impulses in order to explain how moral behavior is possible. And, in fact, Xunzi neither mentions any such incipient impulses nor does he assign any role to them in human moral cultivation. So we see that Xunzi wishes to distance himself from Mengzi on this point. But why does this lead Xunzi to assert that human nature is evil? Why does Xunzi not say only that human nature is morally neutral?

It would be clear why human nature is evil for Xunzi, if he held that we have a natural taste for evil, per se. We find such a doctrine in some versions of Christianity—Augustine and Aquinas both seem to hold that humans are, at least in some circumstances, capable of evil for evil's sake.[78] But Xunzi never, to my knowledge, advocates such a position.

One possible interpretation stems from the fact that Xunzi thinks our natural desires, if pursued unreservedly, would lead us to do evil. Perhaps Xunzi's position, then, is that human nature is evil in a derivative sense, in that the desires which make up our nature, if uncultivated, will make us do evil as a means of satisfying them.[79] But this answer is not entirely satisfactory, for (as we saw) Mengzi was also a self-cultivationist and would agree with Xunzi that we must transform ourselves before we can become fully moral. Mengzi and Xunzi agree that life in a society of uncultivated individuals would be "nasty, brutish, and short."

I think we can gain some insight into why Xunzi wished to insist that human nature is evil if we look at a series of passages in which Mengzi argues against a contemporary named Gaozi, who held the view that human nature is intrinsically morally neutral. We know little if anything about Gaozi besides what we read in the *Mengzi*, unless as David Nivison suggests this is the same Gaozi mentioned briefly in chapter 48 *Gongmeng* 公孟 of the *Mozi* 墨子.[80] (But more about this later.) The exchange between Gaozi and Mengzi is fascinating and complex. Here I can only summarize the major issues which arise. Gaozi certainly assented to at least the following doctrines: (1) Intrinsically, human nature is neither good nor evil.[81] (2) Human nature is characterized primarily by our desires for such things as food and sex.[82]

(3) Humans are made good or evil by the influence of their environment, analogously to the way in which cups and bowls can be carved out of wood.[83]

There are several other issues on which it is difficult to determine Gaozi's position. One passage suggests that Gaozi thought human nature itself is always morally neutral, regardless of whether the possessors of that nature are themselves good or evil.[84] But another passage suggests that, according to Gaozi, although there is no inherent tendency in human nature toward good or evil, our natures can be molded by the environment so that they become either good or evil.[85] Also unclear are: (1) whether Gaozi held that human nature is to be distinguished at all from that of other animals,[86] and (2) whether Gaozi thinks that feelings of kinship for close relatives are also a part of human nature.[87] But, fortunately, such details are not crucial to our purpose here.

What is important is that the positions of Gaozi and Xunzi seem to have much in common: Gaozi (like Xunzi) held that human nature is characterized primarily by our desires, and (again like Xunzi) he uses metaphors of molding raw material to describe the effect of morality upon human nature.[88] Why, then, does Xunzi not simply agree with Gaozi in saying that human nature is morally neutral?

An answer to this question is suggested by one passage in the *Mengzi* and by a historical hypothesis suggested by David Nivison. The *Mengzi* passage is 2A2, and in it Mengzi criticizes Gaozi. Interspersed with the criticisms of Gaozi is the claim that we become moral via a gradual process of "accumulating righteousness," rather than through "random" acts of righteousness. In addition, Mengzi tells us that, in cultivating our sprouts of virtue, we must not be like the "farmer from Song." The farmer from Song was said to have pulled on his stalks of grain in an effort to make them grow faster, succeeding only in ripping out their roots. The point of the analogy evidently is that we can do more harm than good by trying to force our moral development to move faster than is possible.

This suggests that one of Mengzi's criticisms of Gaozi was that the latter was too much of a "voluntarist" in ethics. That is, Gaozi may have held that all that is required in order to become moral is a simple act of choice on one's part. Mengzi, in contrast, being a self-cultivationist, held that we must gradually grow to become fully moral humans. This interpretation is supported by David Nivison's suggestion that the Gaozi we meet in the *Mengzi* is the same one mentioned briefly in part of the Mohist writings. The Mohists were, as

Nivison observes, voluntarists themselves, who wished to dispense with what they saw as the wasteful and useless process of self-cultivation that the Confucians advocated. So if Gaozi were a Mohist or Mohist schismatic, it would fit that he too should be a voluntarist.

If this hypothesis is correct, then we can see how Xunzi's position differs from that of Gaozi—for Xunzi was committed, as are all Confucians, to gradual self-cultivation as the only way to become moral. And this also explains, I think, why Xunzi found it necessary to say that human nature is evil, and not just morally neutral. Xunzi thought, contra Mengzi, that our innate feelings cannot be relied upon as the primary means for moral cultivation. Hence, he denied that human nature is good in the Mengzian sense. Furthermore, he repudiated the voluntarism of Gaozi, holding that more than a simple act of choice is needed in order to become moral. We must, Xunzi claimed, engage in the moral equivalent of war against our desires, and submerge ourselves in ritual (under the guidance of a good teacher), for a large part of our lives, before we will truly be fully moral. Had Xunzi stated that human nature is morally neutral, given the background of the debate between Mengzi and Gaozi, the claim would have been understood by Xunzi's contemporaries as an endorsement of Gaozian voluntarism. Hence, Xunzi denied that human nature is morally neutral in the Gaozian sense.

VI. Conclusion

So we see that the positions of Mengzi and Xunzi (and, in fact, Gaozi) in regard to human nature are predicated upon more fundamental claims about human agency. Mengzi held that we must do that which will obtain for us what we most desire. Furthermore, according to Mengzi, genuinely virtuous behavior requires non-selfish motivation. Consequently, in order for it to be the case that any human is capable of being virtuous, it must be the case that all humans are capable of acting out of virtuous motivations. Mengzi's explanation for why this is possible is that every human has incipient virtuous inclinations, which can be strengthened through use. Hence, even the most reprobate human is capable of performing at least some virtuous acts from virtuous motives. Mengzi uses the slogan "human nature is good" to label his views.

In the "Essay on Rectifying Names," Xunzi denies Mengzi's thesis about human agency. Humans do not, according to Xunzi, have to do what they most desire to do. And in fact, overriding one's desires via "approval" is the first stage along the road of self-cultivation.

Ultimately, the goal of self-cultivation is to have what we approve of be congruent with what Confucian morality directs, and to have our desires congruent with what we approve of. But the beginner in moral cultivation (like Aristotle's "continent" person) is capable of making herself do what she does not yet desire to do.

I think the thesis of this paper is of more than antiquarian interest. If I am right, the disagreement between Mengzi and Xunzi turns out to center on an issue in action theory. Mengzi and Xunzi, then, take opposing sides on a controversial topic in contemporary philosophy, yet their overall systems are unique and possess elements different from any alternatives in the current debate. My own opinion is that Xunzi is correct in claiming that humans can choose to do other than what they most desire to do. At the same time, I submit that Mengzi has something important to say about the resources for self-cultivation offered by our innate desires. But the defense of these claims I must reserve for a future paper.[89]

Notes

1. D. C. Lau, *Mencius* (New York: Penguin Books, 1970) 21.

2. Burton Watson, trans., *Hsün Tzu: Basic Writings* (New York: Columbia Univ. Press, 1963) 158.

3. Lau 21.

4. Graham uses the spellings "Hsün Tzu" and "Mencius," but my practice in this paper will be to convert all romanization into Pinyin (except for romanized spellings occurring in titles of works in English) to make life easier for readers who are not Sinologists.

5. A. C. Graham, *Disputers of the Tao* (La Salle, Ill.: Open Court, 1989) 250. I discuss Graham's interpretation at more length below.

6. Donald Munro, *The Concept of Man in Early China* (Stanford: Stanford Univ. Press, 1969) 77.

7. Ibid. 77-78.

8. Antonio Cua, "The Conceptual Aspect of Hsün Tzu's Philosophy of Human Nature," *PEW* 27 (1977), 374.

9. Antonio Cua, "The Quasi-Empirical Aspect of Hsün Tzu's Philosophy of Human Nature," *PEW* 28 (1978), 15.

10. See the Preface to his *Xunzijijie* 荀子集解, in *Sibubeiyao* 四部備要, hereafter *SBBY*.

11. See especially Lau 21-22; Graham 251; Munro 78; and Cua (1978) 12 ff.

12. *Mengzi* 7A15.

13. D. C. Lau, "Theories of Human Nature in *Mencius* and *Xunzi*," chapter nine in this volume, n. 43.

14. In approaching the issue in this way, I shall differ from the usual (and seemingly sensible) practice of focusing on Xunzi's essay "[Human] Nature Is Evil."

15. I will use the account offered in *Disputers of the Tao*, rather than the one in "The Background of the Mencian Theory of Human Nature," since the former is later and hence, presumably, represents Graham's most carefully developed account.

16. *Disputers* 125.

17. Ibid. 129.

18. Ibid. 128.

19. Ibid. 129.

20. Ibid.

21. Ibid. 130. Emphasis mine.

22. Ibid. 131.

23. And I will insist that the distinction between explaining a thinker's views and endorsing them be observed in evaluating my own analysis. See below, part II.

24. *Disputers* 130.

25. Ibid. 129.

26. All translations are my own unless otherwise noted. Other translations I have consulted include Lau, *Mencius*; James Legge, *The Works of Mencius* (New York: Dover Books, 1970); Yang Bojun 陽伯峻, *Mengzi yizhu* 孟子議譯注 (北京: 中華書局, 1984); Yang Yong, *Mengzi yijie* (Xianggang: Dazhong Shuju, 1970); and Uchino Kumaichir 內野熊一郎, *Moshi*, vol. 4 of *Shinshaku Kambun Taikei* 新釋漢文大系 (Tokyo: Meiji Shoin, 1962). In addition, I have examined the commentaries of Zhao Qi 趙岐 (*Mengzi zhaozhu* 孟子趙注, SBBY) and Zhu Xi 朱熹 (*Mengzi sishu jizhu* 孟子四書集注, SBBY). Section numbering follows that in *A Concordance to the* Mengzi 孟子逐字索引, ed. D. C. Lau and Fong ching Chen, ICS series (Hong Kong: The Commercial Press, 1994).

27. Herrlee Creel, *Chinese Thought from Confucius to Mao Tse-tung* (Chicago: Univ. of Chicago Press, 1953) 87.

28. The Chinese is 可欲之謂善 *keyu zhi weishan*. Antonio Cua reads the line, "What ought to be desired is the good." See his *Ethical Argumentation* (Honolulu: Univ. of Hawaii Press, 1985) 191, n. 61.

29. Mengzi has surely overstated his case here. We know that people will often debase themselves in order to preserve their lives. It is also true, however, that even the most desperate people often have a sense of pride. I have encountered street people who insist on giving me a ragged magazine that they have scrounged from a trash bin in exchange for the coffee I have offered them—just to preserve the illusion that they are not beggars. And Mengzi is surely right that people who kowtow to their employers often show less integrity than such homeless people.

30. See "Two Roots or One?" in *The Ways of Confucianism: Investigations in Chinese Philosophy*, Bryan W. Van Norden, ed. (Chicago: Open Court, 1996) 133-48; and "Motivation and Moral Action in Mencius," Ibid., 91-120.

31. On my translation of 思 *si*, compare Arthur Waley, *The Analects of Confucius* (London: George Allen and Unwin, 1956) 44-46.

32. I am not inclined to put much weight on 4A13 in any event, because I suspect that it is an interpolation. Note that it appears, not attributed to Mengzi, in the *Zhongyong* 中庸 and the *Kongzijiayu* 孔子家語.

33. On these uses, compare 7B37 (two occurrences) and 5A2. This is not an exhaustive list of the uses of *si*.

34. The Chinese of this line is, 弗思耳矣 *fusi eryi*. Most translators (cf. Lau, Legge, Yang Bojun) give this the sense of, "It just never dawned on them." But given that *si* is a technical term for Mengzi, referring to the intellectual process by which we "extend" our sprouts, the translation I give is more likely to be correct.

35. Mengzi's view of humans as essentially evaluative animals sharply contrasts with that of his contemporary, Zhuangzi 莊子. Zhuangzi held that the best human life is one in which we attempt to escape the "trap" of evaluative distinctions. To make evaluative distinctions, Zhuangzi held, was to become attached to the world, and thereby to expose oneself to the danger of loss.

36. As James Legge noted long ago. See Legge 418, n. 15.

37. What is *qi*? This topic deserves a paper of its own. Suffice to say for now that it has many meanings in ancient China. The *qi* was originally the mist that arose from heated sacrificial offerings. Later, it came to refer to breath, wind, and—more esoterically—the *qi* was some sort of vital fluid in the body associated with emotional states, as well as some primal material out of which things such as the stars came to exist. For more on *qi*, see "The Early History of Yin-Yang and the Five Phases," the appendix to A. C. Graham's *Ying-Yang and the Nature of Correlative Thinking* (Singapore: Institute of East Asian Philosophies, 1986) 70-92, passim.

38. See note 37 above on the many meanings of *qi* in early China.

39. The use of *yi* here is notoriously puzzling. Lau and Jeffrey Riegel

follow Zhao Qi's gloss, according to which *yi* means blocked. See Riegel's "Reflections on an Unmoved Mind: An Analysis of *Mencius* 2A2," *JAAR* (Thematic Issue) 47 (1980) 454, n. 29; and Lau's "Some Notes on the *Mencius*," *Asia Major*, n.s., 15 (1969) 72, n. 8. But *yi* seems to have often been used in connection with psychological terms like *zhi* and *qi* to mean something other than "blocked." Consider *Zhuangzi, Renjianshi* 人閒世, where we find the imperative "Unify your intention *zhi*!" Riegel states that a translation such as mine is "literal but difficult to comprehend in the context." But I suggest that for the *zhi* to be unified is simply for it to be firmly focused on some object.

40. For more on Gaozi, see part V below.

41. Corresponding to the emphasis in the translation is the emphatic final particle 矣 *yi* in the Chinese.

42. 荀子: 正名 22/111/6-12. I have consulted the translations of Burton Watson, n. 2 above; Homer Dubs, *The Works of Hsüntze* (London: Arthur Probsthain, 1928); and John Knoblock, *Xunzi* (Stanford: Stanford Univ. Press, 1988), vol. 1. In addition, I have examined the commentaries of Yang Liang 楊倞, Wang Xianqian 王先謙, Liang Qixiong 梁啟雄 in *Xunzijianshi* 荀子簡釋 (北京: 古記出版社, 1956), and the "Beijing University *Xunzi* Annotation and Translation Team" in *Xunzixinzhu* 荀子新注 (北京: 中華書局, 1979).

43. The only previous reference I have been able to locate regarding the similarity of 6A10 to this passage from "Rectifying Names" are passing comments in David S. Nivison's "Xunzi and 'Human Nature,'" [*The Ways of Confucianism: Investigations in Chinese Philosophy*, Bryan W. Van Norden, ed. (Chicago: Open Court, 1996) 308] and in Liang Qixiong's commentary. He makes the terse observation that "[I]n the *Mengzi* [we find the phrase]: 'Forsake life and select righteousness'. 'Righteousness' means 'propriety'. And 'the proper' is 'what is approved of'," *Xunzijianshi* 荀子簡釋 322. But, to the best of my knowledge, no one up until now has fully explored the implications of the disagreement between Mengzi and Xunzi as expressed in these passages.

44. Although Freud thought this was necessarily the human condition.

45. 荀子: 修身 2/7/18-9, Knoblock 2.10. Cf. also the following: "(0) Those who do not follow ritual and value ritual are called people without direction to their lives. (1) Those who follow ritual and value ritual are called scholars with a direction to their lives. (2) Those who dwell in ritual and study it, are said to be able to ponder 慮 *lü*. (3) Those who dwell in ritual and can be unchanging, are said to be capable of being steadfast. (4) One who can ponder *lü* and be steadfast, and in addition loves [ritual], such a one is a sage." 荀子: 禮論 19/92/16-8, Watson 95. Note also that *lü* is a technical term for Xunzi. See "Rectifying Names," where he writes: "When the emotions are thus and the heart selects [which of them to attempt to satisfy], this is called *lü*." 荀子: 正名 22/107/23-4, Watson 139.

46. M. F. Burnyeat, "Aristotle on Learning to Be Good," in A. O. Rorty, ed., *Essays on Aristotle's Ethics* (Berkeley: Univ. of California Press, 1980) 78.

47. Ibid. Cf. Xunzi's "gentleman."

48. Ibid. 81.

49. One of the major differences between Xunzi and Aristotle on self-cultivation is that Aristotle thinks one must have gone through the first stage by the onset of middle age, whereas Xunzi, in common with other Confucians, sees self-cultivation as a more long-term process. Compare *Analects* 2:4.

50. 荀子: 勸學 1/4/17-18. Compare Watson 22.

51. 荀子: 性惡 23/1114/2-4, Watson 159-60.

52. Chad Hansen, *Language and Logic in Ancient China* (Ann Arbor: Univ. of Michigan Press, 1983) 80. Emphasis in original.

53. "Assertable" is Hansen's translation of *ke*.

54. Hansen 98.

55. 荀子: 樂論 20/100/16-17, Watson 117.

56. For a more extensive criticism of Hansen's interpretation, see my "Hansen on Hsün Tzu," *JCP* 20:3 (1993) 365-82. Philip J. Ivanhoe also raises similar objections to Hansen's interpretation in his "One View of the Language-Thought Debate: A Review of 'Language and Logic in Ancient China'," *Chinese Literature: Essays, Articles, Reviews* 9 (1987) 119, 121-22.

57. 荀子: 解蔽 21/102/5, Watson 121.

58. 荀子: 禮論 19/92/4-8, translation by Watson 94.

59. 荀子: 樂論 20/100/14, Watson 117.

60. 荀子: 正名 22/112/2, translation by Watson 153.

61. 荀子: 性惡 23/115/1-2, Watson 162. As "Rectifying Names" makes clear, Xunzi is a conventionalist about language in some sense. Xunzi is a linguistic conventionalist in the sense that he thinks that, for example, the Chinese could have used some other word besides "善 *shan*" to describe what is *shan*. This is perfectly consistent with the claims (which I think Xunzi endorses) that (1) "*shan*" has, as a matter of fact, always been used in Chinese to describe what is *shan*, and (2) the distinctions among things in the world picked out by the (arbitrarily chosen) words of Chinese are themselves objective. On this point, contrast Hansen 62.

62. Philip J. Ivanhoe defends a similar interpretation of Xunzi in his "A Happy Symmetry: The Foundation of Xunzi's Ethical Thought," *JAAR* 59:2 (1991) 309-22.

63. Curiously, Hansen suggests, but does not pursue, this interpretation: "Objectivist or absolute justifications of 'realist' traditionalism are available by making maximizing survival and effectiveness the test of *the correct* system of names" (Hansen 182, n. 46, emphasis in original).

64. 荀子: 正名 22/112/5-7, amending 嫌 *xian* to 慊 *qie*. Compare Watson 154, n. 21, and *Xunzixinzhu* 386, n. 5. Perhaps the phrase "choose subjectively by oneself," 內自擇 *nei zize*, is a subtle criticism of Mengzi for relying upon internal standards.

65. 荀子: 禮論 19/90/3-6, Watson 89.

66. Thomas Hobbes, *Leviathan*, ed. Crawford B. Macpherson (New York: Penguin Books, 1968), section I.6 120.

67. Hobbes 128.

68. 荀子: 勸學 1/3/7-8. Translation by Watson 19. Compare Knoblock 1.8.

69. 荀子: 勸學 1/3/20-1/4/1, Watson 20-21. Compare Knoblock, 1.10-11.

70. 荀子: 修身 2/8/1, Knoblock, 2.11. Compare Watson 30.

71. 荀子: 性惡 23/115/12-13, Watson 163.

72. 荀子: 性惡 23/115/24, Watson 164-65.

73. This section draws much from the comments of Bratman, Cartwright, and Cohon (see n. 89 below).

74. Throughout this section, the reader should bear in mind that "approval" and "desire" are to be understood as labels for the Chinese *ke* and *yu*. We are not interested, per se, in what criteria would distinguish the mental states identified by the English "approval" and "desire" in their normal usages.

75. See the "Rectifying Names" passage quoted above.

76. And note that in the "Rectifying Names" passage Xunzi speaks of the heart "stopping" certain actions.

77. Perhaps we may distinguish a third phenomenological state as well: desiring to perform an act just because it is good. This seems distinct both from Xunzi's "approval," since it does not involve compulsion, and from the sort of desire brought out in the case of helping one's daughter. The ideal parent loves his daughter and, consequently, wishes to help her. The fact that it is the right thing to do may not figure in his thoughts at all.

78. See Augustine's *Confessions*, Book 2, Chapters 4-10; and Aquinas' *Summa Theologiae* I-II, q. 78, a.1.

79. Compare Cua (1978) 3.

80. David S. Nivison, "Philosophical Voluntarism in Fourth Century China," in *The Ways of Confucianism: Investigations in Chinese Philosophy*, ed. Bryan W. Van Norden (Chicago: Open Court, 1996) 121-32. A. C. Graham has also suggested that the *Jie* 戒 chapter of the *Guanzi* 管子 represents some of Gaozi's doctrines. See "The Background of the Mencian Theory of Human Nature," in *Studies in Chinese Philosophy and Philosophical Literature* (Albany: SUNY Press, 1990) 22-26.

81. *Mengzi* 6A6.

82. *Mengzi* 6A4.

83. *Mengzi* 6A1.

84. *Mengzi* 6A6. This is implied by Gongduzi, who distinguishes Gaozi from those who say that human nature can be made to be good or evil.

85. *Mengzi* 6A1. 6A2 may also suggest this, although the intent of the water analogy is less clear.

86. *Mengzi* 6A3 is an attempted reductio of Gaozi's position, but perhaps he is happy to accept the implication that Mengzi draws there: that the nature of an ox is no different than the nature of a human.

87. In *Mengzi* 6A4, Gaozi seems to identify human nature with desires for food and sex, but then he immediately says that "benevolence," by which he means kinship feelings, is "internal."

88. Cf. "If there were no human nature, there would be nothing for conscious activity to work upon, and if there were no conscious activity, then human nature would have no way to beautify itself." 荀子: 禮論 19/95/1, Watson 102.

89. I am indebted to Michael Bratman, Nancy Cartwright, Rachel Cohon, Eric Hutton, P. J. Ivanhoe, T. C. (Jack) Kline, Julius Moravcsik, Donald J. Munro, David S. Nivison, and an anonymous referee from *IPQ* for making insightful comments on earlier versions of this paper. Any errors that remain are, of course, my responsibility.

Six

Xunzi on Moral Motivation

David B. Wong

"Virtue" is valuable to have, and praiseworthy to have; and so one is moved to seek it, even to compete for it. Yet it is gained through self-denial—and, it must seem, squandered by self-seeking.

—David Nivison[1]

One of the most distinctive contributions of David Nivison is his focus on issues of moral psychology in thinkers such as Mencius and Xunzi. His treatment of these issues manages to be impeccable in scholarly terms and at the same time to show how Chinese concerns, problems, and solutions are and should be relevant to us. This essay attempts to make a contribution to the tradition Nivison has established. I want to start with Xunzi's moral psychology and show that he has serious problems explaining how we achieve virtue when we start from a "self-seeking" nature. These problems lead me to suggest a reconstruction of his theory that places it closer to Mencius. The result is a theory of moral motivation that is naturalistic in the way Xunzi intended but that is clearer than he was about the way we achieve virtue.

From a modern, secular, and naturalistic perspective, Xunzi is of great interest. He denies Mencius' view that somehow rightness is revealed in certain shared emotional reactions of the heart-mind 心 *xin*,[2] a view that will seem mysterious on a naturalistic perspective, especially if the moral reactions are given by a Heaven 天 *tian* that is somehow sympathetic to the human ideals of morality. For Xunzi, morality is a system of rules devised by human beings, and Heaven is indifferent to the fulfillment of these rules. Therefore, we must not expect Heaven to have given us a nature that would dispose us toward morality.

There is nothing in our nature that Xunzi thinks can be called good. He defines human nature 人性 *renxing*, as that which is inborn and not acquired through human effort, and clearly, he argues, moral goodness is an achievement. What is inborn is the motive for gain 好利 *haoli*, a self-seeking tendency to satisfy desires 欲 *yu* of the ear and eye and liking 好 *hao* of sound and beauty. These desires are responses to feelings such

135

as pleasure, joy, anger, and sorrow, and they have no natural limit. This makes for chaos when combined with scarcity of resources:

> Man is born with desires. If his desires are not satisfied for him, he cannot but seek some means to satisfy them himself. If there are no limits and degrees to his seeking, then he will inevitably fall to wrangling with other men. From wrangling comes disorder and from disorder comes exhaustion. The ancient kings hated such disorder, and therefore they established ritual in order to curb it, to train men's desires and to provide for their satisfaction. They saw to it that desires did not overextend the means for their satisfaction, and material goods did not fall short of what was desired. Thus both desires and goods were looked after and satisfied. This is the origin of rites.[3]

Many have observed that this story of the origin of ritual 禮 *li* anticipates Hobbes' story of why human beings need to escape from the state of nature. One way in which Xunzi's story differs, however, is that after recognizing the need to restrain their search for satisfaction of desire, human beings see the need not only to restrain their behavior but to transform their very characters through ritual, music, and righteousness 義 *yi*.[4] They see that it is in their interests to love these things, and not merely to be curbed by them. As Nivison has observed, Xunzi's conception of the requirements of enlightened self-interest includes not merely the belief that the Way is best for everyone concerned, but also the cultivation of behavior and a love of what one believes in.[5]

By contrast, Hobbes never expected the self-interested motivation of human beings to change in the transition from the state of nature to civil society.[6] His egoistic psychology allows the internalization of no standards other than that of direct concern with individual preservation and contentment. This psychology creates a problem for his theory that only the state can solve. The rules that curb the pursuit of desire are mutually beneficial to all, but individuals can benefit even more if they can cheat on them while others generally comply. Since everyone knows this fact, no one will have confidence that others will comply, and therefore no one will have a self-interested reason to comply. The solution to this problem is the state as the enforcer of the rules. It must create a risk of punishment that makes it irrational for any individual to try to cheat. Only with the state does it become perfectly rational for the egoist to obey the rules.

By comparison, Xunzi recognized force as a necessary means, but not the primary means: "One who truly understands how to use force does not rely upon force."[7] While he may have been skeptical of most people's willingness and ability to become truly moral, he saw the need for a ruling elite to transform themselves so that they come to love and delight in virtue and morality. This elite, with supreme benevolence, righteousness, and authority, would attract the people and inspire them with respect. In this, Xunzi seems to affirm the Confucian belief in the ability of a ruler with 德 *de* to win the hearts and minds of the people.

Hobbes' solution to the egoism of human beings has some serious disadvantages. As David Gauthier has observed, his use of the state to make it irrational for individuals to cheat is a political solution to the problem, not a moral one.[8] A morality that gives one reason to obey only by virtue of the threat of punishment is not a genuine morality. A moral reason to obey should be one that is more internal to the motivations of individuals. This is not to deny that compulsion may have some role to play. Ideally, we need enough enforcement of the moral rules so that we would not be fools to obey the rules. We would be fools if we obeyed while others did not. Xunzi assigns enforcement the role of creating enough security so that we feel safe enough to embark on the project of transforming our characters: "Encourage [men of perverse words and deeds] with rewards, discipline them with punishments, and if they settle down to their work, then look after them as subjects; but if not, cast them out."[9] But also crucial to that security is the character of the ruling elite. It is because they have transformed their characters that they can be trusted. They love benevolence 仁 *ren*, are benevolent to the people, and so are trusted by the people. Their moral influence and not just their capacity to punish affects the characters of others so that a general climate of security is created.

Xunzi, then, has in this respect offered a better solution to the problem of the self-interested behavior of human beings. His solution is a moral solution because it envisions an internal change in human beings that makes a reliance on force unnecessary. Moreover, in locating the greatest transformation in a ruling elite, Xunzi offers a solution to another problem Hobbes has. It has often been pointed out that Hobbes did not adequately address the problem of corruption of the state. His solution to the state of nature requires the assumption that the state will be an impartial enforcer of the rules. But given that the state is run by human beings with the same egoistic nature as their subjects, Hobbes seems not entitled to this assumption. By contrast, Xunzi avoids this problem by requiring a moral transformation of those who run the state. Therefore Hobbes' solution to the dangerous nature of human beings is unstable without an envisioned change in their motivations.

So, both Hobbes and Xunzi begin with similar premises about human nature and its propensities to seek the satisfaction of desires that if unchecked would lead to chaos. But they end with very different visions of what people can become. For Hobbes, self-interested human beings accepted the authority and power of the state on the basis of their long-term interests. While the same is true for Xunzi, he also holds that one's long-term interests dictate a radical transformation in one's character. As we have seen, his vision can claim certain advantages over Hobbes'. But Xunzi's vision has its own problems in explaining how moral transformation is effected. The question is how one becomes a person who loves rites, benevolence, and righteousness when one starts with a repertoire of "very unlovely" emotions that cause a man to neglect his parents once he acquires a wife and children, or to neglect his friends once he has satisfied his cravings and desires, or to cease to serve a sovereign with a loyal heart once he has attained high position and a good stipend.[10]

There is another way to put the problem for Xunzi. In a beautiful and illuminating essay on Xunzi and Zhuangzi, Nivison finds a Daoist theme in Xunzi's recognition of moral rules as conventional, as the result of cool calculation on how to maximize the satisfactions of one's desires.[11] The Daoist theme furthermore includes an acceptance of one's basic social, political, and psychic commitments as inevitable. Where Xunzi goes beyond the Daoist Zhuangzi, however, is in recognizing the human world of institutions, ideals, and norms as the flowering of what is most fundamental in nature. Even though they are conventional, these human forms are an inevitable part of nature precisely because they are the best answer to the chaos that threatens all human beings.

On this interpretation, Xunzi goes one step beyond Daoism in accepting not just the nonconventional part of nature but that more inclusive whole that contains human forms. Such an interpretation of Xunzi, offers Nivison, would explain the two contrasting Xunzis: the cool detached observer who sees morality as a set of conventions designed to maximize self-interest; and the one who bursts out in "paeans of praise" of rites and the gentleman as having a place in the cosmic order. At the end of his essay, Nivison addresses a question similar to the one I posed above: how could the sage-kings have created morality unless morality were already a part of their nature? They created it not only out of a recognition that it is required by self-interest, but also out of an awareness of human nature and the inescapable human situation. They recognized their moral order "as having the same sort of ordering authority over all human life as do the rising and setting of the sun."

And through their "superior creative intelligence," they moralized themselves.[12]

This interpretation explains the exalted place that Xunzi gives to rites and to the human beings who devised them. Even though rites were created, they are discovered in another sense as the single best way to order society and therefore have supreme authority over human beings who must live in and through society. And Nivison is undoubtedly right in saying that for Xunzi the sage-kings must have moralized themselves through a heroic use of their superior creative intelligence. But just *how* did they use that intelligence to transform themselves? The question seems difficult to answer precisely because Xunzi shares with Hobbes a pessimistic (from the moral viewpoint) conception of human nature. How did they, with their "unlovely emotions" and self-regarding desires, turn themselves into beings who loved and delighted in morality? To accept rites and morality as not only necessary to self-interest but as part of the natural order is not yet to love and delight in them. It is not yet to make oneself willing to die for them, as Xunzi thinks the sage-kings were. Nivison identifies precisely this unresolved problem in a later essay on Xunzi.[13]

A clearer view of how moral transformation could take place seems to require a clarification of the mind's power over innate desire and emotion. Bryan Van Norden draws an interesting contrast between Mencius' and Xunzi's views of agency. According to Van Norden, Mencius held that what we do is determined by what we most desire. In order for us to be capable of acting out of unselfish motivation, we must have incipient virtuous inclinations that can be cultivated to be our strongest motivations. By contrast, Xunzi believes that we can override our desires through what we approve of. The beginner in moral cultivation can make herself do what she does not yet desire to do through approving of an action. Such action would include submission to rites and the dictates of righteousness, and would if practiced rigorously and consistently, result in the transformation of the desires themselves. Ultimately, the mind's power over desires results not just in overriding them but in retraining them.[14]

Van Norden's interpretation of Xunzi receives some *prima facie* support from the following passage from "Rectifying Names":

There is nothing a man desires more than life and nothing he hates more than death. And yet he may turn his back on life and choose death, not because he desires death and does not desire life, but because he cannot see his way clear to live, but only to die. Therefore, although a man's desires are excessive, his actions need not be so, because the mind will stop them short. If the dictates of the mind are in accord with just principles, then, although the desires are manifold, what harm will this be to good government? Conversely, even though there is a deficiency of desire, one's actions can still come up to the proper standard because the mind directs them. But if the dictates of the mind violate just principles, then, although the desires are few, the result will be far worse than merely bad government. Therefore, good or bad government depends upon the dictates of the mind, not upon the desires of the emotional nature.[15]

Van Norden is clearly onto something in Xunzi when he emphasizes that the mind's approval can override desire. Nevertheless, I think his interpretation cannot help us with the problem of explaining how we can make the transition from self-interest to truly moral behavior. The power of the mind to override desire might seem to provide such an explanation, but I shall argue that it does not.

To begin to see why not, let us distinguish between a weak and a strong sense in which the mind's approval can override desire. In the weak sense, the mind's approval can cause an agent to act contrary to what the agent desires most immediately, but what the mind approves is ultimately based on what it will take to best satisfy over the long term the total set of the agent's desires. On this view, the mind's function is to determine what desires are possible to satisfy given the world as it is, and whether actions dictated by our immediate desires might be self-defeating in the end. The weak sense is closer to a means-ends view of the role of practical reason. Reason is a Humean "slave of the passions," but it can manage the passions for the sake of their long-term optimal satisfaction. The more sophisticated versions of the means-ends view need not limit reason to a purely instrumental determination of what actions will have the greatest likelihood of satisfying an agent's desires. It also allows an adjudicative function of selecting among desires to be satisfied when there is conflict between them. But the basis of this decision will have to be something like the comparative intensity of conflicting desires, or which of the conflicting desires are tied to the greater number of other desires.

In the strong sense, approval can override desire even when it has no relation at all to what will satisfy over the long term the agent's total set of desires. The western analogue to this interpretation would be the Kantian view of the efficacy of pure practical reason, or the different view that moral qualities can be perceived and that such perception is intrinsically motivating. Notice, however, that if approval overrides desire in this strong sense, there must be some basis for approving of an action other than its relation to the satisfaction of desire. Kant, of course, held that pure practical reason yielded the categorical imperative, which applies to all rational agents regardless of the content of their particular desires and emotions. On the moral perception view, it is simply the apprehension of moral qualities that is the basis of approval.

If the possibilities of interpretation are divided in this way, then it would seem that only a weak sense of the mind's overriding desire can emerge from Xunzi's philosophy. The only basis for approval of an action given in his philosophy is desire—that the action is best, given the agent's long-term interests, even if it is not dictated by her immediate desires. Even if the mind can override emotions and desires, it does so in their interests, so to speak:

> [As for the king's officials] let them understand clearly that to advance in the face of death and to value honor is the way to satisfy their desire for life; to spend and to supply what goods are needed is the way to satisfy their desire for wealth; to conduct themselves with respect and humility is the way to satisfy their desire for safety; and to obey ritual principles and good order in all things is the way to satisfy their emotions. He who seeks only to preserve his life at all cost will surely suffer death. He who strives only for profit at all cost will surely suffer loss. He who thinks that safety lies in indolence and idleness alone will surely face danger. He who thinks that happiness lies only in gratifying the emotions will surely face destruction.[16]

This quote certainly rules out the Kantian option of holding that the mind can act on the dictates of pure practical reason. Nor can Xunzi hold that the mind can act on an approval based on perception of irreducible moral properties, because he does not think there are such properties. In short, Xunzi cannot allow any sense in which approval can override desire except the weak sense. And if Xunzi had in mind only the weak sense, then there cannot be as dramatic a contrast between Xunzi's and Mencius' views of agency as Van Norden claims there is.

On both views, the ultimate motive force of the mind's judgments would derive from desire. In both theories, the mind makes decisions as to which desires to act on. In Xunzi's case, it is a choice between one's immediate sensual desires on the one hand, and the desires arising out of reflection on one's long-term interests. In Mencius' case, the mind must make a choice between one's moral desires and sensual desires that come into conflict with them. Consider Mencius' explanation of why some people become greater than others even though they are equally human: "He who is guided by the interests of the parts of his person that are of greater importance is a great man; he who is guided by the interests of the parts of his person that are of smaller importance is a small man."[17] [*Mencius* 6A15] Mencius goes on to say that the difference comes down to the heart-mind performing its function of thinking. If this interpretation is right, then we need not interpret Mencius as believing that we act simply on the strongest desire of the moment.[18] Rather, he allows for the mind's approval to have an effect on what we desire.

What is the relevance of this discussion to the problem of explaining the moral transformation from self-interest to love and delight in morality? If for Xunzi approval can override desire only in the weak sense, any path to self-transformation must start from the self-interested nature of human beings, and not from a capacity for an approval that can motivate independently of self-interest. Changing oneself on the basis of approval would be changing oneself on a more sophisticated and long-term view of what is in one's self-interest, but it would be self-interest after all that.

We still have the problem of explaining how approval based on self-interest can lead to a transformation of one's selfish desires. How does one become a person who sacrifices himself for morality when the raw material for such a transformation is a self-interested nature? We can see the self-interested grounds for transforming our characters, but what remains unclear is how the transformation takes place given the nature of what we have to start with. Of course, Xunzi is not trying to convince his audience to undertake the transformation from self-interest to morality. The audience, after all, has already been transformed to at least some extent. His account is a retrospective explanation of how we came to be the way we are. But the question is how to fill in the explanation.

Even if we attribute to Xunzi a belief in the strong sense of the mind's overriding power, we still have essentially the same problem of explanation. If the mind has a non-self-interested motivation that is separate from selfish desires, there is still a need to explain how the mind can actually *reshape* selfish desires and create new ones for morality. How are desires to be transformed or created, instead of merely being overridden by the mind's approval? We cannot attribute to Xunzi a belief in a magical ability to transform desire, for that would make no sense of his emphasis on the *training* of desire through rites and music. But when we take this emphasis into account, we still have a problem of explanation. If we continually submit ourselves to rites and to righteousness, we may form a habit of practicing them, but how do we come to delight in them and be willing to die for them?

Philip J. Ivanhoe has noted that Xunzi thinks of human nature as highly plastic, like hot wax that can be shaped by something external.[19] At the same time, Ivanhoe notes that on Xunzi's account we encounter new sources of satisfaction by adopting morality. The question is how we can *take* satisfaction from such new sources given our nature. For example, Ivanhoe has written illuminatingly of Xunzi's conception of rites as "bringing human needs and Nature's bounty into a harmonious balance by achieving a *happy* symmetry."[20] Xunzi's gentleman clearly takes this kind of delight in ritual, and it is important to note that the delight is not simply based on the fact that rites provide for the satisfaction of human needs. The delight is in the balance, the symmetry itself between human need and what Nature provides. But how does the gentleman acquire the capacity to take this delight in symmetry? The capacity clearly goes beyond the mundane and self-seeking drives highlighted by Xunzi when he is trying to persuade us that human nature is evil. The theme of the plasticity of human nature seems to obscure the question. It is mysterious how a motivationally efficacious delight in symmetry can be imprinted on the heart-mind like the impression of a seal on hot wax. How can a completely new motivation be imparted to the heart-mind?

Xunzi carried the theme of the plasticity of human nature too far, creating for himself the problem of explaining moral transformation. He may have been grappling with this problem in "Human Nature Is Evil." There he directly opposes Mencius in denying that goodness is part of the innate endowment of human beings. He turns to the question of the origin of goodness if it is not in human nature already. The answer he gives is quite curious:

> Every man who desires to do good does so precisely because his nature is evil. A man whose accomplishments are meager longs for greatness; an ugly man longs for beauty; a man in cramped quarters longs for spaciousness; a poor man longs for wealth; a humble man longs for eminence. Whatever a man lacks in himself he will seek outside. But if a man is already rich, he will not long for wealth, and if he is already eminent, he will not long for greater power. What a man already possesses in himself he will not bother to look for outside. From this we can

see that men desire to do good precisely because their nature is evil.[21]

One interesting feature of this passage is the mention of the *desire* to do good, indicating that the difference between agency by desire and agency by approval cannot be so stark for Xunzi, and further supporting the interpretation that he must have had the weak sense in mind when he said that the mind can override desire. But the other way in which this passage is interesting is its very oddness. We have trouble figuring what Xunzi is up to here. He seems to be saying that human nature is evil because we desire goodness. What sense can we make of this?

Antonio Cua suggests that the truth in the above passage is a conceptual point about desire. Desire, by its very nature, is premised on a perception that one is lacking what one desires. Therefore, if one desires goodness, one lacks it, and human nature is evil or at least morally neutral. Cua observes that such an argument does not prove that human nature is not good. One could desire more of something that one already has, as long as one is not satisfied with the degree to which one has it.[22] But I suspect that Xunzi was not just trying to prove that human nature is evil in the above passage. This passage occurs after the question is raised about the origin of goodness, and in particular, the question of how human beings can become good if they do not already have some goodness in them. Xunzi is attempting to show how human beings could transform themselves into moral beings when their original nature is to seek the immoral. The basis of transition is precisely this seeking after what they lack. So perhaps the point of the passage is not so much a proof that human nature is evil, but to show, *contra* those who think that goodness must come from goodness, that goodness can come from evil.

And this would be an answer to the question of transformation we have been raising. If besides the motive for gain, we have a desire to be good, that would explain how we can begin transforming ourselves into moral beings. But at this point, a fair question to raise is whether Xunzi has obliterated any difference between himself and Mencius. Mencius did not, as Xunzi often implies, believe that we are born with full-blown goodness. Mencius only believed that we have the beginnings of goodness, in the four sprouts 端 *duan* of morality. A. C. Graham in fact holds that Xunzi attributed moral desires to human nature and that the difference between him and Mencius is not clear. Graham's interpretation is rooted in the above passages and others in which Xunzi mentions a "love of right"[23] and a "sense of duty."[24]   According to his interpretation, Xunzi thinks that human nature is bad, not because it lacks any good impulses, but because it is an anarchic mix of selfish and moral desires.

Graham's solution would make it clear how the sage-kings could have transformed their characters so as to love virtue and delight in ritual. Their motivations to transform themselves would not only be pure self-interest, but a sense of duty and a desire to do good. And in transforming themselves, they could make use of the raw material of good inclinations they already had. Training in ritual and the rules of morality could reinforce those inclinations and their superiority over selfish desires. But Graham's interpretation has the disadvantage of rendering Xunzi completely mistaken about his disagreement with Mencius. If Graham is right, then Xunzi actually agrees with Mencius in believing that there are sprouts of goodness in human nature. Both agree that the good inclinations would go undeveloped without training and education. Furthermore, Mencius certainly granted that there were tendencies in human nature that could lead us astray.

Now it is true that Xunzi misconstrued in an important respect his relation to Mencius, He argues against Mencius as if they both had the same definition of "nature" 性 *xing*, but in fact Mencius does not define nature as that which is inborn and which need not be acquired through effort. When he says that human nature is good, he cannot mean that we are inborn with a full-blown goodness that requires no effort. And if this is true, then Xunzi misses the mark when he tries to refute Mencius by pointing to the fact that we must work for goodness.

There is one clear difference between Mencius and Xunzi, however, which Graham's interpretation does not capture. The difference comes from Xunzi's naturalistic account of morality. If morality is born of the need to create a social order that will benefit all, then it seems to make no sense to do as Mencius does and posit an original nature to do good or a sense of duty in human nature. Goodness and right are determined by the rules created by the sages. They cannot be prior to the sages in the sense required by their having innate desires for these things. This must be true even if, as Nivison emphasizes, it was inevitable that the sages create such rules.

Because of this problem with Graham's interpretation, we must consider an alternative interpretation: that for Xunzi the desire to do good and the sense of duty are not original to human nature but derived from calculation on what is in our self interest. We come to have these things when we see in terms of our own long-term self-interest that we should have a certain character that we now lack. This certainly would fit with

Xunzi's story of why morality is necessary. Fung Yu-lan gives such an interpretation:

> So-called goodness, says Xunzi, is a combination of social ceremonies, institutions, culture, and moral qualities such as human-heartedness and righteousness, together with just laws. These things are not originally desired by man, but he is left no alternative but to desire them.[25]

This interpretation is consistent with Xunzi's naturalistic account of morality. But if we are to interpret the desire to do good and the sense of duty as derived from a desire to do what is one's long-term interests, we still have no explanation of how self-interest turns into love of and delight in morality. How does one start with the attitude that "one has no alternative but to desire" morality and create within oneself a genuine love for and a delight in it?

In view of the problems with either interpretation and in view of the fact that Xunzi gives no clear signal about the status of the desire to do good, it may well be that he was confused or ambivalent about the status of the desire. And if this is true, there will be no determinate answers from Xunzi about the nature of moral transformation. What we can do, however, is to construct an explanation of moral transformation that is compatible with his theory. I will consider two possible explanations.

One explanation is suggested by J. S. Mill's answer to the question of why moral virtue came to be valued for its own sake. The question is a problem for Mill because he thinks people desire only various kinds of pleasure and the absence of pain. At first glance, it seems that he could only allow virtue to be a means to pleasure and the absence of pain, just as it may seem that Xunzi could only allow moral virtue to be a means to the optimal long-term satisfaction of desire. But Mill, like Xunzi, does not want this result. Mill's answer is an analogy: just as money is originally only a means to pleasure, so virtue is originally only a means; but the constant association of money with pleasure, and virtue with pleasure, results in money and virtue being in themselves sources of pleasure. In other words, we are *conditioned* to take pleasure in virtue.[26]

In order for this idea to help Xunzi, however, there must be an explanation of how the sage-kings could have created the connection between virtue and pleasure in the first place. On Xunzi's account, morality can be a means to satisfying desire over the long-term only when the sage-kings have internalized it and gained the following of the people. Only then will they be able to create the secure social order that benefits all, including themselves. But if that is the story, then the sage-kings cannot *first* condition themselves by associating pleasure with virtue. The constant connection between pleasure and virtue only comes after they have succeeded in transforming themselves and creating a social order that *makes* virtue pleasurable. The problem is a general one. Theories that explain the presence of genuine moral virtue on the basis of transformation of a recalcitrant human nature have difficulty explaining how the conditions favorable to such a transformation are ever effected. The temptation is to illicitly presuppose the presence of those conditions.

We can get a clue to a better interpretation of moral transformation by looking at Nivison's interpretation of those passages in which Xunzi seems to attribute to the heart-mind an original desire to do good and a sense of duty. Nivison rejects Feng's interpretation of the origin of these things in self-interest for the reasons I have given above. His own conclusion is that Xunzi must assume that human beings just have a sense of duty.[27] This sense of duty, for Nivison, amounts to a capability of performing moral duty for its own sake and not for self-interested reasons. So far this interpretation sounds like Graham's, but it is intriguing in the way that it is different from Graham's. Nivison observes that the sense of duty as an original feature of human nature need not have any particular *content*. Thus qualified, Nivison's interpretation of the sense of duty may be compatible with Xunzi's naturalism in a way that Graham's interpretation is not.

As noted above, the heart-mind can have no original capability to discern any particular content to the ideas of right and wrong because the content is invented (or discovered as the best way to promote the interests of all). Even if the human heart-mind has an original capability to perform moral duty for its own sake, the content of morality cannot be there in the capability from the beginning. Now, without implying that Nivison would approve the way I use his interpretation, let me suggest that we must look for capabilities that satisfy three requirements: when attributed to human nature, they must be consistent with Xunzi's claim that human nature is evil; they must not have moral content; but they must provide some motivational efficacy to beliefs about duty when duty is invented/discovered.

We find such capabilities in those chapters where Xunzi describes the transforming effect of ritual and music. Consider the chapter on rites and in particular the discussion of the rationale for the three-year mourning period for the death of a parent. Why this particular period? Xunzi explains that this is the time when the pain of grief is most intense. But why is grief the emotion felt upon the death of a parent? Xunzi explains that nothing that possesses consciousness fails to love its own kind and that "Among creatures of blood and breath, none has greater understanding than man; therefore man ought to love his parents until the day he dies."[28] On the subject of sacrificial rites, Xunzi says that they "originate in the emotions of remembrance and longing for the dead," which come to those who lose loved ones. Rites are needed to give expression to these emotions, which otherwise will be "frustrated and unfulfilled." Rites "express the highest degree of loyalty, love, and reverence."[29]

In the chapter on music, Xunzi says that when performed in an ancestral temple it produces harmonious reverence. When performed in the household, it produces harmonious kinship. When in the community, harmonious obedience. Music, says Xunzi, is a necessary requirement of human emotion. When it enters deeply into men, it transforms them deeply. When it is stern and majestic, the people become well behaved and shun disorder. If seductive and depraved, the people become abandoned and fall into disorder. "If people have emotions of love and hatred, but no ways in which to express their joy or anger, they will become disordered."[30]

In the chapters on rites where Xunzi is as specific as he ever is on the way that the human heart is transformed, he *presupposes* human emotions that are quite different from the ones he cites in arguing for the evilness of human nature. There is love for and grief and remembrance of lost parents. There is the suggestion that love of one's own kind is natural to all creatures, and greatest among human beings. In the chapter on music, Xunzi sometimes speaks as if music writes noble emotions on the slate of the mind, which if not blank, is at any rate not good. But at other times, he writes as if music expresses emotions that are latent within the heart. The middle and most plausible path between these extremes is the view that in one respect music does express latent emotion, but that it serves to stimulate and connect its expression to various situations defined by the rites.[31] The capacity to be inspired by a musical expression of harmony, for Xunzi, may be closely related to the capacities to be inspired by harmony between human beings and by the happy symmetry between human needs and Nature's bounty.[32]

Given the loves and feelings Xunzi describes in the chapters on rites and music, there is a way to see how the sage-kings could have transformed themselves. Rites and music work on some raw material in human nature that is amenable to being shaped toward a love of virtue and a delight in ritual. Human beings may have a desire for harmony and coherent wholes and may therefore delight in the harmony between each other and between the human world and nature that is established by rites. The virtue of filial piety 孝 *xiao* strengthens, refines, and directs the primitive impulse of love of one's parents and the primitive impulse to reciprocate for the greatest of benefits—one's life and nurturance. The three-year mourning period and sacrificial rites strengthen, refine, and direct the natural feelings of grief and remembrance. We can come to love morality because it allows full expression of natural and deep human emotion.

Scholars have often observed that Mencius de-emphasizes the role of ritual in the shaping of character, while Xunzi gives it a very strong role. One reason for this difference is that Mencius believes the innate moral feelings provide a kind of direction for action and attitudes while Xunzi obviously cannot rely on any innate direction toward the moral. If the interpretation offered here is right, there is another reason for Xunzi's emphasis on ritual: his insight that rituals are especially effective in shaping and channeling human feeling because they regulate and partially define occasions on which human beings have strong feelings of the sort that can become moral feelings.

So far I have addressed the requirement that capabilities attributed to human nature provide beliefs about right and wrong and some motivational efficacy once these beliefs are acquired. But what about the requirement that the capabilities have no original moral content? The natural feelings that rites and music work upon are not yet moral in content. They are primitive responses not yet refined and regulated by moral rules. One originally delights in harmony and in wholeness of various sorts, with no thought that it is somehow morally right. One mourns for a parent simply, with no thought of its rightness or of the forms it should take. By contrast, Mencius holds that our natural feelings of mourning are feelings that reveal the rightness of mourning and that identify certain sorts of actions that ought to be taken. Consider *Mencius* 3A5, in which the story is told of people who did not bury their deceased parents. Not only do they eventually bury the bodies, not being able to bear looking at the bodies thrown into a ditch, but Mencius describes the covering of them as right. So on the proposed reconstruction of Xunzi's theory of moral transformation, he still denies the Mencian claim that innate, shared reactions reveal rightness to us. The proposed reconstruction is consistent with Xunzi's claim that morality is constructed out of self interest. But he now has a picture of human nature that allows him to explain the transformation from self interest to a love and delight in morality. On this view, we love it because it expresses, channels, and strengthens some of our natural human feelings.

And it is quite plausible that we do have some natural feelings that are congenial to morality even if they aren't moral feelings. For example, David Nivison has observed that the feeling of a debt of gratitude for a kindness or a gift is something we all know, and that in Chinese society that feeling is greatly magnified.[33] Such a feeling, as an innate impulse, need not be interpreted as a moral feeling, but simply a strong impulse to return good for good.[34] It becomes a moral feeling after the rules of morality are devised. The rules come to govern and even be embedded in the intentionality of the feeling (feeling that it is one's duty to return good for good). Further, there is good reason to think that the rules of morality would require reciprocity as well as define its acceptable forms. As Xunzi argued, human beings cannot get along without helping each other. And it seems plausible, as Lawrence Becker has observed, that helping behavior would be extinguished if it were systematically unreciprocated.[35]

But what about the requirement that capabilities attributed to human nature be consistent with Xunzi's claim that human nature is evil? Even if the feelings of love of parents and grief and remembrance when they die are not yet moral feelings, how could human nature be evil if it contains them? How could it be evil if it contains feelings that are congenial to morality? The answer, I think, lies in construing his claim that human nature is evil to be more sophisticated. Human nature is not evil because it contains nothing but selfish desire and feeling. It is evil because these kinds of desire and feeling *dominate* in conditions of insecurity and lack of order. It is evil in precisely the sense that Xunzi says it is: without the transforming effect of rites, music, and righteousness, human beings would act for themselves. So interpreted, Xunzi's claim has a great deal of plausibility to it. It also should be noted that love and grief may be expressed in a wide range of ways, only some of which are compatible with morality. These feelings must be moralized in order for them to result in moral behavior.

To conclude, let me make a case for the idea that we have not only found a plausible way for Xunzi to explain the path to moral transformation, but that the path found is of general significance for moral psychology. An exploration of Freud's moral psychology by Richard Wollheim results in some of the same conclusions reached here. Much of Freud's explanation of the growth of the moral sense, Wollheim observes, paints a rather unhappy picture of our relation to morality. Human beings are first bullied into internalizing morality. The child first experiences anxiety and terror at a parent or someone upon whom he is utterly dependent. He perceives that figure as obstructing or threatening the satisfaction of his sensual desires. The child internalizes the demands of the external figure as a way of dealing with his terror:

> We are frightened in childhood, we interiorize the fear by substituting an internal for an external object, we placate the internal representative of fear by the sacrifice of instinctual gratification, the gain in tranquillity outweighs the crippling loss in satisfaction, but the sacrifice has nothing independently to recommend it. . . . A happier interpretation of morality would be deserved if it could be shown that there are some needs, some desires, other than the avoidance of fear, and not shallow ones, that the establishment of the superego satisfies.[36]

The basis for a happier interpretation that Wollheim derives from Freudian and neo-Freudian theories is a postulated need to control aggression toward a loved person. Wollheim's conclusion parallels the conclusion we have reached about Xunzi. Human nature is for him still evil in a very substantial sense. But there are elements in that nature that make it possible for human beings to be fulfilled by morality. And by "fulfilled," I do not mean simply have one's narrow self-interest satisfied. Morality serves to express certain latent emotions such as love and the desire to reciprocate for benefits received. Further, righteousness, ritual, and music not only allow expression of these emotions but channel and shape them so that originally narrow self-interest becomes much broader and more firmly connected to the interests of others. Morality does not eliminate nonmoral sensual desires but limits them in such a way that they are more compatible with moralized emotions and desires. Morality can provide a coherence to our characters that was not there before. It seems to me that only such a view of human nature could make possible what many of us, not only Xunzi, envision: the possibility of genuine love and delight in morality.[37]

Notes

1. David S. Nivison, Feature Book Review of *The World of Thought in Ancient China* by Benjamin Schwartz, *PEW* 38 (1988) 415.

2. For such an interpretation of Mencius, see David S. Nivison, "Two Roots or One," Presidential Address delivered before the Fifty-fourth Annual Pacific Meeting of the American Philosophical Association, 28 March 1980, in *Proceedings and Addresses of the American Philosophical Association* 53 (1980) 739-61; Nivison, "Philosophical Voluntarism in Fourth Century China," in *The Ways of Confucianism: Investigations in Chinese Philosophy*, Bryan Van Norden, ed. (Chicago: Open Court, 1996) 121-32;

Kwong-loi Shun, "Mencius' Criticism of Mohism: An Analysis of *Meng Tzu* 3A:5," *PEW* 41 (1991) 203-14; and Shun, "Mencius and the Mind-Inherence of Morality: Mencius' Rejection of Kao Tzu's Maxim in *Meng Tzu* 2A:2," *JCP* 18 (1991) 141-69.

3. 荀子: 禮論 19/90/3-5; Burton Watson, *Hsün Tzu: Basic Writings* (New York: Columbia Univ. Press, 1963) 89.

4. This comparative point has been made by Bryan W. Van Norden, "Mengzi and Xunzi: Two Views of Human Agency," chapter five in this volume.

5. Nivison, Review of *The World of Thought in Ancient China*, 416.

6. He did believe, however, that our self-interest can become more expansive in civil society. Part of his account in *Leviathan* of the growth of civility and civilization hinges on an explanation of how we can come to appreciate the arts and sciences as answering to an expanded sense of self-interest.

7. 荀子: 王制 9/37/2, Watson 40.

8. David Gauthier, *Morals by Agreement* (Oxford: Clarendon Press, 1986) 162-63.

9. 荀子: 王制 9/35/6-7, Watson 34.

10. See 荀子: 性惡 23/116/25-6, Watson 168.

11. David S. Nivison, "Xunzi and Zhuangzi," chapter eight in this volume.

12. Ibid. 186.

13. David S. Nivison, "Hsün Tzu on 'Human Nature'," in *The Ways of Confucianism: Investigations in Chinese Philosophy*, Bryan W. Van Norden, ed. (Chicago: Open Court, 1996) 203-14.

14. Bryan W. Van Norden, "Mengzi and Xunzi: Two Views of Human Agency," chapter five in this volume.

15. 荀子: 正名 22/111/8-11, Watson 151.

16. 荀子: 禮論 19/90/14-7, Watson 90-91.

17. D. C. Lau, *Mencius* (Harmondsworth: Penguin, 1970) 168.

18. This seems to be Van Norden's interpretation of Mencius. See "Mengzi and Xunzi: Two Views of Human Agency," 107-17. Van Norden here draws our attention to *Mencius* 6A10, where the beggar, in refusing food, desires rightness more than life. Van Norden interprets this to mean that the beggar is moved by a stronger desire for rightness. However, as Kwong-loi Shun has pointed out to me in personal communication, this passage might be read in a different way: it is not that the beggar has a desire for life that is overridden by a stronger desire for rightness; rather, the beggar

has a desire for rightness over life which might be a consequence of the approving activity of the mind. Shun notes, however, that the passage probably does not provide enough material for a conclusive reading of Mencius' view of human agency.

19. Philip J. Ivanhoe, "Human Nature and Moral Understanding in the *Xunzi*," chapter eleven in this volume.

20. Philip J. Ivanhoe, "A Happy Symmetry: Xunzi's Ethical Thought," *JAAR* 59 (1991) 315.

21. 荀子: 性惡 23/114/18-21, Watson 161-62.

22. See Antonio S. Cua, "The Quasi-Empirical Aspect of Hsün Tzu's Philosophy of Human Nature," *PEW* 28 (1978) 3-19.

23. A. C. Graham, *Disputers of the Tao: Philosophical Argumentation in Ancient China* (La Salle, Ill.: Open Court, 1989) 248.

24. 荀子: 王制 9/39/11-3, Watson 45-46.

25. Fung Yu-lan, *A History of Chinese Philosophy*, Vol. 1, Derk Bodde, trans. (Princeton: Princeton Univ. Press, 1952) 294.

26. John Stuart Mill, *Utilitarianism*, chap. 4, in *Utilitarianism, On Liberty, Essay on Bentham* (New York: World Publishing, 1962) 290-91. There is a basis in Mill for a less reductive explanation of the pleasures of virtue, even though this is not the explanation he gives in *Utilitarianism*. Mill does not have an egoistic psychology, so he can acknowledge the existence of sympathetic emotions that are not based on any calculations of self-interest. The pleasures of virtue may on this view be derived from the satisfaction of our concerns for others. Below, I shall suggest a similar move for Xunzi.

27. Nivison, "Hsün Tzu on 'Human Nature'."

28. 荀子: 禮論 19/96/13, Watson 106.

29. 荀子: 禮論 19/98/1-2, Watson 109-10.

30. 荀子: 樂論 20/99/25, Watson 115.

31. There is a tradition in Western aesthetics that focuses on the relation between music, emotion, and the way that music can transform emotion. See, for example, H. R. Haweis, *Music and Morals* (New York: Harper, 1871) 1-54. Haweis holds that music stimulates certain "indefinite" feelings, i.e., feelings without definite objects or accompanying thoughts. When music is mixed with words, he says, the stimulated feelings may be wedded with definite ideas. His description of the effects of "patriotic, or languishing, or comic," "sublime or degraded" music is similar to Xunzi's.

32. The work of Claude Lévi-Strauss draws our attention to a human striving for coherent wholes, in music, myth, kinship structures, and science. See *The Savage Mind (La Pensée Sauvage)* (London: Weidenfeld and

Nicolson, 1962); *Structural Anthropology* (trans. C. Jacobson and B. G. Schoepf (New York: Basic Books, 1963); *Totemism*, trans. R. Needham (Boston: Beacon Press, 1963); *The Raw and the Cooked*, trans. J. & D Weightman (London: Jonathan Cape, 1969); and *The Elementary Structures of Kinship*, trans. J. H. Bell, J. R. von Sturmer, & R. Needham (ed.) (Boston: Beacon Press, 1969).

33. David Nivison, "'Virtue' in Bone and Bronze," in *The Ways of Confucianism: Investigations in Chinese Philosophy*, Bryan Van Norden, ed. (Chicago: Open Court, 1996) 17-30.

34. This does not mean that the good that is returned must be of the same kind as the good received. A child cannot return the same kind of good that is received from the parents, but can return a good nevertheless.

35. See Lawrence Becker, *Reciprocity* (London: Routledge & Kegan Paul, 1986) 90-91. Also see pp. 347-59 for an excellent bibliography of anthropological, sociological, and psychological works on the appearance of reciprocity in various cultures. He also gives references for theories of reciprocal altruism arising from evolutionary biology,

36. Richard Wollheim, *The Thread of Life* (Cambridge, Mass.: Harvard Univ. Press, 1984) 205.

37. I have greatly benefited from comments on an earlier version from Kwong-loi Shun and Amélie Rorty.

Seven

Moral Agency and Motivation in the *Xunzi*

T. C. Kline III

According to Xunzi 荀子 the story of the origin of the moral order is a simple tale to tell.[1] Before the emergence of the ancient sages the world was in chaos. Human beings did not possess the proper rituals or institutions to create and maintain a well-governed and harmonious society. The use of natural resources was unregulated, and abuse led to war, famine, flood, and pestilence. Life was, as Hobbes described so concisely, "solitary, poor, nasty, brutish and short." Fortunately for Chinese civilization there arose sages who were able to create ritual forms and build lasting institutions that provided the framework for an ordered society and individual cultivation. They regulated the use of resources and were thus able to provide for the needs of the populace and avoid natural disaster. In short, the sages were able to turn a chaotic, conflict-ridden people into a moral society that manifests the Dao. Although Xunzi vividly portrays this transformation of early Chinese civilization in numerous places in the text—most prominently at the beginning of the *Lilun* 禮論 chapter—he leaves parts of the explanation unfilled. Xunzi does not, for instance, explicitly describe how someone growing up in a chaotic society without ritual, teachers, or institutions to guide moral cultivation could possibly become a sage. How did those in the Confucian "original position" ever manage to transform themselves? Most of Xunzi's writing is focused on how teachers, ritual, and institutions created by the sages guide moral cultivation and structure the harmonious society. However, before the sages these guides did not exist. To borrow an image from the *Dalue* 大略 chapter: if rivers were not created with markers for where to ford them, and it was up to the sages to plant markers for the rest of us, how did the sages ever manage to get across?

155

The importance of this question lies in its ability to focus our attention on the core of moral cultivation for Xunzi, his conception of moral agency. As Bryan W. Van Norden and David B. Wong have pointed out, in order to arrive at a satisfactory explanation of the original transformation from chaos to moral order there has to be a full accounting for how human beings are capable of cultivating themselves so that they become moral or virtuous.[2] Moreover, this account requires a conception of moral agency that can allow for moral cultivation even in the period before the first sages. The purpose of this chapter is to examine Van Norden and Wong's interpretations of Xunzi's understanding of moral cultivation, and in so doing to reopen, or perhaps continue, the discussion between them concerning Xunzi's conception of moral agency. The chapter begins with a brief summary of Van Norden's and Wong's interpretations of the text, as well as David Nivison's response to Wong. It ends with my own interpretation that builds on the work of these scholars, and in so doing suggests further elements to a plausible explanation of the dilemma of the early sages.

Van Norden

In considering Van Norden's interpretation of Xunzi we should first note that he does not directly address the question of cultivation for the early sages. However, regardless of a difference in focus, Van Norden examines Xunzi's conception of moral agency and provides the groundwork for the present inquiry. The purpose of Van Norden's chapter, "Mengzi and Xunzi: Two Views of Human Agency," is to lay out a detailed interpretation of the core differences between Mengzi's and Xunzi's conceptions of human nature.[3] According to Van Norden, these two early thinkers differ in their understanding of the basic psychological mechanisms of moral agency. This difference in conceiving of the mechanisms of moral agency in turn underlies their differing polemical slogans of "human nature is good" 性善 *xingshan* for Mengzi and "human nature is bad" 性惡 *xing'e* for Xunzi. For this chapter we will not be concerned with Mengzi's side of this disagreement, though it should be understood to be in the background at all times. What we will focus on is Van Norden's interpretation of moral cultivation and agency for Xunzi.[4]

In order to grasp Xunzi's view of moral cultivation we must have some understanding of his notion of human nature. Unlike Mencius, Xunzi does not believe that we are born with incipient moral reactions that can guide us in moral cultivation. Human nature consists in that portion of our being with which we are born, that cannot be learned.[5] Among the psychological elements of our nature are the desires of the different sense organs and the rudimentary movements of the emotions 情 *qing*, as well as our capacity to understand. Left to their own devices human beings would simply be led by these inborn impulses and desires into a situation of chaos and conflict, as Xunzi describes at the beginning of the *Lilun* chapter. Given that chaos results from following the ordinary uncultivated prompting of our nature, Xunzi declares that human nature is bad.

One result of this conception of human nature is that moral cultivation cannot be understood with the agricultural metaphors of planting and cultivating so prevalent in Mengzi's writings. Human nature does not have inherent moral responses that will gradually grow into fully blossoming moral sensibilities. Instead, Xunzi conceives of cultivation as analogous to the bending and steaming and squaring involved in crafts. A craftsman takes raw material and shapes it into the desired form. The finished product does not grow out of the form of the raw material. Rather it is shaped and molded by the intentional activity of the craftsman. Only with the active and sustained intervention of the craftsman's effort is the finished product even conceivable. This is not to say that the properties of the material itself can be ignored. To be successful the craftsman must understand the properties of the raw material and as far as possible work with the grain as opposed to against it.

This analogy illustrates that Xunzi conceives of moral cultivation as a process of working from the outside in, rather than one of working from the inside out. Teachers, classical texts, ritual, and music become the instruments that shape the person's moral sense from the outside. These factors, external to the self and one's nature, socialize a person by developing moral perceptions and dispositions and eventually shaping one into a cultivated Confucian, a person who understands the patterns of the Dao and is able to act for the good in any given situation. Van Norden sums up this process well when he says:

> . . . the process of self-cultivation begins with performance of ritual activities which one does not yet delight in, and in the study of ritual, literary, and historical texts which one cannot yet appreciate or fully understand. Through determined and prolonged effort, one eventually comes to delight in the ritual practices for their own sakes, and to understand and appreciate

the canonical texts. According to Xunzi, one must be *trained* to delight in ritual and morality. [Van Norden 123]

In this passage, Van Norden also brings out one form of a general problem that David Nivison has referred to as "the paradox of virtue."[6] When first beginning on the path of cultivation the choice is a prudential one. There is no spontaneous love or delight in following ritual as it manifests the way for human beings. Following ritual is the means to other ends, ends such as gaining power as a ruler, avoiding harm and conflict, or ordering a chaotic situation. However, persistent effort and a skillful teacher will eventually lead to the transformation of perceptions and desires such that they are in accord with the Dao. At this point one will love ritual for its own sake and not as a means for anything else. Ritual will not simply be a tool but will become expressive of the internal psychological states that it helped to shape in the first place. Acting according to the Dao will be the obvious and easy path rather than one that we must seek and arduously follow. This transformation from a prudential motivation that treats ritual as means to one that treats it as end is the paradox that Nivison describes. Moreover, it constitutes part of the problem of cultivation for the original sages. Xunzi's way out of this paradox begins with his conception of moral agency.

As Van Norden explains, at the core of Xunzi's understanding of moral agency is the distinction between the volitional mechanisms of approval 可 *ke* and desire 欲 *yu*. According to Xunzi, desires are the specific and more particular responses of the emotional states 情 *qing* that are part of our nature 性 *xing*. [Watson 151] Approval, on the other hand, arises out of understanding 知 *zhi*. [Watson 127]   Through approval or disapproval brought about by understanding, the heart/mind 心 *xin* controls action.   Desires need not be translated into action regardless of how strongly they are felt; approval and disapproval can control the search for their satisfaction. Furthermore, approval can motivate an action even though there is insufficient or even contrary desire. As an extreme example, people are able to act contrary to their most strongly felt desires and dislikes. Even though they love life and hate death more than anything else, they can intentionally follow courses of action that lead to their death in pursuit of some ideal or principle of which they approve. [Watson 151]   In the end this human capacity to approve or disapprove of actions makes moral cultivation possible. As Xunzi states, "The mind must first understand the Way before it can approve it, and it must first approve it before it can abide by it and reject what is at variance with it."[7] [Watson 127]   At the final stages of moral cultivation we will approve of only those actions that are in accordance with ritual, and our desires will accord with what we approve of. There will be no need for approval to override errant desires. [Van Norden 128] However, this congruence of desire, approval, and ritual is an ideal goal for most people. It will be fully manifest only in the actions and psychology of the sage.

Wong

Given that Van Norden is primarily interested in contrasting the two conceptions of human nature, he does not concentrate on giving a fuller explanation of moral cultivation. Rather, it is Wong who raises the challenges of both the paradox of virtue, with regard to cultivation after the creation of ritual, and offering a plausible explanation for the emergence of the original sages. According to Wong, focusing on a distinction between approval and desire seems to shed some light on how Xunzi may have explained both of these processes. However, he raises objections to the interpretation offered by Van Norden. Deciding to reject the straightforward interpretation, he suggests an alternative, which he then uses to answer his own challenge.

Wong objects to Van Norden's interpretation by arguing that the distinction between approval and desire is not really as strong a distinction as it appears. According to Wong there are two possible ways to understand the capacity to approve or disapprove. He labels these two conceptions the "strong interpretation" and the "weak interpretation." Under the strong interpretation "approval can override desire even when it has no relation at all to what will satisfy over the long term the agent's total set of desires." [Wong 140] This is the interpretation that Wong understands Van Norden to be advocating. However, Wong argues that this model cannot be a plausible interpretation of Xunzi's position. His objection relies on considering what the plausible explanations for such a capacity, which is separate from desire, could be. He suggests that there are only two kinds of explanation possible. Either approval is based on the perception of "irreducible moral properties"—the Platonic solution—or else it is based on the activity of pure practical reason alone—the Kantian solution. Since Xunzi does not believe that there are irreducible moral properties, nor does he believe that approval is the functioning of pure practical reason alone, there are no plausible options left. Approval cannot be given the strong interpretation. What is left is the weak interpretation.

According to the weak interpretation the capacity to approve of an action is the capacity to act contrary to what one desires most strongly in the short term, yet the mind's approval of any given action rests on a consideration of what will satisfy the "total set of the agent's desires" over the long term. [Wong 140] The difference between approval and desire as motivations for action is simply the scope of the desires that they represent. "[I]t is a choice between one's immediate sensual desires on the one hand, and the desires arising out of reflection on one's long-term interests." [Wong 141] On this account, according to Xunzi's conception of agency, desires are the only psychological states that can motivate action. However, if desires are the only psychological states that motivate action, the problem of the transformation of people in the original position has become even more difficult than under the strong interpretation. Given the strong interpretation it seems that there is at least one factor in our moral psychology that could act as a force contrary to the "unlovely" emotions and sensual desires that are part of our original nature. Now it seems that there are only different types of competing desires, some pushing along the path of moral cultivation, some pulling away from it. Wong does have a plausible explanation for how the sages might have managed to become moral under these circumstances. Yet, before we consider his solution there is an alternative to both the strong and weak interpretations that should be considered.

Xunzi, and the early Confucian tradition as a whole, can be understood as advocating a virtue tradition.[8] Approaching the examination of moral agency with this assumption is worthwhile for two reasons. First, by considering Xunzi as part of a virtue tradition we make room for an alternative to Wong's "strong" and "weak" interpretations. Second, by doing so we also provide a framework for understanding approval as something other than simply the desires arising from consideration of long-term satisfaction of a total set of desires, or either option under the strong interpretation—Plato or Kant. Instead, approval can be understood as a motivational mechanism distinct from desire as such, yet not completely separate from desire. Xunzi connects approval to understanding, to our cognitive capacities to describe and evaluate our internal motives as well as the external situation. "The desire itself, which arises before one knows whether or not it can be satisfied, comes from the nature received at birth, while the search to satisfy it as best one can is directed by the mind. Thus a single desire which has sprung from the inborn nature may be directed and controlled in many different ways by the mind, until it becomes difficult to identify it with the original desire."[9] [Watson 151] This process of direction and control by the mind transforms the original desire into a more complex motive than the particular response to an emotional state that sprang from the inborn nature. This motive now can incorporate a wide range of cognitive descriptions and evaluations as well as rest on sensitive perception and understanding of the nature of external factors. For example, according to Aristotle this is the transformation that takes place in practical reasoning and produces a practical judgment. Wong's interpretation suggests that we ought to still call this transformed motive a desire, one that now takes into consideration a larger scope of time and other competing and complementing desires. However, calling this new motive a desire goes against Xunzi's definition of a desire as a response to an innate emotional state. [Watson 151] This new motive is explicitly described as a result of deliberative activity 偽 *wei*. It is definitely not a naturally occurring state of mind, emerging from human nature. Moreover, concluding that this new motive should be labeled a desire simply assumes that there are no other psychological states that motivate action other than desires.[10] The alternative would be to suppose that approval represents another kind of motive, perhaps something we could call a practical judgment, that combines both cognitive and conative elements. Unfortunately, there is not room to fully argue for this alternative here, and it goes beyond the proper scope of this chapter. Furthermore, although Wong relies on the weak interpretation for purposes of understanding cultivation, his solution to the problem of cultivation can be made to incorporate either interpretation.

Wong's explanation of the moral cultivation of the sages goes beyond earlier attempts by bringing together two different observations. The first of these observations is that Xunzi believes there are elements of our psychological makeup that can be conscripted into the service of the Dao after being worked upon by the ritual, regulations, music, and learning created by the sages. Xunzi gives examples such as grief at the loss of and love for one's parents, as well as the joy and exuberance accompanying victory and companionship. These emotions, like the desires of the five sense organs, are inevitable and deeply felt components of human life. In themselves, these psychological states are not moral. As they arise from our nature they are without any moral direction or tendency, and, in fact, without further transformation they lead to forms of expression that encourage chaos and conflict. Yet, they lend themselves to being given moral shape.[11] Furthermore, and this is the second observation, it is ritual and music that are the most efficacious means for transforming these pre-moral emotional states: "rituals are especially effective in shaping and channeling human feeling because they regulate and partially define occasions on which human beings have strong feelings of the sort that can become moral feelings." [Wong 149] By gradually creating new ritual and music—activities that are able to perform this double function of both expressing emotion and defining the occasions on which, and the forms in which, it should be expressed—the sages transformed those who participated in the very rituals that they were creating, including themselves. The transformation from engaging in ritual and music as a means to loving it as an end in itself now has a plausible explanation. Those who practice cultivation through Confucian ritual "love it because it expresses, channels, and strengthens some of our natural human feelings." [Wong 149] As we travel further along the path of cultivation the fit between external ritual forms and the internal emotional reactions becomes closer and closer. For the sage there is no deviance between the two. Ritual fully expresses their emotional reactions and defines the occasions and circumstances in which these emotions arise. They have become fully cultivated and see a life lived within ritual structures as the only one that fully satisfies their need for personal expression of grief, love, joy, etc. At this stage ritual becomes an end in itself and not simply a means. The sage delights in the practice of ritual. Moreover, with this explanation we can understand why Xunzi believes that human nature is bad in itself, yet can be transformed through a process that works from the outside in.

Nivison

Nivison, in his response, agrees with Wong's picture of moral cultivation and goes on to add one more element to the explanation of the creation of ritual and moral order by the early sages.[12] What Nivison adds to the explanation is a sensitive attention to Xunzi's conception of the creative process. Xunzi himself uses craft analogies to present his understanding of the creation of ritual and regulation. When the potter molds a pot out of clay, or the carpenter carves a utensil out of wood, the pot and the utensil are products of the *deliberative activity* 偽 *wei* of the craftsman. They are not the product or part of the craftsman's *nature* 性 *xing*, neither are the clay or wood, the design of the object, or the method by which it is made. All of these parts of the process are originally external to the craftsman and are learned or acquired during the process of learning how to mold clay or carve wood. [Watson 160, 164] From this analogy we are to understand that the sages create rituals and regulations in the same manner that the potter and carpenter create their products. It is a process of intentional creation from raw materials that are available to the sage. "The sage gathers together his thoughts and ideas, experiments with various forms of deliberative activity, and so produces ritual principles and sets forth laws and regulations." [adapted from Watson 160]

So far Nivison has only pointed out another facet of Xunzi's conception of (moral) agency, but he makes a profound and important discovery in pushing the analogy further than just the superficial level. Looking deeper into the analogy he suggests it implies that rituals and regulations were not made overnight. They were created over an extended period of time. The sage works like any other craftsman on the cutting edge of his craft. "He must see a need, and then must mold simple rules, or make simple adjustments in existing rules. Conceivably this sage may not himself see the finished 'product' or even have intended to 'produce' it." [Nivison 328] What Nivison believes this notion of creative activity leaves room for is the possibility that Xunzi "does not need to have an 'individual genius' concept of 'sagehood'; the development of institutions under the fashioning hand of the sages may well take ages." [Nivison 328] If Xunzi did in fact think of the process as one that required a slow and steady process of experimentation and adjustment guided by those with the perception and insight to recognize solutions to present problems, then it appears even more plausible that the sages were able to accomplish the task of ordering a chaotic and conflict-ridden society. The transformation from a chaotic society of self-interested individuals competing with one another to a harmonious society of cultivated individuals cooperating to manifest the Dao and form a triad with Heaven and earth need not have been accomplished in a matter of years or even a generation. Each sage built on the wisdom and insight passed on through the tradition, adding as much as he could to the overall design.

Although Nivison himself does not point to other parts of the *Xunzi*, and in fact believes that there is no definitive support for his interpretation, circumstantial support for this conception of gradually accumulated effort over time can be seen in discussions of individual cultivation rather than the creation of ritual. Two passages are of particular note:

> If, however, you set a limit to your journey, then you will arrive there sooner or later, before others or after them, but how can you fail to arrive at your goal some time?[13] [Watson 28]

> If the man in the street applies himself to training and study, concentrates his mind and will, and considers and examines

things carefully, continuing his efforts over a long period of time and accumulating good acts without stop, then he can achieve a godlike understanding and form a triad with Heaven and earth. The sage is the man who has arrived where he has through the accumulation of good acts.[14] [Watson 167]

Both of these passages refer to the process of moral cultivation. And both suggest that, at least for the case of individual cultivation, the model of a gradual process proceeding through a slow accumulation is an accurate interpretation of Xunzi's ideas. It does not seem that far of a stretch to conceive of the creation of ritual as likewise a gradual process of accumulation. However, as Nivison correctly points out, while this interpretation remains plausible and consistent with other parts of Xunzi's writings, it lacks explicit evidence to back it up.

Building on the Wisdom of Ancestors

Following in the spirit of Nivison's critique of Wong, this last section of the chapter concentrates on suggesting further aspects of Xunzi's philosophy that can be brought fruitfully into the discussion of moral agency and cultivation, both for explaining cultivation through ritual and music as well as the sages' creation and maintenance of the ritual order and moral society. Before turning to these further suggestions it may be helpful to summarize the elements that have been contributed above. Van Norden provided the framework of cultivation, a process that has sagehood as its ultimate goal, and the important focus on Xunzi's conception of moral agency. Wong has correctly pointed to the transformative power of ritual, its ability to control, express, and eventually shape our strong emotions, emotions that constitute the raw material shaped by ritual cultivation. Nivison has added to this the need to conceive of the work of the sages as a gradually accumulated achievement spanning generations. There was no need, as he says, for the genius sage. Sages only needed to have better than average understanding of human beings and their environment and the perseverance to find solutions to the social problems of their time.

Brought together these insights create a philosophically plausible and textually supportable explanation of moral cultivation in the *Xunzi*. However, there are further areas of Xunzi's thought that have not been directly discussed and which lend additional support and depth to the interpretation: Xunzi's metaphysical assumptions about the Dao, his conception of the efficacy of ritual, and the understanding of moral charisma or virtue 德 *de*. Within the *Xunzi* these topics are connected together, but we will begin with the metaphysics of the Dao and move toward discussion of moral charisma.

Unlike much of the earlier philosophical tradition, Xunzi does not anthropomorphize the cosmos. He believes that there is a fixed, objective pattern to the workings of the cosmos.[15] Heaven has its patterns of movement 天行 *tianxing*. The seasons follow one another in sequence, night follows day, the moon waxes and wanes through its monthly cycle, the stars travel through their yearly journey, and wind and rain follow the cycles of weather. Earth, on the other hand, has its natural resources. The plants and animals each follow cycles of birth, maturation, reproduction, and death. The sages looked to these patterns, along with the patterns of human nature, and created the Dao that ordered behavior and brought human beings into harmony with each other and the natural world. It should be emphasized that the Dao embodied in the Confucian ritual order was not so much discovered among, as it was inspired by, the patterns of Heaven and earth. Through careful observation and gradual experiment, the sages created and shaped ritual until it reached the height of perfection in the ritual order of the early Zhou kings.

The Dao of human beings that is manifest in the ritual and music created by the sages constitutes not simply a pattern of interaction that orders the state by keeping people out of conflict. It is not simply a prudential order. It is the proper set of practices and activities that bring human beings into harmony with their own natures as well as the patterns of the rest of the cosmos. The Dao is the moral order. It is the way in which human beings ought to pattern their actions. When properly following these patterns, a person's actions harmonize with the actions of other human beings as well as the natural world. Rather than running into resistance from other people and things, they are instead aided by them, and actions are easily brought to completion. Moreover, the ritual order and regulations of the sage-kings allow human beings to form a triad with Heaven and earth. By following the regulations for the use and development of natural resources—when to cut wood, plant, hunt, and trap—there is no fear that they will be insufficient to satisfy the basic needs of the people. Even natural disasters, such as flood and drought, will be properly prepared for. The patterns of the Dao permeate all aspects of the movements of the human and natural world.

Although this belief in the Dao as the proper pattern of the moral order, as well as the order of the entire cosmos, rarely gets discussed at great length, it cannot be stressed enough for understanding why Xunzi believed that cultivation through ritual was both effective and necessary. Ritual embodies the patterns of activity leading to harmonious and supportive interactions with other people and with the natural world. It embodies not just *a* set of patterns, but *the unique* and most fully harmonious patterns of activity. Ritual is efficacious in that it embodies and follows the Dao. Xunzi repeatedly describes, in no uncertain terms, the alternative to following the patterns of the ritual order. "A man without ritual cannot live; an undertaking without ritual cannot come to completion; a state without ritual cannot attain peace."[16] [Watson 25] Regardless of the scope and level of activity, to go against the ritual patterns is to try to swim upstream against the Dao. The inevitable result will be constant and unrelenting resistance from other people and the natural world. Nowhere can this fact be seen more readily than in relation to individual moral cultivation.

> No man who derides true principles in his mind can fail to be led astray by undue attention to external objects. No one who pays undue attention to external objects can fail to feel anxiety in his mind. No man whose behavior departs from true principles can fail to be endangered by external forces. . . . In such a case, a man may be confronted by all the loveliest things in the world and yet be unable to feel any gratification.[17] [Watson 154-5]

> If he does not possess ritual principles, his behavior will be chaotic, and if he does not understand them, he will be wild and irresponsible.[18] [Watson 162]

The patterns of activity set down in the ritual order of the sages provide the optimal patterns for human action in the world. Any deviation results in a loss of efficacy of one's own efforts.

The consequences of living outside of the ritual order are extreme. Yet, Xunzi believes that there is no need for anyone to suffer these consequences. Xunzi is an epistemological optimist.[19] Although he argues for boundaries to the proper scope of human knowledge, he still believes in the human capacity to understand all within those bounds. Everyone has the cognitive capability to understand the patterns of the Dao. Through study of ritual and classical texts, perseverance, and concentration on the things at hand, and the continued effort to apply this knowledge in good acts, anyone "can achieve a godlike understanding and form a triad with Heaven and earth."[20] [Watson 167] Xunzi's optimistic assessment of human cognitive capacities further supports the plausibility of his model of cultivation. As mentioned in the discussion of Van Norden, in order to abide in the Dao, approving and disapproving of the appropriate actions, we must first understand the Dao. [Watson

127] If it were almost impossible to come to any understanding of the Dao, moral cultivation would seem to be a rare phenomenon indeed.

As much as Xunzi is optimistic about our capacity to understand the Dao, he believes few people manage to acquire anything close to comprehensive knowledge. "As for ritual, the common people take it as their standard but do not understand. The sage takes it as his standard and also understands it."[21] [adapted from Knoblock 30.1] Only the sages fully understand the Dao and its embodiment in ritual. Nevertheless, Xunzi allows for different and significant levels of understanding. The common people do not need the same understanding of the Dao as does the man of breeding, the gentleman, or the sage. Within the ritual order the common people do not require full understanding of the patterns within which they are acting. They need only comprehend which actions are efficacious and in harmony with ritual. Although the common people understand less of the Dao, their understanding differs from the sage's in degree rather than in kind. "Any man in the street has the essential faculties needed to understand benevolence, righteousness, and proper standards, and the potential ability to put them into practice. Therefore it is clear that he can become a Yu."[22] [Watson 166] The sage does not have cognitive faculties that others lack. Rather, he simply has put more effort into developing and refining the innate faculties with which we are all born.

Connected to understanding of the Dao is the recognition of virtue. Even at the lowest levels of understanding the Dao Xunzi believes people are able to recognize virtuous and vicious behavior in others:

If you are respectful in bearing and sincere in heart, if you abide by ritual principles and are kindly to others, then you may travel all over the world and, though you may choose to live among the barbarian tribes, everyone will honor you. If you are the first to undertake hard work and can leave ease and enjoyment to others, if you are honest and trustworthy, persevering and meticulous in your job, then you can travel all over the world and, though you choose to live among the barbarians, everyone will want to employ you. But if your bearing is arrogant and your heart deceitful, if you follow dark and injurious ways and are inconsistent and vile in feeling then you may travel all over the world and, though you penetrate to every corner of it, there will be no one who does not despise you. If you are shiftless and evasive when it comes to hard work but keen and unrestrained in the pursuit of pleasure, if you are dishonest and insincere, concerned only with your desires and inattentive to your work, then you may travel all over the world and, though you penetrate to every corner of it, there will be no one who does not reject you.[23] [Watson 27]

Barbarian tribesmen, outside of the Confucian ritual order, not only recognize the virtuous and vicious behavior in others but respond appropriately, honoring and employing the worthy while despising and rejecting the vicious. Yet, this response to another's behavior cannot be due to the barbarians' *understanding* of ritual and the Dao. They have absolutely no understanding of the ritual order. Within the Confucian worldview, the barbarians occupy the lowest end of the cultural spectrum. Nevertheless, Xunzi claims that they recognize virtue and vice. If it is not due to understanding the Dao, how then do they perceive and respond appropriately to virtue and vice?

One important clue can be found in the *Bugou* 不苟 "Nothing Indecorous" chapter. Here Xunzi suggests that at a basic level the recognition of and response to virtue has nothing to do with understanding. "When the gentleman purifies his character, those of a kindred spirit join with him. When he refines his speech, those who are of his kind respond. Just as when one horse neighs, other horses respond to it [and when one cow lows, other cows respond to it]. This is not because of any knowledge on their part, it is because such is their inner constitution."[24] [Knoblock 3.8] If we understand the barbarians' response in this way, then they need have no understanding of Confucian ritual and the Dao. Their simply being human means that they will respond to the virtue of others. Xunzi does not claim that the barbarians will act virtuously, only that they will respond appropriately to another's virtue. The barbarians' appropriate actions are properly understood as *reactions* to the qualities of the virtuous person. The barbarian is not motivated by reflection on inner moral reactions but drawn along by the external qualities of the virtuous person. Here again we see Xunzi emphasizing the outside-in, rather than the inside-out, character of moral cultivation.

From a historical point of view, this optimism about the recognition of virtue seems somewhat out of place given the number of vicious people who appear to have done quite well in the turmoil of the Warring States. Yet, it is a reasonable extension of Xunzi's beliefs about the causal efficacy of ritual and the unerring patterns of the Dao. Following ritual insures that we are in harmony with others and the natural world. We are able to peacefully rely on the cooperative efforts of social organization.

If you treat old people as they ought to be treated, then young people too will come to your side. If you do not press those who are already hard pressed, then the successful too will gather around you. If you do good in secret and seek no reward for your kindness, then sages and unworthy men alike will be with you. If a man does these three things, though he should commit a grave error, will Heaven leave him to perish?[25] [Watson 31]

With regard to the recognition of virtue, we are inevitably on both sides of the relationship, at some times recognizing the virtue in others and responding to it, at other times having our virtue recognized and responded to. Nevertheless, the recognition of virtue and vice does not always work for the good. Xunzi believes that this system of mutual recognition can work both to the good and to the bad. If one understands and accepts the Dao then one will be able to recognize virtue in others and will draw close to those people one recognizes as virtuous. If one does not understand or rejects the Dao, when choosing friends and associates, one will instead recognize those of a likewise vicious temperament. Those who recognize virtue will gather around them other virtuous people and thus reinforce their own tendencies to be virtuous. Those they associate with will support and encourage their endeavors. Contrary to this, the vicious will draw themselves further and further into disorder and chaos by attracting and associating with other vicious individuals. [Watson 127] In this way human behavior functions in a system of positive and negative reinforcement. However, it is a system in which only the virtues and dispositions cultivated by ritual take advantage of the natural patterns of activity and response that are manifest by the Dao. Xunzi believes they have an internal logic that when properly followed almost guarantees success in achieving one's goals. Here we can see the beginnings of the concrete effects of moral charisma 德 *de.*

Moral charisma is the final element to be added to the previous explanation of moral cultivation. Moreover, with the addition of moral charisma we set in place the linchpin of Xunzi's theory of moral cultivation. All the mechanisms discussed above, to varying degrees, rely on the dynamics of personal interaction expressed in his understanding of moral charisma. The patterns of the Dao created by the sages and embodied in ritual presuppose the functioning of moral charisma. Ritual efficacy due to harmonious and supportive interactions with others rests on the dynamics of moral charisma. And, most directly, the recognition of virtue occurs because of the influence of moral charisma.

What then is the character of moral charisma and how does it function to fulfill these various roles?

To begin, Xunzi believes we acquire moral charisma through the accumulation of good actions. In a passage near the beginning of the *Quanxue* 勸學 chapter, Xunzi explains that if we gradually pile up earth to make a hill, wind and rain will naturally come and bring weather patterns to the new mountain. If we gradually pile up water into a deep pool, dragons will come of their own accord to dwell in its depths. Likewise, for human beings, "if we pile up good deeds to complete our moral charisma, then godlike understanding will come of its own and the mind of the sage will be completed in it."[26] [adapted from Watson 17-8] Moral charisma is not mandated by Heaven. Instead, it accrues to those who participate in moral cultivation. It is the result of their continuous effort and devotion to practicing the virtues embodied in the ritual order.

It is goodness made manifest in the demeanor and actions of the cultivated individual, and, via the mechanisms of recognition and reinforcement described above, it has the power to attract and transform others. At the highest levels of virtue the sage-king rules through the force of his moral charisma alone. At lower levels moral charisma is the power generated through the recognition by others of one's virtue. Moral charisma can be thought of as a power emanating from the virtuous individual, since the recognition of higher virtue in another elicits a response of support and admiration from those who properly recognize it. This admiration and perceived charismatic power on the part of the virtuous encourages others to emulate their virtue. Those of greater virtue can transform those of lesser virtue around them. In the case of the sage, moral charisma has the ability to transform even those who have little or no understanding of the Dao. Such virtue will elicit virtuous responses from even the barbarian tribesmen.

Xunzi describes the power of the gentleman or sage to order society as the power to transform 化 *hua* those around him. In order to explain this transformation, Xunzi often uses the metaphor of resonance in sound.[27] The tone of the gentleman's moral charisma 德音 *deyin* resonates with those with whom he interacts and causes them to vibrate to the tone of his moral charisma as well. We can unpack this metaphor by considering elements of Xunzi's theory discussed above. Since the gentleman acts in accordance with the patterns of ritual he acts with a greater efficacy and ease than those not as far along the path of cultivation. Petty people, who have undertaken little or no moral cultivation, recognize his virtue and the benefits accrued through his actions. He is honored and employed by those for whom he works. He effectively generates admiration for his accomplishments, and therefore petty people come to see the gentleman as a model. Recognizing their own deficiency, petty people are motivated to make up for this moral lack. In turn, this admiration and recognition provides the gentleman with the community standing needed to carry out the ordering and transforming of social arrangements such that the people begin to participate in ritual cultivation and to improve their situation. Although petty people may describe this transformative power by ascribing magical potency to the gentleman, we need no such ascription of a magical power associated with moral charisma in order to explain its dynamics. Moral charisma constitutes the intersection in the individual of the various synchronic and diachronic elements of moral agency as they interact with the community as a whole. Bringing together the synchronic and diachronic elements of agency in the dynamics of moral charisma allows us to knit the various elements together into a coherent and plausible conception of moral cultivation and moral agency.

Although this system of recognition and support may at first sound somewhat implausible to a modern Western thinker, it may in fact be more ordinary than we tend to first acknowledge. It should be noted that there are those in the Western tradition who work with very similar conceptions. Most prominently, Max Weber, the German sociologist, spends a great deal of time in *Economy and Society* describing the type of government and institutions that accompany charismatic authority. His conception of the charismatic leader is not that dissimilar from Xunzi's notion of the sage-king. He too develops a system of recognition and admiration that translates into the ruler being understood as morally and politically charismatic. This perceived charisma then translates into political authority and power. Xunzi, however, goes beyond Weber in relating moral charisma to individual moral cultivation. Moreover, for Xunzi the force of moral charisma can play an important role in explaining the process of transformation from the chaotic to the harmonious society.[28]

Conclusion

Now that we have further examined the context within which moral agency functions, the capacities that partially constitute moral agency and make cultivation possible, and the mechanisms that support and reinforce moral cultivation, this analysis can all be brought together with the work of Van Norden, Wong, and Nivison to create a broader picture of moral cultivation both for those in the original position as well as for those who came after the ritual order was created. The early sages found themselves in a world in which there were already patterns that could be seen in the movements of the cosmos and the behavior of human beings and animals. Through their natural cognitive ability to perceive and understand these patterns sages were able to begin fashioning rituals and regulations that brought the human and natural orders into harmony with one another. This process built up gradually over a long period of time, each sage responding to the most pressing needs of the present situation, modifying and creating ritual as the need arose. Through participation in these rituals the natures of the participants were both expressed and transformed so that they were capable of even greater expression. The process was supported by the natural mechanisms of recognition and moral charisma. As the sages got closer and closer to perfecting the ritual order, the moral charisma of the most virtuous individuals became greater and greater. They were able to attract and be supported by more and more people. The end result being that, with the perfection of the moral and ritual order, the sage-king was able to rule all under Heaven by virtue of his moral charisma alone.

Combining all these elements of Xunzi's philosophy, we end up with a richer and more plausible interpretation of his conception of moral agency and cultivation. This more robust interpretation then provides the resources necessary to answer Wong's challenge. As a closing note, it should be noticed that this project in itself exemplifies some of Xunzi's claims about the mechanisms for creation of the ritual order. By building on the work of those who came before we are able, with no greater cognitive capacities, to get one step closer to the best possible interpretation of Xunzi's philosophical system, an interpretation that will bring all the various elements of his thought into play and at the same time be the most plausible explanation possible.

Notes

1. For the purposes of this chapter I will assume that the text of the *Xunzi* 荀子 represents a reasonably coherent and unified vision of either a single author or editor or a like-minded group of either. In making reference to "what Xunzi believes" or similar locutions I am referring to the assumed directing vision behind the extant text.

2. The two main articles that I will be referring to are Bryan W. Van Norden, "Mengzi and Xunzi: Two Views of Human Agency," chapter five in this volume, and David B. Wong, "Xunzi on Moral Motivation," chapter six in this volume. All further references to these works will be in the text in brackets by author's last name and page number.

3. Furthermore, Van Norden narrows his examination to a comparison of two passages: *Mengzi* 孟子 6A10 and a passage from the *Zhengming* 正名 chapter of the *Xunzi*.

4. To a large extent this interpretation is one shared by much modern scholarship on the *Xunzi*. The major tenets of this interpretation are shared by at least David S. Nivison, "Xunzi on 'Human Nature'," in *The Ways of Confucianism: Investigations in Chinese Philosophy*, Bryan W. Van Norden, ed. (Chicago: Open Court, 1996) 203-13, and Philip J. Ivanhoe, "Human Nature and Moral Understanding in the *Xunzi*," chapter eleven in this volume, as well as Jonathan W. Schofer, "Virtues in Xunzi's Thought," chapter three in this volume, and Lee Yearley, "Hsün Tzu: Ritualization as Humanization" (unpublished manuscript).

5. *Hsün Tzu: Basic Writings*, Burton Watson trans. (New York: Columbia Univ. Press, 1963) 102, 139, 151. All further references to the Watson translation are in the text in brackets as "Watson" followed by page number. Where Watson's text has been quoted, the Chinese text is included in an endnote. References for the Chinese text are to D. C. Lau and Fong Ching Chen, eds., *A Concordance to the* Xunzi 荀子逐字索引 (Hong Kong: The Commercial Press 商務印書館, 1996). In addition, references to Knoblock's translation, using his own chapter and section numbers, can be found in the endnotes. John Knoblock, *Xunzi: A Translation and Study of the Complete Works* (Stanford Univ. Press, 1988) 3 vols.

6. David S. Nivison, "The Paradox of Virtue," in *The Ways of Confucianism: Investigations in Chinese Philosophy*, Bryan W. Van Norden, ed. (Chicago: Open Court, 1996) 31-44.

7. 曰:心知道然後可道。可道然後能守道以禁非道。[荀子: 解蔽 21/103/21] Watson 127, Knoblock 21.5c.

8. See especially Ivanhoe, "Human Nature and Moral Understanding in the *Xunzi*," and Schofer, "Virtues in Xunzi's Thought."

9. 欲不待可得所受乎天也。求者從所可受乎心也。所受乎天之一欲制於所受乎心之多求。 固難類所受乎天也。[荀子: 正名 22/111/6-8] Watson 151, Knoblock 22.5a.

10. Some of the disagreement here may be caused by the philosophical use of the term "desire." As Richard Wollheim has pointed out, in "From Voices to Values: The Growth of the Moral Sense" *The Thread of Life* (Cambridge, Mass.: Harvard Univ. Press, 1984) 197-225, the philosophical use of the term "desire" as a broad category representing any sort of want, craving, impulse, or other volitional mental state does not in fact help the analysis of moral agency but rather obscures distinctions, distinctions that Xunzi and others, especially those in virtue traditions, have made between different types of volitional states that arise from different psychological processes. To properly understand a volitional state requires an explanation of its history as much as its ability to motivate action. Simply indicating that a mental state motivates action and has a direction of fit by calling it a

"desire" is not sufficient. In the case of Wong's analysis of "approval" and "desire," his understanding of desire as a broad umbrella term may have obstructed his ability to see that there is a alternative to the weak and strong interpretations of the distinction.

11. As Wong mentions, the conception of morality being constructed out of originally non-moral elements of our psychology is shared by Richard Wollheim, "From Voices to Values: The Growth of the Moral Sense," in *The Thread of Life* (Cambridge, Mass.: Harvard Univ. Press, 1984) 197-225. Wollheim, however, is not interested in the Chinese tradition but in interpreting Freud. He sees the introjection of the superego and its subsequent modifications and development as constituting the core of moral psychology. This process of development begins with the creation of the superego from decidedly non-moral elements of our psychology. Wollheim's theory, in fact, is a way that one might connect Xunzi's insights to discussions in contemporary Western philosophy.

12. David S. Nivison, "Critique of David B. Wong 'Xunzi on Moral Motivation'," in *Chinese Language, Thought, and Culture: Nivison and His Critics*, Philip J. Ivanhoe, ed. (Chicago: Open Court, 1996) 323-31. All further references will be in the text in brackets as author's name and page number.

13. 將有所止之則千里雖遠亦或遲或速或先或後胡為乎其不可以相及也。[荀子: 修身 2/7/9-10] Watson 28, Knoblock 2.8.

14. 今使塗之人伏術為學專心一志思索孰察加日縣久積善而不息則通於神明參於天地矣。 [荀子: 性惡 23/116/13-14] Watson 167, Knoblock 23.5a.

15. The discussion of the metaphysics of the Dao owes much to Edward Machle's excellent commentary on the *Tianlun* 天論 chapter. See Edward Machle, *Nature and Heaven in the* Xunzi: *A Study of the Tian Lun* (Albany: SUNY Press, 1993).

16. 故人無禮則不生。事無禮則不成。國家無禮則不寧。 [荀子: 修身 2/5/15] Watson 25, Knoblock 2.2.

17. 志輕理而不重物者無之有也。外重物而不內憂者無之有也。行離理而不外危者無之有也。... 故嚮萬物之美而不能嗛也。[荀子: 正名 22/112/9-12] Watson 154-5, Knoblock 22.6d.

18. 人無禮義則亂。不知禮義則悖。 [荀子: 性惡 23/114/22] Watson 162, Knoblock 23.2b.

19. I am borrowing the phrase "epistemological optimism" from Thomas A. Metzger, "Some Ancient Roots of Modern Chinese Thought: This-worldliness, Epistemological Optimism, Doctrinality and the Emergence of Reflexivity in the Eastern Chou," *Early China* 11-12 (1985-87) 61-117.

20. . . . 通於神明參於天地矣。 [荀子: 性惡 23/116/14] Watson 167, Knoblock 23.5a.

21. 禮者、眾人法而不知，聖人法而知之。 [荀子: 法行 30/143/20-1] Knoblock 30.1.

22. 然而塗之人也，皆有可以知仁義法正之質，皆有可以能仁義法正之 具；然則其　可以為禹明矣。 [荀子: 性惡 23/116/7-8] Watson 166, Knoblock 23.5a.

23. 體恭敬而心忠信，術禮義而情愛人，橫行天下雖困四夷人莫不貴。 勞苦之事則爭先，饒樂之事則能讓，端愨誠信枸守而詳，橫行天下雖困四 夷人莫不任。體倨固而心埶詐，術順墨而精雜汙，橫行天下雖達四方人莫 不賤。勞苦之事則偷儒轉脫，饒樂之事則佞兌而不曲，辟違而不愨，程役 而不錄，橫行天下雖達四方人莫不棄。 [荀子: 修身 2/6/16-2/7/3] Watson 27, Knoblock 2.6.

24. 　君子絜其辯而同焉者合矣，善其言而類焉者應矣。故馬鳴而馬應 之，非知也，其埶然也。 [荀子: 不苟 3/10/18-3/11/1] Knoblock 3.8.

25. 老老而壯者歸焉。不窮窮而通者積焉。行乎冥冥而施乎無報而賢不 肖一焉。人有此三行雖有大過天其不遂乎。 [荀子: 修身 2/8/9-10] Watson 31, Knoblock 2.12.

26. 積善成德，而神明自得，聖心備焉。 [荀子: 勸學 1/2/9] Watson 17-8, Knoblock 1.6.

27. For two paradigm examples see 荀子: 富國 10/43/20, Knoblock 10.5, and 荀子: 王霸 11/55/21-4, Knoblock 11.12.

28. The connection between Weber's conception of charismatic authority and early Chinese conceptions of moral charisma was probably first noted by Herrlee G. Creel in *The Origins of Statecraft in China* (Chicago: Univ. of Chicago Press, 1970) 65. Yet, the most interesting discussion of Weber within the context of Chinese philosophy is found in Herbert Fingarette, "How the *Analects* Portrays the Ideal of Efficacious Authority" *JCP* 8 (1981) 29-50. Julia Ching also makes good use of Weber in her book *Mysticism and Kingship in China: The Heart of Chinese Wisdom* (Cambridge: Cambridge Univ. Press, 1997). She uses Weber's notion of the routinization of charisma to explain changes in the conception of kingship in the Chinese tradition.

Eight

Xunzi and Zhuangzi

David S. Nivison

There are puzzling features of Xunzi's philosophy, and one suspects that they are related. Xunzi argued that language, understood as names for things, is artificial, having been invented and decreed by the sage kings to satisfy human and administrative needs; yet he also thinks the language we have is right, and deplores the confusions of the sophists who treat names as merely conventional. He thought that the sage kings likewise created "rites and norms," i.e., the ordinary moral rules and standards of civilized society; and yet he also thinks that these rules and standards are universally binding on us and are not merely conventions. And when he tries to analyze the reasons an individual has for accepting the moral order (e.g., in the latter part of the essay "Rectifying Names"), he tries to show that a cool calculation will lead one from one's ordinary desires to acceptance of the moral "Way" as the best means of optimizing satisfactions. Yet when he explains how one should "cultivate oneself " (see the essay by that name) so as to make this acceptance effective, he portrays the cultivated gentleman as one who loves the "Way" so that he is willing to die for it, as one who has trained himself to think, see, say, do only what is right, as one who has been transformed by this "learning" so that it penetrates his entire being. And at times Xunzi bursts out in paeans of praise of the "rites" and the "gentleman" as having a place in the cosmic order coequal with heaven and earth (e.g., in "A Discussion of Ritual" and in "The Regulations of a King").

At a deeper level, to some Xunzi has seemed to have two contrasting concepts of the mind: (1) There is the mind as fully engaged in the life of the self, as "director," choosing which desires to satisfy and proceeding to suitable action—and so, in the "cultivated" self, the mind so conceived is completely committed to the "Way" of the gentleman. And (2) there is the mind as disengaged, as "spectator" of the self, enabling one to be "unattached" to one's own passions and actions, letting passions defuse themselves harmlessly without disturbing one's peace of

176

mind or interfering with calm decision. Such a mind would be ultimately uncommitted.

The first of these concepts, one might argue, takes shape in Xunzi's criticism of Mencius, who wrongly supposed that the self's natural movement is toward "appropriate" (good) action, without the need of "direction." Here one may look at the way Xunzi advises us to look at and manage ourselves in "Human Nature Is Evil." But perhaps one sees it also expressed in the many strongly hortatory passages and essays throughout the book, and especially in the "paeans" I have referred to.

One might argue that the second is revealed in the cool, distanced analytical attitude that enables Xunzi to counsel this kind of engagement. And one might even be tempted to say that Xunzi comes to the second by accepting Zhuangzi's idea that for inner peace and steadiness we must be "detached": One seems to see this concept of the mind most clearly in Xunzi's essay "Dispelling Obsession," in which there are obvious Daoist overtones. Thus the enlightened man's mind is like a still pan of water,[1] reflecting reality without distortion. It is able to be "empty," in that while filled with stored past impressions it can be detached from these and so can accept and evaluate impartially a new impression. It is able to be "unified," in that while constantly occupied with many things, it is able to single out and attend to the one thing that is its business. And it is able to be "still," in that while always active, it is able to stand back from itself and see clearly the distinction between what it is really perceiving and what it is merely dreaming or imagining. In all of these ways the mind maintains its autonomy by distancing itself from and observing, at a higher level, the buzzing confusion of its own activity at a lower level.

Here I describe a Xunzi that is readily found. It is now tempting to suggest that in taking this stance Xunzi does follow Zhuangzi, but rejects the Daoist assumption that to be the disengaged "spectator" one must "withdraw from the world": the mind is "subtle" enough, Xunzi thinks, to be able to be engaged in action and emotion yet be, as "spectator," detached at the same time. The former ("mind as director") aspect of Xunzi, oriented toward his critique of Mencius, is the obvious and "exoteric" side of him; the latter ("mind as spectator") aspect, derived from Zhuangzi, is the unrecognized but more basic "esoteric" side. The real Xunzi is "unattached" even to the Confucian moral-ritual Way, seeing it ultimately as merely "conventional," not "universal." Xunzi's occasional rhapsodic paeans to the cosmic beauty of the order of "Heaven," the order of the "rites," and the role of the "gentleman" belong to his "exoteric" side, and have no logical place in his thinking, thus forcing us to recognize the "esoteric" aspect as the real Xunzi.

Against this picture, I shall argue that there is no need to suppose that Xunzi's thought has both an "exoteric" and an "esoteric" aspect. This will require that I reexamine and criticize the picture of Zhuangzi that was assumed here, and of the way Xunzi responded to him.

In fact, the picture of Mencius is not quite right. We can read *Mencius* 6A15 as saying quite explicitly that our senses can move us toward inappropriate sensual gratification if the mind fails to perform its superintending function; to this extent, Mencius too has a concept of the mind as "director." But our mind does this ideally not by forcing the self but by "seeking," bringing into focus and encouraging natural good-tending impulses, and giving them priority over the selfish ones;[2] whereas for Xunzi all our impulses are selfish, though some are such that the wise man will try to satisfy them and some not; and the ones we wisely satisfy are not the immediately compelling ones, so stern discipline is necessary. Xunzi does, indeed, criticize the thought in Mencius 6A15: it is there that Mencius identifies "obsession" 蔽 *pi* as a psychic danger; but for Mencius this danger is only a danger that our senses will be "obsessed" by beguiling objects, if the mind fails to perform its "directing" job. Xunzi's opening point in "Dispelling Obsession" is that the really serious danger is that the directing mind itself will be obsessed by a beguiling but wrong idea.

The basic difficulty, I think, is that we have got Zhuangzi wrong. This is easily done, since there is such a mad variety of ideas in the *Zhuangzi*—a book that is obviously not by a single author, as we all agree. I grant that one does find in it the idea that detachment is the way to Daoist fulfillment, together sometimes with the idea that detachment requires withdrawal from the world; further, one can find this idea in the first seven chapters, that I and most others would accept as the "basic" *Zhuangzi*, whether or not actually the work of one person: consider, for example, the picture of the Daoist saint Liezi in chapter seven.

The trouble, however, is that the more characteristic idea in the earliest strata of the *Zhuangzi* is precisely the idea that we have suggested was Xunzi's "esoteric" improvement on Zhuangzi—that detachment is desirable, but that it does not require disengagement. In fact, Zhuangzi goes farther than this: we are caught in the world as it is, and we cannot get out of it. Even a posture of withdrawal would itself be a form of engagement, and could be dangerous unless recognized as such.

Before I proceed, this claim calls for proof. Here I accept the suggestion of the late Henri Maspero that ancient Chinese philosophical

Daoist mysticism, like other mysticisms, had a conception of a realization that was the goal of a *via mystica*.[3] And I accept also a further suggestion of Maspero's, that we have in the *Zhuangzi* an account that (whether true or not) is to be understood as Zhuangzi's own entry upon such a "path." Entry upon the path, Maspero argues, is thought to require a "conversion experience" that may be brought on by an experience of shock.

In Zhuangzi's case, this experience is found in the semi-final section of chapter twenty ("the Mountain Tree"; not one of the earliest, but containing matter similar to the first seven chapters). Zhuangzi is wandering in a private park, intent on a bit of poaching, crossbow in hand. He sees a huge bird, and takes aim—but just then notices that the bird, oblivious to the danger to itself, is about to snatch up a mantis, which in turn fails to see the bird because it is intent on making a meal of a cicada, blissfully relaxing in a spot of shade.[4]

Zhuangzi the philosopher is fascinated: each of these creatures has forgotten its real interest—i.e., "attached" to immediate gratification, is about to lose its life, which could have been preserved, we might suppose, only by "withdrawal" from mindless pursuit of "profit." He shudders; "Ah!—things do nothing but make trouble for each other—one creature calling down disaster on another!" He throws down his bow and runs—but is almost too late: the gamekeeper, spying him, is in hot pursuit. In a state of shock, Zhuangzi stays home for three months.[5]

A. C. Graham, in his translation and study, *Chuang-tzu: The Inner Chapters, and Other Writings from the Book Chuang-tzu*, also, like Maspero (and acknowledging a suggestion by my colleague Lee Yearly), recognizes this as a traumatic conversion experience. But Graham does not notice one important part of the content of this experience. To fix it, I follow Graham himself: Graham argues that Zhuangzi began as a follower of (or of the school of) the early fourth century recluse-philosopher Yang Zhu, who taught that it is hopeless to take office seeking to reform the world, and dangerous to do so seeking fame or gain, and that the best personal course is to realize that self-preservation and equanimity can be attained only by an ascetic withdrawal from social life.

If this was Zhuangzi's persuasion when he went wandering in the park of Diaoling, his experience had a double meaning for him: what he observed showed him that existence is a net of mutual trouble-making in which all creatures are caught, by their attachments; but his own experience of being rudely surprised by the game keeper showed him that the philosopher's conceit that he can distance himself by simply observing is itself a mode of involvement; you are in the world, and you can't get out of it. It was his philosophy of withdrawal itself that caused him to be so fascinated by the three creatures he was watching, and to watch them so intently, that he forgot his own safety. That philosophy at that instant had "self-destructed." Withdrawal itself is an entanglement. "Staring at muddy water, I have been misled into taking it for a clear pool."[6]

Perhaps Zhuangzi's own teacher had suggested the way out: "I have heard my master say, 'When you go among ordinary men, accept the ordinary ways'."[7] I.e., withdrawal has to be an inner withdrawal, while one "plays the game," engages in the ordinary activities that are normal in one's situation. Returning now to the "inner" chapters, we find this idea explored again and again. Chapter four is especially rich: "Have no gate, no opening, but . . . live with what cannot be avoided. . . . Walk without touching the ground."[8] So Zhuangzi has Confucius say to his disciple Yan Hui, bent on taking office in Wei, in the parody Zhuangzi constructs in the opening section.[9]

Carried to its extreme, Zhuangzi's attitude can even imply that one must recognize as inevitable those basic social, political, and psychic commitments, such as loyalty to ruler and love for parents, that are prized by the Confucians. In this context, even fixation on one's own personal safety can be a form of entanglement that can threaten one's peace of mind and, paradoxically, can threaten personal safety itself.[10] The real adept has attained a degree of detachment-in-engagement that is so subtle that he can actually concentrate with complete singleness of mind on the execution of the skill that is his in his role, without being in the least "worn" by so doing; this is why the philosopher-cook, the Complete Butcher in chapter three, is said to teach us "how to care for life."[11]

If I am right in all this, then we cannot say that Xunzi took over Zhuangzi's goal of detachment, but improved on Zhuangzi by noticing that detachment does not require literal withdrawal from the world—for this is Zhuangzi's own position. If the "real" Xunzi is not simply a Daoist rather than a Confucian moralist, he must be saying something else. What might it be?

Just as Zhuangzi's Daoist cannot disengage from the world, but must at best be active yet unattached, so also he cannot step outside himself in a meditative withdrawal, to view the self as an other, an object of analysis that would reveal its structure and its "true ruler,"[12] for (we can fill in his thought) the adoption of such a stance is just another posture of the self: the "I" is "systematically elusive," and so (as Wang Yangming was to notice centuries later) any philosophically saving "spectator"-like "quiescence" must be concomitant with ongoing psychic and emotional "activity." Nor can he make the Dao, the "Way" of everything, the object of his thought, for that attitude itself is part of what the "Way" is the way of. "The Way has never known boundaries."[13] One can only empty the mind of its "underbrush" of prejudices, Zhuangzi hopes,[14] and let the Way "gather" in "emptiness."[15] This inner freedom from "attachment" is itself the tranquillity that all men desire—for the Daoist.

For Xunzi, tranquillity is a common-sense good: the ease of mind that makes simple goods enjoyable, where riches and privileges would make one fret lest they be lost.[16] But Xunzi makes this point only to make it obvious that the Dao—the Confucian Way of an ideal society, in which my desires are subjected to order—is the best way of life I can choose. There is no suggestion whatever here of a "Way" that is beyond conception, or of an *ataraxia* as a supreme personal religious goal. It is true that Xunzi values mental detachment, and one can point rightly to the "Dispelling Obsession" chapter's analysis of the mind's capacity for "emptiness," "unity," and "stillness," in Xunzi's carefully defined senses, as explaining how the mind can concentrate on a problem without getting "stuck" on it. I suspect that one would be right, also, in suggesting that Xunzi is led to this matter by reflecting on Zhuangzi's idea of detachment (indeed, Zhuangzi's idea of detachment-in-engagement).

But this state of mind in Xunzi is a means to clear thinking and correct judgment, not a religious goal, not an end in itself. Xunzi is quite explicit in the "Dispelling Obsession" chapter: "The mind must first understand the Way before it can approve it, and must first approve it before it can abide by it and reject what is at variance with it".[17] The mind can do this by being "empty, unified and still"—detached, if one wants the word, but in the sense Xunzi proceeds to explain. Xunzi's concept of "obsession" comes from Mencius, as we noted; but Mencius speaks of "obsession" as a danger that besets the physical senses only, and then only when the mind 心 *xin* fails to do its natural job of noticing the distinction between the "higher" 大體 *dati* and "lower" 小體 *xiaoti* parts of the self. Xunzi sees that the mind itself can be "obsessed," so that it is drawn to pursue a wrong end, while thinking it to be right. The danger can be met only by cultivating the mind's capacity to keep itself in order as it is functioning: to be open to new impressions no matter how "full" it is, to keep its contents clear and distinct no matter how diverse they are, and to maintain a sense of reality no matter how free the constant movement of thought and imagination. Xunzi probably did notice Zhuangzi's idea of mental balance (in chapter two of the *Zhuangzi*), and he may have been reflecting on it in the "Obsession" chapter; but he obviously didn't accept it. For Zhuangzi, for a mind to be partial to anything at all is for it to be unbalanced. For Xunzi, balance is necessary if the mind is to make appropriate choices.

But Xunzi's Confucianism really is something new; it is a Confucian vision that no philosopher could have conceived until after Zhuangzi's Daoism had happened. And if I have to reject the idea that it is an ultimately "unattached" Confucianism, in a supposed "esoteric" aspect, ultimately seeing even basic Confucian norms as a kind of conventional "game," I can nonetheless see why one is tempted to say this of Xunzi. Xunzi does have two quite different modes—the engaged, committed, almost poetic and passionate, and the cool, detached, objective, analytical; and he can shift from one to the other disconcertingly. Further, there is a distinct Daoist echo in him. Over and over, I think we can see Xunzi's thought taking forms that we can understand only if we think of him as having first thought his way through Zhuangzi.

Zhuangzi in the second section of chapter four says, through the persona of Confucius himself, some startlingly Confucian things: "In the world, there are two great decrees: one is fate and the other is duty 義 *yi*. That a son should love his parents is fate—you cannot erase this from his heart. That a subject should serve his ruler is duty—there is no place he can go and be without his ruler. . . ."[18] We can always suppose a Confucian interpolation in a book that all admit is textually out of control; but the trouble is that this is something, as I have already argued, that one can see a Zhuangzi with his concept of detached engagement as being quite willing to say; and the text continues in just this way. If Zhuangzi can go this far, could we perhaps say that Xunzi's Confucianism is the logical outcome of Zhuangzi's Daoism, in some sense—even if not the sense we tried? Let us see.

"Detachment"—our word, not Zhuangzi's—is misleading, in suggesting that we are "attached" only to things we want or favor. But the mental attitude that prevents equanimity can as easily be toward something we fear. The paradigm is the fear of death. Many Daoists have thought that we can escape death, by a hermit-like life and by other means, and there are vestiges of this view even in the *Zhuangzi* book; but the idea is not Zhuangzi's. He took it for granted that we all die. Here, then, is something that we cannot remove ourselves from through a choice of lifestyle. We can only escape "attachment" to it, by an appropriate change of attitude.

By what change? The only answer Zhuangzi gives is one that is similar to his approach to other attachments: we all have received attitudes toward everything—this is good, that bad, this to be hoped for, that to be feared; but these are merely prejudices. This is so, also, of death: we do not know what our state is to be after death, so we have no reason to fear it; we have to accept the thing, death, but the accepted attitude is silly. Zhuangzi says this most memorably in chapter two; there is much more in chapter six, where we also find the thought, almost a Zhuangzi trademark, that death, as part of the Process 道 *dao* of all nature, is to be accepted as a marvellous transformation. "If I think well of my life, for the same reason I must think well of my death."[19]

Zhuangzi could have gone farther, and the book hints at the possibility when talking of the attitude to be taken toward the death of another, in the anecdote about the death of Zhuangzi's wife in chapter eighteen, part two. Huizi finds his friend beating on a tub and singing, and reproaches him. Zhuangzi says, "When she first died, do you think I didn't grieve like anyone else?" The hint is that it was perfectly natural to grieve; but the lesson drawn is that it was too common to be short-sighted about it, which the Daoist is not: Zhuangzi reflected that his wife's death was part of the process that included her birth and her life; it would betray a lack of understanding of fate if he continued to grieve; "So I stopped."[20]

The next step in the dialectic, which Zhuangzi does not take, would have been to say, is it not fate also that I should grieve? Seeing this, I need not stop; but at least I should see what I am: bereaved husband, I grieve, naturally, perhaps inevitably; but becoming "spectator" to myself as mourner, I can at a second level of myself maintain tranquillity of mind; my grief need not interfere. While Zhuangzi does not take this step vis-à-vis death and grieving, it is precisely the step he does take, in the persona of Confucius, in chapter four, part two: you are a man, says Confucius; therefore you have a ruler, and you have parents, and you cannot escape the obligation of loyalty to the one and love to the other; indeed the love is not just an obligation: a person "cannot erase this from his heart." But if you can recognize this and accept it, you can still be at peace—you can "serve your own mind so that sadness or joy do not sway or move it; to understand what you can do nothing about and to be content with it as with fate—this is the perfection of virtue."[21]

This is still the attitude of a Daoist. There is one more step in the dialectic that is possible, and if Zhuangzi had taken it he would have thought his way to the Confucian Dao. Xunzi took that step. Consider again grief, and consider with it the attitude Zhuangzi does take toward death—lyrical acceptance of it as part of the marvellous process of nature. He might have applied this latter attitude to grief itself: grieving is not just "what I did at first like anybody else," until I realized I was being silly; on the contrary, grief is fitting, and it is beautiful. If one can see this, one can as easily see that the institutional forms for the expression of grief—not tub-thumping, but the decorous forms of mourning—are likewise fitting and beautiful; and the history of human culture, that gives us these forms, is to be recognized as an aspect of the *dao*-process just as much as the process of individual life and death. A Confucius with this point of view would have said, in chapter four, not that inner peace can be maintained *in spite of* our involvement in loyalty and love, but that it is gained *through* those "involvements," once we really understand them, seeing them as essential to a complete humanity.

The most obvious example of this viewpoint in Xunzi is his treatment of ritual, grief and mourning at the close of the long chapter nineteen, "A Discussion of Rites." "The sacrificial rites originate in the emotions of remembrance and longing, express the highest degree of loyalty, love, and reverence, and embody what is finest in ritual conduct and formal bearing. . . . How full of grief it is, how reverent!"[22] One could quote and quote. It is no accident that earlier on in this chapter we find one of the most eloquent of Xunzi's rhapsodic "paeans" to the rites as part of his whole vision of the world: "Through rites Heaven and earth join in harmony, the sun and moon shine, the four seasons proceed in order, the stars and constellations march, the rivers flow, and all things flourish; men's likes and dislikes are regulated and their joys and hates made appropriate."[23] Xunzi's vision is more explicit in chapter nine, "The Regulations of a King," "Heaven and earth are the beginning of life, rites and norms are the beginning of order, and the gentleman is the beginning of rites and norms."[24]

The vision is that the human world, centrally man's world of institutions, ideals and norms, is the flowering of what is most fundamental in the entire world of nature, and is deserving of just that savoring, admiration and reverence that the Daoist accords to his *dao*, the order of nature and all of that order's manifestations; and like the Daoist, Xunzi focuses his attitude of wonder on both the whole of his world and on its detail; but unlike the Daoist, he does not exclude social and religious forms as being at best non-obstacles to realization; on the contrary they are the very substance of it. Accordingly, realization can't be *ataraxia*; reading Xunzi's chapter "On Music," one might almost say that it is ordered passion. But—here perhaps one may see a Daoist tone—the ordering, by way of "rites" and "music," is a systematic distancing, and is liberating: our passions continue for a time, but no longer possess us.

The most interesting, and to us the most puzzling, aspect of this vision is the way it leads one to see value and obligation as natural "facts," even, in Xunzi, data for which one can give a ("detached"?) naturalistic or historical account, without their in any way ceasing to be, really, values and obligations. The viewpoint is simply blind to the "facts/values" dichotomy that is natural to most of us. Here, I think, Xunzi reveals a way of thinking that just seemed obvious to 4th and 3rd century China (and to much of later China too). The text that follows is a paragraph from *Xugua* of the *Yijing* appendices:

> Only after there were Heaven and Earth were there the myriad things. Only after there were the myriad things were there male and female. Only after there were male and female were there husband and wife. Only after there were husband and wife were there father and child. Only after there were father and child were there sovereign and minister. Only after there were sovereign and minister were there superiors and subordinates. Only after there were superiors and subordinates did propriety and righteousness have a medium in which to operate.[25]

Here is a chain of necessary causal conditions; but since the standards of "propriety and righteousness," or "rites and norms" 禮義 *liyi* do exist, the chain implies that the explanation for "rites and norms" must be the basic structure of the universe.

The magical and religious assumptions that many readers of the *Yi* would have brought to this text were not Xunzi's, and here Xunzi and Zhuangzi are alike: for neither of them is Heaven a divine being in the usual sense. For both, Heaven, nature and all its works are the object of an ecstatic wonder, religious in tone: "all," that is to say for each according to his point of view, and Xunzi's was more inclusive than Zhuangzi's. It was a view large enough for him to see human customs, "rites" and norms, as both products of human invention, and so "conventional," and yet as "universal." They had to happen, come to be, in more or less the form they have, sooner or later; and the fact that we see they are man-made does not insulate them from our commitment to them: their "artificiality" thus in no way renders them not really obligatory and normative.

Xunzi's gentleman cannot, therefore, be seen as "detached" from his Confucian commitments, so to speak "playing" them as ultimately a kind of "game"—the commitments being Xunzi's "exoteric" side, and the "spectator" stance, the "detachment," the "game" perspective, being his "esoteric" side. Like all of us, Xunzi must have developed with time; and like most of us, he had his difficulties making completely consistent sense of his own position. But I cannot see that Xunzi saw himself—or his ideal "gentleman"—as having two faces, apparently completely committed, actually completely detached.

Perhaps, then, here at last is the solution to the puzzle Xunzi struggles with in "Human Nature Is Evil": How could the sage kings, in the beginning of things, have created morality unless morality were already a part of their "nature"? Xunzi insists they did it through their superior creative intelligence; but (we keep wondering) wouldn't morality then have been, from their own point of view, merely a "noble lie"? But no: through their superior intelligence they understood human nature and the inescapable human situation, and so also saw that the introduction of order was necessary (see the opening paragraph of "A Discussion of Rites"). So seeing, they formulated laws and norms, and then not only promulgated them to other human beings, but also recognized them as binding on themselves—seeing their moral order as having the same sort of ordering authority over all human life as do the rising and setting of the sun. Through their intelligence they moralized themselves as well as us.

Notes

In working out this essay, I have derived much profit from reading and thinking about Professor Lee H. Yearley's article "Hsün Tzu on the Mind: His Attempted Synthesis of Confucianism and Daoism," in *Journal of Asian Studies* 39.3 (May 1980) 465-480.

1. Compare this image to the Daoist image of the mind as a mirror. See Burton Watson, *The Complete Works of Chuang Tzu* (New York: Columbia Univ. Press, 1968) 97.

2. Cf. *Mencius* 2A2, 6A6, 7A3, etc.

3. Henri Maspero, "Essai sur le Taoisme," IV, Appendix 1, "Les techniques d'immortalité et la vie mystique dans l'école Taoiste au temps de Tchouang-tseu," *Mélanges Posthumes sur les Religions et l'Histoire de la Chine*, vol. II, *Le Taoisme* (Paris: Musée Guimet, 1950) 215-6.

4. This is a tale, not biography: the magpie-mantis-cicada drama is a literary set-piece expressing the Yang Zhu 揚朱 viewpoint. See *Shouyuan* 説苑, 四部叢刊, 9 *Zhengjian* 正諫 4b-5a.

5. Some texts have "three days," but the point is the same. For this and the following, compare translations in Watson 219, Maspero 215-6, and

A. C. Graham, *Chuang-tzu: The Inner Chapters, and Other Writings from the Book of Chuang-tzu* (London: George Allen and Unwin, 1981) 117-8.

6. My translation, following Maspero. Graham has "I have been looking at reflections in muddy water, have gone astray from the clear pool," 118.

7. My translation, again following Maspero. Graham's "If it's the custom there, do as you're told" (118), like Watson's (219), implies that Zhuangzi's discomfort was due merely to his flouting park rules.

8. Watson 58. Graham has "leave off making footprints," 69.

9. The parody is of Mencius 2A1-2. Compare the "fast of the mind" with Gaozi's recipe for psychic steadiness, and notice how the roles of ears, mind and 氣 *qi* are exactly reversed.

10. See section two of the same chapter, on the anxieties of the Duke of She.

11. The story is allegorical: just as Yan Hui is to "walk without touching the ground," so Zhuangzi's cook carves without letting his knife (sic. self) touch bone that would dull it.

12. Watson, chapter two.

13. Watson 43.

14. Watson 54-8.

15. "Let higher daemonic energies enter," as Graham puts it, 68-9.

16. See chapter twenty-two, "The Correct Use of Names," *Zhengming* 正名, Burton Watson, *Xunzi: Basic Writings* (New York: Columbia Univ. Press, 1963).

17. 荀子: 解蔽 21/103/21, Watson, *Xunzi* 127.

18. Watson 60.

19. Watson 85.

20. Watson 113.

21. Watson 59-60. Graham has, "of *de*, 'power'," 70.

22. 荀子: 禮論 19/98/1-9, Watson, *Xunzi* 110-1.

23. 荀子: 禮論 19/92/4-5, Watson, *Xunzi* 94.

24. 荀子: 王制 9/39/1-2, Watson, *Xunzi* 110-1. I am reading "rites and norms" for Watson's "ritual principles."

25. Richard John Lynn, *The Classic of Changes* (New York: Columbia Univ. Press, 1994) 106.

Nine

Theories of Human Nature[1]
in *Mencius* (孟子)
and *Xunzi* (荀子)[2]

D. C. Lau

I

The problem of how human nature is constituted, we have good reason to believe, was current before Mencius[3] and, from the time of Xunzi onward, has been one of the central problems throughout the history of Chinese philosophy. The point at issue between Mencius and Xunzi has traditionally been taken to be something like this. There is a thing called human nature, which is good according to Mencius, but bad according to Xunzi. The same thing cannot be both good and bad at the same time, hence at least one of the two philosophers must be wrong. That this was how most thinkers of subsequent ages understood the position can be seen from the remedies they recommended.

There were two ways of reconciling the conflicting views.

(1) Human beings can be divided into three grades. First come the sages who are purely good, last come the incorrigibly wicked, while in between, where all average people fall, who form the majority of mankind, are those who are capable of becoming either good or bad. This view is derived from two passages in the *Analects*: "The Master said, 'By nature men are near to one another, but they move apart through training;'" and "The Master said, 'Only the wisest and most stupid are unchangeable.'"[4] Wang Chong and Xun Yue 荀悦 subscribed to this view.[5] Wang Chong says:

From Mencius down to Liu Xiang 劉向, there were great scholars with extensive learning, yet there was no agreement in their views concerning human nature. Only the followers of Shi

Shi[6] and Gongsun Nizi more or less grasped the correct view on the matter. . . . . Hence I consider that, in saying that human nature is good, Mencius considered only human beings who are above the average, while, in saying that human nature is evil, Xun Qing [i.e. Xunzi] considered only those below the average.[7]

In Xun Yue's *Shenjian* 申鑒, we find the following: "Someone asked about the mandate of heaven and human effort. The answer was, 'there are three grades [of human beings], the high and the low are unchangeable, while in the middle there is room for human effort.'"[8]

(2) In the make-up of human beings, apart from 性 *xing* (nature), there is a further factor 情 *qing*. *Xing* is good. *Qing* is bad. Mencius had overlooked *qing*, while Xunzi had mistaken *qing* for *xing*. Dong Zhongshu 董仲舒, according to Wang Chong, held this view.

Dong Zhongshu, having read the works of Mencius and Xunzi, propounded his own view of *qing* and *xing*, saying: 'The great principles 經 *jing* of heaven are 陰 *yin* and 陽 *yang*. The great principles in man are *qing* and *xing*. *Xing* is born of *yang*, *qing* is born of *yin*. The nature of the 陰氣 *yinqi* is mean; the nature of the 陽氣 *yangqi* is kind. Those who say human nature (*xing*) is good see only the *yang* in it; while those who say it is bad, see only the *yin* in it.'[9]

The solution suggested by the Song 宋 philosophers was essentially the same. There are two ingredients of human nature: 氣 *qi* and 性 *xing*. *Qi* is of variable quality, but *xing* is always good.

I [i.e. the compiler] asked about the difference between the doctrines concerning *xing* as found in Confucius and Mencius. Answer: 'The *xing* Mencius talks about is the original state of *xing*. When Confucius says that by nature men are near to one another, he is talking about that with which they are endowed and which does not vary much. Human nature is always good. . . .' I further asked whether talent comes out of *qi*. Answer: 'When the *qi* is pure the talent is good, when the *qi* is impure the talent is bad. One who has received the purest *qi* is a sage, while one who has received the most impure *qi* is a wicked man.'[10]

The terminology of the Song philosophers may differ from that of the Han scholars, but the idea behind their solution is the same. The same entity cannot be both good and bad. But if we add a further entity, then we can have one good and one capable of bad. Both Mencius and Xunzi erred in being aware of only one of the two, while Xunzi further erred in taking *qi* at its worst.

What would Mencius and Xunzi have said to these two methods of reconciliation? The first, I think, they would have rejected, because it accuses them of arriving at a general view of human nature from what is true of only a section of human beings—and a very small section at that—in Mencius' case, the sages and, in the case of Xunzi, the incorrigibly wicked, and that they both overlooked the average man, who makes up the majority of mankind. Both Mencius and Xunzi are very explicit that what they say applies to all men alike.

Mencius says: "Things of the same kind are all alike. Why should we have doubts when it comes to men? The sage and I are of the same kind."[11] Again, when he was told that a prince had sent someone to try to find out wherein he was different from other men, his reply was: "In what way should I be different from others? Even Yao and Shun are the same as others."[12] Mencius was positive that every man could become a Yao or a Shun.[13]

Xunzi was equally explicit on the point. "As far as the nature of all men is concerned, Yao and Shun on the one hand, and Jie and Zhi on the other, have the same nature, and the gentleman and the small man have the same nature."[14] He, too, was positive that every man was capable of becoming a Yu.[15]

We see that both Mencius and Xunzi insist on the universality of their doctrines. Human beings belong to the same kind, and have, therefore, a similar nature. What these philosophers have discerned in human nature is not incidental to it but is an essential part of human nature as found in every man, true of the man in the street as well as of Yao and Shun and Yu. The suggestion that they have each overlooked one grade of human beings would therefore be unacceptable to them.

With regard to the second method, that of multiplying entities, it is not possible to be as definite in conjecturing what the reaction of Mencius and Xunzi would have been, since views of this kind did not seem to have been current in their time. All one can say is that the word *qing* appears only four times in Mencius, and of the four the use in 4B18 ("When one's reputation goes beyond what is really so 聲聞過情") has nothing to do with human nature. As to the other three cases, it is exceedingly unlikely that the word was used as a technical term.

In *Xunzi*, *qing* is indeed a technical term, but it is said to be the "content" of *xing*, which is defined purely formally. Hence it is quite impermissible, on Xunzi's definitions, to set up *qing* as a second entity coordinate with *xing*.

All we can say is that the Han dualism of *xing* and *qing* belonged to a climate of thought quite different from that of either Mencius or Xunzi. As to the Song philosophers they belonged to a climate of thought even more remote. The whole notion of *qi* as a sort of stuff of which everything in the universe is made was unknown to both Mencius and Xunzi, and it would be idle to speculate on whether it would have meant anything to them or not.[16]

I hope I have made clear from the solutions offered in subsequent ages how the doctrines of Mencius and Xunzi have traditionally been interpreted. They are taken to be flatly contradictory to each other and also incompatible with the actual facts about human conduct, which is the manifestation of human nature. In the rest of this paper I shall attempt to show that this interpretation is too simple-minded. It rests essentially on the assumption that human nature was a thing which cannot be both good and bad at the same time. Questioning this, I shall attempt to show that it is not very helpful to look upon the doctrines of Mencius and Xunzi as mutually contradictory, even though they both apply to human beings universally, and that neither doctrine is incompatible with the actual facts of human conduct. It is more illuminating to consider the two from the point of view of disagreement over the nature of, or, if one prefers, the way of looking at, morality, which leads in turn to a difference in the method of moral education. I do not, of course, mean to say that there is any issue concerning morality which is not, at the same time, in some way an issue concerning human nature, but only that it is more illuminating to look at it from one point of view rather than from the other.

II

Before examining the doctrine that human nature is good by looking at actual passages from *Mencius*, let us look at an interpretation of this theory by Chen Li 陳澧, an eminent scholar of the 19th century (1810-1882). He writes:

> When Mencius said that human nature is good, what he meant was only that in the nature of all men there is good, and not that the nature of every man is purely good. He says that all men have the heart[17] of commiseration, all men have the heart of shame, all men have the heart of respect, and all men have the heart of right and wrong; that all men have the heart of the

parent; that not only the wise have such hearts but that everyone has them; that if any man were to see, all of a sudden, a child about to fall into a well, he would have a feeling of apprehension and pity; that all men have the heart that cannot bear the suffering of others; that there are things a man cannot bear and things he would not do. Mencius could not have said more clearly than this that in all men there is good. Again, he said that it cannot be the case that in man there is no feeling for morality; that whoever has not the heart of commiseration is not human, whoever has not the heart of shame is not human, whoever has not the heart of keeping oneself back in order to make way for others is not human, and whoever has not the heart of right and wrong is not human. He could not have said more clearly than this that there is no man who is completely devoid of good. Gong Duzi said: 'Some say that there are men who by nature are not good; that is why with Yao as ruler there was Xiang.' Mencius' reply was: 'If one follows one's natural inclinations one can be good. This is what I mean by human nature being good.' In this Mencius was trying to make use of Gong Duzi's view that there are those born not good in order to clear up his perplexity, viz. by saying that although such people have a nature which is not good, they are still not completely devoid of good. How can this be shown to be so? By the fact that their inclinations are capable of being good we know that they are not by nature completely devoid of good, and that is what Mencius meant by saying that human nature is good. For instance, Xiang's nature was indeed bad, yet when he saw Shun he felt ashamed; this means that his inclinations can be good, that even in his nature there is good. This is what Mencius meant by saying that human nature is good. If he had in mind the nature of Yao, how could he have said merely that it was possible for it to be good? For the nature of the sage is purely good, that of the ordinary man has some good, while even that of the bad man is not purely bad. By human nature being good is meant this, and by no man being completely devoid of good is also meant this.[18]

I have quoted this passage at length because I think it is interesting to examine an interpretation which, in point of time, is some 2,000 years later than the Han scholars we have looked at, and yet is, in content, not so very much different. There are points of difference, of course, and we can say they are improvements. Instead of the three grades of men, we have now only two. The sage being purely good is still set apart from the rest of humanity, but the wicked is no longer looked upon as purely bad and so incorrigible, but is regarded as belonging to the same class as the ordinary man who is not purely good either. Further, and this is certainly a great step forward, Mencius' theory is no longer taken as true only of the sage. On the contrary, as it is taken to mean simply that there is good in man, it is precisely as applied to the sage that it is false by implication, for to say that there is good in man is to imply that there is also bad in him, but the sage is said to be purely good. To the ordinary man, this applies without qualifications.

There are, however, two difficulties in this interpretation. Firstly, to consider the sage as above the application of the theory is contrary to the explicit statement of Mencius, who, as we have seen, says that the sage is the same as anybody else. Secondly, there is a difficulty in interpreting the statement that human nature is good as simply meaning that in all men (apart from the sages), there is good and not that all men are completely good. For, as we have seen, to say that there is good in all men is to say that there is also bad in all men, as is evident from the inclusion of the bad man. Now if human nature is, indeed, a mixture of good and bad, and this is taken as ground for saying that human nature is good, then there is no reason why on the same ground we should not say human nature is bad. We must do better than this to defend Mencius as reasonable in putting forth his doctrine. But these two difficulties arising out of Chen Li's interpretation will prove to be instructive and will help us to see more clearly the conditions a successful interpretation must fulfill.

It is time to turn to Mencius. Let us examine a passage which has been partially quoted by Chen Li in his exposition.

> Mencius said: 'Men all have the heart that cannot bear the suffering of others. The Former Kings, because they had the heart that cannot bear the suffering of others, showed this in the way they governed the people. With such a heart practicing such government, ruling the world was like rolling it on one's palm. This is what I mean by saying that all men have the heart that cannot bear the suffering of others. Now if any man were, all of a sudden, to see a little child about to fall into a well, he would experience the feeling of apprehension and pity, not for the sake of gaining the favor of its parents, nor the praise of his neighbors and friends, nor yet because he dislikes the

reputation he would otherwise get of being callous. Judging from this, whoever has not the heart of commiseration is not human, whoever has not the heart of shame is not human, whoever has not the heart of keeping oneself back in order to make way for others is not human, and whoever has not the heart of right and wrong is not human. The heart of commiseration is the beginning[19] of humanity; the heart of shame is the beginning of righteousness; the heart of keeping oneself back in order to make way for others is the beginning of observing ritual; the heart of right and wrong is the beginning of wisdom. A man has these four beginnings as he has four limbs. To have these four beginnings and to say to oneself that one is incapable of being good is to do harm to oneself, and to say that one's prince is incapable of being good is to do harm to one's prince. If having these four beginnings in oneself one knows to extend them, it is as if a fire is beginning to blaze or a spring beginning to flow through. If one is able to extend them, one has all that is required to maintain peace within the four seas. If one does not extend them, one will be incapable even of serving one's parents.'[20]

Since this passage contains, I think, practically the whole of Mencius' doctrine of human nature, it is worth examining it in some detail. The four beginnings have traditionally been taken as if they were parallel and coordinate factors. This I believe to be an error, and one that is at least in part responsible for the failure to understand Mencius.

First of all there is the 是非之心 *shifei zhi xin*, which I have rendered as "the heart of right and wrong." *Shifei* has two senses: (a) right and wrong, and (b) approval of the right and disapproval of the wrong. Hence in saying that every man has *Shifei zhi xin*, Mencius is making the double point that (a) all men are able, by nature, to distinguish right (*shi*) from wrong (*fei*), and (b) they not only draw the distinction but also approve of (*shi*) the right and disapprove of (*fei*) the wrong. In other words, the distinction between right and wrong is not purely a theoretical one, for once the distinction is made one also feels the right ought to be done and the wrong ought not to be done.

Then there is the heart of shame or, in more idiomatic English, the sense of shame. One feels ashamed when one has done the wrong, and not the right, thing. Mencius places great emphasis on the importance of shame. He says, "A man must not be devoid of shame,"[21] and again, "Important indeed is shame to man."[22]

So far we see that every man is equipped with the ability to distinguish right from wrong, to feel he ought to do the right and to feel ashamed if he does not do it. Now assuming that we often do what is wrong, so long as we also sometimes do the right thing, we can see that there is a sense in which we can say that human nature is good. This is because even in cases where we have in fact done wrong, we know that we have done wrong and feel ashamed of it, while in cases where we have done right, we know we have done right and approve of ourselves for what we have done. This disposes of the major objection which was raised in connection with Chen Li's interpretation. The objection was that if we sometimes do good and sometimes do bad or, in Chen Li's terminology, if we are neither purely good nor purely bad, how was Mencius justified in saying that human nature is good rather than bad? Now we see that Mencius' justification does not at all lie in the actual way in which human beings behave, but in the fact that they possess a sense of morality and a sense of shame. Since these have to do with what men *ought to do*, an assertion which is based on this cannot be invalidated by evidence as to what men *in fact do*, unless it could be shown that human beings can never do what is right, for in that case it would be odd to say that human nature is good. This also solves the difficulty about the sages. We may admit, for argument's sake, that a sage is one who never *in fact* does anything wrong. This would still leave the possibility open that he *can* do wrong. In that case we can treat him in the same way as an ordinary man, the only difference between him and the ordinary man being that the latter in fact often does wrong, and this, as we have seen, does not touch Mencius' theory.

I have admitted that it would be awkward for Mencius' theory if man, as a matter of fact, can never do the right thing. Fortunately this has been taken care of by Mencius in the above passage. He shows there that there are tendencies in a man's nature which can furnish him with the motive force for doing good. Both "the heart of commiseration" and "the heart of keeping oneself back in order to make way for others" are such tendencies. The first renders us capable of feeling sympathy towards the misery of others and of desiring to do something about it. The second renders us capable of putting others first. In situations where there is any conflict of interest between ourself and others, this will prompt us to be considerate towards them.

Mencius ought, of course, to show that by nature man in fact possesses these four beginnings. Unfortunately he has done so only in the case of the heart of commiseration. Let us look at this part carefully. Note that he says, "Now if any man were, *all of a sudden*, to see a little child about to fall into a well . . ." The phrase "all of a sudden" was, I think, put in deliberately and has great significance in connection with the point under discussion. It shows that the reaction is instantaneous and therefore not the result of deliberation but entirely spontaneous. Now in one sense of the word "natural," our spontaneous reactions are natural, while our reactions after due deliberation are not. We often say, for instance, that a man is liable to show his true nature in moments when he is caught off his guard. On this criterion, if a man unexpectedly sees a child about to fall into a well and feels apprehension and pity, this shows that to feel this way in such situations must be part of his nature. There is a further purpose in inserting the phrase "all of a sudden." Mencius was anxious to show that the feeling was not due to self-interest, because one can only act out of self-interest after deliberation or calculation. Here there is no time for such deliberation. Moreover, Mencius says that he would not be feeling pity for the sake of gaining the favor of the parents of the child or of winning the praise of his neighbors and friends, or even to avoid the name of callousness which he might otherwise incur. If his feeling had any ulterior motives at all, these would be the most likely ones, so, if he was not prompted by any of these motives, one may take it that his feeling was genuinely spontaneous.

Mencius' purpose was only to show that men have natural motives to do good; he did not want to exaggerate the strength of such motives. It is worth noticing that Mencius does not say that this feeling of apprehension and pity would necessarily lead to any action at all. This serves to show that this feeling is only literally a "beginning," which needs cultivation before it can become a strong motive force. It also serves to show that in our nature we may be corrupt to the extent of doing nothing about the child, and yet not so corrupt as to feel nothing.

Not only did Mencius admit that men, more often than not, do the wrong thing, but he offered an explanation for it. This, according to him, is due to the corrupting influence of environment.

"In good years the young people are mostly slack; in hard years they are mostly violent. It is not that heaven has thus endowed them differently, but that what ensnares their hearts are what they are (sic). . . ."[23] That human nature can be corrupted by environment into doing wrong in no way conflicts with Mencius' view, for even when a man does wrong in his corrupted state, he would still know that what he is doing is wrong and feel ashamed of himself. Even the wicked brother of Shun was ashamed when, after making what he thought was a successful attempt on Shun's life, he saw Shun coming into the room.[24]

Moreover, such an account of the corruption of human nature shows that Mencius had his eyes firmly on the facts of human behavior.

It will be helpful to our understanding of Mencius' theory if we ask the question: "Under what circumstances would we be entitled to say, in the same sense in which Mencius says that human nature is good, that human nature is bad?" We have seen that it would not do just to point out that human beings do very often act contrary to their duties. Man would need to approve of the wrong as such and feel ashamed of doing the right as such. But this would be a contradiction in terms, for when we approve of anything we do so because it is right, and when we disapprove of anything we do so because it is wrong, and so if we try to say that we approve of a thing because it is wrong, we feel that either it is a contradiction in terms or that "wrong" really does not mean wrong but right. One cannot really have an immoral morality. The true contrast to morality is the lack of it. That is to say, the opposite to Mencius' view that human nature is good is not the apparent contradictory view that human nature is bad but the view that human nature is amoral. Men would, then, be in a state in which they would not draw the distinction between right and wrong and, therefore, would feel no approval or disapproval. Once we put the matter in this way, we see that the doctrine that human nature is good amounts to no more than that human beings are moral agents, because for a man to be a moral agent is simply for him to be capable of distinguishing right from wrong, to approve of right and disapprove of wrong, and to be able to choose to do the right. Put in this way, it can at once be seen that Mencius' theory was not in conflict with the facts of human behavior at all.

It may be felt that if that is all the contribution made by Mencius to moral philosophy, it is not much. We must, however, realize that though it may not seem very much if we consider Mencius as a contemporary philosopher, it certainly marked a great advance in his time. We must remember that Mencius was combating views current at his time, according to which human nature consists only of desires, morality is decreed by heaven 天命 *tianming* and, this being external, it is not at all certain whether men can be moral or not. Mencius' theory serves to break down the barrier between *ming* and *xing*, and insists that morality is not something "that comes from outside to adorn me, but something that I had originally."[25] He quotes with approval from the *Book of Poetry*:

Heaven produced the common people;
And when Heaven produces anything it also provides it with a

standard,
The common people, if they hold firm to the norm,
Will be attracted to the beautiful virtues.

He goes on to quote Confucius as saying "Whoever wrote this poem must have had knowledge of the 道 *dao*."[26] Mencius quotes this poem with such approval because it lends support to his "internalization" of morals, which may be described as the substituting of "self-legislation" for "external divine command."[27] It is not surprising that Mencius could cite support for his theory from the Zhou poems, as it is really a working out of a view of morals, the germ of which could be found in the thought of the early Zhou rulers as embodied in parts of the *Book of History* 書經 *Shujing* and the *Book of Poetry* 詩經 *Shijing*. This was certainly no mean achievement.[28]

III

We can best begin our account of Xunzi's doctrine of human nature by his definition of it.

> Human nature is what is accomplished by heaven. It is something which cannot be learned and to which one cannot apply oneself. . . . That in man which cannot be learned and to which he cannot apply himself is called his nature.[29]

In defining human nature thus, the purpose is to contrast it with human artifice 偽 *wei*[30] which, later in the same passage, Xunzi defines as "That in man of which he can become capable through learning and which he can perfect through application is called human artifice."[31] Now this definition of human nature is a formal one. It only gives us a criterion for deciding, when faced with any human capacity, whether it falls under human nature or human artifice, given that we know whether this capacity can be learned or not and whether it can be improved through application or not. It is the sort of definition which may continue to hold even if human nature were to change, so long as there are still certain capacities which can be learned and others that cannot be. So this definition does not tell us what exactly human nature is, and for it to be informative on this point it is essential that Xunzi should further specify what it is that cannot be learned or improved through application. This we find in his chapter on Rectification of Names:

> Human nature is that which is accomplished by heaven; emotions 情 *qing* are the content of human nature, desires are emotions manifesting themselves as responses.[32]

The substance or content of human nature is the emotions and these are enumerated as "love, hate, pleasure, anger, sorrow, and joy."[33] They are not important in themselves, but only in so far as they manifest themselves as responses to outside things and thus become desires, which are important for our present purpose, as they lead to action, and it is only when there is action that the question of human nature being good or evil arises.

> Man has desires from birth, and when he desires a thing which he has not got, he necessarily seeks it.[34]

There is no harm in our desires leading us to seek for what we have not got. But Xunzi brings in two other factors which change the complexion of the situation. Firstly:

> Men cannot live without society.[35]

This is because:

> The fruits of the hundred crafts contribute to the sustenance of one man whose capacities cannot be directed towards all the crafts and who cannot attend to all tasks, with the result that if he cuts himself off from society, he would find himself in an impossible position.[36]

Herein lies our superiority to animals,[37] but it is also responsible for the difficulty man finds himself in. Man cannot live without others; but it is not easy for him to live with them either. Secondly:

> Desires and aversions are for the same things. Desires are many while things are few. This scarcity necessarily leads to strife.[38]

We can now see the whole argument. Men cannot but live in society, but they have desires for the same things. The number of things available is limited and is not enough to satisfy all desires if everyone indulges his desires to the full. The result is strife,[39] and "strife is disastrous."[40] To say that strife is disastrous 禍 *huo* is Xunzi's way of saying that strife is bad. Since the content of human nature is desire, and desire given free rein leads necessarily to strife which is bad, we can see why Xunzi says that human nature is bad.

In Xunzi's time there was current a doctrine which solved the problem we are now concerned with by advocating either (a) the complete elimination of desires, or (b) the cutting down of the number of desires.[41] This, of course, goes directly against the teaching of Xunzi, according to which desires, since we are endowed with them by heaven, are beyond our power to change or influence. Xunzi is very positive in his rejection of such a view.

> Whoever in talking about order says we must first rid ourselves of our desires is one who does not know at all how to guide his desires, and so is embarrassed by his desires. Whoever in talking about order says we must first cut down the number of desires is one who does not know how to control his desires and so is embarrassed by having too many desires. Having desires is different in kind from having no desires—the difference between the living and the dead, not the difference between orderly and disorderly states of the same kind of thing. Having many desires is different in kind from having few desires—the difference in the number of emotions, not the difference between orderly and disorderly states of the same kind of thing.[42]

Here Xunzi points out that that which has desires is totally different in kind from that which has no desires, and they are contrasted as the living and the dead, or the animate and the inanimate. Similarly that which has many desires is totally different in kind from that which has few desires. To say that they are different in kind is to say that unless we can change the nature of the one, we cannot hope to transform it into the other, but by definition the nature of a thing is determined by heaven and cannot be changed by the doing of man. Hence it is idle to advocate either ridding ourselves totally of our desires or cutting down the number of desires, for to hope to be able to do this is to hope to transform ourselves into something other than men, which is impossible.

Further, since having desires and having no desires belong to different classes they cannot be the orderly and disorderly states of the same thing. That is, we cannot hold the view that for men to have no desires will give rise to order while for men to have desires will give rise to disorder, for men without desires would no longer be men. The mistake of the doctrine under examination lies, according to Xunzi, precisely in this false belief that even after ridding themselves of their desires (or cutting down their desires) men would still be men.

Having rejected this solution, Xunzi offers his own. This is based on the distinction between desiring something and seeking it.

Whether we desire something or not does not depend on whether that something is obtainable or not; but whether we seek what we desire depends on whether what is desired is possible 可 *ke*[43] or not. Desires do not depend on the obtainability or otherwise of their objects because desires are what we are given by heaven; seeking depends on whether we think the object possible or not because seeking depends on the mind.[44] When what is originally the same in all of us, viz. the desires given us by heaven, is controlled by the mind which differs greatly in different people, it is natural that what results is not much like what we originally got from heaven.[45]

We are all given by heaven the same desires which it is beyond our power to change. What is within our control is whether we proceed to seek the objects of our desires. If the mind realizes that the securing of an object is impossible (or impermissible), then we stop seeking the object. To illustrate this, Xunzi points to cases where a man's action falls short of his desire or goes beyond his desire. In such cases, says Xunzi, it is the mind which keeps the man back or urges him on. An example of the former would be a man who sacrifices his life, because holding on to life would be impermissible. As all men love life more than anything else, the action of a man who sacrifices his life, Xunzi argues, falls short of the strength of his desire for life which would be more than enough to carry him through any action that may be necessary to escape death.

But, it may be asked, if, as a result of the difference between our minds, some of us may consider the securing of any given object as possible (or permissible) and so pursue it, while others consider the same thing impossible (or impermissible) and so desist from pursuing it, is that not evidence that we have been given different desires by heaven? It is to forestall this that Xunzi makes the point that the desires given us by heaven were originally the same, and that it is only because our minds exhibit such diversity that the final result, viz. our desires as modified by the control of our minds, bears so little resemblance to our original desires. At any rate the main point Xunzi wants to establish is that in spite of our desires, our minds have a good degree of control over what we actually do.

Now we are in a position to understand a further definition of human artifice given by Xunzi:

When emotions are what they are (sic), the choosing between them by the mind is called reflection. When the mind reflects and puts our capacities to use, this is called human artifice.

What is accomplished through the accumulation of reflection and the practice in the exercise of our capacities is called human artifice.[46]

This definition completes the description of the marks which distinguish human artifice from human nature. Not only is what can be learned and improved upon by application human artifice, but also what is the result of reflection by the mind. The importance of this will be seen when we come to discuss the role played by the sages in Xunzi's doctrine. The two parts of the definition are designed to bring out the point that there are two distinct ways in which the mind can modify our action. First it can think out the course of action for a particular occasion, and make use of our original capacities for the carrying out of the planned course of action. Secondly, it can accumulate reflections and, more important, it can habituate our capacities to carrying out the planned actions even though these may be contrary to the natural use of these capacities.

Now, it being established that the mind has the ability to control our actions, it is easy to see that the next task is to show that whether we have order or disorder (in ourselves or in society) will depend on the principle underlying the mind's decision whether or in which way to act. If that principle is reasonable then we will have order; if not, disorder.

If what the mind permits 可 *ke* is reasonable, even if desires are numerous, what harm is this to order? . . . If what the mind permits is not reasonable, then even if desires are few, what is there to prevent disorder? This is why order and disorder depend on what the mind considers permissible (*ke*) and have nothing to do with what our emotions desire.[47]

With this, Xunzi seems to have contradicted his own main thesis that desires are responsible for strife and disorder, which is his ground for saying that human nature is evil. But he can be defended against the charge of self-contradiction. When he says that desires lead to strife and disorder, what he means is that desires as they originally are will, if unchecked, lead naturally to strife and disorder. What desire as controlled by the mind leads to is not the same as what desire in its original state would naturally lead to.

Now this principle which, if it underlies the mind's decisions, would lead to order is, of course, morality. Morality, Xunzi insists, was an invention of the sages:

Human nature is what is accomplished by heaven. It is something which cannot be learned and to which one cannot apply oneself. Morality is what has been produced by the sages. It is that of which a man is capable through learning and which he perfects through application.[48]

Morality consists in the creating of social distinctions, which carry with them the delimitation of the extent to which it is permissible for members of each social class to indulge their desires. This Xunzi calls 分 *fen*. As we have seen, strife was attributed to living in society without such delimitation. "Not to have social distinctions (*fen*) is the greatest evil to man; to have social distinctions is the greatest benefit to man."[49] Again, "When there is strife, there is disorder, and when there is disorder, the position would be impossible. The Former Kings disliked disorder. Hence they made morality for the sake of assigning people to their social classes (*fen*)."[50]

The cure for strife and disorder is to lay down rules concerning the position and status of individuals and classes in society. This would define what everyone is entitled to and the precedence of different claimants. This is Xunzi's conception of morality, which is to enable people to reap the benefit of living in society while avoiding the accompanying evils.

In inventing morality the sages had to do more than merely see that this is a solution to the problem of how to reconcile the fact that individuals possess desires with the fact that they have to live in society. They had also to be able to see that what is required of the ordinary man is comprehensible to him, and that there is a genuine possibility of so disciplining man that he will behave in accordance with the prescriptions of morality as if it were second nature to him. And when the ordinary man understands what is required of him, and succeeds in cultivating the habit of being moral, then he is no different from a sage in his behavior.

What does it mean to say that ordinary men can become a Yu? Answer: What makes a Yu a Yu is his being moral and correct. Now morality and norms have in them that which makes them intelligible and practicable. And ordinary men are all so constituted that they are able to understand morality and norms and are all capable of putting them into practice. It is obvious then that an ordinary man can become a Yu. Now, if you consider morality and norms as beyond the possibility of understanding and practice, then even Yu could not have understood them and practiced them. On the other hand, if the man in the street has not the capacity to understand morality and the norms nor the capacity to practice them, then he would not be able to understand, when in the family, the right relation between father and son or, when abroad, the correct relation between ruler and subordinate. Now that is not so; ordinary people are all able to understand, when in the family, the right relation between father and son and, when abroad, the correct relation between ruler and subordinate. It is obvious then that the man in the street has the capacity both to understand and to practice them. Now if the man in the street, with his capacity both to understand and to practice morality and norms, bases himself on the intelligibility and practicability of morality and the norms,[51] then it is obvious that he can become a Yu. And if the man in the street applies himself to learning, and sets his whole heart on it, reflects upon it and examines it carefully, then after a long period of ceaselessly accumulating goodness, he will be in communion with the gods and form a triad with heaven and earth. That is why the position of the sage is attained by the accumulation of human effort.[52]

The common man, if he perseveres in the accumulation of morality (i.e. the gradual acquisition of the habit of behaving morally) will become a sage. It is worth noting in passing that even then he would not really be the equal of the ancient sage kings, for he has only succeeded in becoming a sage after the sage kings had invented morality. Xunzi does not say, and the tenor of his whole teaching is against the view, that any and everybody who thinks hard enough will be able to invent morality.[53]

At this point the question naturally arises: If it is possible for every man to become a sage, why is it not, in fact, true that every man does become a sage? To answer this, Xunzi draws the distinction between its being possible for anyone to become something and his actually succeeding in becoming it.

Question: If the position of the sage is attained by accumulation, why is it not the case that all men are capable of this accumulation? Answer: They are capable of it but cannot be made to do it. The small man is capable of becoming a gentleman but he refuses to become one; the gentleman is capable of becoming a small man but refuses to become one. It is not impossible for small men and gentlemen to become each other; yet they do not, in fact, become each other, because although they can do so they cannot be made to do so. Hence it is the case that the man in the street can become a Yu, but it is not necessarily the case that he will become a Yu. Even if he does not succeed in becoming a Yu, that does not interfere with his being capable of becoming a Yu. The foot is capable of walking all round the world, but there is yet no foot which has succeeded in walking all round the world. It is not impossible for the craftsman, the farmer and the merchant to do one another's jobs, yet they do not in fact succeed in doing so. Judging from this, 'capable of becoming' is not necessarily 'successful in becoming'; and 'not succeeding' does not interfere with 'being capable of becoming.' Hence, 'succeeding and not succeeding,' and 'capable and not capable' are very far apart.[54]

We are now in a position to sum up Xunzi's view of human nature. Human nature consists of emotions which are manifested as desires in response to outside things. Desires naturally lead to seeking the objects desired. Unfortunately man has to live in society, and the supply of goods is limited. Hence, if everyone were to give unchecked rein to his desires, there would not be enough things to go round. This would result in strife and disorder, which are evils. We would still be living in such a state had it not been for the sage kings who invented morality. This consists in assigning to everyone a position in society which defines all that he is entitled to. Because rights to goods are prescribed (presumably with an eye on the available resources) there is harmony and order in place of strife and disorder. That morality is possible is because of three facts. Firstly, our minds have a certain amount of control over the seeking of the objects of our desires, though not over the desires themselves. Secondly, we are creatures capable of habituation. Once a habit is formed, it becomes second nature. This increases the control the mind has over our actions. Lastly, morality, once invented, is intelligible to the man in the street. Every man has within him the makings of a sage. That he does not always succeed in becoming one is because he does not exert himself. Thus Xunzi not only makes room for, but actually accounts for, the fact that there are people who behave morally and people who behave immorally. Like Mencius, he does not fly in the face of facts about human behavior. His thesis that human nature is evil is based solely on the view that an analysis of human nature, as he defines it, shows that, if something is not done to it, it leads inevitably to strife.

IV

We have seen that neither the doctrine of Mencius nor that of Xunzi goes against the facts of human behavior. Let us turn now to a comparison between these two doctrines. We have seen that it is unprofitable to take these two doctrines as being embodied in the two simple assertions, viz. that human nature is good, and that human nature is bad, and consider them as flatly contradicting each other. Rather we should look at the grounds for these doctrines. In the case of Mencius, the grounds are: (a) human beings all have a sense of right and wrong and a sense of shame, and (b) it is possible for human beings to do the right thing, i.e. in the make-up of human nature there are various tendencies which can furnish the motive force for doing the right thing. In the case of Xunzi, the grounds are: (a) morality is not part of human nature but the invention of the sages, (b) if human beings were to act in accordance with their original nature, this would lead to strife. It is obvious that Mencius and Xunzi disagree on both these issues. The basis of disagreement in both cases lies in Xunzi's distinction between human nature and human artifice. Let us, first of all, recall this distinction: human nature is that which (1) is made what it is by heaven, (2) cannot be learned, (3) cannot be improved through application and (4) is not the result of reflection by the mind; while human artifice is that which (1) is invented by the sages, (2) can be learned, (3) can be improved through application and (4) is the result of reflection by the mind.

With this in mind, let us turn back to the two points at issue between Mencius and Xunzi. Let us take the second first. According to Xunzi, human nature consists of desires which, if unchecked, lead to strife. He is implicitly denying that there are desires which are not of this kind, desires which would lead to harmony rather than to strife. Mencius, on the other hand, believes that in the original nature of man there are tendencies that would prompt him to act in a moral way. The contrast between Mencius and Xunzi comes out most clearly in a passage in which Mencius also states this point in terms of what one has to learn before being able to know or do it and what need not be learned.

> That which a man knows without having to reflect is what he really knows; that which he is able to do without having to learn it is what he really knows how to do.[55] There are no young children who do not know to love their parents, and who when they grow up do not know to respect their elder brothers. To love one's parents is 仁 *ren*; to respect one's elder brothers is 義 *yi*.[56]

Here then we have an irreconcilable difference between the two views. But the issue is not quite so clear-cut as regards the other point of difference, for in this statement of what a man knows without reflection and can do without having to learn, Mencius has only named *ren* and *yi* which, we may remember, answer to only two of the four beginnings man is said to have, viz. the heart that cannot bear the suffering of others and the heart of keeping oneself back in order to make way for others. No mention is made of the other two of the four beginnings, viz. the heart of right and wrong and the heart of shame.[57] One suspects that Mencius was aware of the difficulty if he included the other two. It may not be self-evident that children all naturally love their parents and respect their elder brothers, but it can still be said to be plausible. But it is not even plausible to say that young children are naturally able to distinguish between right and wrong and have a sense of shame. To be fair to Mencius, neither is it obvious that morality is an invention of the sages as Xunzi would have it.

The inconclusiveness on both sides is due mainly to the intrinsic difficulty of the issue before us. We are in reality faced with the unenviable task of deciding whether something is learned or not, which is all the more difficult since the character in question is one which does not seem to manifest itself until a certain stage in the development of the human being. Babies do not show a sense of morality. On this point probably both philosophers agree. But as the child grows older, he gradually shows signs of being able to draw moral distinctions and capable of genuinely moral behavior, as against behavior which is prompted solely by love for his parents. We can interpret this fact in two ways. We can, of course, say that the child has learned morality as he has learned so many other things, e.g. speech. On the other hand, we can also say that although he does not show any awareness of morality until he is some years old, morality is really part of his initial make-up, but that the child must reach a certain maturity of mind and be given the right environment and opportunity before his moral consciousness will manifest itself. In this respect moral behavior is rather like sexual behavior. Although it is part of original human nature, it does not manifest itself at birth.[58] We have here two ways of looking at morality in relation to human nature. To put it in another way, we are not as sure of the nature of our moral consciousness as we are of the nature of speech and sex. That is why we find it illuminating to look upon morality as similar to one or the other of these two types of human capacities. If morality is really like speech, it is acquired, but if it is really like sex, it is part of original human nature. If we can decide to adopt either of these ways of looking at morality, we seem to have a clearer conception of the nature of morality, because we are enabled by our choice to arrive at further conclusions about morality simply by pushing our analogy further. If in so doing we are only making clear to ourselves the nature of morality, it may seem immaterial which we choose. But unfortunately in looking upon morality as similar to either we are doing something more. The clarification of the nature of morality carries with it also a decision as to its significance, because it seems natural to feel that morality, if it is acquired, does not possess the same significance as it would if it were part of original human nature.[59]

What is at stake appears to be the nature of morality rather than the nature of man. This point can also be brought out by looking into a weakness in Xunzi's argument. Given that the mind is part of human nature, it is inevitable that someone or other (a sage in Xunzi's terminology) will sooner or later think out a solution which will enable man to escape from the awkward situation he finds himself in as a result of his desires, and on Xunzi's showing there is one, and only one, possible solution, viz. morality. There is no reason why we should not extend the name human nature to cover the capacity of invention possessed by the mind which is part of it. Xunzi's refusal to grant this is reminiscent of the arguments put forth by pious Christians when the motor car was first invented that if we were meant by God to travel on wheels we would have been born with them. There is no reason why God should not have given us a mind and left us to do all our inventing, as there is no reason why the capacity of invention of the mind should not be classified as part of human nature. All this does, of course, nothing to remove the distinctions Xunzi had drawn; it only shows that the distinctions are not the kind that would serve as basis for a theory of human nature. Yet looked at from the point of view of morality what Xunzi says is important, for whether the capacity of invention of the mind is classified as part of human nature or not, it is important, as we have seen, to decide whether or not morality itself is an invention.

Corresponding to this difference as to the nature of morality is a difference between the roles Mencius and Xunzi assigned to the sages or sage kings.

For Xunzi, the sages or sage kings invented morality.[60]   They created morality out of human nature, just as the potter created a vessel out of clay. Also just as the potter is able to do what he does, not *qua* man but *qua* potter, so the sage is able to do what he does, not *qua* man but *qua* sage.[61] The sage, with his special qualifications as a sage, was able to see a way out of the human predicament, and this is the morality he invented. A good example of what a man can do by nature is sight. We either can see or cannot see; we cannot either learn to see or improve our seeing.[62] Any craft will serve as a good example of what is invented by an expert. A good craftsman can discover, say, how to make a vessel. After he has invented it, of course, everyone with average skill can learn to make it. Every craftsman can now make a vessel, but that does not mean that we did not need a genius to invent it in the first place. The argument is sound so far, but there is a certain difficulty. Before any invention in any given craft was made, there must have been a first step, and this first step could only have been taken by someone who was not a specialist. In other words, before the sage invented morality there can have been no sages. If someone invented morality, he must have done so *qua* man after all and not *qua* sage. All that can really be said is that the sage was a more intelligent man who saw a solution where no one had seen one before. It is for this reason that I said earlier on that the definition of human artifice in terms of reflection is important in this connection.[63] That human artifice can be learned and made habitual does not concern the sage who invented morality, except in so far as in making his invention he had to keep in mind that it must fulfill these two conditions.

With Mencius the sages, though they cannot be assigned this role, are assigned some part. Yi Yin 伊尹 is quoted twice as saying that when heaven produced this people it made those who were first to know and to awaken, awaken the others.[64] Their role is not one of invention but of awakening others and making them realize what is within themselves. In 6A7 Mencius says: "What is common to all hearts is reason and morality. A sage is only he who first got hold of that which is common to all hearts. Hence reason and morality please my heart just as meat pleases my mouth."[65] We are all delighted with what is moral, but it needs a sage to find out what it is that we are delighted with. He finds out what is common to all moral acts, and systematizes moral principles. A sage in regard to morality may be compared, say, to a grammarian in regard to our speech. We can all recognize correct forms of speech, but it needs a grammarian to find out the system that runs through our speech habits. That Mencius was well qualified to carry out this task of the sage can be seen from the way that he dealt with King Xuan of Qi.[66] This ability to analyze clearly what pertains to the mind is the ability of the sage. The sage does not invent but awakens others to what is really within themselves.

It may be said that all ancient Chinese philosophers were mainly concerned with practical problems. They were concerned with how people could be made morally good and how government could result in order. In other words they were all concerned with the problem of moral education. Any difference in their way of looking at morality was bound to reflect itself in their methods of moral education. We can go even further and say that it is in the field of moral education that we see clearly the significance of the difference between their moral theories. This is particularly true of Mencius and Xunzi. For Xunzi, since morality is only a device invented by the sages and does not answer to anything which forms part of original human nature, the only way of instilling it into people is by sheer drill and habituation. The favorite analogies resorted to by Xunzi are the straightening of crooked wood by the pressing frame and the sharpening of metal through grinding. Our only hope of success is that if the drilling is thorough enough morality may become second nature to men. For Mencius the position is radically different. Morality is part of original human nature, though as yet only a slender beginning. The way to go about educating people morally is to awaken them to the realization that they have got it within themselves. The analogy of the pressing frame and the grindstone is not only mistaken but vicious. In his criticism of Gaozi on precisely this point Mencius is emphatic in his denunciation:

> Gaozi said: 'Human nature is like the willow, and morality is like cups. To make human nature moral is like making cups out of the willow.' Mencius said: 'Is it by following the nature of the willow that you can make it into cups, or do you have to do violence to the willow in order to make it into cups? If you have to do violence to it to make it into cups, then do you also have to do violence to man in order to make him moral? Nothing could be more calculated to lead men to bring disaster upon morality than your words.'[67]

Mencius' criticism is not simply that the analogy is inept, for inept analogies, though necessarily useless, may yet be harmless. It is that the misleading implications are positively vicious. It suggests distorting and torturing human nature before it can be made moral. From Mencius' point of view the situation is totally different. Becoming moral is only a cultivating and a nurturing of what was there in human nature originally. This is very well summed up in the following passage.

> Mencius said: 'The gentleman penetrates deep into the Way, for he wants to find it within himself. If he finds it within himself, then he can feel at home in it. If he can feel at home in it, he can

draw greatly on its help. If he can draw greatly on its help, he can take from it left and right and always meet with its source. Hence the gentleman wants to find it within himself.'[68]

It is only if a man finds morality within himself that he can abide by it and can draw on its resources without the fear of its failing him. Considering the moral demand stated by Mencius that when life and duty are incompatible one ought to "forgo life in order to be moral,"[69] it is not surprising that he should have emphasized the possession by the gentleman of endless moral resources. Compared with this it is not easy to see how habituation as advocated by Xunzi could cope with such difficult duties. Habit is all very well in cases where the difficulty is not too great and no conflicts arise in one's mind. In a case where one is called upon to sacrifice one's very life, the difficulty in Xunzi's theory is acute, for, in the last analysis, the only reason Xunzi offers for being moral is the avoidance of strife and disorder, which are harmful. Arguing within the framework of benefit and harm, what is more harmful than death? And if a man is willing to give up his life in order that harm should not befall the world, this is no longer acting from habit, and Xunzi's whole theory that human nature is evil is in peril. It is significant that Xunzi's examples of moral actions are never cases of great sacrifices but only comparatively trivial cases like letting one's elders eat first even though one is hungry and working in their place though one is tired,[70] for these may well be cases where habit alone will see one through. In fact they are the kind of thing that could easily be done without thinking at all. When Xunzi tried to show that a man sometimes embraces death because he thinks life impermissible, it is, as we have seen, the equivocation on the word *ke*[71] which has prevented the weakness of his argument from being transparent. As Mencius and Xunzi both belonged to the Confucian tradition, they held more or less similar views concerning the demands made by morality on man. On Xunzi's theory of human nature, it is more difficult to show with any plausibility that man can be morally educated so as to live up to the most stringent of those demands. That this is so is a serious drawback, at least when judged from within the tradition to which both philosophers belong.

Notes

1. The word here translated as "human nature" is 性 *xing*, which strictly speaking means merely "the nature (of something)," but was used by Mencius (and probably before him) to mean specifically "human nature." However, the term "人性 *renxing*" is also occasionally used (e.g. 6A1 and 2). It is certain that the word *xing* is etymologically either the same word as, or closely

cognate with, the word 生 *sheng*, which means "to give birth to, to produce, to come into being." For discussion of this problem, see the excellent work by the late Fu Sinian 傅斯年, *Xingmingguxunbianzheng* 性命古訓辯證 (Commercial Press, second ed., 1947).

2. In this paper I propose to discuss theories of human nature as found in the books *Mencius* and *Xunzi*. For this purpose it is unnecessary to consider the authorship and authenticity of these texts. That *Mencius* contains the genuine teachings of Mencius has rarely been called in question. The case of *Xunzi* is, however, different. The fact that the present text duplicates to a considerable extent what is to be found in the *Liji* 禮記, the *Dadailiji* 大戴禮記 and the *Hanshiwaizhuan* 韓詩外傳 seems to show that *Xunzi* is a work of a very heterogeneous nature. Fortunately in the present paper I draw mainly on two chapters of *Xunzi*, viz. chapter twenty-two, 正名 *Zhengming* "The Rectification of Names," and chapter twenty-three, 性惡 *Xing'e* "That Human Nature Is Evil," supplemented by only a few quotations from three other chapters. As the doctrine that human nature is evil, which is the concern of this paper, has since the earliest times been associated with the name of Xunzi, there is a good chance that the passages I have used are more or less authentic. At any rate, the question of authenticity is of no great importance, as my purpose is philosophical rather than historical or textual. So long as the thought contained in these passages is of intrinsic interest, it matters little whether they were genuinely the work of Xunzi or only attributed to him. However, having given this warning, I shall speak freely of what is said by Mencius and Xunzi, and assume that I shall be understood as saying no more than that such and such is found in the books *Mencius* and *Xunzi*.

3. See Wang Chong 王充, *Lunheng* 論衡: "Shi Shi 世碩 of the Zhou 周 Dynasty considered that there are both good and bad in human nature, and that if the good nature in man is singled out for nurture then the good will develop, but if the bad is singled out for nurture then the bad will develop. . . . He therefore wrote a book called *Yangshu* 養書. Fu Zijian 宓子賤, Qi Diaokai 漆雕開, Gongsun Nizi 公孫尼子 and the like also discussed human nature, holding views which agreed with Shi on some points and disagreed on others, but they all considered that there are both good and bad in human nature." [*Sibucongkan* (*SBCK*) 四部叢刊 ed. juan 3 pp. 14b-15a.]

4. *Lunyu* 論語 17.2 and 3.

5. Although this view does not appear in the Bohutong 白虎通, Ban Gu 班固 makes use of this principle of grading human beings in his Gujinrenbiao 古今人表 (*Hanshu* 漢書, juan 20), and further subdivides each of the three grades into three.

6. Omit the word 儒.

7. *Lunheng*, juan 3 pp. 18b-19a.

8. *SBCK* ed. juan 5 p. 5a.

9. *Lunheng*, juan 3 p. 17b. This is not found in the extant work of Dong Zhongshu. In the *Chunqiufanlu* 春秋繁露 we find a rather different view of human nature. My purpose here is merely to show that the dualist view was current in Han times. Dong was considered, rightly or wrongly, by Wang Chong as holding this view.

10. *Erchengquanshu* 二程全書, *Sibubeiyao* (*SBBY*) 四部備要 ed., *Erchengyishu* 二程遺書 juan 22A pp. 10b-11a. This distinction is sometimes alternatively stated as between the material nature 氣質之性 *qizhi zhi xing* and the moral or rational nature 義禮之性 *yili zhi xing*. Zhu Xi 朱熹 writes: "Mencius never mentioned the material nature of man. The greatest contribution Chengzi 程子 made to morals in his discussion of human nature was his elucidation of this material nature. Once we bring in material nature, all the differences between those who discuss human nature disappear completely." *Zhuziyuleijilue* 朱子語類輯略, *Congshujicheng* 叢書集成 ed. juan 1 p. 26.

11. *Mencius* 6A7; Legge, *Chinese Classics* (second ed., rev., Oxford, 1895) vol. ii pp. 404-5. All translations used are my own and, because I wish to make these translations as literal as possible, they are often written in English which is not very idiomatic, but I hope they are at least intelligible. References to Legge are, however, included for the convenience of the reader who may not otherwise have easy access to the Chinese texts.

12. Ibid. 4B32; Legge, p. 340.

13. Ibid. 6B2; Legge, p. 424.

14. 荀子: 性惡 23/115/22-3, Knoblock 23.4a. (All the chapters in Xunzi I quote from have been translated by Prof. Homer H. Dubs in his *The Works of Hsüntze* (London: Arthur Probsthain, 1928), but as it does not contain the Chinese text I shall not give detailed references to it.) Elsewhere, in chapter five, 非相 *Feixiang* "Against Physiognomy," we find: "Past and present are the same [omit the word 度]. Things of the same kind, though they are far apart in time, have the same principle underlying them." [荀子: 非相 5/19/4, Knoblock 5.5] It is interesting to note in passing that Dr. Hu Shih took this passage as evidence that Xunzi believed in the immutability of species, translating it as follows: "The past and the present are the same. The species are not mutable: they are governed by the same principle, no matter how long they have lasted." *The Development of the Logical Method in Ancient China* (Shanghai: The Oriental Book Company, 1922) 153; see also *Zhongguozhexueshidagang* 中國哲學史大綱 (1919) 311-12. The text does not seem to warrant such an interpretation. All that is said is that *if* things are of the same kind, then irrespective of the position in time they may happen to occupy, the same principle underlies them all; it says nothing as to whether things can change from one species into another or not. If they do, then since they would have become things of a different kind it follows as a matter of course that the principle that used to underlie them before the change would no longer hold. For our present purpose this passage embodies the

general principle of which the truth that all men being of the same kind are alike is but a special case.

15. 荀子: 性惡 23/116/12-3, Knoblock 23.5a.

16. An objection may be raised here that even if *qi* is not used as a technical term in *Xunzi*, it seems to be so used in *Mencius*, and this may, in some respects at least, be akin to the notion of *qi* of the Song philosophers. Such an objection would, of course, be based solely on *Mencius* 2A2, where the famous 浩然之氣 *haoran zhi qi* occurs. As it would be too long to go into details concerning the interpretation of the *haoran zhi qi*, my answer is briefly this. I am aware that there have been attempts to read metaphysical implications into this phrase of Mencius, but I am inclined to think that the purpose of the whole passage was merely to give a description of what it feels like to be a morally cultivated man so as to provide a criterion for anyone who would like to test his own progress in the acquiring of such cultivation. In its use here *qi* would have very much its ordinary meaning of "breath," something which, in Mencius' own words, "fills the body." As a man who is angry is puffed up with *qi*, so a man of moral cultivation who has right on his side is filled with the *haoran zhi qi*. By using the word *qi* for both, Mencius draws our attention to the resemblance while, by adding the epithet *haoran*, he is drawing our attention to the difference. In being filled with righteous indignation, we are not really puffed up with breath as in the case of anger. Nevertheless, there is something akin between the two such as to make this way of speaking illuminating in our search for some subjective sign which can enable us to recognize our success in moral cultivation.

17. In this paper I have sometimes rendered the word 心 *xin* as "heart," because, though it is perhaps more natural to render it as "mind," in some contexts "mind" would be misleading. As the word "heart" in English can be used to denote the seat of the emotions, it is an extension rather than a violation of its usage to use it to denote other aspects of the mind.

18. *Dongshu Dushuji* 東塾讀書記, *SBBY* ed. juan 3 pp. 1a-1b.

19. The word here translated as "beginning" is 端 *duan*, which means literally a new shoot, a sprout, and therefore something which needs nurture before it can develop fully into a plant.

20. *Mencius* 2A6.

21. Ibid. 7A6.

22. Ibid. 7A7.

23. Ibid. 6A7.

24. Ibid. 5A2.

25. Ibid. 6A6.

26. Ibid. 6A6. The quotation from *The Book of Poetry* is from *Zhengmin* 蒸民 in the *Daya* 大雅.

27. This naturally reminds one of Bishop Butler's sermon on the text "For when the Gentiles, which have not the law, do by nature the things contained in the law, these, having not the law, are a law unto themselves." Indeed the resemblance between Mencius' moral philosophy and that of Butler was pointed out long ago by Legge (see "Mencius and His Disciples: His Influence and Opinions," *The Chinese Classics*, vol. 2 (Oxford: Clarendon Press, 1895) 60-76. I wish, however, to draw attention to the difference between them. Butler, as has often been pointed out, had a hankering after the view that enlightened self-interest and conscience, in the last resort, really point the same way. But Mencius was most uncompromising in his attitude towards self-interest 利 *li*, as can be seen from, for instance, 7A25, where he says, "One who gets up with the crowing of the cock and untiringly works for goodness is the same sort of man as Shun; one who gets up with the crowing of the cock and untiringly works for profit (*li*) is of the same sort as Zhi. If you want to know the difference between Shun and Zhi, it is nothing else than this: it is the difference between profit and goodness."

28. I cannot here go into the problem of the relation between *ming* and *xing*, interesting though it is. For treatment of the history of both notions and their relation I refer the reader to the book by Fu Sinian mentioned in n. 1.

29. 凡性者、天之就也，不可學，不可事。⋯不可學、不可事之在人者謂之性。[荀子: 性惡 23/113/17-8] Knoblock 23.1c.

30. The word *wei* as used in *Xunzi* is free from the pejorative sense of "hypocritical." It is possible that the word originally used by Xunzi was simply 為 *wei* "to do." At any rate, *wei* is used in *Xunzi* as a technical term in opposition to *xing* (human nature). It covers both the human activities of doing something and making something, e.g. moral behavior and the making of articles by a craftsman. Since there is no English word which covers the same range of meaning, I have chosen arbitrarily the term "human artifice," which should therefore be understood in the sense just described.

31. 可學而能、可事而成之在人者謂之偽。 [荀子: 性惡 23/113/18-9] Knoblock 23.1c.

32. 荀子: 正名 22/111/14, Knoblock 22.5b. There are two further translations of this chapter which may be consulted: (a) by Prof. J. J. L. Duyvendak, *T'oung Pao* 22 (1924) 221-254, (b) by Prof. Y. P. Mei, *PEW* 1:2 (July, 1951) 51-66. Both contain the Chinese text.

33. 荀子: 正名 22/107/23, Knoblock 22.1b.

34. 荀子: 禮論 19/90/3, Knoblock 19.1a.

35. 荀子: 王制 9/39/15, Knoblock 9.16a; also 荀子: 富國 10/43/9, Knoblock 10.4.

36. 荀子: 富國 10/42/16-7, Knoblock 10.1.

37. 荀子: 王制 9/39/9-13, Knoblock 9.16a.

38. 荀子: 富國 10/42/16, Knoblock 10.1.

39. Although Xunzi uses only the argument that the number of things fall short of that which would satisfy all the desires of all the men to the full, he need not have relied completely on this. Even were there enough things to go round, there may still be strife when different people desire one and the same thing. For the solution of this sort of conflict, there need to be rules to establish the precedence of claims.

40. 荀子: 富國 10/42/16, Knoblock 10.1.

41. The cutting down of the number of desires is put forth in *Mencius* 7B35, as the best means for nourishing the mind.

42. 荀子: 正名 22/111/4-6, Knoblock 22.5a.

43. The word *ke* means (1) possible, and (2) morally permissible. The argument here is that we stop seeking a thing once we realize that it is *impossible* (i.e. unattainable). But then it is assumed that what has been established is that we stop seeking a thing once we realize that it is *impermissible*. This sliding from something which is at least plausible to something which is palpably false is, of course, unacceptable. Fortunately this defect in the argument is not of very great importance to our present purpose. It is enough that we do *sometimes* stop seeking a thing once we realize that it is morally impermissible though we may continue to desire it.

44. In some versions there are nine extra characters here: 天性有欲心為之制節, "There are desires by nature, but the mind exercises control over them." See Kubo Ai (Chikusui) 久保愛 (筑水), *Junshi Zochu* 荀子增注, Kan 16 p. 13b.

45. 荀子: 正名 22/111/6-8, Knoblock 22.5a.

46. 情然而心為之擇偽之慮。心慮而能為之動謂之偽。慮積焉、能習焉而後成謂之偽。[荀子: 正名 22/107/23-4] Knoblock 22.1b.

47. 荀子: 正名 22/111/9-11, Knoblock 22.5a.

48. The first half of this quotation has already appeared on p. 198, where the original Chinese text is given in n. 29. The Chinese text then goes on as follows: 禮義者、聖人之所生也，人之所學而能，所事而成者也。[荀子: 性惡 23/113/17-8] Knoblock 23.1c.

49. 荀子: 富國 10/43/9-10, Knoblock 10.4. Read 大利 *dali* for 本利 *benli*.

50. 荀子: 王制 9/36/2, Knoblock 9.3.

51. Read 可知可能之理 for 可知之理可能之具.

52. 荀子: 性惡 23/116/6-15, Knoblock 23.5a.

53. In chapter 21, 解蔽 *Jiebi* however, in answer to the question, "How does the mind get to know the Way 道 *dao*?" we are given what seems to be a general recipe for attaining knowledge of the *dao*, viz. emptying, unity and

tranquillity (of the mind). This seems to dispense with the necessity of the sages as inventors of morality. As I have pointed out above (see n. 1), the present text of *Xunzi* is a very heterogeneous collection, and it is rather to be expected that there should be inconsistent views in different parts of the work. In our present case, the theory of mind and knowledge as found in chapter 21 is Daoist in flavor rather than Confucianist. See Yang Yunru 楊筠 如, *Xunziyanjiu* 荀子 研究 in *Guoxuexiaocongshu* 國學小叢書 (Commercial Press, 1933) 58-62.

54. 荀子: 性惡 23/116/17-23, Knoblock 23.5a.

55. The word I have here rendered as "really" is 良 *liang*. A word of explanation may not be out of place, as, since the Song philosophers, the phrases 良知 *liangzhi* and 良心 *liangxin* have been taken to mean "original morally good knowledge" and "original morally good capacities." Zhu Xi, for instance, says in his commentary, "By '*liang*' is meant 'originally good.'" (*Mengzijizhu* 孟子集注, *SBBY* ed. juan 15 p. 4b 11. 6-7). By the time of Wang Yangming 王陽明, this interpretation was so firmly established that *liangzhi liangneng*, in the sense of the originally good knowledge and capacities, became the corner-stone of his whole philosophy. But there seems to be no good grounds for this interpretation. The normal adjective for "morally good" is 善 *shan*. Apart from twice being used as a personal name, *liang* occurs only twelve times in *Mencius*, of which seven times are in the combination 良人 *liangren*, which approximates very closely to the English phrase "good man" in its idiomatic meaning of "husband." This has nothing to do with the use of the word under discussion. Of the other five occurrences, two seem to mean not "morally good" but "good of its kind": (1) 3B1 天下之良工也, "the *best* charioteer (lit. the best craftsman) under heaven"; (2) 6B9 今之所謂良臣古之所謂民賊也, "What is today called a *good* minister would in ancient times have been called a pest to the people." In 6A17 非良貴也 decidedly means "not *truly* (genuinely, really) noble," while in 4A15 we have 存乎人者莫良於眸子, "Of what is in man there is nothing more *genuine* (i.e. incapable of deceit) than his eyes." Lastly in 6A8 we have 其所以放其良心者亦猶斧斤之於木也, "His letting go of his *true* (original) heart is like what is done to the wood by axes and bills." These last three passages point to the use of the word *liang* as meaning, "truly, genuinely, really." I have therefore followed Pei Xuehai 裴學海 in extending this interpretation to the present passage. (See *Mengzizhengyibuzheng* 孟子 正義補正, in *Guoxueluncong* 國學論叢 2:2 (Tsing Hua University, 1930) 188-9. The gloss given by Zhao Qi 趙岐 in his commentary is 甚 *shen* (very, greatly), which would give an interpretation of *liangzhi* and *liangneng* as "know well (best)" and "to be well (best) able to do," which does not differ materially from the present one.

56. *Mencius* 7A15.

57. See above, p. 194.

58. Mencius did not compare moral behavior with sexual behavior, but I have chosen it as an illustration because, when Gaozi said, "Sex and eating

are human nature," Mencius did not dispute the statement (6A4), for his view was not that sex and eating are not human nature, but that human nature is not merely sex and eating. As he accepted sex as part of original human nature, and sex in Mencius' day could only have been understood in the narrow sense of sex behavior between man and woman, his view of sex must have been the common sense one assumed here. Needless to say, my point here has nothing whatever to do with modern psychological views about sex.

59. Something of this kind can be seen in the contemporary issue between the Sociological school of moral theory which claims that morality has grown out of tribal custom and the Intuitionist school which holds that morality is part of the nature of things. Great importance seems to be attached to this issue. See, for instance, Sir David Ross, *The Right and the Good* (Oxford: Oxford Univ. Press, 1930) 12-14. The reason why Ross feels so strongly about the matter seems to be found in the following quotation: "But beliefs have the characteristics which bodies have not, of being true or false, of resting on knowledge or of being the product of wishes, hopes, and fears; and in so far as you can exhibit them as being the product of purely psychological and nonlogical causes of this sort, while you leave intact the fact that many people hold such opinions *you remove their authority and their claim to be carried out in practice*." [Ross 13, my italics]

60. It is interesting to note in this connection that it is never very clear whether in Xunzi's view one particular sage king invented morality or a number of sage kings invented it. It would be difficult to know what the other sage kings were responsible for, if only the first was responsible for the invention. It is equally difficult to see how a number of sage kings coming at fairly long intervals could have been jointly responsible for the invention. This seems to be a case of the form of a particular language being the cause for a philosopher failing to make an important distinction by not requiring such a distinction to be made, for, as there is no "number" in Chinese, it was unnecessary for Xunzi to make any distinction between "sage king" and "sage kings." The same linguistic form being used in both cases, Xunzi had no need to think clearly even to himself whether it was one or more. If he had been aware of the need for making such a distinction and the difficulty involved in saying specifically that morality was invented at a definite time by a particular sage, he might have had second thoughts about the theory of its being invented at all.

61. 荀子: 性惡 23/114/8-10, Knoblock 23.2a.

62. 荀子: 性惡 23/114/19-20, Knoblock 23.1d.

63. See above, p. 202.

64. *Mencius* 5A7, 5B1.

65. Ibid. 6A7.

66. When the king, after he had spared an ox about to be sacrificed because he could not bear seeing the poor animal going to its death, ordered

that a lamb be substituted, he was suspected by the common people of being parsimonious, and had to admit that on the surface the affair must have looked so to the people and that he was really unable to say exactly what his motive was. Mencius pointed out to him that there was a difference between sending the lamb to its death and sending the ox. The king had seen the ox trembling at its imminent fate but he had not seen the lamb. The king then said, "I did the act, and yet, when I looked into my own heart, I failed to discover my own intention. You say it for me and I feel within me that you have hit upon what I was really after." Ibid. 1A7.

67. Ibid. 6A1.

68. Ibid. 4B14.

69. Ibid. 6A10.

70. 荀子: 性惡 23/114/2-4, Knoblock 23.1e.

71. See above, n. 43.

Ten

Does Xunzi Have a Consistent Theory of Human Nature?

Eric Hutton

Xunzi is most famous for his claim that "human nature is bad." However, the exact meaning of this phrase is a disputed matter among scholars, and the debate is complicated by various passages in the text, which may seem to contradict this idea. In a recent essay, Donald Munro has written, "Had developing a theory of human nature been his interest, I doubt that Xunzi would have left it in such a mess."[1] Munro then lists several such problematic passages as evidence of an intellectual sloppiness, which he takes to indicate that Xunzi was not primarily concerned with articulating a theory of human nature. Of course, one could try to explain away these difficult passages as interpolations that have crept into the text through errors during transmission of the work. Yet, until such errors can be demonstrated conclusively, we should try to find a way to show how these passages are consistent with the rest of the text. In this chapter, I will attempt such a project, analyzing passages Munro mentions as well as some he does not. Along the way, I will also consider David S. Nivison's proposed solution to one of the problems noted by Munro. My intention is not to show that Xunzi really was primarily interested in human nature, since I question the helpfulness of isolating some single idea as the core of all of Xunzi's beliefs. If my arguments are successful, they remove an obstacle to seeing the theory of human nature as at least one of Xunzi's major concerns and an important part of a larger consistent web of teachings. More positively, I hope that in the process of "cleaning up" the "mess" which Munro finds in the text, we will ultimately arrive at a more nuanced and accurate understanding of Xunzi's position.

Obviously, the degree to which any passage appears to conflict with Xunzi's view of human nature depends on one's interpretation of that view in the first place. Hence, I will begin by briefly summarizing my understanding of Xunzi's claim that human nature is bad. Hopefully, the extent to which I can reconcile the problematic passages with Xunzi's view of human nature will count as evidence in favor of the proposed interpretations of both sides of the question.

I take the core of Xunzi's theory of human nature to consist of four related claims. First, Xunzi believes that we naturally have certain desires, which are neither good nor bad in themselves. Second, Xunzi believes that we have no innate moral knowledge or tendencies that would naturally lead us to control the strength of these desires or to satisfy them in a morally appropriate way. Third, Xunzi believes that without such guidance, our desires and emotions tend to bring us into conflict with each other, which is bad. Therefore, he declares that human nature is bad. Fourth, Xunzi believes that we do not naturally enjoy imposing such restraints on our desires, but that we can come to see such restraints as both enjoyable and intrinsically valuable.[2]

By the end of this essay, I will offer a more refined account of Xunzi's view. In the meantime, given this sketch of his theory, let us now turn to the examples cited by Munro. The first he cites is "one that says that people are born with an innate moral sense (義 *yi*)" [Munro 198]. The passage he has in mind is the following:

> Water and fire have 氣 *qi* but are without life. Grasses and trees have life but are without awareness. Birds and beasts have awareness but are without *yi*. Humans have *qi* and life and awareness, and, moreover, they have *yi*. And so they are the most precious things under Heaven. They are not as strong as oxen or as fast as horses, but oxen and horses are used by them. How is this so? I say it is because humans are able to form communities while the animals cannot. Why are humans able to form communities? I say it is because of hierarchical divisions. How can hierarchical divisions be carried out? I say it is because of *yi*. And so if they use *yi* in order to make hierarchical divisions, then they will be harmonized. If they are harmonized, then they will be unified. If they are unified, then they will have more power. If they have more power, then they will be strong. If they are strong, then they will be able to overcome the animals. And so they can get to live in homes and palaces. . . . There is no reason for this other than that they are able to get these hierarchical divisions and *yi*. And so human life cannot be without community. If they form communities but are without hierarchical divisions, then they will struggle. If they struggle,

then there will be chaos. If there is chaos then they will disband.
If they disband then they will be weak. If they are weak then
they cannot overcome the animals. And so they will not get to
live in homes and palaces. This is what is meant by "You may
not let go of ritual 禮 *li* and *yi* for even a moment."[3]

There is a crucial ambiguity in this passage because of the word 有 *you*
("have"). The Chinese text merely says that humans "have *yi*," but what
sense of having does Xunzi intend? In distinguishing between elemental
forces, plants, and animals, Xunzi picks out attributes (*qi*, life, and
awareness) that are not acquired; they are properties intrinsic to the
entities in question. Therefore, by parallel, *yi* should also be an inborn
characteristic, and this is why one might easily be tempted to consider it
a "sense of duty." Xunzi, however, specifically denies that *yi* is part of
human nature in his doctrine that human nature is bad: "People's nature
is originally without ritual and *yi*, and so they must force themselves to
study and seek to have them. Their nature does not know of ritual and *yi*,
and so they must think and reflect and seek to know them."[4] Thus, if
"have" in the above passage means "have innately," then there is
obviously a serious contradiction in the text of the *Xunzi*.

In his essay "Xunzi on 'Human Nature',"[5] David S. Nivison has
suggested one solution to this difficulty that deserves careful
consideration. In a later essay he sums up his idea as follows:

> Xunzi uses the same word that Mencius uses for an innate
> incipient sense of duty. But if Xunzi is consistent, and also says
> . . . that human nature is "bad," . . . then he must mean
> something else: perhaps, a bare capacity that enables men to
> form societies with hierarchical social distinctions and to
> apprehend an obligation as a *moral* obligation: yet a capacity
> that has no positive *content*. And since there is no *content*, a
> Mencian cannot say, "See! Xunzi admits a crucial element of
> goodness in human nature after all!" For it is obviously possible
> for this disposition to be filled out in a duty-like commitment to
> some *immoral* end . . . thus Xunzi's *yi* . . . is . . . *nonmoral*.[6]

On Nivison's view, this "unfilled" capacity for regarding something as a
duty is given its proper content only when the sages create the
appropriate duties for it, and these are what Xunzi usually refers to by the
term *yi* in the other contexts in which it appears.

While this solution is ingenious, certain features of the passage work
against it. First, as before, *qi*, life, and awareness do not seem to be

simply "unfilled" capacities for the elements, plants, and animals. For in a sense, without these things, none of these entities would exist in the first place. Of course, one could try responding that these really are capacities which can be filled or unfilled, since plants and animals can certainly exist without life and awareness, in the sense that their corpses remain after they die. In the same way, human beings could remain alive without *yi*, though they would really be less than human. However, it seems much less plausible to try the same argument for the case of fire and water existing with only an unfilled capacity for having *qi*.[7]

Second, if *yi* were only a bare nonmoral capacity to regard something as a duty which could be filled out to immoral ends, it then seems unlikely that Xunzi would want to claim, as he does at the beginning of the passage, that *yi* is what makes humans the most precious creatures in the world.[8] At one point Nivison notes that *yi* is somehow derivative from humans' distinctive ability to make distinctions 辨 *bian*, and that this ability is also the source of obsession 蔽 *bi*. In reading over the *Feixiang* 非相 chapter, where Xunzi discusses distinctions, it is important to note that he describes them rather neutrally.[9] He indicates that some distinctions lead to the rituals of the sage kings, but this leaves open the possibility that other distinctions are not good. Accordingly, he never makes the claim that these distinctions are what makes humans the most valuable creatures, and this might indicate that when he speaks of *yi* in the 王制 *Wangzhi* chapter he has something more in mind than a neutral capacity.

Thirdly, in the passage cited, Xunzi says that people can successfully form societies simply if they use their *yi* to make hierarchical divisions. Certainly in this case, he must mean something more than the bare capacity, since the capacity while still unfilled would not lead to any advance whatsoever, and Xunzi does not say anything here about filling it in with something. Lastly, in summing up at the end of the passage, Xunzi speaks of the possibility of "letting go of ritual and *yi*." "Ritual and *yi*" is Xunzi's usual phrase for the inventions of the sage kings, and so if *yi* here were still an unfilled capacity, "ritual" here would also have to be such, but Xunzi never makes any such claim in the passage, and to import this idea back into the passage would make it even more difficult to preserve his theory of human nature. Moreover, the very idea that one could "let go of" (i.e., lose) even this barest innate capacity seems implausible, and this seems to work against any interpretation that would want to read "having" here as "having innately." These considerations are not decisive against Nivison's interpretation, since it could be that Xunzi is using *yi* in slightly different senses throughout the passage, and we are simply supposed to be able to figure out which is which. Even so, the *Wangzhi* passage seems to be the only case in the *Xunzi* where *yi* might plausibly be construed in Nivison's sense as an unfilled capacity, and this fact alone should make us hesitate to adopt it.[10]

Fortunately, "having *yi*" does not have to be read as "having innately." The passage can also be understood as simply listing the most significant characteristic of each of the various things it describes without regard to the origin of that characteristic. On this reading, the claim that humans "have *yi*" means that they "possess" or "own" it in the same sense, for example, that they have tools. It is not something inborn. Rather, it is something external and acquired. An important piece of evidence in support of this interpretation is that Xunzi says that humankind's success in overcoming the animals is for no other reason than that we are able to get *yi*. The use of the word "get" 得 *de* is particularly revealing in that, according to Xunzi, human nature is "that which cannot be learned and which cannot be achieved through practice."[11]   Hence, his use of the word "get" in connection with *yi* implies it is outside the bounds of human nature. On this reading, there is no conflict with Xunzi's claim that human nature is bad, because the passage is not making any claims about our innate tendencies. The fact that only humans can have *yi* does logically imply that humans have a unique capability, as Nivison argues,[12] but the passage here is using *yi* in its full sense as the set of norms created and handed down by the sage kings. Having *yi* in this way is very different from having an innate tendency towards *yi*. The former is entirely compatible with Xunzi's view of human nature as I have described it; the latter is not.

At this point, I want to bring up a related passage which Munro does not mention, but which at first glance might seem to cause even more serious difficulties than the first one. The *Dalüe* 大略 chapter contains the following remarks:[13]

> *Yi* and profit 利 *li* are the two things that humans have. Even Yao and Shun could not get rid of the common people's desire for profit. However, they were able to cause their desire for profit not to overcome their fondness for *yi*. Even Jie and Zhou could not get rid of the common people's fondness for *yi*. However, they could cause their fondness for *yi* not to defeat their desire for profit. And so, when *yi* defeats profit, it is an ordered age. When profit overcomes *yi*, then it is a disordered age.[14]

To begin with, note that the same ambiguity with the word "have" occurs again in this passage. Second, though the passage starts off by talking only of *yi* and profit, it quickly becomes clear that by this Xunzi really means a "fondness for *yi*" and a "desire for profit." Now a desire for profit is something that Xunzi clearly lists among the elements of human nature (cf. 荀子: 性惡 23/113/3, Knoblock 23.1a), and since he makes a fondness for *yi* as parallel to this desire, it might seem to suggest strongly that *yi* is likewise to be considered part of human nature.

This impression might be further strengthened by the following reflections. If *yi* were something originally external to human nature, then it seems as though in principle it could be separated from people. Or in other words, if it is something that can be gotten, it should also be the sort of thing that can be lost. Given Xunzi's views of the effects of education and one's environment on one's character, it seems quite reasonable to think that it would in fact be lost if one's control over the natural tendencies of human nature were allowed to slip. Indeed, he states that if we give in to the promptings of our nature, virtue and proper conduct will actually "perish" 亡 *wang*,[15] as opposed to simply not arising in the first place. Here in the *Dalüe* passage, even during the rule of the tyrants Jie and Zhou when such tendencies were allowed to re-emerge and run wild, the common people do not lose their fondness for *yi*. Thus this fondness would seem to be an indelible part of them, as though it were part of their nature. If such were the correct reading, it would be even worse for Xunzi's theory of human nature, because then this passage would be making the even stronger claim that not only do people naturally have a moral sense, but moreover they naturally enjoy morality.

There are two plausible ways to avoid drawing this conclusion. First, one might note that the political situation depicted is neither the state of nature, nor a complete return to the state of nature from a state of civilization. For under Jie and Zhou human society did not totally disintegrate, but was rather just very chaotic. Therefore, one could argue that the passage does not show that people's fondness for *yi* is something inborn. Instead, it can be interpreted as saying that *yi* was taught to them by the sages before Jie and Zhou came along, and they managed to appreciate enough of it so as not to lose all of their fondness for it even under corrupting circumstances. Moreover, even Jie and Zhou had to preserve the most basic structure of society in order to pursue their own goals, so there still would have been some incentive for people to retain their fondness for *yi*.[16]

This approach may adequately resolve the problems in this passage, but there are other passages for which it will not work (see below, p. 228). I therefore prefer a second way of reading the passage to avoid concluding that humans have a natural tendency toward morality, which works by noticing that there is an ambiguity in the use of the word 好 *hao* ("like" or "be fond of"). When I say, "I like volleyball," I can mean either that I like to play volleyball myself, or that I like to watch other people play volleyball. In the same way, when Xunzi says the people like *yi*, he does not necessarily have to mean that they like to participate in it themselves. Rather, he can mean that people like for *other* people to act morally toward them.[17] For example, I may not enjoy being nice to other people, but that certainly does not inhibit me from wanting other people to be nice to me. Indeed, from a selfish point of view, it is all the better if other people behave morally while I can get away with whatever I want. In fact, this is precisely the insight that lies behind the "free rider" problem in Hobbesian political theory, and since Xunzi seems similar to Hobbes in many other respects, it is not surprising that he should pick up on this aspect of human psychology too. However, as we shall see, he uses it to a very different effect.

When the notion of "liking *yi*" is viewed thus, there is nothing in the *Dalüe* passage that is incompatible with Xunzi's theory of human nature, if the claim that human nature is bad is understood primarily as the idea that humans have no inborn tendency to practice morality or to enjoy practicing it. On this reading, the passage is stating that even Jie and Zhou could not rid the people of a natural basic expectation to be treated well, but they could cause the people to care less about being treated well than benefiting themselves. The significance of such a claim is threefold. At one level, it explains both why the people could tolerate misrule for so long and why the people would behave badly to each other, namely because there was not sufficient social pressure to get them to treat each other well. At a second level, this claim is perhaps intended as a rebuttal to Mozi and other thinkers who seem to view humans as completely plastic and infinitely susceptible to manipulation by their superiors. For example, Mozi cites the stories of King Ling of Chu, whose love of slender waists induced the people to starve themselves almost to death, and King Gou Jian of Yue, who trained his people to such bravery that his soldiers trampled each other in their haste to plunge into fire and water.[18] Xunzi's point would then be to emphasize that there is ultimately a limit on the extent to which people can be shaped by their rulers, because of their fundamental nature. Thus, even the worst governments could not corrupt the people totally.[19]

As a third consequence, the claim would explain how the sage kings were able to get the common people to follow them. For if people were by nature repulsed by others' acts of goodness, it would be very hard for

ntators have taken him to be saying that our natural
arrowly self-directed. However, nowhere that I know
citly exclude other-directed desires or claim that all
im only at our own benefit. The idea of "selfishness"
early China; Yang Zhu's idea of acting for the sake
ei wo was certainly taken by Mencius to be
certainly knew of Yang Zhu[29] and could have easily
he chose, but he did not. If the badness of human
esires know no natural bounds and tend to bring us
is no reason to exclude other-directed desires. For
ight selflessly love his son, but if he is willing to do
stealing and killing, to provide for his son's welfare,
why Xunzi would not condemn even this apparently
n. Xunzi would probably deny that such altruistic
najor part of our natural inclinations, but even if he
does not contradict his theory of human nature.
very little about the psychology of desire. He neither
natural desires aim at our own pleasure, as a
nist might, nor does he say that all our natural desires
od, as a psychological egoist would claim, and the
ld be taken as counterevidence to both these views.
Xunzi's picture of human nature to rule out people's
sires for things which they understand will bring them
r benefit. Xunzi's examples merely lead one to think
any, would be few and far between.
might be uncomfortable with this idea, for does it not
people are in fact by birth inclined to some moral
ld seem to mean that Xunzi is giving in to the kind of
cius uses when he talks about how children's love of
example of their innate knowledge and powers (良知
ng neng). Up to this point, I have not made use of the
f *yi*, but here is a place where a finer understanding of
cepts becomes useful. Elsewhere, I have argued that the
ween *yi* and the other major Confucian virtue, 仁 *ren*
is that for Xunzi *ren* primarily involves affection for
imarily involves adhering to certain social norms, most
which delineate one's proper social role.[30] Now insofar
ndency which is being attributed to people is a concern
me kind, it would seem to be saying that people have a
o *ren*. However, there is one passage in the *Xunzi* that
at Xunzi would deny that this is in fact a tendency to

the sage kings to win their loyalty. This bears on the interpretation of
another supposedly problematic passage that Munro mentions, so let us
now turn to it. Munro states that according to Xunzi, people naturally
"love the virtues of ritual propriety, duty, loyalty, trustworthiness, and
so forth" [Munro 198]. Apparently, the passage he has in mind is the
following:

> Jie and Zhou were the descendants of sage kings. . . . However,
> the people all rebelliously hated Jie and Zhou but honored Tang
> and Wu. Why is this? Why did Jie and Zhou fail? Why did
> Tang and Wu succeed?[20] I say it is for no other reason than that
> Jie and Zhou were good at doing what people hated, while Tang
> and Wu were good at doing what people liked. What is it that
> people hate? I say it is corruption, arrogance, contentiousness,
> and greediness for profit. What is it that people like? I say it is
> ritual, *yi*, deference, loyalty, and trustworthiness.[21]

Here again the word *hao* is used somewhat ambiguously, but I think
from the context it is quite obvious that what the people liked was that *it
was Tang and Wu who were displaying these virtues* toward them, not
that they themselves naturally enjoyed being virtuous or desired to be so.
What is most interesting is that this natural fondness on the part of the
people is what allows good sage kings to wrest control away from the
tyrants. As noted earlier, for Hobbes, people's hope for goodness from
others while not desiring to act morally themselves creates problems and
threatens the social contract. It creates an air of mistrust, and the power of
the sovereign to impose punishments is needed to make the contract
binding. However, Hobbes is very pessimistic about the people's ability
to form and abide by the contract in the state of nature, and for that reason
he thinks that contract by coercion is more likely to happen than contract
by un-coerced agreement. For Xunzi, on the other hand, this desire of
good treatment from others is such that it makes people amenable to
those who satisfy the desire, and thus accounts precisely for the reason
why the sages can take control of the people without compulsion, and
without an explicit contract (though a Hobbesian might still want to
interpret this as a kind of tacit contract).

This same approach can also be used to resolve a third apparent
difficulty that Munro brings up. He writes, "people carry the sentiment in
favor of rules that bring social order" [Munro 198], and his footnote refers
us to a passage in the 王霸 *Wangba* chapter. In order to make the full
sense of the quote apparent, it is necessary to quote its context at length.
It reads:

To be honored as the Son of Heaven, to have the wealth of possessing the whole world, for one's reputation to be that of a sage king, to control other people and not be controlled by other people, these are what the essential nature 情 *qing* of people is alike in desiring, but only a true king has them all. To wear clothes of many colors, to eat food of many flavors, to have control over many kinds of goods, to bring together all under Heaven and be lord over them, for one's food and drink to be most abundant, for one's music to be most magnificent, for one's terraces and pavilions to be most high, for one's parks and gardens to be most broad, to make the feudal lords one's ministers and unite all under Heaven—these are also what the essential nature *qing* of people is alike in desiring, but only the ritual regulation of the true Son of Heaven is thus. For one's regulations to be implemented, for one's orders to be upheld, for officials who fail in important tasks to suffer death, for dukes and feudal lords who do not treat one according to ritual propriety to suffer imprisonment, for states at the four borders which are filled with a rebellious spirit to be destroyed, for one's reputation to shine as brightly as the sun and moon, for one's accomplishments to be as great as Heaven and Earth, for all the people under Heaven to respond to one like a shadow or echo—these are also what the essential nature *qing* of people is alike in desiring, but only a true king is one who possesses them all.[22]

Munro seems to be focusing on the last part of this passage, and here it is indeed made very clear by context that people do in fact favor the rules that promote social order. Moreover, in contrast to the previous passages, which said nothing explicit about human nature, the fact that this tendency is part of human nature is made undeniable by the statement that this is part of the human *qing*, which Xunzi elsewhere defines as part of human nature.[23] (Note, therefore, that the first approach outlined on p. 225 above, which takes the fondness for morality as something acquired, will not work here.[24]) However, it is clear that all these claims are being made *in the context of each person's natural desire to be emperor*, and the natural sentiment in favor of social order is a natural desire for others to obey and submit to one if one is the emperor.[25] Again, there is nothing here to suggest that people naturally have any tendency to do what is good. Moreover, the very principle of interpretation I have been suggesting is explicitly stated by Xunzi at the beginning of the passage

when he remarks th
without being cont
contradiction simply

One of Munro's
endowment or natura
[Munro 198]. I will
claimed that it was ag
and so as stated abc
equipped for practicing
human nature is bad.
Xunzi believed people
them to do so. In fac
become a sage like Yac

The last example N
writes that people "hav
involved in love of kin
Lilun chapter. There we

> All living creatures
> and breath must
> possesses conscious
> animals or great bi
> herd or flock . . . it
> when it passes its
> hesitate and drag it
> among tiny creature
> sorrow for a little wl
> blood and breath, n
> therefore man *ought*
> (Translation from Bu

The original Chinese te
passage should be read lit
their parents. That seems
goodness of human nature
"ought." Of course, it m
some people naturally lov
this would still not get hin
the claim that human natur
inborn altruistic tendencies
understanding of human na
often use examples of selfis

and so many comm
desires are all only
of does Xunzi expl
our natural desires a
was not unknown in
of oneself 為我
selfishness.[28] Xunzi
adopted his terms i
nature is that our d
into conflict, there
example, a father n
anything, including
there is no reason
altruistic motivation
tendencies form a
does allow them, it

Xunzi tells us
says that all our
psychological hedo
aim at our own g
Lilun passage cou
There is nothing in
naturally having de
neither pleasure n
that such desires, i

Yet, one still
really mean that
actions? This wou
example that Men
their parents is an
liang zhi, 良能 *lie*
specific meaning
Xunzi's moral con
basic division bet
("benevolence"),
others, while *yi* pr
specifically those
as the supposed te
for those of the sa
natural tendency
makes me think t

ren. The passage also comes from the *Dalüe* chapter, and it reads, "The gentleman dwells in *ren* by means of *yi*, and only then is it *ren*. He carries out *yi* by means of ritual, and only then is it *yi*. In regulating affairs with ritual, he returns to the roots of things and completes the branches of things, and only then is it ritual. When all three are thoroughly mastered, only then is it the Way."[31] In other words, even if Xunzi were to admit that people do naturally love their parents, this would not constitute a tendency toward virtue for him, because it would become a virtue only when given the proper form, and there is no natural tendency to do that.[32] In fact, if one thinks about it, insofar as Xunzi does maintain that filial piety is one of the most important virtues, he would have to think that love of parents is in some way compatible with human nature, but as noted earlier, love of parents can be a far cry from virtue, if it is accompanied by a total lack of constraints on the way to go about manifesting that love. Indeed, such unrestrained natural affection would perhaps ultimately be self-defeating. For if a person A harms another person B's father in order to care for his own, that other person B is likely to retaliate by harming A's father, but hardly anyone would want to call a love that tends to the harm of its object virtuous. I think that in this passage we may also see Xunzi taking a subtle jab at Mencius. His point would be that love of kin is as natural to animals as it is to humans, and therefore it may be part of nature, but it is not at all what makes us human, because it is worthless without the teaching that enables one to form it properly.[33] In an enlightening article, Bryan W. Van Norden has pointed out how Xunzi may be seen as trying to distinguish himself from the earlier thinker Gaozi.[34] In this case, we may perhaps extend Van Norden's insight by noting that Gaozi wants to say that *ren* is internal, which is an assumption he shares with Mencius, but Xunzi sets himself apart from both by rejecting even this idea.[35]

If all of what I have said above is correct, then the difficulties Munro points out are not really problems for Xunzi after all, and they can all be resolved while keeping his theory of human nature consistent and substantive. Nevertheless, we should be thankful to Munro for raising interesting questions that have brought to our attention certain under-appreciated or overlooked aspects of Xunzi's philosophy. In concluding, I would like to sum up the revised picture of Xunzi's conception of human nature that has emerged over the course of responding to Munro's challenge. Specifically, we are now in a position to offer a more nuanced account of the desires and dispositions which constitute human nature according to Xunzi. First of all, in addition to the desires for food, sex, and other fairly concrete bodily comforts which he frequently cites, we have noted that Xunzi thinks that humans also have a natural desire for less tangible goods such as power and honor. Now these desires for power and honor consist in a desire for others to behave in a certain manner toward oneself (i.e., with obedience and admiration), and correspondingly Xunzi posits that people are naturally disposed to react in certain ways to certain sorts of treatment by others. In particular, he believes that people are naturally disposed to react positively when treated well, especially when they are shown the kind of respect and deference that follows from ritual and *yi*. This is the second nuance in Xunzi's view revealed by our investigation. As a third and final point, Xunzi seems to allow that people's inborn tendencies need not all be narrowly self-centered, but that people may also naturally have certain feelings of love and concern for others.

To my mind at least, it is important to recognize these features of Xunzi's view, because they make his conception of human nature seem a more plausible one. The question is then whether or not Xunzi can maintain his claim that human nature is bad in light of these aspects of human nature, and I have argued that he can indeed do so. The first two pose no threat to that idea, because the tendencies in question do not dispose people to act virtuously themselves. Nor does the third feature create a contradiction in Xunzi's view, because he could reasonably deny that such natural other-directed concerns are in themselves virtuous. These points, I suggest, push us to revise our understanding of Xunzi's claim that human nature is bad, by making us consider that it rests as much on a theory of virtue as it does on a theory of psychology, and that the disagreement between Xunzi and Mencius must be analyzed in terms of both of these elements, though it is beyond the scope of this essay to say which of their two positions is ultimately more plausible. The interaction of these two kinds of theory seems important for moral philosophy more generally, especially for moral education, and so even though I ultimately find no "mess" in Xunzi's position, I think we can also thank Munro for spurring us to reflect on issues that reach beyond the confines of Chinese thought alone.[36]

Notes

Portions of this chapter are taken from an earlier paper of mine, "On the Meaning of *Yi* (義) for Xunzi," unpublished M.A. thesis, Department of East Asian Languages and Civilizations, Harvard University, 1996.

1. Donald J. Munro, "A Villain in the *Xunzi*," in *Chinese Language, Thought, and Culture: Nivison and His Critics*, Philip J. Ivanhoe, ed. (Chicago: Open Court, 1996) 198.

2. My basic understanding of Xunzi's view of human nature follows the interpretation given by Philip J. Ivanhoe. For fuller arguments in favor of this reading, see Ivanhoe, "Human Nature and Moral Understanding in the *Xunzi*," chapter eleven in this volume, and chapter 3 of *Confucian Moral Self Cultivation* (Indianapolis: Hackett Publishing Co., 2000).

3. 水火有氣而無生，草木有生而無知，禽獸有知而無義，人有氣、有生、有知、亦且有義，故最為天下貴也。力不若牛，走不若馬，而牛馬為用，何也？曰：人能群，彼不能群也。人何以能群？曰：分。分何以能 行？曰：以義。故義以分則和，和則一，一則多力，多力則彊，彊則勝 物，故宮室可得而居也。…無它故焉，得之分義也。故人生不能無群，群 而無分則爭，爭則亂，亂則離，離則弱，弱則不能勝物，故宮室不可得而 居也，不可少舍禮義之謂也。 [荀子: 王制 9/39/9-16] Knoblock 9.16a. All references to the *Xunzi* will be according to the numbering system of the Chinese concordance by D. C. Lau and Fong Ching Chen, eds., *A Concordance to the Xunzi* 荀子逐字索引, Hong Kong: The Commercial Press 商務印書館, 1996. All translations are my own unless otherwise noted. For comparison, I have also provided references to the translation by John Knoblock, *Xunzi: A Translation and Study of the Complete Works*, vols. 1-3 (Stanford: Stanford Univ. Press, 1988-1994).

4. 今人之性，固無禮義，故彊學而求有之也；性不知禮義，故思慮而求知之也。 [荀子: 性惡 23/114/21] Knoblock 23.2b.

5. This essay is published in *The Ways of Confucianism: Investigations in Chinese Philosophy*, Bryan W. Van Norden, ed. (Chicago: Open Court, 1996) 203-13. It should be noted that, since the time when this essay was first written, Nivison has changed his opinion about the *Wangzhi* passage and now views it in a way quite similar to the interpretation I suggest here. See his "Response to Jim P. Behuniak" (forthcoming in *PEW*). For that reason, my criticisms of Nivison here should be taken more in the spirit of additional arguments in support of his new position.

6. Nivison, "Critique of David B. Wong, 'Xunzi on Moral Cultivation'," in *Chinese Language, Thought, and Culture*, 324.

7. Moreover, even in the case of bad people, Xunzi seems unwilling really to relegate them to the status of animals: "Why do people struggle with one another? . . . I desire to class them with the birds and beasts, but I may not, because their form is still that of human beings, and their likes and dislikes are mostly the same [as those of humans]." 人之有鬥，何哉？…我欲屬之鳥鼠禽　獸邪？則不可，其形體又人，而好惡多同。 [荀子: 榮辱 4/13/9-10] Knoblock 4.3.

8. At least, at 荀子: 榮辱 4/13/4-5, Knoblock 4.3, Xunzi seems to say that bad humans are not even as good as animals.

9. 荀子: 非相 5/18/13-19, Knoblock 5.4.

10. Moreover, when Xunzi does want to speak of a bare capacity for goodness, he does have the vocabulary to do so. For example, in the 性惡 *Xing'e* chapter, he speaks of how people all have the "material" 質 *zhi* and

"tools" 具 *ju* for coming to know and practice *ren*, *yi*, lawfulness, and correctness [荀子: 性惡 23/116/7-8] Knoblock 23.5a.

11. 不可學，不可事。[荀子: 性惡 23/113/18] Knoblock 23.1c.

12. I owe this point to Bryan W. Van Norden.

13. The *Dalüe* has been suspected of being a later addition to the text by Xunzi's students. Of course, if such were the case, it would absolve Xunzi of any guilt of contradicting himself. However, the passage I quote does in some ways fit well with what Xunzi says in better attested chapters, and I think it can be reconciled with his view of human nature, so there is no need to be so eager to throw it out.

14. 義與利者、人之所兩有也。雖堯、舜不能去民之欲利，然而能使其欲利不克其好義也。雖桀、紂亦不能去民之好義，然而能使其好義不勝其欲利也。故義勝利者為治世，利克義者為亂世。 [荀子: 大略 27/132/1-3] Knoblock 27.63.

15. Cf. 荀子: 性惡 23/113/1-4, Knoblock 23.1a.

16. I was helped in formulating this argument by T. C. (Jack) Kline III.

17. It is important to see that the distinction I am drawing on Xunzi's behalf here is between different possible objects of the natural desires (i.e., what one wants to do versus what one wants to receive), and not between groups of agents having natural desires for different things. Thus, the interpretation I am offering is perfectly consistent with Xunzi's view that all human beings share the same nature. I am simply claiming that, in the case of *yi*, the natural desire which all humans share is to receive such treatment, rather than to give it to others.

18. Cf. Burton Watson, *Mo-Tzu: Basic Writings* (Columbia Univ. Press, 1963) 47-8. These stories are also cited by Han Feizi, who likewise seems to think that there is no limit to the ways in which human beings can be shaped. Cf. *Han Fei Tzu: Basic Writings*, tr. by Burton Watson (Columbia Univ. Press, 1964) 33.

19. In fact, Xunzi himself apparently refers to the story of King Ling at 荀子: 君道 12/58/12, Knoblock 12.4, though there the king is said to be King Zhuang of Chu. However, whereas Mozi claims that *all* the king's ministers starved themselves (*Mozi* HYIS 23/15/22) and that this change was brought about in the space of a single year or single generation (HYIS 23/15/23, 27/16/74), Xunzi says only that there were *some* starving people in the king's court, and he makes no comment about how long such a transformation required. Thus, in Xunzi's hands the story makes much weaker claims about the malleability of people. Moreover, neither there nor anywhere else in the text does Xunzi allow that human beings are *infinitely* plastic. On the contrary, in the 正名 *Zhengming* chapter, Xunzi clearly states that the desires constitutive of human nature cannot be eliminated, but only redirected [荀子: 正名 22/111/14-17] Knoblock 22.5b.

20. Alternatively, "How is it that Jie and Zhou lost them? How is it that Tang and Wu obtained them?"

21. 夫桀、紂，聖王之後子孫也，⋯反然舉疾惡桀、紂而貴帝湯、武，是何也？夫桀、紂何失？而湯、武何得也？是無他故焉，桀、紂者善為人之所惡，而湯、武者善為人之所好也。人之所惡者何也？曰：汙漫、爭　奪、貪利是也。人之所好者何也？曰：禮義、辭讓、忠信是也。[荀子: 彊　國 16/76/24-16/77/3] Knoblock 16.4.

22. 夫貴為天子，富有天下，名為聖王，兼制人，人莫得而制也，是人情之所同欲也，而王者兼而有是者也。重色而衣之，重味而食之，重財物而制之，合天下而君之；飲食甚厚，聲樂甚大，臺謝甚高，園囿甚廣，臣使諸侯，一天下，是又人情之所同欲也，而天子之禮制如是者也。制度以陳，政令以挾；官人失要則死，公候失禮則幽，四方之國有侈離之德則必滅，名聲若日月，功績如天地，天下之人應之如影響，是又人情之所同欲也。而王者兼而有是者也。 [荀子: 王霸 11/53/12-17] Knoblock 11.7b.

23. 荀子: 正名 22/111/14, Knoblock 22.5b.

24. Speaking most precisely, because the first approach claims that the fondness for morality is an acquired fondness, it can allow that fondness to be interpreted as a delight in actively adhering to the moral order. If, however, we must admit that Xunzi is referring to an inborn fondness, then in order to avoid contradicting his theory of human nature, the fondness must be viewed as a delight in being treated well by others adhering to the moral order. The first approach can admit this reading of fondness and would then claim that this came about only after the initial instruction of the sages, but this is what the current passage seems to deny. It is still possible that Xunzi would agree to the story that the people managed to appreciate enough of morality to pursue it to some degree even in corrupt times, and that there was incentive for them to do so even during the reigns of Jie and Zhou, but then that would not be the primary reasoning underlying the *Dalüe* passage.

25. Admittedly, there is a slight ambiguity in the Chinese that might allow one to read the passage as saying that people desire for others to follow the emperor, whoever he is. This would make a stronger point for Munro's claim, but I think this reading is quite clearly ruled out by the context.

26. 荀子: 性惡 23/116/6-15, Knoblock 23.5a.

27. 凡生乎天地之間者，有血氣之屬，必有知；有知之屬，莫不愛其　類。今夫大鳥獸則失亡其群匹，⋯則必反鉛，過故鄉，則必徘徊焉，鳴號焉，躑躅焉，踟躕焉，然後能去之也。小者是燕爵，猶有啁叫之頃焉，然　後能去之。故有血氣之屬，莫知於人，故人之於其親也。至死無窮。[荀子: 禮論 19/96/10-13] Knoblock 19.9b. Burton Watson, *Hsün Tzu: Basic Writings* (New York: Columbia Univ. Press, 1964) 106.

28. Cf. *Mencius* 3B9 [孟子 6.9/34/13-35/10], 7A26 [孟子 14.26/76/6-7].

29. Yang Zhu is mentioned by name at *Xunzi* 荀子: 王霸 11/53/25, Knoblock 11.7d.

30. Cf. "On the Meaning of *Yi* (義) for Xunzi," op. cit.

31. 君子處仁以義，然後仁也。行義以禮，然後義也。制禮反本成末，然後禮也。三者皆通，然後道也。 [荀子: 大略 27/128/2-3] Knoblock 27.21.

32. David B. Wong seems headed toward this conclusion in his essay "Xunzi on Moral Motivation," chapter six in this volume, p. 149ff. If correct, this view of the virtues raises some interesting and difficult questions. Is full moral status conferred on impulses merely when they are restrained in the right way? Or must the agent moreover *intend* to restrain them in the right way? Does the agent furthermore have to understand why it is right to restrain them in this way, and how theoretical does this understanding have to be? The answers to these questions will determine to what extent, if any, the common people, and not just the gentleman and sage, will be able to achieve virtue. Xunzi wants to attribute to them some kind of virtue, but it is not immediately clear how much.

33. Contrast this with *Mencius* 7A15 [孟子 13.15/68/26-8]: "That which people are capable of doing without learning is their innate ability. That which people know without pondering is their innate knowledge. Among small children, none do not know to love their parents, and when they are grown, none do not know to respect their elder brothers. To love one's parents is *ren*, and to respect one's elders is *yi*. There is nothing more to do than to extend these to all under Heaven." Here the innate impulse simply *is ren* from the very beginning.

34. Bryan W. Van Norden, "Mengzi and Xunzi: Two Views of Human Agency," chapter five in this volume, especially pp. 125-7.

35. Cf. *Mencius* 6A4 [孟子 11.4/57/7-21].

36. I want to thank Philip J. Ivanhoe, T. C. (Jack) Kline III, Paul Goldin, David Nivison, Miranda Brown, Joel Sahleen, and the anonymous reviewers at *Philosophy East and West* for their comments on earlier drafts of this chapter.

Eleven

Human Nature and Moral Understanding in the *Xunzi*

Philip J. Ivanhoe

I want to explore the question of how an early Chinese philosopher named Xunzi (310-219 B.C.E.) thought one could come to be moral, both in the sense of recognizing what morality requires one to do and possessing the corresponding and proper motivations.[1] Answering this question is critical to the task of understanding his ethical philosophy. In particular, it will help us to understand what is arguably the basis of his ethical philosophy, his well-known teaching that "human nature is bad" 性惡 *xing'e,* and how it differs from the view that it directly challenges: the competing claim by the older philosopher Mencius (391-308 B.C.E.) that "human nature is good." I will begin with a brief description of Mencius' position.[2]

Mencius believed that we can come to know what is moral through a kind of intuition: one that is more a felt *sense* than an *intellectual insight.*[3] To be precise, he claimed we are endowed with four nascent moral senses, or, on another interpretation, that our innate moral sense has four basic modes. Unlike his later, Neo-Confucian followers, Mencius did not regard these nascent senses as full-blown faculties like sight or smell (two favorite examples of Neo-Confucians).[4] He referred to them as "sprouts" 端 *duan.* His choice of metaphor is critical, for like sprouts, our moral sense is an observable and active—not hidden and latent—part of the self. These fragile moral capacities need considerable protection, attention and cultivation in order to mature to the point where they inform and direct a majority of our actions.

In order to prepare the ground for the present inquiry, I want to draw attention to three aspects of Mencius' position. First is his claim that everyone is endowed with these moral "sprouts." According to Mencius, we begin life with an ability—albeit limited—to understand and appreciate what is moral.[5] As long as we are paying attention to the

237

appropriate aspects of our "heart-and-mind" 心 *xin*,[6] at least in certain paradigmatic cases, we will recognize the good when we see it. Mencius makes two other important and related claims: first, when we act in accordance with morality and reflect on what we have done, we feel a special sense of joy, and second, this joy helps the moral sprouts to grow.[7]

Xunzi disagrees with all of Mencius' picture, as I have described it above. Specifically, he disagrees with the three claims that I have singled out. He denies that we are endowed with an innate moral sense; he does not subscribe to the related claim that we naturally enjoy moral action, and, *a fortiori*, he rejects the claim that such joy helps our innate moral sprouts to grow. I want to offer an explanation of why he rejects these claims, how this fits in with other aspects of his ethical philosophy and how, in particular, this helps us to understand his claim that human nature is bad.

Xunzi would agree with the view that one can't fully delight in moral actions until one sees them as moral, in the full-blooded sense of worth doing in their own right. But, as pointed out earlier, he denies that we are endowed with a moral sense. As a consequence, before we learn to be moral, we are incapable of appreciating the right actions we may encounter or do as moral in the requisite way. This seems to be our plight as long as we remain in the pre-socialized, amoral state. When all we have to deploy are our natural faculties, we will not experience any recognizably moral responses to the events and situations we encounter in the world.

Xunzi does seem to believe that certain extremely gifted individuals (i.e. a series of primordial sages who both discovered and developed human culture) were able to see parts of the moral way by means of incisive intellectual insights; these were the first people to develop a nascent moral understanding of the world. But even they could not grasp the whole, for it took considerable time and repeated trial and error in order to understand the complex and interrelated aspects of human needs and desires and how these fit into the greater scheme of Nature. The earliest sages seemed to have contributed pieces of the moral puzzle, but even they did not see and appreciate the entire picture.[8]

For those of us who are less gifted, the only way to gain the needed understanding of ourselves and our place in the world is through a prolonged and difficult process of learning. There is a specifically moral aspect to acquiring certain kinds of knowledge. We simply don't know what morality is until we come to understand how we and what we do fit into the world at large. As we learn and reflect on what we know, we come to realize that certain courses of action and states of affairs regularly produce desirable results. In some cases, we discover that behaving in certain ways allows us to enjoy satisfactions that were not available to us in our pre-social state; we come to see and appreciate the many benefits of living a distinctively moral kind of life. When we reflect on these combined experiences we realize that the most satisfying life is the one described by the Confucian *dao* and so we come to "approve" 可 *ke* of the set of practices and norms that constitute the Confucian Way. As this diverse sense of approval accumulates, it gives rise to an increasingly powerful commitment to the *dao*. And so for Xunzi, one must have an adequate grasp of how a given act or type of action fulfills the grand plan of Confucian society in order to fully understand and appreciate its moral qualities.[9] Such understanding in turn produces a commitment to follow the grand plan of the *dao* as good in itself, not only the means to but a symbol of the best kind of life.[10]

Contrasting Xunzi's view with two alternative idealized pictures of how one might acquire an understanding of morality and then go on to develop a moral sense may help to make clear the distinctive character of Xunzi's position. In what I will refer to as the *constructivist* account, we come to understand morality through reason alone and these insights guide and motivate us to perform virtuous actions. For example, I see that acting in a certain way meets the constraints incumbent upon me as a rational agent (e.g. the imperative that, *ceteris paribus*, my actions be universalizable). This gives me a reason, the only truly moral reason, for action. Furthermore, this kind of reason itself provides motivation to act in the prescribed way. According to the constructivist account, this is a critical feature of what it means to have and recognize a moral reason to do something. Over time, such performances produce in us the proper affective states; we come to feel filial love in addition to and as a result of acting filially.[11]

In what I will call the *intuitionist* account, we begin with a nascent and imperfect moral sense. In addition, we have the ability to steer the focus of our attention to this moral response when considering an actual or hypothetical moral choice and concentrate upon it.[12] By concentrating on this sense and reflecting on how to apply it in the world around us, we refine and strengthen it. This leads to a greater understanding of the nature of morality and develops the strength and accuracy of our moral sense. This, in brief, is my understanding of the Mencian position.

Xunzi's view, which I will refer to as the *re-formation* account, is distinct from either of these positions.[13] According to Xunzi, one's moral sense is grounded neither in pure reason nor in some nascent faculty.

The moral sense is almost wholly acquired; it emerges as one engages in and reflects upon a specific set of ritual practices and traditional norms whose significance is illustrated and elaborated by examples and teachings found in the classics. The process of learning leads one to recognize and appreciate how to curb one's worst tendencies and regularly satisfy a wide range of one's basic needs and desires. In addition, it opens up new ways of finding and appreciating satisfaction and meaning in human life. This process eventually leads to a strong commitment to the overall form of life that allows one to realize and balance these various goods in a way that locates one in a greater harmonious vision of society and the world.

The Confucian rituals lead to the most satisfying of lives because they harmonize our needs and abilities with the way the world is. They provide a way to realize an orderly design inherent in the world.[14] The critical claim of Xunzi's position is that we truly begin to understand the value of such rituals and norms only *after* successfully embarking upon the arduous course of Confucian learning. We acquire true moral understanding only through our critical participation in the Confucian way of life. According to Xunzi, before we engage in learning, we simply lack the cognitive equipment to "see" the value of the Way, and it clearly follows that before we appreciate the value of moral action, we lack any ability to enjoy acting in accordance with it.

It is important to realize that Xunzi is making a radical claim about the nature of the understanding that arises from mastery of Confucian ritual practices and traditional norms. He is not making the related but weaker claim that one needs to be situated in *some* world view before one even has the possibility of acting intentionally and developing some kind of morality. That would be Heidegger, not Xunzi. Nor is he claiming simply that practical experience is needed to augment a nascent moral faculty. Something like this latter view is the charitable reading of Mencius. Xunzi claims that a proper sense of right and wrong and the ability to unwaveringly pursue the former and turn away from the latter can only arise out of the reflective practice of a particular set of rituals and norms: those of Confucianism. Only this particular set can shape, direct and orient human beings in ways that satisfy their basic needs and desires and expand the horizon of their meaningful activities in ways that provide an optimally satisfying life. The Confucian Way brings order to society and harmoniously situates the human realm within the larger natural order.

It is true that for Mencius, practical knowledge is a necessary part of moral perfection: one needs to understand how to apply one's moral sense to the complex situations of the actual world in order to successfully cultivate one's sprouts.[15] It does seem that for Mencius the only way one can come to possess such an understanding is through the reflective consideration of a variety of experiences. But even if we read him this way, there remains an important difference with Xunzi: for Mencius, the process of acquiring practical knowledge *refines* the moral sense; for Xunzi, this sense *arises* from such practice.

One way to understand this critical difference is to compare the respective theories of Mencius and Xunzi with some of the characteristic debates between language empiricists and language innatists.[16] First, let us consider an important issue about which these opposing positions agree. Language empiricists and language innatists agree that human beings can learn language. In a similar way, Mencius and Xunzi agree that we all can learn to be moral. Disagreement arises though when we turn to more interesting questions. For example, unlike their empiricist competitors, language innatists believe that if we can understand the deep structure of human language we will understand something very important about the structure of the human mind. They believe this because they claim it is this deep structure that both enables and disposes us to learn natural languages. In a similar way, unlike Xunzi, Mencius believes that the structure of the *xin* both enables and inclines us to learn morality. By implication, if we could understand the deep structure of morality we would, at the same time, understand something very important about the human heart-and-mind. In particular, we would see that its very structure predisposes it to learn morality.[17] I take this to be the essence of Mencius' claim that human nature is good.

Beyond this lie some very important implications. In the case of language acquisition, according to innatists, the ability for an infant to learn a language is, in all probability, species specific. According to this view, if human infants were raised by creatures significantly different from themselves—if, for example,[18] they were raised by warm, glowing, blue-green rhomboids, who communicated with one another by flashing binary code—these children would in all probability never come to understand these creatures and follow their ways. Similarly, according to Mencius, it seems that if human infants were raised by creatures who morally were significantly different from themselves, they would probably never understand these creatures or follow their ways. The overwhelming probability is that such children would never develop into full moral agents—human or otherwise—since their abilities and inclinations would be so much at odds with their environment.

Xunzi and the language empiricists present a significantly different view. Language empiricists view the human mind as being, to varying degrees, plastic. At the extremes the mind can be thought of as if it were soft wax that readily takes on and is shaped by the impressions it receives or as hard and resistant marble that nevertheless can be etched and encoded with new impressions. Xunzi focuses on human nature, not just the mind, and describes its ability to change by comparing it to formless and rather recalitrant materials—for example clay or metal—that can and must be shaped and sharpened through the application of concerted and persistent effort. In any event, according to both language empiricist views of the mind and Xunzi's view of human nature, there is nothing inherently problematic with human infants learning the language of the glowing, blue-green rhomboids. While Xunzi would probably insist that because of its inherent unruly tendencies human nature would resist taking on the language of these alien teachers, on neither account is there any inherent structure or grain to the mind or nature channeling and informing the acquisition of language. The only constraints that exist on what kinds of language can be acquired are the obvious ones imposed by the child's physical capacities: e.g. having visual perception over a particular part of the electromagnetic spectrum and the ability to hear only a certain range of frequencies.

There are further significant similarities between Xunzi's view of the moral sense and empiricist views about language. For example, for Xunzi, understanding the nature of morality tells us almost nothing about the structure of the human heart-and-mind; morality does not directly manifest any of its inherent features. Deference to elders or the feeling of alarm and concern one might feel when suddenly seeing a child about to fall into an open well[19] do not directly manifest any inherent features of one's *xin*. According to this view, if human infants were raised by creatures significantly different from themselves—our glowing, blue-green rhomboids—these children could come to understand these creatures and follow their ways and would, as long as doing so satisfies the children's basic needs and desires. If the way of the rhomboids provided greater overall, long-range satisfaction than the way of the sages, then these children would have new sages.

It is hoped that this exploration helps us to understand and appreciate important features of Xunzi's view of the character of human nature. Specifically, it is intended to help us see that Xunzi believed we begin life bereft of any moral sense and that this is the crux of his disagreement with Mencius. Morality for Xunzi is not a blossoming of human nature; it is that system of behaviors that in the short run regulates our basic desires and maximizes their satisfaction and in the long run shows us the most and best new sources of satisfaction, while harmonizing all our needs and desires with a pattern inherent in Nature. At this point, it is appropriate to say a bit more about what I think Xunzi means by his claim that human nature is bad. I will begin by arguing against two popular interpretations of his position.

The first position finds its clearest representative in Homer H. Dubs.[20] Dubs claims that Xunzi's position represents what I will refer to as an *Augustinian turn* in the Confucian tradition (he himself likens Xunzi's position to that of Augustine). Dubs argues that Xunzi believed human nature was essentially *evil* and that it therefore needed to be restrained. And so, he devised the *xing'e* slogan (which Dubs translates as "human nature is evil") in order to counter the overly tender-hearted Mencius. Dubs sees this move, by Xunzi, as initiating an "authoritarian" theme in Chinese thought, a theme which Dubs sees as the *de facto* dominant tendency in the Confucian tradition.

Whatever merits Dubs' analysis may possess, this aspect of his interpretation appears to be both wrong and misleading. It is unwarranted to ascribe to Xunzi, or any early Chinese thinker, the view that our nature, in whole or part, is fundamentally and incorrigibly bad. There is nothing in Xunzi's thought that approaches the Augustinian notion of sin as a willful rejection of God's will. There is no hint in his writings that might lead one to think he believed we take a perverse *pleasure* in doing wrong.[21] This is an important point, for in order to have a position that is truly opposite of Mencius' in the way that Dubs believes Xunzi's theory is, this is precisely what Xunzi would have to be saying.

The second interpretation I wish to argue against is what I will call the pessimistic *complement* interpretation.[22] Essentially, proponents of this position argue that Xunzi's "pessimistic" theory complements Mencius' more "optimistic" view of human nature. They see Mencius as cheerfully pointing out that the glass is half full (i.e. we already are partially good) whereas Xunzi glumly focuses on the glass being half empty (i.e. we still are half-bad). Mencius offers an ideal toward which we are to strive and is seen as encouraging us to develop the good already within us. Xunzi sets forth restrictions on our actions and warns us to curb our innate tendencies to err. A crucial feature of this position is the contention that the two views are essentially the same, differing only in what they emphasize.

Both of these interpretations miss what I take to be the defining and most critical aspect of Xunzi's position; namely, that we begin life in a state of utter moral blindness. According to Xunzi, initially, we have no conception of what morality is; we can't recognize the moral dimensions of even paradigmatic actions or situations. Of course we can see an act of cruelty, for example we might perceive some children setting a slumbering, old philosopher on fire, but we fail to perceive it *as* an act of cruelty. Instead, we might see it as necessary, amusing, exciting, an "interesting case" or simply be indifferent to this course of events. Prior to undergoing a proper course of learning, moral categories simply do not color our view of the world, any more than an appreciation of irony and the other beauties of literature are innately part of our nature. In the pre-social state of existence, we are led exclusively by our physical desires. In a world of limited goods, inhabited by creatures of more or less unlimited desires, it is inevitable that the result is destructive and alienating competition. This is what Xunzi means by the claim that human nature is bad.

In order to reform our bad nature, we must sign up for and successfully pursue a thorough, prolonged and difficult course of learning. We must re-form our nature—as a warped board is re-formed by steam and pressure—so that it assumes an orderly shape and can fit into the grand Confucian design. Those first embarking upon the study of the Way can't fully appreciate this. They are driven to a study of the *dao* largely out of fear of the life they know and understand: the chaotic, dangerous and profoundly unfulfilling life outside the Way. Under the guidance of one who does understand the Way, the uninitiated can come to appreciate its more simple and direct advantages. With further study, new possibilities and profound satisfactions come into play.

Appealing once more to the empiricist view of language acquisition may help to illustrate my understanding of Xunzi's view.[23] According to language empiricists, we begin life without language or any innate affinity to acquire natural languages. A person espousing this view of language acquisition might argue that when placed among competent language users, we acquire language purely as a tool in the service of our basic needs and desires. But, as we are led to see and understand certain features about ourselves and the world around us, instead of using language exclusively in an instrumental fashion—purely as a means to satisfy our basic needs and desires—we may come to see it as intrinsically valuable—as a new source of satisfaction. If our hypothetical student has the necessary talent, training, energy and luck, she may become a true poet: someone who regards the right kind of literature as life itself. She would then achieve the literary equivalent of the Confucian sage; her love of and devotion to her art would mirror the sage's delight in and dedication to the Way.

An appreciation of literature—and this includes the wonder of it as a unique creation of human societies—is an acquired taste. An illiterate person *literally* cannot understand these beauties. According to Xunzi, this is what morality is like: something the uninitiated can only understand in terms of its immediate usefulness in the quest to satisfy their basic desires; they have no innate taste for it, no real appreciation of it. But if they acquire enough knowledge about themselves, the world and how it works, they will discover that there are new sources of profound satisfaction, things more valuable than life itself. The longer one studies, the more one understands, the deeper will be one's appreciation of the Way.

It is misleading to say simply that Xunzi is more "authoritarian" than Mencius or less "optimistic."[24] The former claim is much too crude to be helpful and the latter obscures the profound *optimism* of the Xunzian position. One might reasonably argue that such optimism is unwarranted, when one reflects on the history and present state of human beings. Nevertheless, one cannot deny that it is a characteristic of the Confucian tradition in particular and Chinese thought in general, especially the thought of the early period.[25] It should also be clear why I believe it is wrong to say that the theories of Mencius and Xunzi complement one another in the way described earlier. The difference between the theories of Mencius and Xunzi on human nature and moral education is not just one of degree but of kind. It is not that Xunzi thought it is more difficult to develop one's innate moral sense, he did not believe we *have* an innate moral sense at all. Morality is something we can and must acquire in order to lead a fully satisfying life, but we can acquire it only by coming to understand and appreciate the accumulated wisdom of human culture; it is not something we have an innate feeling of or taste for. This is why Xunzi emphasized the importance of the classics and the sages more strongly than did Mencius and why he wrote extensively about the role of the teacher, a topic about which Mencius has surprisingly little to say.

This interpretation of Xunzi's thought helps us to understand why he saw Mencius' intuitionism as a serious threat to the Confucian tradition. For if, as Mencius claimed, we are endowed with an innate moral sense of what is right and wrong, the role of the classics, the sages and teachers is much less clear. Xunzi's *xing'e* slogan was directed at the Mencian assumption that we are endowed with some nascent moral sense and that we can come to understand morality—the *dao*—by reflecting upon how this sense responds to the things we do, think and say. For Xunzi, our understanding of morality only emerges as we acquire knowledge about how one can organize self and society in ways that provide for the peaceful and harmonious satisfaction of human needs and desires. Such an understanding is simply beyond the compass of our innate abilities; it is something we must acquire from our tradition under the guidance of good and proper teachers. And until one acquires such knowledge, one cannot perceive, let alone appreciate, the moral dimensions of life.

Notes

The present essay is a revised and expanded version of an article that was published under the same title in *IPQ* 34:2 (June, 1994) 167-175. In reworking the essay, I have benefited particularly from the comments of T. C. (Jack) Kline III and Eric Hutton.

1. Here, I am attempting to provide a theoretical framework for thinking about the differences among various positions on moral understanding that I see as helpful in grasping central features of the thought of Mencius and Xunzi. I shall not provide detailed textual evidence to support the interpretations of Mencius and Xunzi that I rely on to describe these distinctions here but I have done so elsewhere. Readers who are interested in examining and evaluating such evidence should refer to the articles cited in the following notes.

2. For a more complete account of my understanding of Mencius' ethical views, see my *Ethics in the Confucian Tradition: The Thought of Mencius and Wang Yang-ming* (Atlanta: Scholars Press, 1990). For an essay contrasting aspects of Mencius' view with those of Xunzi, see "Thinking and Learning in Early Confucianism," *JCP* 17:4 (December, 1990) 473-493.

3. By "moral sense" I mean something like what thinkers like Hutchenson and Hume had in mind when they described an innate human capacity to feel the inherent rightness or wrongness of certain kinds of actions. I describe this more fully in my discussion of Mencius' position below and in my description of what I call the "intuitionist account" which follows. What I have in mind is close to what Stephen Darwall calls "sentimentalist theories." See his *The British Moralists and the Internal 'Ought': 1640-1740* (New York: Cambridge Univ. Press, 1995). By a moral "intellectual insight" I mean the cognitive recognition of the value of certain actions, both as means to the satisfaction of an agent's basic desires and as critical to the realization of larger, long-range goals to which the insight contributes. As I will argue below, for Xunzi, such insights are not purely or even primarily theoretical. They arise only through reflective participation in a certain form of life.

4. The examples are from the *Great Learning*. These are Wang Yangming's (1472-1529) favorite examples of his teaching concerning "the unity of knowing and acting." See Wing-tsit Chan, tr., *Instructions for Practical Living and Other Neo-Confucian Writings by Wang Yang-ming* (New York: Columbia Univ. Press, 1963) 10, etc.

5. For example, see *Mencius* 2A6, 7A15, etc.

6. Early Chinese thinkers tended to believe that the human *xin* (lit. "heart") possessed cognitive affective and something like volitional capabilities. Hence I translate it as "heart-and-mind."

7. For example, see *Mencius* 4A27, etc.

8. In his faith in the value of the inherited wisdom embodied in social practices and norms, Xunzi is not unlike Edmund Burke (1729-1797). However, Burke believed that tradition provided the best means to carry on in a fundamentally imperfect and imperfectable world, while one waited for one's Heavenly reward. In contrast, Xunzi believed that the society worked out by the former sages provided the one and only way to a happy and flourishing world. Burke's views are best represented by his *Reflections on the Revolution in France* (Indianapolis: Hackett Publishing Co., 1987).

9. For my understanding of this aspect of Xunzi's thought, see "A Happy Symmetry: Xunzi's Ethical Thought," *JAAR* 59:2 (1991) 309-322.

10. The *dao* possesses value as the unique means to the various goods it promotes. Above and beyond such value, it gives us an inspiring metaphor by means of which we can organize and carry out our lives. Robert Adams puts this well, "Symbolically I can be for the Good as such, and not just for the bits and pieces of it that I can concretely promote or embody" (p. 12). See Robert M. Adams, "Symbolic Value," in *Midwest Studies in Philosophy*, Vol. 21, "The Philosophy of Religion" (Notre Dame: Univ. of Notre Dame Press, 1998) 1-15. The commitment to the *dao* that Xunzi sees as arising out of our appreciation for all that it can provide is a good example of how ethical beliefs are not simply expressive of desires or even norms but rather imply a form of ethical realism. For an illuminating discussion of this topic see Marcel S. Lieberman, *Commitment, Value and Moral Realism* (Cambridge: Cambridge Studies in Philosophy, 1998).

11. This picture of moral understanding and development is obviously inspired by Kant, though he would probably not subscribe to parts of it.

12. Bryan W. Van Norden provides the most sophisticated and incisive account of this aspect of Mencius' thought. See his "Mengzi and Xunzi: Two Views of Human Agency," chapter five in this volume.

13. Jon Schofer first recognized this unique characteristic of Xunzi's view of moral education. See his "Virtues in Xunzi's Thought," chapter three in this volume. Aristotle seems to have held something close to the Xunzian position, though there are important differences between the two. Aristotle affords the intellect greater powers of insight and more strength in its ability

to guide and shape the uncultivated self. Other important differences include but are not limited to: Xunzi's emphasis on ritual action, his allegiance to a specific set of ritual practices and classical texts, and his linkage of this scheme with a grand ecological vision.

14. See "A Happy Symmetry."

15. For example, see *Mencius* 4B19.

16. My discussion of the differences between language innatists and empiricists is based largely on the analysis to be found in Ian Hacking, *Why Does Language Matter to Philosophy?* Reprint (Cambridge Univ. Press, 1990) 57-69.

17. I mean by this that the heart-and-mind has an innate ability to recognize morality, and the joy that accompanies the contemplation of moral actions one has performed strengthens one's moral disposition. While the heart-and-mind is also capable of other things and indeed inclined toward less laudable ends, reflection upon those cases where one has pursued such ends not only does not reinforce these tendencies, it tends to lead one away from such pursuits.

18. Cf. Hacking 59.

19. These are two paradigmatic examples of the moral sense for Mencius. See *Mencius* 2A6, 6A6, 7A15, etc.

20. Homer H. Dubs, "Mencius and Sun-dz on Human Nature," *PEW* 6 (1956) 213-222.

21. Compare Augustine's description of stealing pears: "I should be gratuitously wanton, having no inducement to evil but the evil itself. It was foul and I loved it." *The Confessions* in *Basic Writings of Saint Augustine*, Whitney J. Oates, tr. (New York: Random House, 1948) 24.

22. The clearest proponent of this view is Antonio S. Cua. See his *Ethical Argumentation: A Study in Xunzi's Moral Epistemology* (Honolulu: Univ. of Hawaii Press, 1985) 15, and *passim.*

23. Note that here I depart from a strict behaviorist interpretation of the empiricist view in that at more advanced stages of language acquisition, the agent contributes significantly to the processing of raw inputs and outputs. In a similar way, I believe that Xunzi sees a significant degree of autonomy in advanced moral agents in that they develop the sense of when and how to apply the rites and the lessons of the classics. I discuss this issue in considerable detail in the case of Confucius in my "Reweaving the 'one thread' of the *Analects*," *PEW* 40:1 (January 1990) 17-33. In "Thinking and Learning in Early Confucianism," *JCP* 17 (1990) 473-493, I argue that, in this regard, Xunzi is closer to Confucius than is Mencius.

24. I have benefited from conversations with Derek Fung Ling on this issue.

25. Thomas A. Metzger discusses what he refers to as the "epistemological optimism" of early Chinese thinkers in his "Some Ancient Roots of Modern Chinese Thought: This-Worldliness, Epistemological Optimism, Doctrinality, and the Emergence of Reflexivity in the Eastern Chou," *Early China* 11-12 (1985-1987) 61-117. Though his use of this term is not altogether clear to me, it does seem to include the sense I intend: i.e. that human beings have the capacity to understand themselves and the world in critically important and comprehensive ways, which allow them to realize a grand utopian vision of human flourishing.

Contributors

Antonio S. Cua has published extensively on ethics and Chinese philosophy, especially on the philosophy of Xunzi. His book-length study of Xunzi's ethics is entitled *Ethical Argumentation: A Study in Hsün Tzu's Moral Epistemology*. He is Professor Emeritus of Philosophy at Catholic University of America.

Eric Hutton is writing his dissertation on Xunzi's conception of virtue. He received his B.A. from Stanford University (1994) and an M.A. in Asian Languages from Harvard University (1996), and he is presently a Ph.D. candidate at Stanford University.

Philip J. Ivanhoe has special interests in Chinese religious and ethical thought. His work focuses on Chinese views on character, self-cultivation, virtue, moral agency, environmental philosophy, relativisim, and skepticism. He is an Associate Professor of Philosophy and Asian Languages and Cultures at the University of Michigan. He received both his B.A. (1976) and Ph.D. (1987) from Stanford University.

T. C. Kline III spends most of his time reading, trying to understand, and writing about Xunzi's philosophy, especially the connection between ethics and tradition. Presently, he teaches Chinese philosophy at Loyola University of Chicago. He earned his B.A. from Dartmouth College (1988), an M.A. in East Asian Languages and Civilizations from the University of Chicago (1992), and a Ph.D. in Philosophy from Stanford University (1998).

Joel J. Kupperman is a Professor of Philosophy at the University of Connecticut. Although his main interest lies in Western ethics, he has written many articles on both comparative and Chinese philosophy. He received his B.A. from the University of Chicago and a Ph.D. from Cambridge University (1963).

D. C. Lau is a world-famous translator and scholar of Chinese philosophy. He is currently a Professor of Chinese Language and Literature at the Chinese University of Hong Kong. He has published a great deal of material on Chinese philosophy and helped pave the way for later scholars.

David S. Nivison is Professor of Philosophy Emeritus at Stanford University. He was the first Walter Y. Evans-Wentz Professor of Oriental Philosophy, Asian Languages, and Religious Studies. In 1996 he published many of his published and unpublished articles in an edited volume entitled *The Ways of Confucianism: Investigations in Chinese Philosophy*. He is still hard at work solving dating issues related to events of the early Zhou dynasty. He earned his B.A. (1946), M.A. (1948), and Ph.D. (1953) from Harvard University.

Henry Rosemont, Jr., has recently published a new translation of the *Analects* with Roger Ames. His interests are primarily in Chinese philosophy. He is a Professor of Philosophy at St. Mary's College of Maryland and consulting professor at Fudan University in Shanghai. He received his B.A. at the University of Illinois (1962) and a Ph.D. at Washington University (1967).

Jonathan W. Schofer is completing his studies at the Divinity School of the University of Chicago. His dissertation examines the ethical thought of the rabbis of late antiquity through an analysis of the text of *Avot de Rabbi Natan*. This project was partially inspired by his earlier work in Chinese philosophy.

Bryan W. Van Norden is presently working on an edited volume of articles on the *Analects*. His primary interest is in Chinese philosophy, especially early Confucian philosophy. Presently he is Assistant Professor of Philosophy at Vassar College. He received his B.A. from the University of Pennsylvania (1985) and a Ph.D. from Stanford University (1991).

David B. Wong has published in both Western ethics and Chinese philosophy. He is Professor and Chairman of the Department of Philosophy at Brandeis University. He studied at Macalester College for his B.A. (1971) and at Princeton University for his Ph.D. (1977).

Bibliography

This bibliography of scholarship on Xunzi in English is divided into two parts. The first part contains articles, books, and dissertations that focus on Xunzi's writings. The second part includes general studies of Chinese philosophy that have a section on Xunzi. When feasible, the specific chapter or section of these general studies is cited. For references to secondary literature in East Asian languages see the bibliographies in either John Knoblock, *Xunzi: A Translation and Study of the Complete Works*, or Paul R. Goldin, *Rituals of the Way: The Philosophy of Xunzi*.

Works on Xunzi

Allinson, Robert E., "The Debate Between Mencius and Hsün-tzu: Contemporary Applications," *JCP* 25:1 (1998) 31-50.

Campany, Robert F., "Xunzi and Durkheim as Theorists of Ritual Practice," in *Discourse and Practice*, Frank Reynolds and David Tracy, eds. (Albany: SUNY Press, 1992) 197-231.

Cheng, Andrew Chih-yi, *Hsün Tzu's Theory of Human Nature and Its Influence on Chinese Thought* (Beijing, 1928).

Cook, Scott, "Xun Zi on Ritual and Music," *Monumenta Serica* 45 (1997) 1-38.

Creel, Herrlee G., "Confucius and Hsün-tzu," *Journal of the American Oriental Society* 51 (1931) 23-32.

Cua, Antonio S., "The Conceptual Aspect of Hsün Tzu's Philosophy of Human Nature," *PEW* 27 (1977) 373-89.

———, "The Quasi-Empirical Aspect of Hsün Tzu's Philosophy of Human Nature," *PEW* 28 (1978) 3-19.

———, "Dimensions of *Li* (Propriety): Reflections on Hsün Tzu's Ethics," *PEW* 29 (1979) 373-94.

———, "Hsün Tzu's Theory of Argumentation," *Review of Metaphysics* 36:4 (1983) 867-94.

———, *Ethical Argumentation: A Study in Hsün Tzu's Moral Epistemology* (Honolulu: Univ. of Hawaii Press, 1985).

———, "Hsün Tzu and the Unity of Virtues," *JCP* 14 (1987) 381-400.

Cua, Antonio S., "Review of *Xunzi: A Translation and Study of the Complete Works*, vol. 1, books 1-6, John Knoblock" *PEW* 41:2 (1991) 215-27.

————, "The Possibility of Ethical Knowledge: Reflections on a Theme in the *Hsün Tzu*," in *Epistemological Issues in Classical Chinese Philosophy*, Hans Lenk and Gregor Paul, eds. (Albany: SUNY Press, 1993) 159-84.

Dubs, Homer H., *Hsüntze: Moulder of Ancient Confucianism* (London: Arthur Probsthain, 1927).

————, "'Nature' in the Teaching of Confucius," *Journal of the American Oriental Society* 50 (1931) 233-7.

————, "Mencius and Sun-dz on Human Nature," *PEW* 6:213-22.

Duyvendak, J. J. L., "Hsün-tzu on the Rectification of Names," *T'oung-Pao* 23 (1924) 221-54.

————, "The Chronology of Hsüntzu," *T'oung-Pao* 26 (1929) 73-95.

————, "Notes on Dubs' Translation of *Hsün-tzu*," *T'oung-Pao* 29 (1932) 1-42.

Goldin, Paul R., *The Philosophy of Xunzi*, Ph.D. Dissertation, Harvard Univ., 1996.

————, *Rituals of the Way: The Philosophy of Xunzi* (Chicago: Open Court, 1999).

Hsieh, Shan-yuan, "Hsün-tzu's Political Philosophy," *PEW* 29 (1979) 69-90.

Hutton, Eric, "On the Meaning of *Yi* for Xunzi" (Unpublished manuscript).

Ivanhoe, Philip J., "A Happy Symmetry: Xunzi's Ethical Philosophy," *JAAR* 59:2 (Summer) 309-22.

————, "Thinking and Learning in Early Confucianism," *JCP* 17 (1990) 473-93.

Kensig, Steve, "Ritual Versus Law in *Hsün Tzu*," *JCP* 3 (1975) 57-66.

Kline III, T. C., *Ethics and Tradition in the* Xunzi, Ph.D. Dissertation, Stanford Univ., 1998.

Knoblock, John, "The Chronology of Xunzi's Works," *Early China* 8 (1982-3) 28-52.

————, *Xunzi: A Translation and Study of the Complete Works*, 3 vols. (Stanford: Stanford Univ. Press, 1988, 1990, 1994).

Kuller, Janet A. H., *Early Confucian Resistance to Taoist Thought: A Study of Anti-Taoism in the* Hsün Tzu, Ph.D. Dissertation, Univ. of Chicago, 1974.

————, "The 'Fu' of the *Hsün Tzu* as an Anti-Taoist Polemic," *Monumenta Serica* 31 (1974-5) 205-18.

————, "Anti-Taoist Elements in Hsün Tzu's Thought and Their Social Relevance," *Asian Thought and Society* 3:7 (1978) 53-67.

Machle, Edward, "Hsün Tzu: A Revisionist View," *Iliff Review* 32:3 (1975) 19-31.

————, "Hsün Tzu as Religious Philosopher" *PEW* 26 (1976) 443-61.

————, "The Mind and the *Shen-ming* in the *Xunzi*," *JCP* 19 (1992) 361-86.

————, *Nature and Heaven in the* Xunzi: *A Study of the Tian Lun* (Albany: SUNY Press, 1993).

Malmquist, Göran, "Cherng shiang," *Bulletin of the Museum of Far Eastern Antiquities* 45 (1973) 63-91.

————, "A Note on the Cherng shiang Ballad in the *Shyun Tzyy*," *BOAS* 36 (1973) 352-8.

Martin, Michael, "Ritual Action (*Li*) in Confucius and Hsün Tzu," *Australian Journal of Philosophy* 73:1 (1995) 13-30.

Mei, Y. P., "Hsün Tzu on Terminology," *PEW* 1 (1951) 51-6.

————, "Hsün-tzu's Theory of Education," *Qinghua xuebao* 2 (1961) 361-79.

————, "Hsün-tzu's Theory of Government," *Qinghua xuebao* 7 (1970) 36-83.

Munro, Donald J., "A Villain in the *Xunzi*," in *Chinese Language, Thought, and Culture: Nivison and His Critics*, Philip J. Ivanhoe, ed. (Chicago: Open Court, 1996) 202-23.

Nivison, David S., "Xunzi on Human Nature," in *The Ways of Confucianism: Investigations in Chinese Philosophy*, Bryan W. Van Norden, ed. (Chicago: Open Court, 1996) 123-41.

————, "Critique of David B. Wong, 'Xunzi on Moral Motivation,'" in *Chinese Language, Thought, and Culture: Nivison and His Critics*, Philip J. Ivanhoe, ed. (Chicago: Open Court, 1996) 323-31.

————, "Response to Jim P. Behuniak," *PEW* (forthcoming).

Parker, E. H., "Liu Hsiang and Tsien Tahien on Suntsz," *New China Review* 4:6 (1922) 443-9.

————, "The Philosopher Suntsz," *New China Review* 4:1 (1922) 1-19.

Radcliffe-Brown, A. R., "Religion and Society," in *Structure and Function in Primitive Society: Essays and Addresses* (New York: The Free Press, 1968) 153-77.

Shih, Vincent Y. C., "Hsüntzu's Positivism," *Qinghua xuebao* 4 (1963) 152-74.

Shun, Kwong-loi, "Review of *Ethical Argumentation: A Study in Hsün Tzu's Moral Epistemology*, by A. S. Cua," *PEW* 41:1 (1991) 111-17.

Tsui, Chee Yee, *A Study of the* Hsün Tzu, Ph.D. Dissertation, Univ. of Toronto, 1981.

Van Norden, Bryan W., "Hansen on Hsün-tzu," *JCP* 20:3 (1993) 365-82.

Watson, Burton, *Hsün Tzu: Basic Writings* (Columbia: Columbia Univ. Press, 1963).

Yearley, Lee H., "Hsün Tzu on the Mind: His Attempted Synthesis of Confucianism and Daoism," *Journal of Asian Studies* 39 (1980) 465-80.

————, "Facing Our Frailty: Comparative Religious Ethics and the Confucian Death Rituals," *Gross Memorial Lectures*, Valparaiso Univ., 1995.

————, "Hsün Tzu: Ritualization as Humanization," in *Confucian Spirituality*, Tu Wei-ming, ed. (New York: Crossroads Publishing Co., forthcoming).

General Works

Chan Wing-tsit, "Naturalistic Confucianism: Hsün Tzu," *A Source Book in Chinese Philosophy* (Princeton: Princeton Univ. Press, 1963) 115-35.

Creel, Herrlee G., "Chapter Seven: The Authoritarianism of Hsün Tzu," *Chinese Thought from Confucius to Mao Tse-tung* (Chicago: Univ. of Chicago Press, 1953) 115-34.

Eno, Robert, "Chapter Six: Ritual as a Natural Art: The Role of T'ien in the *Hsun Tzu*," *The Confucian Creation of Heaven: Philosophy and the Defense of Ritual Mastery* (New York: SUNY, 1990) 131-70.

Fehl, Noah E., Li: *Rites and Propriety in Literature and Life—A Perspective for a Cultural History of Ancient China* (Hong Kong: Chinese Univ. of Hong Kong, 1971).

Fung Yu-lan, "Chapter Twelve: Hsün Tzu and His School of Confucianism," *A History of Chinese Philosophy: Volume I —The Period of the Philosophers*, Derk Bodde, trans. (Princeton: Princeton Univ. Press, 1952) 279-311.

Geaney, Jane, "Xunzi: Eye/Action and Ear/Speech," *Language and Sense Discrimination in Ancient China*, Ph.D. Dissertation, Univ. of Chicago, 1996, 103-43.

Graham, Angus C., "Hsün-tzu's Confucianism: Morality as Man's Invention to Control His Nature," *Disputers of the Tao: Philosophical Argument in Ancient China* (Chicago: Open Court, 1989) 235-66

Hansen, Chad, "Xunzi: Pragmatic Confucianism," *A Daoist Theory of Chinese Thought: A Philosophical Interpretation* (Oxford: Oxford Univ. Press, 1992) 307-34.

Ivanhoe, Philip J., "Chapter Three: Xunzi," *Confucian Moral Self Cultivation* (Indianapolis: Hackett Publishing Co., 2000) 29-42.

Makeham, John, "Chapter Three: Nominalist Theories of Naming in the Neo-Mohist Summa and Xun Zi," *Name and Actuality in Early Chinese Thought* (Albany: SUNY Press, 1994) 51-64.

Mote, Frederick, "Early Confucianism: Hsün Tzu," *Intellectual Foundations of China*, second edition (New York: McGraw-Hill,

1989) 54-8.

Munro, Donald J., *The Concept of Man in Early China* (Stanford: Stanford Univ. Press, 1969).

Needham, Joseph, *Science and Civilization in China*, vol. 2 (Cambridge: Cambridge Univ. Press, 1954).

Neville, Robert, "Chapter Seven: Ritual and Normative Culture," *Normative Cultures* (Albany: SUNY Press, 1995) 163-95.

Roetz, Heiner, "Xunzi's Rationalism," *Confucian Ethics of the Axial Age: A Reconstruction under the Aspect of the Breakthrough Toward Postconventional Thinking* (New York: SUNY Press, 1993) 213-26.

Schwartz, Benjamin I., "Hsün-tzu: The Defense of the Faith," *The World of Thought in Ancient China* (Cambridge, Mass.: Harvard Univ. Press, 1985) 290-320.

Slingerland, Edward G., "Chapter Six: Wu-wei in the *Xunzi*," *Effortless Action: Wu-wei as a Spiritual Ideal in Early China*, Ph.D. Dissertation, Stanford University, 1998, 345-411.

Twohey, Michael, "Chapter Two: Xunzi and Ancient Chinese Authority," *Authority and Welfare in China: Modern Debates in Historical Perspective* (New York: St. Martin's Press, Inc., 1999) 13-28.

Subject Index

agency: autonomy in, 248; moral,
139, 144, 155-156, 162-163,
164, 197, 241; rational, 239;
role of 德 *de* in, 170-171; role of
desire and approval for, 109-111,
118-119, 158-161, 173;
disagreement of Mencius and
Xunzi about, 104, 117, 127-128
agriculture, 4, 8
anger, 79-80, 135, 214
approval. See 可 *ke*
arete, 76
argumentation: Confucian
conception of, 62-63; phases of,
50-51; standards of, 39, 40,
56-57, 61
art, 12, 29
artifice. See 偽 *wei*
ataraxia, 181, 184
atheism, 3, 25
attachments, 179, 182
authoritarianism, 15, 20-22, 67,
243, 245
authority, 49-50, 57, 137, 139,
175, 186
autonomy, 43, 177, 248

barbarians, 167-168, 170
beauty, 26, 98, 99, 135-136, 143,
177
behavior, 39, 71, 72, 150, 242-243
belief, 47, 48-49, 55
蔽 *bi*. See obsession
辨 *bian* "discrimination," 50-51,
223. See also justification
benevolence. See 仁 *ren*

ceremony. See 禮 *li*

chaos, 155, 157, 161, 163, 171,
225
children, 31, 97, 150-151
China, 4-8, 38
choice, 45, 73, 127, 141-142, 239
civil servants, 7-8. See also
scholar-officials
class. See 分 *fen*
Classics, 12, 43, 57, 69, 157, 166,
240, 245-246
closed society, 3, 13-16, 28, 35
collectivism, 14, 16-18
commerce, 5, 8, 32
commiseration, heart (*xin*) of,
193-195
communism, 14
Confucianism: argumentation in,
49, 62-63; Augustinian turn in,
243; grades of, 67; of Xunzi,
177, 181-182; rituals in, 9,
167-168, 240; view of virtue in,
160, 230
constraint, external, 72, 81,
95-100, 157, 197-198
cultivation: love of *dao* in, 176;
moral, 44, 45, 58, 72, 113, 158,
163, 166, 168, 196, 203;
framework provided by sages,
155-156; motivation for, 114,
160-161; role of 德 *de* in,
169-172; process of, 118-119,
122-124
customs, 6, 7, 10, 22, 95, 185

道 *dao* "Way," 23, 27, 56, 136,
155, 176, 183-184, 231;
adherence to, 63, 158, 161, 247;
Confucian, 69, 81, 82, 239;

knowledge of, 43, 72, 180-181, 198, 157, 216, 240, 244; metaphysical nature of, 164-169, 174; origins of, 120-122; unifying perspective of, 41, 44, 48, 53-54, 60

道貫 *daoguan* "the thread of *dao*," 41, 63

Daoism, 66, 138, 177, 178, 180-183

得 *de* "get," 224

德 *de* "virtue," 52, 76-77, 137, 164, 169-172, 175

death, 25, 109, 117, 139, 141, 147-148, 158, 182-183

delight. See joy

democracy, 14, 16, 61

desire, 23, 46, 52, 69, 81, 92, 104, 173; appropriate, 44, 76; control of, 11, 48, 56-57, 71, 127, 150, 201; for goodness, 124, 144-145, 147-148; natural, 114, 125, 156-157, 197, 205-206, 221, 224-225, 228-232, 234, 238; role in human nature, 109-111, 198-200; role in moral development, 72, 74, 82, 94, 98, 121, 151, 181, 244; satisfaction of, 117, 138-142, 227, 240, 242, 245; transform-ation of, 42, 91, 158. See also 欲 *yu*

detachment, 177-182

德音 *deyin* "the tone of virtue," 170

dictatorship, 14, 16

disposition, 44, 46, 73, 78, 81, 85, 112-113, 122, 157, 248

端 *duan* "sprouts" of morality, 89, 108, 112-113, 117, 126-127, 144-145, 193-195, 206-207, 237-238, 241

duty, 6, 65, 99, 144, 145, 147, 150, 182, 197, 222-223

惡 *e* "bad," 90, 93-94, 98. See also evil

economics, 3, 4-6, 12, 30

education, 9-13; class aspects of, 16; intellectual independence in, 23-25; moral, 145, 209-211, 225, 245-246, 247; use of historical appeal in, 42. See also learning

effort, 78, 81, 95, 157, 166-167, 189, 204

egoism, 136-137

emotion, 15, 46, 71-72, 177; control of, 139-141, 160-161; natural, 147-149, 221; role in morality, 74, 76, 81, 151, 164; role in ritual, 98, 184; transformation of, 138, 153, 161-162. See also 情 *qing*

endurance, 78, 81

environment, 2, 100; role in moral development, 70, 82, 86, 95, 115, 126, 196, 241-242

equality, 4, 31, 97, 190, 192-193

equanimity, 179, 182

ethical development, 69-72, 77-79, 84

etiquette. See manners

evidence, 40, 57-60

evil, 44, 90, 119, 124, 143-145, 150, 243. See also 惡 *e*

examples, use of, 39, 61, 240

excellence, 55, 72, 75, 77, 81, 83, 85, 104

法 *fa* "law," 60, 92, 95-96, 146, 186

分 *fen* "class," 6-8, 15, 203
filial piety, 8, 75, 148-149, 231, 239
force, 55-56, 59, 96, 136
former kings, 45, 193. See also 先王 *xianwang*
freedom, 2, 15, 30, 46, 56-57, 181

gentleman. See 君子 *junzi*
goodness, 124, 147-148, 233; sprouts (*duan*) of, 89, 108, 112-113, 117, 126-127, 144-145, 193-195, 206-207, 237-238, 241
government, 9-13, 76-77
grief, 147-150, 161-162, 183-184
古 *gu* "past." See past

habit, 95-96, 202-205, 210-211
好 *hao* "joy," 81, 225-227. See also joy
harmony: creation of, 148, 171, 205, 221; metaphysical, 165-168; musical expression of, 148; role of ruler in, 6
合 *he* "harmony," 67. See also harmony
heart-and-mind. See 心 *xin*
hierarchy, 7-9, 76, 91, 97, 221, 223
historicism, 18-19
history, 12, 19-20, 39-40, 53-57; appeals to, 41, 42-60
後王 *houwang* "later kings," 41
human nature, 64, 72, 89-93, 95-100, 147-148, 160, 165, 198-205; comparison of Mencius and Xunzi, 117-125, 205-211, 245-246; comparison of Xunzi and Gaozi, 125-127; Mencius' view of, 107-117, 191-198,

237-241; transformation of, 71, 142, 160-162. See also 人性 *renxing*, 性 *xing*, 性惡 *xing'e*

impartiality, 48-49, 52
impulses, 52, 72, 103-104, 111-112, 124, 125, 148-150, 157, 173, 178, 236
individual, 39-40, 45, 61, 65, 73, 123, 163, 203
individualism, 14, 17, 30
institutions, 3-5, 6-8, 11
intellectual insight, 238-239, 247
intuition, moral, 218-219, 237-239, 245

今 *jin* "the present," 39, 41, 45, 48, 54, 57
joy, 77, 79-81, 99, 123-124, 148, 161-162, 238, 248
judgment, 53, 54-60, 73, 74, 160-161
君子 *junzi* "gentleman": as moral model, 46, 69, 74, 168; character of, 24, 52, 79-80, 143, 166, 170, 176, 184, 185; contrasted with sage, 54, 73, 81, 118-119; contrasted with *xiaoren*, 204; cultivation of, 43, 210-211; translation of, 86
justification, 54-57, 59

可 *ke* "approval," 118-119, 124-125, 128, 133, 134, 140-142, 158-161, 173, 200-202, 211, 216
knowledge: historical, 49, 55, 57; inborn faculty of, 98; moral, 42, 63, 238-241; nature of, 54, 98, 166, 221; Plato's definition of,

94; source of satisfaction, 245-246. See also 知 *zhi*

language, 133, 176, 241-242, 244-245, 248. See also names
law. See 法 *fa*
learning, 42-46, 69-70, 72, 80, 84, 95, 176, 231, 238; role in moral development, 122-123, 161,198, 204, 240, 241-242, 244-245; virtues required for, 77-79
利 *li* "profit," 113, 135, 141, 215, 224-225
禮 *li* "ritual": and ruler, 6, 21; Confucian 240; creation by sage kings, 136, 155, 162-164, 176, 223; function of, 27, 33-34, 46, 56, 142-143; love of, 145, 158, 161-162; origins of, 10, 19, 72, 97-98, 120-122, 184-185; practice of, 58, 60, 70, 240; role in moral cultivation, 24, 75, 84, 93, 123-125, 139, 142-143, 158, 161, 164, 168; transformative effect of, 9-13, 16, 27-28, 76, 147-149, 150, 157
logic, 47, 53

manners, 9, 70, 98
Mencius 孟子, 211-212, 213-214
military, 16, 26, 29, 33, 55-56
mind: nature of, 86, 176-178, 181, 208, 241-242; obsession of, 48-49, 99; role of desire in, 160-161, 201-202, 205. See also 心 *xin*
Ming Dynasty, 21
monarch. See ruler
moral sense, 221-225, 237-242, 245-246
morality, 105-106, 142, 147-150,

191, 202-203, 205; Athenian and Spartan, 17-18; intuition of, 218-219, 237-239, 245; love of, 137, 146, 235; origins of, 26-28, 91-93, 135, 207-208, 241-243; re-formation account of, 239-240, 244-245
motivation, 83, 110-111, 123, 136-137, 139, 158, 160-161, 196, 206, 237, 239-240, 244-245
mourning, 147, 183-184
music: effect of, 12-13, 33, 136, 147-149, 150, 153; love of, 161-162; relation to 德 *de*, 77; role in moral cultivation, 99, 123-125, 142-143, 151, 157, 161, 164, 184

names, 117-121, 176. See also language
nature, 183-184, 185, 238, 243
Neo-Confucianism, 237
norms, 9, 13, 185, 186, 203, 224, 240

obsession: danger of, 82, 178; freedom from, 76; hindrance to ethical development, 82; historical examples of, 48-49; remedy for, 181; sources of, 99, 223
Odes. See *Shi* 詩
officials, 6-8, 22
oneness, 77-79, 81
open society, 3, 17
opening-stage nature. See human nature
optimism: epistemological, 166, 174, 248-249; in Mencius, 243; in Xunzi, 168, 245

original nature. See human nature

parents, 147-150, 180, 182, 206-207, 229, 231
passions, 108, 140, 176, 184
past, 11, 19, 39, 41, 45, 48, 54, 57, 61
pessimism, 243-244
philosophers, Song, 189, 191
philosophy, 1, 12, 57, 59, 61, 180
pleasure, 98, 99, 135, 146, 230, 243
poverty, 10, 21, 79-80, 92
precedent, 6-7. See also history, appeals to
progress, 19-20, 25
prudence, 46, 157-158
psychological egoism, 136-137, 153, 230
psychological hedonism, 230
psychology: of childhood, 93; of desire, 158-161, 230; Mencian, 112-115; moral, 135, 150, 173-174
punishment, 22, 95-96, 136, 227

氣 *qi* "ether," 115-116, 189-191, 213-214, 221-223
Qin Dynasty, 96
情 *qing* "emotions," 107, 156-158, 189-191, 198-199, 205

reason, 15, 140-142, 159, 239
refined person. See 君子 *junzi*
relationships, 10, 26-27, 44, 165, 168-169, 203-204
仁 *ren*, 41, 44, 46, 55-56, 58, 75-76, 80, 90-93, 113-114, 137, 206, 230-231, 235
人性 *renxing* "human nature," 135, 211. See also human nature, 性 *xing*
responsibility, 18-20, 28
rewards, 8, 95-96
ritual. See 禮 *li*
ruler: character of, 36, 57, 76, 113; duty to, 180, 182; role of, 6, 8, 20, 29, 37, 61, 96, 158, 226; succession of, 16, 23, 32; Weber's concept of, 171

sage: as moral model, 42-43, 74, 82-83, 229, 242, 245; as purely good, 188, 192-193; character of, 52, 53, 69-70, 76, 80-81, 99, 105, 113, 121, 205, 244; compared to other people, 190, 195; distinguished from *junzi*, 73, 118-119; distinguished from sage kings, 204
sage kings: character of, 8, 21, 124, 169-172, 176, 226-227; creation of morality, 121-122, 136, 138-139, 145, 155-156, 162, 164-167, 171, 186, 202, 205, 206, 208-209, 216, 218, 222-223, 235, 238, 247; creation of ritual, 34, 72; cultivation of, 144-146, 158-159, 161, 171; distinguished from sage, 204; relation to former kings, 57-58
satisfaction, 52, 91; in ritual, 11, 27; in morality, 143, 239, 240, 244-246; maximization of, 138, 158, 242-243; of desires, 140-142, 159-161
scholar-officials, 7-9, 11, 13, 36
science, 13, 20, 24-26
security, 5, 8, 137
self, 71, 94, 176-177, 180-181, 237
self-interest: enlightened, 109-111, 136, 214-215; Hobbes'

conception of, 91-92, 152;
maximization of, 138; Mencius'
conception of, 196;
transformation of, 142, 145-146,
149, 163
self-preservation, 136, 179
selfishness, 29, 110, 226, 229-230,
232
semblances of virtue. See virtue,
semblances of
sentiments, 65, 92
shame, heart of, 194-195, 205, 207
Shi 詩 "*Odes*," 43, 77, 113, 123,
197-198. See also Classics
Shu 書 "*Documents*," 123, 198.
See also Classics
思 *si* "concentration," 112-115,
117, 122, 130
skepticism, 19, 96
social contract, 91-92, 227
social philosophy, 9-13
society, 73, 152, 199, 239-240,
245
"sprouts," of morality. See 端
duan
stages, developmental, 93-94
state, 2-9, 16, 61, 136-137
state of nature, 2, 136, 227
superstition, 13, 14, 82

Tang Dynasty, 21
taxation, 4-5, 8, 20-21
teacher, 11, 43-44, 70, 95, 123,
157-158, 245-246
testimony, 49-50
thought experiments, 46, 64, 99
天命 *tianming* "Heavenly
mandate," 197
天行 *tianxing* "movements of
Heaven," 164
totalitarianism, 14, 15, 29

trade, 5-6, 32
training, 72, 142-143. See also
learning
tranquility, 45, 151, 181, 183-184,
216
transformation: from chaos to
order, 155-156; moral, 42,
92-93, 136, 138, 142-144,
147-149; of emotion and desire,
42, 91, 111-112, 138, 153, 158,
161-162; of sage, 73, 81, 139,
160
trust, 47, 137
tyranny, 14, 16

virtue, 40, 65, 71-75, 77-79, 90,
160, 183, 231; recognition of,
167-170; failures of, 82-83, 225;
moral, 90-92, 100, 146,
239-240; of *junzi*, 79-80; of
sage, 80-81; paradox of,
157-158, 159; pleasure in, 119,
137, 145, 153; semblances of,
74-75, 83, 110; use of 德 *de*,
76-77
virtus, 76

Warring States, 6, 168
Way. See *dao*
wealth, 8, 9, 79-80, 143
偽 *wei* "artifice," 70, 161, 162,
198, 206, 209, 215
微 *wei* "subtlety," 81
wisdom, 39, 72, 119, 245, 247

先王 *xianwang* "former kings," 41,
57-58
孝 *xiao* "filial." See filial piety
小人 *xiaoren* "petty person," 46,
170, 204
心 *xin* "heart-and-mind": desire

and approval in, 118-119; nature
of, 43, 70, 115-116, 135, 143,
147, 158, 181, 237-238,
241-242, 248; role in Mencian
theory, 142, 191-195; translation
of, 148, 214, 247
性 *xing* "nature," 93, 103, 105,
145, 158, 162, 189-191, 197,
211
性惡 *xing'e* "human nature is bad,"
69, 107, 125-127, 143-144, 151,
156-157, 162, 198-205,
220-221, 229, 232, 237-238,
243-245
Xunzi 荀子: authorship of, 62,
172, 211-212, 216, 234;
contradictions in, 222-224; use
of 氣 *qi* in, 213-214

義 *yi* "social norms," 7, 41, 44,
46, 54-56, 58, 75, 77, 108, 131,
136, 182, 206, 221-227,
230-231
Yi 易 "*Changes*," 185
欲 *yu* "desire," 118-119, 124-125,
128, 133, 135-136, 158-161,
173. See also desire

知 *zhi* "to know," 158
志 *zhi* "intention," 43, 115-117
忠 *zhong* "loyalty," 52-53
Zhuangzi 莊子, 178, 182-184

Name Index

Adams, Robert, 247
Ames, Roger, 61
Aquinas, St. Thomas, 84, 125
Aristotle, 4, 31, 84, 96, 101, 114,
    119, 132, 160, 247
Augustine, 69, 115, 125, 134, 248
Austin, J. L., 49, 66

Baier, K., 37
Ban Gu, 212
Becker, Lawrence, 150, 154
Bodde, Derk, 36, 153
Burke, Edmund, 247
Burnyeat, M. F., 119, 132
Butterfield, Herbert, 61

Chan Wing-tsit, 63, 246
Chen Li, 191-195
Chen Xiao, 55
Cheng Yi. See Cheng Yichuan
Cheng Yichuan, 42, 63, 71
Ching, Julia, 175
Chuang Tzu. See Zhuangzi
Confucius, 39-40, 61, 76, 81, 95,
    99, 180, 182-184, 188, 189,
    198, 248
Crawford, Robert, 32
Creel, Herrlee, 33, 62, 67, 110,
    130, 175
Cua, Antonio S., 61, 62, 63, 64,
    65, 66, 67, 75, 86, 87, 100,
    104, 129, 130, 144, 153, 248

Darwall, Stephen, 246
Dietrichson, Paul, 66
Dong Zhongshu, 189, 212
Dray, William H., 68
Dubs, Homer, 5, 40, 62, 67, 86,
    213, 243, 248
Duke Huan, 53
Duke of Zhou, 53
Duke Ping of Lu, 115
Duyvendak, J. J. L., 215

Feng Youlan. See Fung Youlan
Fingarette, Herbert, 175
Fisch, Max, 68
Fogelin, Robert, 65
Foot, Philippa, 74, 87
Freud, Sigmund, 132, 150-151,
    173
Friedman, Edward, 38
Fu Cha, 53
Fu Sinian, 211
Fung Youlan, 62, 145-146, 147

Gaozi, 105, 107, 108, 117, 125-
    127, 187, 210, 217, 231
Gauthier, David, 137, 152
Gongduzi, 107, 134, 192
Gongsun Chou, 116
Gongsun Nizi, 188
Graham, A. C., 71, 86, 103,
    105-107, 128, 129, 131, 134,
    144-145, 147, 153, 179, 186
Guan Zhong, 53

Hacking, Ian, 248
Han Feizi, 22, 234
Hansen, Chad, 120, 132
Haweis, H. R., 153
Hegel, G. W. F., 14
Heidegger, Martin, 240
Ho Ping-ti, 33
Hobbes, Thomas, 91-92, 98, 99,

101, 109, 121-122, 133, 136-138, 155, 226, 227

Hoffman, Martin L., 101
Hu Shih, 213
Hucker, C. O., 36
Huizi, 183
Hume, David, 65, 90, 92, 101, 246
Hutchenson, Francis, 246

Ivanhoe, Philip J., 71, 86, 87, 88, 100, 132, 143, 153, 172, 173, 232-233, 246, 247, 248

Jie (tyrant), 19, 42, 45, 52, 59, 68, 190, 224-226, 227, 235

Kant, Immanuel, 66, 100, 141, 159, 160, 247
Karlgren, Bernhard, 116, 131
Kierkegaard, Søren, 38, 94, 101
King Gou Jian of Yue, 226
King Ling of Chu, 226, 234
King Wen of Zhou, 42, 53, 56, 63
King Wu of Zhou, 42, 56, 59, 63, 68, 227
King Xuan of Qi, 108, 110, 114, 209
King Zhuang of Chu, 234
Knoblock, John, 85
Kohlberg, Lawrence, 90, 100
Kracke, E. A., 33

Lau, D. C., 61, 86, 88, 103, 105, 106, 115, 128, 129, 131, 152
Legge, James, 115
Lévi-Strauss, Claude, 153-154
Lieberman, Marcel S., 247
Liezi, 178
Liu Wu-chi, 62
Liu Xiang, 188
Lynn, Richard John, 187

Machle, Edward, 174
MacIntyre, Alasdair, 73, 87
Mair, Victor, 65
Marx, Karl, 3, 14
Maspero, Henri, 178-179, 186
Master Tai, 48
Mei, Y. P., 37, 64, 215
Mencius. See Mengzi
Mengzi, 40, 47, 69, 71, 83-84, 89-93, 95, 99, 103-128, 130, 136, 139, 141-145, 149, 156-157, 177, 181, 188-198, 205-211, 217, 222, 230-232, 237-243, 245
Metzger, Thomas A., 174, 248
Milgram, Stanley, 100, 102
Mill, John Stuart, 146, 153
Mo Tzu. See Mozi
Mote, Frederick, 62
Mozi, 47, 65, 82, 226, 234
Munro, Donald, 31, 61, 88, 103, 129, 220, 221, 224, 226-229, 231-232, 235

Needham, Joseph, 61
Nivison, David S., 76, 88, 111, 126-127, 134, 135, 136, 138-139, 145, 147, 149-150, 151, 152, 154, 156, 157-158, 162-164, 171, 172, 173, 174, 220, 222-224, 233

Passmore, John, 65
Pei Xuehai, 217
Piaget, Jean, 89, 93, 94, 101
Pincoffs, Edmund, 73, 87
Plato, 3, 4, 6, 12, 14, 15, 94, 159, 160
Pope, Alexander, 25
Popper, Karl, 3, 13-16, 17, 18-19, 23-24, 27, 28

Rescher, Nicholas, 49, 66
Roberts, Robert C., 87
Rosemont, Henry, 34, 88
Ross, David, 218
Russell, Bertrand, 31

Santayana, George, 11
Schneewind, J. B., 73, 87
Schofer, Jonathan W., 172, 173, 247
Selden, Mark, 38
Shensheng, 48
Shi Shi, 188
Shih, Vincent, 34
Shun (sage king), 4, 42, 56, 63, 86, 190, 192, 196, 215, 224, 229
Shun Kwong-loi, 87, 151
Sima Qian, 32
Socrates, 29
Song Keng, 117
Stevenson, C. L., 66
Swann, N. L., 32

Tang (king), 42, 48, 56, 59, 63, 68, 227

Urmson, J. O., 67

Van Norden, Bryan W., 73, 86, 87, 139-141, 152, 155-158, 159, 164, 166, 171, 172, 231, 247

Waley, Arthur, 32, 130
Wang Chong, 188-189, 212
Wang Xianqian, 104
Wang Yangming, 63, 180, 217, 246

Watson, Burton, 47, 62, 65, 128, 186, 234
Weber, Max, 171, 175
Wei Zhengtong, 63
Wen. See King Wen of Zhou
White, Morton, 34
Williams, Bernard, 73, 87
Wollheim, Richard, 150-151, 154, 173
Wong, David B., 155-156, 159-162, 164, 171, 172, 236
Wu. See King Wu of Zhou

Xiqi, 48
Xun Yue, 188-189

Yan Hui, 180, 187
Yang Yunru, 62, 216
Yang Zhu, 179, 230, 235
Yao (sage king), 4, 19, 42, 45, 56, 63, 124, 190, 192, 224, 229
Yearley, Lee, 71, 73-75, 83, 86, 87, 88, 172, 179, 186
Yi Yin, 209
Youzi, 81
Yu (sage king), 24, 42, 45, 52, 56, 63, 68, 167, 190, 203-204, 229

Zang Cang, 115
Zhao Meng, 113
Zhao Qi, 217
Zhi (robber), 45, 190, 215
Zhou (tyrant), 42, 59, 224-226, 227, 235
Zhu Xi, 212-213, 217
Zhuangzi, 47, 82, 130, 138, 177-186
Zi Xu, 53